INTERPRETING THE
GENERAL LETTERS

HANDBOOKS FOR NEW TESTAMENT EXEGESIS
John D. Harvey, series editor

Interpreting the Pauline Letters: An Exegetical Handbook
John D. Harvey
Interpreting the General Letters: An Exegetical Handbook
Herbert W. Bateman IV
Interpreting the Gospels and Acts: An Exegetical Handbook (forthcoming)
David L. Turner
Interpreting the Apocalypse: An Exegetical Handbook (forthcoming)
C. Marvin Pate

INTERPRETING THE GENERAL LETTERS

An Exegetical Handbook

Herbert W. Bateman IV

AUTHOR

John D. Harvey

SERIES EDITOR

Kregel *Academic*

Interpreting the General Letters: An Exegetical Handbook
© 2013 by Herbert W. Bateman IV

Published by Kregel Publications, a division of Kregel, Inc., P.O. Box 2607, Grand Rapids, MI 49501.

The Greek font GraecaU and the Hebrew font New JerusalemU are both available from www.linguistsoftware.com/lgku.htm, +1-425-775-1130.

ISBN 978-0-8254-2768-8

Printed in the United States of America
13 14 15 16 17 / 5 4 3 2 1

Dedicated to
Herbert W. Bateman Jr.

CONTENTS IN BRIEF

CONTENTS

PREFACE

INTERPRETING THE GENERAL LETTERS: AN EXEGETICAL HANDBOOK, the third of a four-volume series, intends to shape the way people think and go about studying and communicating eight books of the New Testament: Hebrews, James, the Petrine letters, the Johannine letters, and Jude. Instructional handbooks or guides like those in Kregel's Handbooks for New Testament Exegesis emerge because authors like me were introduced to and then further developed skills passed on to us from other people. I am truly grateful for the Old and New Testament Departments at Dallas Theological Seminary who taught, cultivated, and fostered the exegetical skills compiled in this book. Yet there are others to whom I am grateful for their instruction, guidance, and affirmation.

During my seminary years at Dallas Seminary, Darrell Bock instilled in me skills to think and continues to patiently stretch my thought processes (1983–present). During the early years of my conversion, Tom Larmore taught me skills to evangelize and disciple the ethnically and socially diverse people of east Camden (1978-82). Together with my best friend Bill Rehrer, I learned skills for growing up and navigating life (1968-2001, d. 2005). During my employment at Kushner's Hardware, Paul Wendt granted me opportunities to develop business skills and extended levels of responsibilities that shaped my work ethic and people skills (1972-80, d. 1996). These people were *living handbooks* whose instruction and lives have guided and shaped me. Yet the *living handbook* to whom this book is dedicated is Herbert W. Bateman Jr., my grandfather, who was born one hundred years ago this year (November 1913).

Herb (or as he was known by family members, Bud) never earned a Ph.D. He never went to college. He never finished high school. He sold sporting goods his entire life and retired as the manager of Strawbridge and Clothier's sporting goods department in 1976. Yet he has been the most significant *living handbook* of my life. He infused the importance of family and passing on our family heritage through stories of William H. Bateman's immigration from England in 1870s[1] and many other people in our family. More importantly, he imparted the importance of family by faithfully providing for his immediate and extended family members during and after the Great Depression. After his father, Herbert W. Bateman Sr., lost everything in 1929 and died of depression in 1933, Bud provided and cared for his mother until she died in 1964.[2] Furthermore, while I was growing up in South Jersey, holidays such as Memorial Day, Fourth of July, and Labor Day were always special times at his home. At such traditional family events, he would always grill hamburgers, hotdogs, and of course our family traditional favorite, Texas Tommies.[3] These times were exceptional events when sisters, brothers, aunts, uncles, first cousins, second cousins, and grandchildren would get together, relax, tell stories, listen to the Phillies ballgame, play yard games, and just hangout. He had a knack for putting people at ease, relaxing, and just enjoying himself and his family. Finally, he had a keen sense of humor and a hearty as well as contagious laugh.

Although he died in July 1997, I will never forget our family gatherings and those occasional projects we did together: painting the house, stripping and re-roofing the garage, remodeling his kitchen, building furniture together, tilling his vegetable garden every spring, and building a fish pond in his backyard. All of these memories, our relationship, the life skills, and the values he passed on to me are mine for as long as I live. It is for these reasons that I dedicate this book to Herbert (Bud) W. Bateman Jr., who one hundred years ago was born and continues to have an impact on people because he was a *living handbook*.

—HERBERT W. BATEMAN IV
Author

---

1   William H. Bateman arrived from England in America at the age of 40 on the Ship Britannic (September 29, 1879). Accompanying him was Alice, his wife, who was 30 years old and two sons: Fred age 4 and Jack age 2. After settling in South Jersey, he and Alice had six other children: Herbert W. Bateman Sr. (April 1881), Maybel (January 1884), Wallace (June 1885), Robert (May 1888), Clyde (November 1889), and Clare (September 1891).

2   Prior to FDR and Truman, there was no Social Security deductions or subsequent payments when one's spouse died. So Elizabeth Agin Bateman, like other women of her day who tended to have no labor skills except for being a stay-at-home mom, was without any source of income. In those days, family had to provided for family. See David McCullough, *Truman* (New York: Simon & Schuster 1992).

3   Texas Tommies are hotdogs sliced down the center with a sliver of cheese placed inside and wrapped in pre-cooked bacon. Grill them and put them on a toasted hotdog bun and you have a "Texas Tommie," although they have no connection with Texas.

ABBREVIATIONS

AB	Anchor Bible
BSA	*Annual of the British School at Athens*
ABD	*Anchor Bible Dictionary*
ANTC	Abington New Testament Commentaries
ASV	American Standard Version
BSac	*Bibliotheca Sacra*
BCE	Before the Common Era (equivalent of B.C.)
BDAG	A Greek-English Lexicon of the New Testament and Other Early Christian Literature
BDF	*A Greek Grammar of the New Testament and Other Early Christian Literature*
BECNT	Baker Exegetical Commentary on the New Testament
CBQ	*Catholic Biblical Quarterly*
CE	Common Era (equivalent to A.D.)
CEB	Common English Bible
CEV	Contemporary English Version
DJD	*Discoveries in the Judean Desert*
DSS	Dead Sea Scrolls
EDNT	*Exegetical Dictionary of the New Testament*
EEC	The Evangelical Exegetical Commentary
EncDSS	*Encyclopedia of the Dead Sea Scrolls*
ESV	English Standard Version
ICC	The International Critical Commentary
ISBE	*International Standard Bible Encyclopedia*
JAOS	*Journal of the American Oriental Society*
JBL	*Journal of Biblical Literature*
JETS	*Journal of the Evangelical Theological Society*

Jos	Josephus
JSNTSup	Journal for the Study of the New Testament Supplemental Series
JSJ	*Journal for the Study of Judasim*
JSOT	*Journal for the Study of the Old Testament*
KJV	King James Version
LXX	Septuagint
NASB	New American Standard Bible
NAV	New American Version
NET	New English Translation
NICNT	New International Commentary on the New Testament
NIGTC	New International Greek Testament Commentary
NIV	New International Version
NKJV	New King James Version
NLT	New Living Translation
NRSV	New Revised Standard Version
OEAGR	*Oxford Encyclopedia of Ancient Greece and Rome*
PNTC	Pelican New Testament Commentaries
RCRD	Rule of the Community and Related Documents
SBLDS	Society of Biblical Literature Dissertation Series
SBLMS	Society of Biblical Literature Monograph Series
SP	Sacra Pagina
RSV	Revised Standard Version
RV	Revised Version
TDNT	*Theological Dictionary of the New Testament*
TDOT	*Theological Dictionary of the Old Testament*
TJ	*Trinity Journal*
TLNT	*Theological Lexicon of the New Testament*
TNIV	Today's New International Version
TynBul	*Tyndale Bulletin*
USQR	*Union Seminary Quarterly Review*
WBC	Word Biblical Commentary
WEB	World English Bible
ZNW	*Zeitschrift fur die Neutestamentliche Wissenschaft*

APOCRYPHA

1 Esd.	First Esdras
2 Esd.	Second Esdras
1 Macc.	First Maccabees
2 Macc.	Second Maccabees
3 Macc.	Third Maccabees
4 Macc.	Fourth Maccabees

Bel	Bel and the Dragon
Judith	Judith
Sir.	Wisdom of Jesus the Son of Sirach (Ecclesiasticus)
Tobit	Tobit
Wisd. Sol.	*Wisdom of Solomon*

OTHER EXTRA BIBLICAL SOURCES

Ant.	Antiquitates Judaicae
Ap.	Contra Apionem
Barn.	*Epistle of Barnabas*
Ep. Arist.	*Epistle of Aristeas*
Jub.	*Jubilees*
Odes Sol.	*Odes of Solomon*
Poly *Hist.*	Polybius *History*
Pss. Sol.	*Psalms of Solomon*
Sib. Or.	Sibylline Oracles
T. Adam	Testament of Adam
T. Benj.	Testament of Benjamin
T.Dan.	Testament of Dan
T. Levi	Testament of Levi
T. 12 Patr.	Testaments of the Twelve Patriarchs
T. Sol.	Testament of Solomon
War	*Bellum Judaicum*

QUMRAN SOURCES

CD	*Damascus Document*	
1QM	*1QWar Scroll*	
1Q28	*1QS*	*1QRule of the Community*
1Q28a	*1QSa*	*1QRule of the Congregation*
1Q28b	*1QSb*	*1QRule of Blessings*
4Q161	*4QpIsaᵃ*	*4QIsaiah Pesherᵃ*
4Q174	*4QFlor*	*4QFlorilegium*
4Q175	*4QTest*	*4QTestimonia*
4Q246	*4QpsDan ar*	*4QAramaic Apocalypse*
4Q252	*4QcommGenᵃ*	*4QCommentary on Genesis A*
4Q266	*4QDᵃ*	*4QDamascus Documentᵃ*
4Q285	*4QSM*	*4QSefer ha-Milhamah*
4Q376	*4QapocrMosesᵇ*	*4QApocryphon of Mosesᵇ*
4Q382	*4QParaphrase of the Kings*	
4Q458	*4QNarrative A*	
4Q521	*4QMessianic Apocalypse*	

1

THE GENRE OF THE GENERAL LETTERS

AS WE BEGIN THIS CHAPTER ABOUT "The Genre of the General Letters," it is helpful to bear in mind that we are talking about a certain type of literature. Speaking in very broad terms, there are four categories or types of genre in the New Testament: Gospels (Matthew, Mark, Luke, and John), historical narrative (Acts), apocalyptic (Revelation), and the most represented genre, the letter. Of the twenty-seven books of the New Testament, twenty-one are letters. They are pen-and-ink correspondences that reflect the personality of the sender, that make direct and sometimes indirect references to a person or group of people as though they stood in the author's presence, and that represent only one half of a conversation. Paul's material and the General Letters (Hebrews, James, 1 and 2 Peter, 1–3 John, and Jude) are all deemed letters. This chapter seeks to answer two questions: what do we know about ancient letter writing, and how does what we know affect how we study, interpret, and teach the General Letters?

Tracing developments in ancient letter writing within the Greco-Roman world is at times difficult. Nevertheless, this chapter strives to describe, illustrate, compare, and contrast extant letters written during the first century. More specifically, this chapter identifies and illustrates the component parts of an ancient letter; it describes and demonstrates similarities and differences of a letter's opening salutation; it compares and contrasts the different types of epistolary correspondence within the Greco-Roman world; and finally it divulges information about and displays examples of letters written by trained letter-writers known as amanuenses. Yet at every turn, our goal is to provide a proposal for interpreting the General Letters.

COMPONENT PARTS OF A LETTER

The purpose of this section is to identify and illustrate the component parts of an ancient letter and how they might affect our studying, interpreting, and teaching the General Letters. In order to spot the component parts of an ancient letter, we begin with a contemporary illustration, email. In 1982, the developments of digital messaging known as electronic mail (email) not only exploded here in the United States, it transformed one-way communication universally. Unlike any other development in communication (e.g., the telegraph and the telephone), email has surpassed the effectiveness of communication globally on every level of society. Yet as you know, today's electronic mail messages consist of two components parts: the message *header* and the message *body*. The message *header* generally includes the following fields though the order may vary:

- From: The email address and perhaps the name of the author(s).

- To: The email address indicates primary recipient (multiple allowed) and for secondary recipients indicated below with Cc and Bcc.

- Subject: A brief summary of the topic of the message.

- Date: The local time and date when the message was written.

The message *body*, that larger box where a message is typed, is where our one-way communication occurs. The content may concern personal or private matters, report on or record business transactions, or enlighten someone concerning political, philosophical, or religious issues. In fact, there are instruction manuals with proposals for how to write a proper email.[1] An email message, however, may or may not end with a person's signature block of information. A personally designed signature block is optional. So, email has a twofold structure: a header and a body, but a person's signature block to close the email message is optional. A personal computer, a phone with email capabilities, or an e-reader is a necessary component for message submission or retrieval as opposed to the use of paper, pen, ink, a stamp, and envelope. As we will discover, however, there are similarities and differences. We will address the differences when discussing the need for trained letter-writers later in the chapter, but for now we pause to examine the similarities.

Concerning similarities, the ancient non-canonical Greco-Roman and Jewish letters tend to follow the same structure. A typical letter consisted of three component parts: (1) the letter's opening address and greeting, (2) the letter's body, and (3) the letter's closing salutation. Available today are numerous Greco-Roman and Jewish letters that exemplify this threefold structure. Many of the Greco-Roman letters were found among the Oxyrhynchus Papyri collection discovered in an ancient rubbish dump near Oxyrhynchus, Egypt, a town that flourished during the Roman period in Middle Egypt about 125 miles south of Cairo.[2] Greco-Roman examples chosen for this chapter were written around the same time as the author of Hebrews,[3] Peter, John,

---

1.   Janis Fisher Chan, *E-Mail: A Write It Well Guide—How to Write and Manage E-Mail in the Workplace* (San Francisco: Write It Well, 2005); *The Microsoft Manual of Style for Technical Publications* (Microsoft Press, 3rd edition, 2004).

2.   Excavations at the dump near Oxyrhynchus, Egypt began as early as 1882. The finds include the writings of Euripides, Sophocles, Menander, OT texts, OT apocrypha, NT texts, NT apocrypha, etc. Yet, ninety percent of the finds are public and private letters, public and private records, and public and private deeds written by or about ordinary people of antiquity who lived between 301 BCE (Ptolemaic Period) and into the 400s CE (Roman-Byzantine Periods). See W. Hersey Davis, *Greek Papyri of the First Century: Introduction, Greek Text, English Translation, Commentary, Notes* (Chicago, IL: Ares Publishing, 1933).

3.   It is my belief that we are unable to determine who wrote the Epistle to the Hebrews. Nevertheless, for those who wish to know the options and weigh the pros and cons of each, see the series of charts on debated considerations about authorship in Herbert W. Bateman IV, *Charts on the Book of Hebrews* (Grand Rapids: Kregel, 2012).

James, and Jude composed their letters. The first letter is an official letter of *commendation* of a new governor, Pompeus Planta, written by the
Roman Emperor Trajan, to the city of Alexandria, Egypt (98 CE).

LETTER'S OPENING	Imperator Caesar nerva Traianus Augustus Germanics Potifex Maximus tribuniciae potestatis II cousul, to (the city of?) Alexandrians . . .
LETTER'S BODY	(Being well aware of) your city's outstanding loyalty towards the emperors, and having in mind the benefits which my deified father conferred on you . . . of his reign, and for my own part also, (over and above?) these claims (of yours), saving a personal feeling of benevolence towards you, I have commended you first of all to myself, then in addition to my friend and prefect Pompeius Planta, so that he can take every care in providing for your undisturbed tranquility and your food-supply and your communal and individual rights. From which (it will be?) clear . . .
LETTER'S CLOSING	(the end of the letter is lost)[4]

The second letter is also a letter of *commendation*, and though it is not
stated, the writing style of this letter from Theon to Tyrannus on behalf
of his brother Heraclides (25 CE) was written by a trained letter-writer,
an amanuensis (N.B.: Theon *to his esteemed . . .*).

LETTER'S OPENING	Theon to his esteemed Tyrannus, many greetings.
LETTER'S BODY	Heraclides, the bearer of this letter, is my brother. I therefore entreat you with all my power to treat him as your protégé. I have also written to your brother Hermias asking him to communicate with you about him. You will confer upon me a very great favour if Heraclides gains your notice.
LETTER'S CLOSING	Before all else you have my good wishes for unbroken health and prosperity. Good-bye.[5]

4.   P. J. Parsons, ed., *The Oxyrhynchus Papyri*, vol. 42 (London: Oxford University Press, 1974), 76–77.

5.   Bernard P. Grenfell and Arthur S. Hunt, eds., *The Oxyrhynchus Papyri*, Part 2 (London: Oxford University Press, 1899), 292.

The third is a *conciliatory* letter from a son, Harpocras, to his father, Thracidashis (76 CE). In a very formal manner, a son informs his father of his recovery from an illness, recounts his delight in receiving a letter from his father, and informs his father of a pair of sandals he has sent.

LETTER'S OPENING	Harpocras to Thracidashis father, very many greetings.
LETTER'S BODY	Knowing that you will be delighted, I feel obliged to write you that there is nothing the matter with me, but that I was rather lethargic for only a very few days and have been feeling better for some time, and there is nothing the matter with me. I was greatly delighted to read through your letter, in which I learned, my lord father, that you were in excellent health; and because I was tremendously elated in spirit on receiving your letter, I at once thought it might be an oracle of the god, and my health improved remarkably. Receive from Petechon, who is bringing you the letter, a pair of sandals worth 4 dr. Quickly tell me whatever else you have need of, as I still have a few days here.
LETTER'S CLOSING	Give my best wishes to Thatres my mother, Thaisous, Sarapion, Ariston, Tycharion, Nice, Eutych( ), and everyone in the house.[6]

The fourth is a *commanding* letter from a man, Ilarion, who has gone to Alexandria (1 BCE). He has written to his sister as well as his wife, Alis, and two other women concerning his whereabouts, provided instructions about the birth of a child, and exhorted them not to worry.

LETTER'S OPENING	Ilarion to Alis his sister, many greetings, and to my dear Berous and Apollonarion.
LETTER'S BODY	Know that I am still even now at Alexandria; and do not worry if they come back altogether (?), but I remain at Alexandria. I urge and entreat you to be careful of the child, and if I receive a present soon I will send it up to

---

6.   R. A. Coles and M. W. Haslam, eds., *The Oxyrhynchus Papyri*, vol. 42 (London: Oxford University Press, 1980), 116–17.

you. If (Apollonarion?) bears offspring, if it is
a male let it be, if a female expose it. You told
Aphrodisias "Don't forget me." How can I forget you? I urge you therefore not to worry.

LETTER'S CLOSING   (No closing salutation.)[7]

The fifth is another *commanding* letter, however, this one is Jewish
found at Engedi in Judea. And though it is fragmented with no final
salutation (*circa* 124 CE), it is important because it was written by Bar-
Kokhba, the leader of the second Jewish revolt against Rome (132–135
CE). He addresses Galgoula to perhaps murder ("destroy") or possibly
punish Galileans. Although Bar-Kokhba's orders appear a bit harsh, it
exemplifies the same sort of structure, though from a different geographical location by a dissimilar ethnic group.

LETTER'S OPENING   From Shimeon ben Kosiba to Yeshua ben
                         Galgoula and to the men of the fort, peace.

LETTER'S BODY   I take heaven to witness against me that un-
                         less you mobilize [perhaps "destroy"?] the
                         Galileans who are with you every man, I will
                         put fetters on your feet as I did to ben Aphlul.

LETTER'S CLOSING   (the end of the letter is lost.)[8]

Although the majority of these non-canonical letters of antiquity tend
to follow a threefold structure, the authors of their respective letters are
not enslaved to it. For instance, letter-writers tend to vary in whether to
include a closing salutation. This is also the case concerning our canonical letters. Whereas 1 Peter, 2 John, and 3 John conform to the threefold
organization of a letter, others like James eliminate the closing salutation,
or in the case of 2 Peter and Jude they close with doxologies. Hebrews
and 1 John,[9] however, are unique in that they open with prologues.

7.   Bernard P. Grenfell and Arthur S. Hunt, eds., *The Oxyrhynchus Papyri*, Part 4 (London:
     Oxford University Press, 1904), 243–44; see the "Letter to a Friend" (2 BCE), which is also
     a letter of commendation written on behalf of a person named Damas to his good friend.

8.   Ibid, 137. Other examples of Jewish letters are provided in Yadin's chapter, "The Letters
     Speak," 124–39. Compare *Encyclopedia of the Dead Sea Scrolls* (2000), "Letters."

9.   Admittedly, 1 John is the least letter-like of all the General Letters. Brown describes it as a
     commentary on the Gospel of John, Smalley depicts it as a paper, and Kruse declares that
     "1 John falls into the category of epideictic rhetoric." Historically Irenaeus (*Haer.* 3.16.8)
     and Dionysisus of Alexandria (Eusebius, *Hist. eccl.* 7.25.8) considered it an epistle. Internally,
     there are three possible features of 1 John that are epistolary: shared joy (1:4), repeated

General Epistle	Letter's Opening	Letter's Body	Letter's Closing
Hebrews	Prologue 1:1–4	1:5–13:19	13:20–25
James	1:1	1:2–5:20	None
1 Peter	1:1–2	1:3–5:11	5:12–14
2 Peter	1:1–2	1:3–3:6	Doxology 3:17–18
1 John	Prologue 1:1–4	1:5–5:21	None
2 John	vv.1–3	vv.4–11	vv.12–13
3 John	vv.1–2	vv.3–12	vv.13–15
Jude	vv.1–2	vv.3–23	Doxology vv. 24–25

There is a greater and more significant difference between the non-canonical Greco-Roman and Jewish letters exemplified from *The Oxyrhynchus Papyri,* Masada letters, and those of our General Letters. It is length. The average length of a typical Greco-Roman letter, according to Harvey, is 87 words.[10] They could be as short as 18 words and as long as 209 words. Even the Greco-Roman and Jewish letters illustrated earlier in this chapter are of average length. The complete

mention of motive for writing (γράφω: 1:4; 2:1, 7, 8, 12, 13, 14, 21, 26; 5:13), and the repeated use of direct address (τεκνίον: 2:1, 12, 28; 3:7, 18; 4:4, 5; 5:2). Raymond Brown, *The Epistles of John* in AB (Garden City, NY: Doubleday, 1982), 86–92; Stephen S. Smalley, *1, 2, 3 John* in WBC (Waco, TX: Word, 1984), xxxiii; Colin G. Kruse, *The Letters of John* in PNTC (Grand Rapids: Eerdmans, 2000), 29.

10. John D. Harvey, in his chapter on genre, identifies the extreme brevity of letters in comparison to Pauline works in *Interpreting the Pauline Letters: An Exegetical Handbook*, vol. 2 in Handbooks for New Testament Exegesis, edited by John D. Harvey (Grand Rapids: Kregel, 2012), 29.

letter of *commendation* from Theon to Tyrannus on behalf of his brother Heraclides (25 CE) consists of 59 words in the Greek, the *conciliatory* letter from Harpocras to his father (76 CE) is 127 words in the Greek, and the *commending* letter from Ilarion, who has gone to Alexandria (1 BCE) consists of 79 words in the Greek.

Nevertheless, other Greco-Roman letters may average more words: Cicero's letters average 295 words;[11] Seneca's letters average 995 words;[12] and Paul's letters average 2,495 words.[13] Like Paul's canonical letters, some of the General Letters are longer than others. Hebrews, the longest epistle, consists of 4,954 words while 3 John, the shortest, consists of 219 words. The total number of Greek words used to compose the eight General Letters is 12,532. Thus, the average number of words per General Epistle is about 1,566 words.[14]

General Epistle	Longest Chapter	Shortest Chapter	Average Number of Words Per Chapter	Total Number of Words Per Book
Hebrews	Chapter 11 (633 words)	Chapter 5 (232 words)	381 words	4,954 words
James	Chapter 2 (415 words)	Chapter 4 (274 words)	347 words	1,737 words

---

11. Cicero was born in 106 BCE, six years before the birth of Julius Caesar. He came from a wealthy family, received a superior education, and served in Rome's political arena. After his political career, he wrote a number of philosophical works until he was assassinated in 43 BCE.

12. Seneca may have been born in 4 BCE, around the same time Herod the Great died in Judea. Although born in Spain, he was educated in Rome. He was a playwright, an orator, and philosopher. He tutored the young Nero. He later served as Nero's advisor for several years, and was an influence on the young emperor from 54–62 CE. After he retired, he lost favor with Nero, was accused of conspiring against Nero, and was forced to commit suicide in 65 CE.

13. Harvey, *Interpreting the Pauline Letters*. For a more extensive presentation see Lars Kierspel, "Paul's Letters: Total Number of Words and Vocabulary" in *Charts on the Life, Letters, and Theology of Paul*, Kregel's Charts of the Bible and Theology (Grand Rapids: Kregel, 2011), Chart #40.

14. The Greek word count was derived from Nestle-Alands, 28th edition. The New Testament chapter and verse divisions do not exist in the original manuscripts. The New Testament text was initially divided into numbered verses by Stephanus and published in his fourth edition of the New Testament (1551). Folklore has it that Stephanus marked the verse division while journeying "on horseback," and that some of the unwelcome divisions by present-day scholars arose from the jogging of the horseback that bumped his pen into the wrong places. Although his son confirms that his father did indeed work on the text while on a journey from Paris to Lyons, in all probability the task was accomplished while resting at the inns along the road.

General Epistle	Longest Chapter	Shortest Chapter	Average Number of Words Per Chapter	Total Number of Words Per Book
1 Peter	Chapter 1 (405 words)	Chapter 5 (206 words)	336 words	1,680 words
2 Peter	Chapter 1 (384 words)	Chapter 3 (341 words)	366 words	1,098 words
1 John	Chapter 2 (586 words)	Chapter 1 (207 words)	428 words	2,140 words
2 John	245 words	245 words	245 words	245 words
3 John	219 words	219 words	219 words	219 words
Jude	459 words	459 words	459 words	459 words

In summary then, what have we learned about the component parts of an ancient letter, and how does what we now know affect how we might study, interpret, and teach the General Letters? First, we know that like present-day email, ancient letters had some semblance of structure. Whereas our email has two component parts, a header and a body with an optional personal block to close, letters of antiquity tend to have three component parts: an opening salutation, a body, and an optional closing salutation. Consequently, there are letter-structured divisions that should be first recognized and then honored when studying, interpreting, and teaching James, 1 Peter, 2 Peter, 2 John, 3 John, and Jude. Second, we learned that the General Letters, on average, tend to be much longer than letters of antiquity, which naturally leads us to ask, why? The why question, however, may be answered in part with a closer look at the "Opening Salutations" of ancient letters and in part in our subsequent section about the "Types of Epistolary Correspondence."

OPENING SALUTATIONS

The purpose of this section is to describe and demonstrate similarities and differences of a letter's opening salutation, and thereby make some suggestions for studying, interpreting, and teaching an opening salutation. A quick re-reading of the opening salutations above reveals the brevity in which a *sender* states his name, the simplicity in which the name of the *recipient* is given, and the succinctness of the *greeting*. Authors of the General Letters, on the other hand, tend to expand their opening salutations. The *sender* may attach a noun or adjective to his name as in the case of James, Peter, and Jude. The *recipient* may receive extensive forms of affirmation as in 1 Peter, 2 Peter, 2 John, 3 John, and Jude. And though James offers a concise *greeting*, others use a more expansive twofold (1 Peter, 2 Peter), threefold (2 John, Jude) or the more traditional wishful greeting (3 John).

General Epistle	Opening Salutations	
Hebrews	Prologue	
James	Sender:	James
	Expansion	slave of God and the Lord Jesus, *who is the* Christ
	Recipient:	to the twelve tribes of the Diaspora
	Greeting:	Greetings
1 Peter	Sender:	Peter
	Expansion	apostle of Jesus, *who is the* Christ
	Recipient:	to the chosen pilgrims of the Diaspora
	Expansion	in Pontus, Galatia, Cappadocia, Asia, and Bithynia
	Greeting:	May God's grace and peace be multiplied to you
2 Peter	Sender:	Simon Peter
	Expansion	slave and apostle of Jesus, *who is the* Christ
	Recipient:	to those who have been granted a faith just as precious as ours
	Expansion	through the righteousness of our God and savior Jesus *who is the* Christ
	Greeting:	May God's grace and peace be multiplied to you
	Expansion	through the knowledge of God and Jesus our Lord
1 John	Prologue	

General Epistle	Opening Salutations	
2 John	Sender:	The Elder
	Recipient:	to the elect lady and her children
	Expansion	whom I love in the truth
	Greeting:	Grace, mercy and peace
	Expansion	from God the Father and from Jesus, *who is the* Christ, the son of the Father, will be ours who live in truth
3 John	Sender:	The Elder
	Recipient:	to beloved Gaius
	Expansion	whom I love in the truth
	Greeting:	Dear friend, I wish you to prosper and to be in good health,
	Expansion	even as your soul prospers.
Jude	Sender:	Jude
	Expansion	slave of Jesus, who is the Christ, and brother of James
	Recipient:	to those Judean believers
	Expansion	who are called, who are loved by God the Father and kept for Jesus, who is the Christ
	Greeting:	May mercy, peace, and love be multiplied to you

Having described and demonstrated similarities and differences of a letter's opening salutation, several observations are worthy of consideration when studying and teaching the diverse opening salutations: sender, recipient, and greeting.

The Sender of a Letter

Concerning the *sender*, some of the General Letters offer no identification (Hebrews, 1 John);[15] in others the sender is either well known (2, 3

---

15.   The Letter to the Hebrews and 1 John tend to break many rules of letter writing. For instance in his excursus on letter writing, Demetrius deplores the use of periods in a letter as if the sender was writing a speech. He avers, it "is absurd." Yet both Hebrews and 1 John begin with a period, which is an extremely long sentence (Heb. 1:1–3; 1 John 1:1–3). And though Hebrews at least has a closing salutation, 1 John does not. Nevertheless, both are deemed letters by most commentators. See Bateman, "The Genre of Hebrews," *Charts on the Book of Hebrews*.

John)[16] or clearly identified by name (James, Peter, and Jude). Typical of all the letters exemplified above, 2 and 3 John offer no expanded or qualifying noun. Yet James, Peter, and Jude offer a rather significant expansion. Whereas James and Jude present themselves as a "slave" (δοῦλος), Peter describes himself as both an apostle[17] and "slave" (δοῦλος).

The noun "slave" (δοῦλος) typically referred to the legal status of a person in the Roman Empire. He or she was attached to a master; was an article of personal property that one buys, sells, leases, gives, bequeaths, jointly owns, and perhaps groups with the animals;[18] and was "duty-bound only to their owners or masters, or those to whom total allegiance is pledged."[19] The calculated use of the word "slave" (δοῦλος) by Peter, James, and Jude tells us something about their attitudes as members of God's kingdom. They present themselves as slaves who were "duty-bound" to Jesus, slaves who were in servitude to and thereby labored for Jesus. Jesus was not just someone they followed for three years (Peter) or a related sibling (James and Jude). Though English translations tend to render "Jesus Christ" (Ἰησοῦ Χριστοῦ) as though "Jesus" is his first name and "Christ" is his last, the term "Christ" (Χριστοῦ) serves as a title that identifies "Jesus" (Ἰησοῦ) as Messiah. Thus in their respective and expanded identifications of themselves, it is not an elevated expansion as we see in Trajan's opening salutation (cited above). Rather Peter, James, and Jude present themselves as slaves who belong to Jesus, who is the Christ (Ἰησοῦ Χριστοῦ).[20] Jesus is their King, and they in turn are his slaves in his kingdom. (This way of describing oneself is radical when considering we today tend to emphasize our friendship or perhaps even a sense of equality with Jesus.)

---

16. In the gospel of John there is a noticeable reticence on the part of the author to identify himself explicitly with the apostle John. In fact, John son of Zebedee is never mentioned by name in the fourth gospel. He refers to himself as the "disciple whom Jesus loved." Consistent with this, it is not inconceivable that John preferred to use the title "Elder" (πρεσβύτερος) rather than "Apostle" as a self-designation, although the churches to whom he ministered and wrote would naturally know who he was and what his status was. Thus, it is conceivable that the apostle John wrote the gospel of John and the Johannine letters.

17. The noun "apostle" (ἀπόστολος) is a favored designation of Paul. It speaks of a person having been *sent* by someone to someone else. Apostles are messengers from God with extraordinary status (BDAG 122b 2). In the LXX, "apostle" (ἀπόστολος) is the Greek rendering for the Hebrew term *saliah*. The prophet Ahijah, for example, was *sent* to deliver a divine message to the wife of king Jeroboam when she came and asked about her sick son (3 Kgdms. [1 Kings] 14:6; cf. *TDNT*, 1:413–14, 423).

18. Spicq, in *TLNT* (1994), "δοῦλος."

19. BDAG 260, δοῦλος. "For Judaism in the time of Jesus, as for the Greek world, the slave was on a lower level of humanity. By law the slave of non-Jewish birth was classed with immobile goods, had no rights at law and could not own property." Karl H. Rengstorf in *TDNT* (1983), "δοῦλος."

20. In all three salutations, Ἰησοῦ Χριστοῦ is a genitive of apposition. See Wallace, *Greek Grammar Beyond the Basics: An Exegetical Syntax of the New Testament* (Grand Rapids: Zondervan, 1996), 95–98.

The Recipient of a Letter

Concerning the *recipients*, most of the non-canonical Greco-Roman and Jewish letters illustrated in this chapter were addressed to an individual, which is also the case for 3 John. But most of the other canonical letters address a group of people either in a geographical region clearly stated (1 Peter) or to a group of people whereby as interpreters we must do some conjecturing (James, 2 John, Jude).[21] Still others cite no recipients at all but merely make reference to a group of people throughout their correspondence (Hebrews, 1 John). Our desire here, however, is to consider the obvious expansions, in particular affirming expansions of 1 John, 2 John, and Jude. All three avow to the recipients of their respective letters a form of "love" (ἀγαπάω), an occurrence that appears to be uncharacteristic among the sampling of the non-canonical Greco-Roman letters exemplified above.

On the one hand, John muses, "whom I love *with respect to the* truth" (ὃν ἐγὼ ἀγαπῶ ἐν ἀληθείᾳ)[22] to both an individual Gaius (3 John) and then again to a community of believers (2 John).[23] Jude, on the other hand, avers that God loves the group of people to whom he writes. They are "the called" (τοῖς κλητοῖς), "who are loved by God the Father" (ἐν θεῷ πατρὶ ἠγαπημέ-νοις). In light of the simplicity in which the name of the recipient is given in the non-canonical Greco-Roman letters illustrated above we might ask ourselves, why the expansion and what does "love" (ἀγαπάω) mean?

---

21. For instance, Jude does not specify a geographical region as Peter does when he named his recipients to be churches located in the Roman regions of Pontus, Cappadocia, Asia, and Bithynia (1 Peter 1:1). Jude merely directed his letter "to those who are called." Nevertheless, Jude's relationship with the ostensible leader of the Jerusalem church, James, appears to support the notion that Jude addressed his letter "to those called" followers of Jesus living in Judea. See Herbert W. Bateman IV, *2 Peter and Jude*, The Evangelical Exegetical Commentary (Bellingham, WA: Logos, forthcoming).

22. The prepositional phrase "in truth" (ἐν ἀληθείᾳ) is probably functioning as a dative of reference, and thereby translated "with respect to truth." It speaks directly to and affirms the belief or the theology of what Gaius as well as the community of believers believed about Jesus. The dative not only identifies belief, but how that belief is closely tied to how they live. Thus the recipients of both letters are loved not merely for what they believe but for how that belief affects how they live. See Bateman, *A Workbook for Intermediate Greek*, 31.

23. The "Elect Lady" (ἐκλεκτῇ κυρίᾳ) in 2 John is a metaphor for either the Church at large or a specific church located at some distance from the community where the author is living. For the sake of brevity, it seems 2 John is a letter of request to a "sister" church to honor God's command "that we love one another" (ἵνα ἀγαπῶμεν ἀλλήλους) in contrast to those who refuse to keep the command and deny Jesus' humanity ("do not confess Jesus, who is the Christ, as having come in the flesh," οἱ μὴ ὁμολογοῦντες Ἰησοῦν Χριστὸν ἐρχόμενον ἐν σαρκί). Thus, the "elect lady" (ἐκλεκτῇ κυρίᾳ) is a personified reference to a particular local church at some distance from the community where John lives, and the phrase "and to her children" (καὶ τοῖς τέκνοις αὐτῆς) is a reference to the people who attend that church. Bateman, *A Workbook for Intermediate Greek*, 94.

Unlike English, the Greeks had four words for expressing love: (1) στέργω, which generally describes familial affection;[24] (2) ἐρος, which generally described the sexual craving of an individual: "So violent was the desire for love that welled up in my heart, pouring out an opaque fog upon my eyes";[25] (3) φιλέω, which is marked by a kindly attitude and good will that came to indicate reciprocal friendship among equals;[26] and (4) ἀγαπάω,[27] which is very close to φιλέω as an expression of a rational kind of love. Unlike φιλέω, ἀγαπάω links people of different *social classes* and *conditions*, namely linking regular people (an inferior within a hierarchal society) with rulers, benefactors, and fathers (examples of a superior who are the hierarchal society).[28]

When tracing the concept of "love" (ἀγαπάω) in the Septuagint (LXX), the theological significance of the word (verb: ἀγαπάω; or noun: ἀγάπη) is not always limited to a special kind of divine love as is often communicated from many pulpits. For instance in 2 Samuel 13:1–15, both the verb and noun forms of love describe Amnon's infatuation with his half-sister Tamar that led to his raping of her. In fact, the majority of the noun appearances of "love" (ἀγάπη) in the LXX describe the love between a man and a woman (Song 2:4, 5, 7; 3:10; 5:8; 7:7; 8:4, 6, 7; cf. Jer. 2:2). Yet God's (a superior) special love for his people (inferiors) is indeed evident and does carry tremendous theological significance in the LXX (cf. Deut. 10:15; Isa. 43:4a; Hos. 11:1). Similarly, divine acts of "love" (ἀγαπάω) extending from a superior to an inferior appear often in the New Testament. It is in this sense that God loves the world (John 3:16) and knows no racial, social, or cultural boundaries.

So for the recipients of John's letters, the expansion appears to be a significant affirmation because John, "the *well-known* elder" (ὁ πρεσβύτε-

---

24. For instance in *Sirach* 27:17 it says, "Love your friend and keep faith with him; but if you betray his secrets, do not follow after him." For other examples see BDAG 943a, στέργω.

25. Archilochus, *Epodes* 8.245. Notice how the example parallel's Amnon's love for his sister, Tamar, whom he rapes. Take note, however, that ἀγάπη and ἀγαπάω are used in 2 Samuel 13. For other examples see Spicq in *TLNT* (1994), ἀγάπη.

26. It has been suggested that φιλέω did not express an emotional attachment, but merely indicated that a person belonged to a social group. It was always marked with a kindly attitude and good will, and yet at times it was employed to be very close to ἀγαπάω. See Spicq in *TLNT* (1994), ἀγάπη; cf. BDAG 1056c, ἀγάπη.

27. Dio Cassius, in his history of Rome, particularly the last years of the Roman Republic and the early Roman Empire, records how Julius Ceasar avers to his troops: "I love (ἀγαπω) you as a father loves his children" (12.27). Thus, the title of "father" given to emperors is "an invitation for them to love their subjects as their children" (53.18; 56.9). Spicq in *TLNT* (1994), ἀγάπη; Stauffer in *TDNT* (1983), "ἀγαπάω, ἀγάπη"; cf. BDAG 6a, ἀγάπη.

28. This discussion about "love" first appeared in *A Workbook for Intermediate Greek*, 115. The discussion was expanded and reapplied in my commentary for *2 Peter and Jude*, forthcoming.

ρος),[29] loves those to whom he writes as a father (a superior) loves his children (inferiors; see note 27). This unique expansion makes public a noteworthy relationship from which John launches a desired compliance to extend hospitality to itinerant preachers (3 John v.8) and a desired obedience of God's command that believers love one another (2 John v.5). For the recipients of Jude's letter, however, Jude's point is simply that people, who are "called" have been loved by God. God (a superior) has already loved the group of people (inferiors) who are called. Thus in verse 21 when Jude avers, "keep yourself" (ἑαυτοὺς . . . τηρήσατε) in God's love, it is an expectation or responsibility of the believers (inferiors) to remain *in* the love relationship with God (a superior), which God himself initiated with the recipients in verse 1. Thus, the striking expansion of the word "love" (ἀγαπάω) serves to reveal a significant relationship upon which all three letters build.

The Greeting of a Letter

Concerning the *greeting*, some salutations are merely "greetings" (χαίρειν) as exemplified earlier from Greco-Roman letters (cf. Acts 15:23; 23:26) or "peace" (*shalom*) as in the Jewish letter from the period of the Bar-Kokhba revolt (132–135 CE). Thus, they are merely, shall we say, a cultural cliché. In a similar way, the opening greeting in James, 2 Peter, and 3 John give the impression to be a mere cultural formality, and thereby add little or nothing to developments in their respective letters.[30] Yet, other greetings look as though they are more than a cliché or formality. Consequently, people differ over how much importance to place on the opening and closing formulas of a given letter, since ancient letter-writers seem to pay little attention to their

---

29. The addition of "well-known" is interpretive based upon a semantical category for the article "the" (ὁ). In this case the articles before "elder" (πρεσβύτερος) in both 2 John v.1 and 3 John v.1 serve to point out something about the elder, namely he is well-known or familiar to the readers. Thus, John need not name himself. See footnote #20 and Wallace, *Greek Grammar Beyond the Basics*, 225.

30. Davids compares James' use of the standard Greek epistolary "greeting" (χαίρειν) with Paul's double formula "grace to you and peace" (χάρις ὑμῖν καὶ εἰρήνη) and reasons "either because he lacked Paul's creativity and mastery of the Greek or because the Hellenistic redactor/scribe had principal responsibility for v 1 and did not think in Paul's more Aramaic terms." Peter Davids, *Commentary on James* in New International Greek Testament Commentary (Grand Rapids: Eerdmans, 1982), 64. "3 John displays," muses Lieu, "many of the features of the ordinary letters surviving from the ancient world, including the framing epistolary conventions such as a health wish (v 2), a thanksgiving (v. 3), a promise of a visit to compensate for the brevity of the letter (vv. 13–14), and the sharing of greetings with a third party before a closing farewell (v. 15). Judith M. Lieu, *I, II, & III John* in The New Testament Library (Louisville: John Knox Press, 2008), 265. For other examples of letter of commendation, see Clinton W. Keyes, "The Greek Letter of Introduction," *Journal of Philology*, 56.1 (1935): 28–44, especially page 35.

opening salutations.[31] Nevertheless, Jude's threefold greeting—"May mercy, peace, and love 'be multiplied' (πληθυνθείη)[32] to you"—looks to be calculated because Jude returns to these three themes later during his admonitions to the godly ones. He exhorts his readers to extend mercy to others (vv. 21b–23), to be different from those who were divisive (i.e., live in peace; vv. 19–20), and to remain in love (v. 21a).

In summary then, what have we learned about the opening salutation of a non-canonical letter; and how does what we now know affect how we might study, interpret, and teach the opening salutation of a General Epistle? First, we know that an opening salutation generally consists of a sender, a recipient, and some form of a greeting. Furthermore, brevity appears to be an outstanding characteristic of ancient non-canonical Greco-Roman letters. This brevity is particularly significant when comparing them to many of the opening salutations of the General Letters. So when a sender of a canonical letter attaches "slave" to his name, it appears to communicate a significant attitude as does the contemplatively inserted term "love" (ἀγαπάω), for it may undergird an epistle's theological concern (2, 3 John) or perhaps even foreshadow at least an aspect of the sender's later admonition (Jude vv.1, 21–23). Consequently, when studying, interpreting, and teaching the General Letters some attention should be given to the various expansions attached to the sender's name, the apparent affirmations extended to the recipients, and the chosen extension for an opening greeting because any one of these may reemerge as a significant theme later in the letter. These significant expansions naturally lengthen the canonical letters, and as we shall see, the type of correspondence also contributes to why the General Letters are longer than the average non-canonical Greco-Roman letter.

TYPES OF EPISTOLARY CORRESPONDENCE

The purpose of this section is to compare and contrast the different types of epistolary correspondence within the Greco-Roman world,

---

31. Stanley K. Stowers, *Letter Writing in Greco–Roman Antiquity* in Literature of Early Christianity edited by Wayne A. Meeks (Philadelphia: Westminster, 1986), 20.

32. The added passive infinitive, 'be multiplied' (πληθυνθείη), may be a noteworthy expansion for not only Jude but for the Petrine Letters because it is a wish for God's blessing. Semantically, Achtemeier avers, "the passive form of the verb "multiply" (πληθυνθείη) is probably a 'reverential passive,' a form used among Jews to avoid mentioning God's name . . ." Paul J. Achtemeier, *1 Peter* in Hermeneia (Minneapolis: Fortress, 1996), 89. God's multiplying of "grace and peace" in the midst of suffering under a hierarchal system might suggest something more in 1 Peter. Certainly in Jude's case "the blessings that Jude emphasizes are woven," according to Green, "into the fabric of his epistle and, therefore, this wish-prayer serves as an introduction to the fundamental themes he will take up." Gene Green, *Jude & 2 Peter*, BECNT (Grand Rapids: Baker, 2008), 50.

and thereby offer some suggestions as to how determining the type of a General Epistle may benefit our studying, interpreting, and teaching them. As we noted above, tracing developments in ancient letter writing within the Greco-Roman world is difficult. Nevertheless, it seems the earliest extant guidelines concerning letter writing come from the renowned Athenian orator, Isocrates.[33] He was the first to treat rhetorical prose as a work of art. His most famous written rhetorical discourse was his plea for Athens and Sparta to join forces against Persia (380 BCE). Isocrates believed, however, that *letter-writing was to differ from written rhetorical discourses.*[34] A variety of his letters have survived over the years. His ten extent letters, written from 385 to 338 BCE, illustrate several very early epistolary types of letters, for he wrote letters that admonished, advised, counseled rulers, exhorted, encouraged and dissuaded, introduced and commended a friend, and petitioned another person.

Letters of Isocrates (436–338 BCE)	Letter to Admonish	Letter to Advise	Letter to Counsel	Letter to Exhort	Letter to Encourage & Dissuade	Letter to Introduce-Commend	Letter to Request-Petition
Busiris (ca. 385)	√						
To Dionysius (368 or 367)		√					
To the Children of Jason (359 or 358)						√	

---

33. Isocrates was born in 436 BCE, eight years before Plato. His birth into a wealthy Athenian family afforded him an excellent education in Athens and he eventually joined the circle of Socrates. His most significant contribution was to the development of rhetorical theory, philosophy, and education in Ancient Greece. Isocrates' model of education guided educators in rhetoric for centuries. Tradition suggests that Isocrates starved himself to death at the age of 98, after Philip of Macedon defeated Athens at the Battle of Charonea (338 BCE).

34. This point strikes me as significant, namely that letters differ from rhetorical discourses because many contemporary commentators look for rhetorical structure within the body of a General Epistle. They study, interpret, and teach canonical letters as though they are rhetorical discourses and not ancient letters. At times, such attempts appear forced and out of sync with the general distinction between rhetorical speech and personal letter.

Letters of Isocrates (436–338 BCE)	Letter to Admonish	Letter to Advise	Letter to Counsel	Letter to Exhort	Letter to Encourage & Dissuade	Letter to Introduce-Commend	Letter to Request-Petition
To Archidamus (356)			√				
To the rulers of the Mytilenaeans (350)							√
To Philip of Macadon (346)			√	√			
To Timotheus (345)						√	
To Antipater (ca. 340)						√	
To Alexander (ca. 342–340)					√		
To Philip of Macadon (338)			√	√			

Based upon these ten letters, Sullivan suggests an Isocratean theory of letter writing.[35]

1. Letters are written communications sent directly from one person to another.

2. These communications may perform a wide variety of rhetorical tasks, of both private and public natures.

---

35. Robert G. Sullivan, "Classical Epistolary Theory and Letters of Isocrates" in *Letter-Writing Manuals and Instruction from Antiquity to the Present*, ed. Carol Poster and Linda C. Mitchell (Columbia: University of South Carolina Press, 2007), 7.

3. As written communications, they have all the strengths and weaknesses of other written forms and may clash with sensibilities more attuned to oral discourse.

4. Letters should be opened with a formulary address of either a long nominative ‹dative› infinitive construction, or a truncated form indicating the receiver in the dative case.

5. Formulary closings are available and optional.

6. Letters of patronage have relatively settled ways of introducing clients and asking for the aid of the receiver in reminding the client of his patron's intercession.

So for Isocrates, it appears letters were to have particular symmetries and stylistics: they should be short, personal, and written in a simpler style than that of a speech, and they were not to be impertinent, ostentatious, or excessively elaborate.

Over time, guidelines for letter writing were developed, duplicated, and distributed for public consumption—in much the same way as "how to" manuals have been produced to guide a person when composing different types of email depending on the situation.[36] Consequently, we have today an excursus on ancient letter writing and two instructional manuals from the Greco-Roman period. These tools were intended to teach and model how to compose different types of letters. We begin with the earliest extant epistolary tool employed for instructing a person in how to write a letter. It is a brief excursus about letter-writing found in a work entitled *On Style*, attributed to Demetrius of Phalerum, and considered by most to be from the first century BCE. Unlike Isocrates from whom we can merely surmise ancient letter writing practices, Demetrius lists guidelines for letter writing from which the following is a selective summary.[37]

1. Letters are written communications as though speaking with a friend.

2. Letters should reveal a glimpse of character that is of reasonable length.

---

36. While White limits ancient letter types to two broad kinds of messages: "(1) the imparting/seeking of information, and (2) the making of requests/commands," he too recognizes that "these epistolary functions come to expression in the body, whereas the broader maintenance of contact is characteristically conveyed by the opening and closing." John White, "The Greek Documentary Letter Tradition Third Century BCE to Third Century CE," *Semeia* 22 (1981): 89–106, especially 95.

37. Abraham J. Malherbe, *Ancient Epistolary Theorists* (Atlanta: Scholars Press, 1988), 16–19.

3. Letters are to be structured with a degree of freedom granted to the author, but extensive use of the period is "absurd."

4. Letter-writers are to "remember there are epistolary topics, as well as epistolary style."

5. Letters ought to evidence both a graceful and plain style.

Although Demetrius spoke about letter-writing as merely an excursus, there are two ancient how-to manuals devoted to writing letters. Both contain a theory of letter-writing followed by a descriptive model for the various types of letters.

Types of Ancient Letters

The first, *Letter Types* (*Typoi Epistolikoi*), is falsely ascribed to Demetrius and frequently referred to as Ps.-Demetrius. Although broadly dated somewhere between the second century BCE and the third century CE, there are six pages of text that indicate some standardized body of epistolary theory. It seems the intended audience was students training to be professional letter-writers. The manual not only names and defines twenty-one different types of letters, it also identifies the goals for each type of letter, explains the formulaic and categorical nature for each type, and offers an example. For instance, the suggestion given to a person who desires to commend someone needs to write *a commendatory type of letter*; a person who desires to expose unworthy conduct needs to write a *vituperative type of letter*; a person who wants to exhort or dissuade someone from something should do so via an *advisory type of letter*; a person who wants to teach what should and should not be done would do so via an *admonishing type of letter*; or if a person desired to express sympathy or console another he would do so in a *consoling type of letter* and thereby consider the following suggestions.[38]

> *The commendatory type*, which we write on behalf of one person to another, mixing in praise, at the same time also speaking of those who had previously been unacquainted as though they were (now) acquainted. In the following manner:
>
>> So-and-so, who is conveying this letter to you, has been tested by us and is loved on account of his trustworthiness. You will do well if you deem him worthy of hospitality both for your sake and his, and indeed for your

---

38. The four examples and translations are from Abraham J. Malherbe, *Ancient Epistolary Theorists* (Atlanta, GA: Scholars Press, 1988), 33, 35, 37.

own. For you will not be sorry if you entrust to him, in any matter you
wish, either words or deeds of a confidential nature. Indeed, you, too, will
praise him to others when you see how useful he can be in everything.

It is *the vituperative type* when we bring to light the badness of someone's character or the offensiveness of (his) action against someone.
In the following manner:

> Even if I should remain silent, you would hear from others how meanly
> and how unworthily of their conduct So-and-so has treated those men
> who have been entrusted with responsibility. For it is proper to write
> concerning matters about which some people might not know. But it is as
> superfluous to write concerning matters that everybody knows about and
> that are being noise abroad by rumor itself, as it is to make known those
> things which are exposed by the very fact of their being kept secret.

It is *the advisory type* when, by offering our own judgment, we exhort
(someone to) something or dissuade (him) from something. For example, in the following manner:

> I have briefly indicated to you those things for which I am held in high
> esteem by my subjects. I know, therefore, that you, too, by this course
> of action can gain the goodwill of your obedient subjects. Yet, while
> you cannot make many friends, you can be fair and humane to all. For if
> you are such a person, you will have a good reputation and your position
> will be secure among the masses.

It is *the admonishing type* one which indicates by its name what its
character is. For admonition is the instilling of sense in the person
who is being admonished, and teaching him what should and should
not be done. In the following manner:

> You acted badly when you ill-treated a man who had conducted him-
> self well and had lived according to reason and had, generally speaking,
> done you no harm. Realize, therefore, that this action (of yours) de-
> serves an apology. Indeed, if you had been so treated by some else, you
> would have taken it amiss and demanded justice for what had been done
> to you. Do not, then, think that the person who would rebuke sins had
> neither parents nor a (proper) upbringing, nor, worst of all, that he has
> no relative or friend.

The consoling type is that written to people who are grieving because
something unpleasant has happened (to them). It is as follows:

> When I heard of the terrible things that you met at the hands of thank-
> less fate, I felt the deepest grief, considering that what had happened
> had not happened to you more than to me. When I consider that such
> things are the common lot of all, with nature establishing neither a
> particular time or age in which one must suffer anything, but often con-
> fronting us secretly, you, I decided to do so by letter. Bear, then, what
> has happened as lightly as you can, and exhort yourself just as you would
> exhort someone else. For you know that reason will make it easier for
> you to be relieved of your grief with the passage of time.

These five examples will prove significant later in this section when
discussing the types of General Letters.

The second manual is entitled *Epistolary Types (Epistolimaioi Kharactêres)*.
Like Ps.-Demetrius, it too has been falsely ascribed to someone, Libanius.
Although difficult to date, it probably dates to the fourth-century CE but
evolved gradually over time at the hands of many authors. Like Isocrates
and Ps.-Demetrius, Ps.-Libanius considered a letter to be a "written conversation" addressed to someone who was not physically present. Unlike
the previous manual, however, the intended audience was apparently
elite members of society who could not afford professional letter-writers
or who wished to write their own letters. The manual begins with an
introduction followed by naming forty-one letter types. It then offers a
summary of epistolary theory and provides a collection of model letters
illustrating each type. For instance, the suggestion given to a person who
needs to exhort a person to avoid something would write a *paraenetic type
of letter*; a person who desires to commend a person would write a *commendatory type of letter*; a person who wants to empower someone would
write an *encouraging type of letter*; a person who wanted to console someone would write an *consoling type of letter*; a person who needs to speak to
someone's character might write a *maligning type of letter*; or finally a person who may need to address more than one issue would write *a mixed
type of letter* and thereby would consider the following suggestions.[39]

> The paraenetic style is that in which we exhort someone by urging him
> to pursue something or to avoid something. Paraenesis is divided into
> two parts, encouragement and dissuasion. Some also call it the advisory
> style, but do so incorrectly, for paraenesis differs from advise. For parae-
> nesis is hortatory speech that does not admit of a counter-statement, for

39. The examples and translations are from Malherbe, *Ancient Epistolary Theorists*. For the
     paraenetic style and letter see pages 69, 75; the commendation style and letter see pages 69,
     75; the encouraging style and encouraging letter see pages 71, 81; the consoling style and
     sympathetic letter see pages 71, 77; maligning style and letter see pages 71, 79; mixed style
     and letter see pages 73, 81.

example, if someone should say that we must honor the divine. For nobody contradicts this exhortation were he not mad to begin with. But advice is advisory speech that does admit of a counter-statement. . . .

> *The paraenetic letter.* Always be an emulator, dear friend, of virtuous men. For it is better to be well spoken of when imitating good men than to be reproached by all men while following evil men.

The commendatory style is that in which we commend someone to someone. It is also called the introductory style.

> *The letter of commendation.* Receive this highly honored and much sought-after man and do not hesitate to treat him hospitably, this doing what behooves you and what pleases me.

The encouraging style is that in which we encourage someone and make them fearless.

> *The letter of encouragement.* Be completely fearless, and hold your ground while living honorably, because God is well disposed toward you. For God everywhere helps the person who lives an upright life.

The consoling or sympathetic style is that in which we console someone over the troubles that befell them.

> *The consoling letter.* I was grieved in soul when I heard of the terrible things that had befallen you, and I besought God to free you from them. For it behooves friends to pray that they may see their friends forever free of evils.

The maligning style is that in which we attack someone's character for what he has done.

> *The maligning letter.* So-and-so, who has a very bad character, has caused me much harm. For, after having acted as though he were my friend, and having received many favors from me when he as not able to repay me measure for measure because he possessed no noble qualities, he brought the greatest evils down upon me. Be on your guard, therefore, against this man, lest you, too experience terrible trials at his hands.

The mixed style is that in which we compose from many styles.

> *The mixed letter.* I know that you live a life of piety, that you conduct yourself as a citizen in a manner worthy of respect, indeed, that you

adorn the illustrious name of philosophy itself, with the excellence of an
unassailable and pure citizenship. But in this one thing alone do you err,
that you slander your friends. You must avoid that, for it is not fitting
that philosophers engage in slander.

As it was the case for the five examples provided from Ps.-Demetrius,
these six examples will prove significant later in this section when discussing the types of General Letters. In conclusion, both manuals offer
suggestions for how to write a commendatory and consoling type letter, so there is overlap between the two manuals. Both manuals look as
though they describe similar types of letters but name them differently
as in the case of the vituperative and maligning types of letters as well
as the advising and paraenetic types of letters.[40] Then there are letters
unique to both, which is the case concerning the mixed, admonishing, and encouraging letter. The following chart lists the various types
of letters identified, taught, and exemplified in the Ps.-Demetrius and
Ps.-Libanius manuals.[41]

Types of Greco-Roman Letters in Ps.-Demetrius and Ps.-Libanius			
Twelve Letters Common to Both	Nine Letters Unique to Ps.-Demetrius	Twenty-eight Letters Unique to Ps.-Libanius	
Blaming	Accounting	Angry	Insulting
Censorious	Accusing	Commanding	Maligning*
Commendation*	Admonishing*	Conciliatory	Mixed*
Congratulatory	Advisory*	Consulting	Mocking
Consoling*	Allegorical	Contemptuous	Paraenetic*

40. Many people refer to the General Letters as paraenetic letters. Yet Demetrius describes the
     "advisory type" letter as exhorting someone to something or dissuading someone from
     something, and in a similar manner Libanius describes the "paraenetic type" letter as involving
     "encouragement and dissuasion." The person is exhorted, by urging, "to pursue something
     or to avoid something." Compare Stowers, *Letter Writing in Greco-Roman Antiquity*, 96 and
     Greene, *Jude & 2 Peter*, 37–38 with Malherbe, *Ancient Epistolary Theorists*, 35, 69.
41. The asterisks (*) are the types of letters defined and exemplified in this chapter. Consoling
     letters in Ps. Demetrius and sympathetic letters in Ps. Libanius are viewed as synonymous
     types of letters.

THE GENRE OF THE GENERAL LETTERS

Types of Greco-Roman Letters in Ps.-Demetrius and Ps.-Libanius			
Twelve Letters Common to Both	Nine Letters Unique to Ps.-Demetrius	Twenty-eight Letters Unique to Ps.-Libanius	
Friendly	Apologetic	Counter-accusing	Praying
Inquiring	Responding	Declaratory	Provoking
Ironic	Supplicatory	Denying	Repenting
Praising	Vituperative★	Didactic	Replying
Reproachful		Diplomatic	Reporting
Thankful		Encouraging★	Reproving
Threatening		Enigmatic	Requesting
		Erotic	Submissive
		Grieving	Suggestive

So just as there are different types of ancient non-canonical letters, there are different types of General Letters.

Types of General Letters

Naturally, any letter's type is reflected in the composition of the body of the letter. In other words, to identify a letter's type we need to *look for performance goals stated or identify specific descriptive features in the body of the letter* to determine the type of letter. As we advance our discussion, however, it will become painfully obvious that assigning *every* biblical letter to any one of these ancient forms of correspondence could be debated. Yet by the same token, merely to limit the labeling of a General Epistle to "an ancient letter" based solely upon structure (an opening salutation, body, closing salutation) seems to ignore the historical reality that ancient non-canonical letters addressed topics that warrant the writing of diverse types of letters. So we need to bear in mind when studying the General Letters that they too are diverse in character, intention, and type that employ rhetorical methods (though different from rhetorical works). So the question to ask is simply: what types of letters are evident among the

General Letters? At this point, we will point out three types of ancient letters represented among the General Letters: a commendation type of letter, a mixed vituperative and admonishing type of letter, and a mixed consoling and paraenetic type of letter.

Commendatory Letter. Moving beyond the fact that 3 John consists of an *opening* salutation (vv.1–2), a *body* (vv.3–12), and a *closing* salutation (vv.13–15), the threefold body of John's letter, visibly marked by way of John's use of "beloved" (ἀγαπητέ),[42] exhibits several features typical of *the commendatory styled* letter. First, "the elder" (ὁ πρεσβύτε-ρος) writes to Gaius (v.1) on behalf of several itinerate ministers of the gospel (vv.6b, 12). Second, the letter praises (commends) Gaius for hospitality he extended to traveling preachers whom he previously did not know (vv.3, 5–6a), but then commends these same itinerant preachers and others as people worthy of further hospitality (v.6b). The reason for further kindness is due to their mission and dependence on fellow followers of Jesus (v.7). Third, John commends Demetrius as having been tested by the elder (v.12). Finally, the intention behind "the elder's" mitigated expectation to extend hospitality to these commended itinerant preachers is ultimately a benefit to Gaius (vv.8, 10).[43] Terms like "tested" and phrases like "loved on account of his trustworthiness," "worthy of hospitality," and beneficial "both for your sake" are the features expected of a letter of commendation.[44] Thus, it would appear safe to say that 3 John exhibits features characteristic of a *letter of commendation*.

---

42. In his letter of recommendation, John first uses "beloved" (ἀγαπητῷ) to describe his friendship with Gaius. In verse 2, John shifts to direct address using the vocative case (ἀγαπητέ). John purposefully addresses Gaius as "beloved" three times (vv. 2, 5, and 11) to transition from one section to another throughout the body of the letter. Although the transitional marker "beloved" (ἀγαπητοί) is a direct address, it is a term of endearment and personal warmth. In Johannine letters it occurs ten times (1 John 2:7, 3:2, 3:21, 4:1, 7, 11; 3 John vv.1, 2, 5, 11).

43. For commentators who consider 3 John to be a letter of commendation see George Strecker, *The Johannine Letters*, Hermenea (Minneapolis: Fortress, 1989), 253–54; Robert W. Yarbough, *1–3 John*, Baker Exegetical Commentary on the New Testament (Grand Rapids: Baker, 2008), 363. Compare Chan-Hie Kim, *Form and Structure of the Familiar Greek Letter of Recommendation*, SBLDS 4 (Missoula, MT: Scholars, 1972).

44. Stowers highlights two fundamental elements of a commendatory letter: "the writer and the recipient share some positive relationship of reciprocity and are most often social peers in some respect (e.g., friends, family, government officials)," and "the writer intercedes on behalf of a third party in order to perform a favor for or through the third party and to establish appositive social relationship between the recipient and the third party." Stowers, however, views 3 John to exhibit freedom in that though a letter of recommendation (vv. 8, 10), it "contains a short invective (*psegin*) in vv.9–10 and exhortation in vv.11–12." Stanley K. Stowers, *Letter Writing in Greco-Roman Antiquity* (Philadelphia: The Westminster Press, 1986), 156. Funk views 3 John as a petition with commendation. Robert W. Funk, "Form and Structure of II John and III John," *JBL* 86, no. 4 (1967): 424–30, esp. 427.

Vituperative & Admonishing Letter. Moving beyond the fact that Jude's letter consists of an *opening* salutation (vv.1–2), a *body* (vv.3–23), and a *closing* doxology (vv.24–25), the *body* of Jude's letter has the look of a mixed letter: a vituperative styled and an advisory (or paraenetic) styled letter.[45] Jude's three-part body begins with a stated performance goal (vv. 3–4) whereby he introduces vituperative and advisory features. Jude then advances to his vituperative disclosures. The ungodly people, namely "godless *people*" (ἀσε-βεῖς) who deny Jesus' Messiahship (v. 3), are unmistakably compared with rebels of a worthless cause and thereby destined for divine punishment (vv. 5–16). Jude exposes several character flaws about a group of people who have maneuvered their way, in a secretive manner, into Judean churches. He draws lucid attention to the "badness" of that group of individuals and the "offensiveness" of their actions, which in Jude's case may be those involved in the mounting atmosphere of rebellion and insurrections against Rome during the 60s. (More will be said about this topic in our next chapter.) The offensiveness of these "godless *people*" (ἀσεβεῖς) is unmistakably evident in several triplet portraits of "these *people*" (οὗτοι). Thus, Jude makes typological comparisons and disclosures of several Old Testament portraits within his "vituperative type" or "maligning type" of letter.

Overview	Threefold Portraits			Jude
OT Paradigm of Divine Punishment of the Rebellious	*Remember the Wilderness generation*	*Remember the Fallen angels*	*Remember Sodom & Gomorrah*	vv.5–7
Unbecoming Scruples	Self-polluting	Rebels	Slanderers	v.8
OT Paradigm of Divine Punishment of the Godless	They are like Cain	They are like Balaam	They are like Korah	v.11
Unbecoming Scruples	Blemishes	Brazen	Selfish	v.12
Unbecoming Scruples	Disgruntled murmurers	Boastful	Patronizing	v.16

---

45. For commentators who consider Jude to be a vituperative and advisory letter see Gene L. Green, *Jude & 2 Peter*, BECNT (Grand Rapids: Baker, 2008), 37–38, 55–56.

After these compelling disclosures about a group of shady characters with questionable scruples, Jude proceeds to advise his Judean readers and instill in them steps to be taken to remedy their situation (vv.17–23). Whereas Jude first advises the churches in Judea "to fight" (ἐπαγωνίζε-σθαι) for their faith (v.3), he now teaches or offers instructions concerning what their "fight" for their faith involves. Jude exhorts: "keep yourselves in God's love" (ἑαυτοὺς ἐν ἀγάπῃ θεοῦ τηρήσατε; v.21a), "be merciful to believers who doubt" (οὓς μὲν ἐλεᾶτε διακρινομένους; v.22), "save other people from the fire" (οὓς δὲ σῴζετε. ἐκ πυρὸς ἁρπάζοντες; v.23a), and "be merciful with fear" (οὓς δὲ ἐλεᾶτε ἐν φόβῳ) to those who disbelieve (v.23b). Thus, the *body* of Jude's letter evidences features of a mixed letter: a vituperative description of the godless (vv.5–16) and strong advice to the godly (vv.17–23) as stated in Jude's preempted performance goals that opened the body of his letter (vv.3–4). In a similar way, 2 Peter is a mixed letter that has vituperative (2:1–22) and advisory (or paraenetic) features (1:5–11; 3:1–18a).[46]

Consoling & Paraenetic Letter. Moving beyond the fact that Peter's letter consists of an *opening* salutation (1:1–2), a *body* (1:3–5:11), and a *closing* doxology (5:12–14), the *body* of 1 Peter looks like a mixed letter: a consoling and paraenetic (or advisory) styled letter. It consists of three parts: a consoling styled opening (1:3–5); a two-part parenesis styled set of advice/exhortations (1:13–2:10 and 2:11–4:11); and a consolation styled closing (4:12–5:11).[47] As is typical of the consoling letter, Peter is aware of the "terrible things" his readers are suffering and thereby is sympathetic to their situation (1:6–7; 2:18–23; 3:9, 13–18; 4:1–4, 12–19; 5:8–10). He begins with a theological consolation about a person's new life in Jesus that appears to govern the entire letter.[48] Thus, the *body* of Peter's letter has features of a mixed letter: a consoling styled letter (1:3–5; 4:12–5:11) and exhortations to persevere as people of God typical of a paraenetic (or advisory) styled letter (1:6–4:11).

In summary then, what have we learned about the types of ancient letters; and how does what we now know affect how we might study, interpret, and teach the General Letters? We learned that letters were different from rhetorical discourses, had divergent styles, and prescribed guidelines existed for each type of letter. So how does what we now

---

46. Green, *Jude & 2 Peter*, 168–69.

47. For commentators who consider 1 Peter a mixed *paraenetic & consoling type letter* see Paul A. Holloway, "*Nihil inopinati accidisse*–'Nothing unexpected has happened': A Cyrenaic Consolatory *Topos* in 1 Peter 4:12ff," *New Testament Studies* 48 (2002): 433–48. Jobes also considers this deserving of further study. Karen H. Jobes, *1 Peter*, BECNT (Grand Rapids: Baker, 2005), 55.

48. David W. Kendall, "The Literary and Theological Function of 1 Peter 1:3–12" in *Perspectives on First Peter*, ed. C. H. Talbert (Macon, GA: Mercer University Press, 1986), 103–20.

know about different types of letters affect how we study, interpret, and teach the General Letters? Distinguishing a General Epistle's type sometimes baffle interpreters, particularly when it comes to Hebrews, James, and 1 John. In fact, Hebrews,[49] James,[50] and 1 John[51] appear to defy classification. Nevertheless, commentators are correct to wrestle with classifying the type represented in any given General Letter for interpretive purposes, which in turn affects the manner in which we eventually study, interpret, and teach the letters. The following chart is a modest proposal about the types of letters found among the General Letters. Nearly all exhibit mixed features of two letter types.

General Letters (45–95 CE)	Advisory or Paraenetic Letter	Commendatory Letter	Consoling Letter	Encouraging Letter	Vituperative or Maligning Letter
Hebrews (64–70 CE)	√		√	√ (?)	

---

49. Hebrews appears to have features similar to that of a consoling letter (2:16, 18; 10:32–34) followed by features of a paraenetic or advisory letter whereby the author strings together strong advice (2:1–5; 2:18; 6:2–8; 4:2–13, 17–19; 10:25–28, 35–38) and at times a seeming admonition (5:11–6:3) and exhortations that exhibit a general ethical content (2:1; 3:1, 13; 4:11, 16; 6:1, 11, 18; 10:22, 24, 32; 12:1; see 13:21). See Stowers, *Letter Writing in Greco-Roman Antiquity*, 96–97; Bateman, "Hebrews: A 'Mixed' Christian Letter of Exhortation," "Words of Exhortation in Hebrews," in *Charts on the Book of Hebrews*.

50. James appears to exhibit features similar to that of a consoling letter (2:2–11) followed by features of a paraenetic or advisory letter whereby the author strings together exhortations that exhibit a general ethical content (1:19–5:11). Donald J. Verseput, "Genre and Story: The Community Setting of the Epistle of James," CBQ 62 (2000): 96–110, esp. 102–04; Stowers, *Letter Writing in Greco-Roman Antiquity*, 96–97, 128; Martin Dibelius, *James: A Commentary on the Epistle of James*, Hermeneia, ed. Heinrich Greeven, trans. Michael A. Williams (Philadelphia: Fortress, 1976), 21.

51. Although readily debated, 1 John appears to be a mixed letter as well. Whereas 1 John opens with a prologue and closes with an exhortation, the body of 1 John appears to exhibit the mixed features of commendation (2:1–2, 6, 12–14, 22, 26; 3:1–3, 21; 4:4, 14–15; 5:1, 10–13) and paraenetic or advisory letter (2:15, 24, 28; 3:18; 4:1, 7, 11; 5:21). Although Klauck argues for 1 John to be deliberative rhetoric of an advisory nature, the point of emphasis is his recognition of 1 John's advisory features. See Hans-Josef Klauck, "Zur rhetorischen Analyse der Johannesbriefe," ZNW 81 (1990): 203–24, especially 208–16. See also Stowers, *Letter Writing in Greco-Roman Antiquity*, 96.

General Letters (45–95 CE)	Advisory or Paraenetic Letter	Commendatory Letter	Consoling Letter	Encouraging Letter	Vituperative or Maligning Letter
James (45–50 CE)	√		√		
1 Peter (63–65 CE)	√		√		
2 Peter (64–68 CE)	√				√
1 John (90–95 CE)	√	√			
2 John (90–95 CE)	√	√			
3 John (90–95 CE)		√			
Jude (65–68 CE)	√				√

The point to be made about teaching a General Epistle is: suppose a male employee were to get a letter of recommendation from a female supervisor, few people would read and then interpret it as though it were a love letter. Similarly it would be odd to teach Jude's vituperatively styled letter during a mission's conference or pastor's ordination service centered on commending a person. Equally unsuitable, it seems to me, is to preach Peter's mixed consoling/paraenetic letter about suffering at a wedding. One further point worth observing: When raising the issue of letter length, as we did at the close of "Component Parts," the fact that all but one epistle (3 John) is a mixed typed of letter obliviously contributes to these canonical letters being above the average length of a Greco-Roman letter. A reasonable question to stop and ponder is: Who in the Greco-Roman world were aware of these fine epistolary distinctions?[52]

TRAINED LETTER-WRITERS AND PSEUDONYMITY

The purpose of this section is to discuss the role of trained letter-writers known as amanuenses within the Greco-Roman world, and thereby offer some suggestions as to how such information benefits our studying, interpreting, and teaching of the General Letters. When studying the General Letters and Paul, it is necessary to be aware and even watchful for clues that may point us to a sender's employment of trained letter-writers. For instance, Paul provides evidence that he himself did not personally write five letters: 1 Corinthians, Galatians, Philemon, Colossians, and 2 Thessalonians. Nevertheless, he authenticates each letter bearing his name when he apparently stopped the amanuensis, provided an obvious change in handwriting, and employed an authenticating phrase "with my own hand" (τῇ ἐμῇ χειρί) at the end of each letter (1 Cor. 16:21; Gal. 6:11; Philem. v.19; Col. 4:18; 2 Thess. 3:17). Furthermore, Tertius wrote Romans (Rom. 16:22). Thus, six Pauline letters appear to have been written by amanuenses and five were authenticated as Paul's own letter in the closing salutation. We might ask ourselves whether such a practice is appropriate.

The Need for Trained Letter-writers

In answering both questions we must consider the time period by considering our current practice of sending email, more specifically the fact that everyone using email is capable of composing, sending, and reading emails. We alluded to this significant difference much earlier in this chapter. Unlike today in the United States, the majority of people in the ancient Greco-Roman world could not read and write. Subsequently, literacy rates were quite low. And though the lack of records hinders our ability for determining with any sense of accuracy the number of literate people,[53] it has been estimated that literacy rates in the Greco-Roman world were seldom more than twenty percent,[54] and

---

52. It is the presupposition throughout this book that these dates are in fact the best options provided by commentators. See D. A. Carson and Douglas Moo, *An Introduction to the New Testament* (Grand Rapids: Zondervan, 1992, second edition 2005); Donald Guthrie, *New Testament Introduction* (Downers Grove, IL: InterVarsity Press, 4th ed. 1990); Robert G. Gramacki, *New Testament Survey* (Grand Rapids: Baker, 1974).

53. Chiappetta argues that there are few accounts of Roman educational process until the second century BCE. Michael Chiappetta, "Historiography and Roman Education," *History of Education Journal* 4, no. 4 (1953): 149–156.

54. The average literacy rate in the Roman Empire was ten percent and perhaps five percent

in Judea during the first century CE the literacy rate was as low as three percent.[55] So the actual number of people who could read and write was limited. Consequently, letter-writers were distinguished as learned people, considered to perform an acknowledged professional skill, and linked with scribes throughout Greco-Roman society. Thus, public and private documents as well as public and personal letters were often dictated to amanuensis (singular). Whether one was literate or not, to employ a trained letter writer was a cultural and acceptable phenomenon. One could only imagine how professional letter-writers would benefit from the letter-writing manuals presented above. An amanuensis composed the following letters.

The first letter is an ancient sales receipt (77 CE) evident in a *reporting type letter* that affirms the sale of an eight-year-old female slave unmistakably written by an amanuensis on behalf of the dispatcher.[56]

LETTER'S OPENING	To the agoramoni . . . from Bacche, citizen, daughter of Hermon, with her guardian Diognetus, son of Dionysius, of the Epiphanean deme.
LETTER'S BODY	I swear by the Emperor Caesar Vespasianus Augustus that I have said to Heliodora, daughter of Heliodora, with her guardian who is her husband Apollonius, son of Dionysius, son of Dionysius also called Didymus, the slave Sarapous who belongs to me, and is about eight years old and without blemish apart from epilepsy and leprosy; and I swear that she is my property and is not mortgaged, and has not been alienated to other persons in any respect, and that I have received the price, 640 silver drachmae, and will guarantee the contract. If I swear truly, may it be well with me, but if false, the reverse.

in the western provinces. William V. Harris, *Ancient Literacy* (Cambridge, MA: Harvard University Press, 1989), 3–24.

55. Catherine Hezser, *Jewish Literacy in Roman Palestine*, Texte und Studien zum Antiken Judentum 81 (Tübingen: J. C. B. Mohr, 2001), 18–26; Meir Bar-Ilan, "Illiteracy in the Land of Israel in the First Centuries C.E." in *Essays in the Social Scientific Study of Judaism and Jewish Society*, eds. S. Fishbane, S. Schoenfeld and A. Goldschlaeger, (New York: Ktav, 1992), 46–61.

56. Catherine Hezser, *Jewish Literacy in Roman Palestine*, Texte und Studien zum Antiken Judentum 81, 474; Allan Millard, *Reading and Writing in the Time of Jesus* (Sheffield: Sheffield Academic Press, 2000), 168; Stowers, *Letter Writing in Greco-Roman Antiquity*, 19.

LETTER'S CLOSING   Signature of Diognetus on behalf of Bacche,
                      and date.[57]

Similarly a trained Jewish scribe (or an amanuensis) wrote our second
letter. It is a *commanding type* letter found in one of the numerous caves
surrounding Engedi where rebels sought shelter while fighting Rome.
The letter concerns a verbal communication too confidential to put in
writing. Thus, Elisha was expected or rather ordered to convey a message face to face, rather than by pen and ink (cf. 2 John v.12; 3 John v.13).

LETTER'S OPENING   Letter of Simeon bar Kosiba, peace! To
                      Yehonatan son of Be'aya

LETTER'S BODY   [my order is] that whatever Elisha tells you do
                      to him and help him and those with him [or: in
                      every action].

LETTER'S CLOSING   Be well.[58]

Obviously, both letters share a similar structure with an opening address and greeting, the letter's body, and the letter's closing salutation.
But they have other shared elements: both are written as if speaking
directly to the recipient in person, one is a letter of recommendation,
and the other a commanding type letter. Thus, it is clear persons other
than the senders wrote the letters on behalf of their respectively named
senders. Yet when studying the General Letters, particularly 1–2 Peter,
James and Jude, the allegation is that someone falsely ascribed these letters to Peter, James, and Jude. This assertion is heightened when considering the fact that unlike Paul there is no authenticating phrase "with
my own hand" (τῇ ἐμῇ χειρί) at the close of each letter. So, how do we
address the issue of authenticity for the Petrine letters, James, and Jude?

Pseudonymity and the General Letters

First, we need to tackle the issue of pseudonymity during the Greco-
Roman world. Often, it is stated that people of the ancient Greco-
Roman world had different values when it came to literary property,
and so the argument promoted is that they did not think the same way
we do when it came to people falsely ascribing works to another person

---

57. Bernard P. Grenfell and Arthur S. Hunt, eds., *The Oxyrhynchus Papyri Part II* (London: Oxford University Press, 1899), 233–34.

58. Yigael Yadin, Bar-Kokhba: *The Rediscovery of the Legendary Hero of the Last Jewish Revolt Against Imperial Rome* (London: Weidenfeld and Nicloson), 126.

(pseudonymity). Thus, some commentators suggest that the Petrine letters, James, and Jude are pseudepigraphical works, but they may concede
that these allegedly pseudonymous letters were not written to deceive
their readers nor did they deceive the readers.[59] The ultimate implication is that they were ruled by a different set of scruples. Wilder, however, points out that both the ancient author and even Greco-Roman
libraries established rules to protect literary works in order to discour-
age the production of pseudonymous works.[60] For instance, an author
could safeguard his work in the following ways by pronouncing a curse
in the document to warn others against altering the work, by binding
the authorial attribution with the text by means of a seal or acrostic, by
making known the document's size by citing the exact number of lines
in it, by informing others of what the work contained in chronological
order, and by using trusted friends to circulate his writings before they
could be altered or distorted.[61] In a similar way, Greeks and Romans
took steps to preserve the authenticity of their library collections of
classical works in the following manner: libraries were established at
Alexandria and Pergamum to collect and preserve the literary writings
of notable authors, forgeries of these collected works were considered
offensive and punishable, and authenticity criticism was developed to

59. Evangelicals and non-Evangelicals alike hold this view. F. W. Beare, *The First Epistle of Peter*
     (Oxford, England: Blackwell, 2nd ed. 1961), 29–30; Kurt Aland, "The Problem of Anonymity
     and Pseudonymity in Christian Literature of the First Two Centuries," in *The Authorship and
     Integrity of the New Testament*, ed. Kurt Aland (London, England: SPCK, 1965), 1–13; Ralph
     P. Martin, *New Testament Foundations: A Guide for Christian Students*, 2 vols. (Grand Rapids:
     Eerdmans, 1975–1986), 2:387; James Dunn, *The Living Word* (London, England: SCM, 1987),
     84; Richard Bauckham, "Pseudo-Apostolic Letters," *JBL* 107 no. 3 (1988): 469–94, esp. 488–
     92. Yet Achtemeier avers, "Falsification of authorship was in fact not routinely regarded as
     harmless; the *Gospel of Peter* was rejected as a falsification, as was the *Acts of Paul* when the true
     author became known." The former was rejected for docetic Christology and the latter for
     falsifying authenticity to Paul as well as for doctrinal grounds. See Achtemeier, 1 Peter, 40;
     Wilhelm Schneemelcher, New Testament Apocrypha, 2 vol., translation ed. R. Mcl. Wilson
     (Philadelphia: Westminister, vol. 1, 1963; vol. 2, 1965), 1:179; 2: 323.

60. Terry L. Wilder, *Pseudonymity, The New Testament, and Deception: An Inquiry into Intention and
     Reception* (Lanham, MD: University Press of America, 2004), 42; *idem.* "Pseudonymity and
     the New Testament" in *Interpreting the New Testament: Essays on Methods and Issues*, David Alan
     Black and David S. Dockery eds. (Nashville: Broadman & Holman, 2001), 296–335. Compare
     Bruce M. Metzger, "Literary Forgeries and Canonical Pseudepigrapha," *JBL* 91 (1972): 3–24.

61. To protect his work, Galen, a second century Greek physician, wrote "On His Own Books"
     in order to foil others from creating and selling forgeries of documents under his name."
     Furthermore, Caesar Augustus (30 BCE–14 CE) has been noted to condemn people who
     wrote under another name (Suetonius, *The Lives of Caesars*, 2.LV). Wilder, *Pseudonymity, The
     New Testament, and Deception*, 42, 49. Josephus appears to protect his material by circulating
     drafts of his work of *War* and by identifying the number of books and the number of lines
     (i.e., 60,000) at the end of *Antiquities* 20.12.1§267. Compare Steve Mason, *Josephus, Judea, and
     Christian Origins: Methods and Categories* (Peabody, MA: Hendrickson, 2009), 57–60.

distinguish the authentic writings of famous authors from inauthentic ones.[62] So it should not surprise us that similar concerns about falsely ascribed writings existed in the early church. For instance, a bishop of Antioch, Serapion (*ca.* 190), reveals his attitude about pseudonymity when he muses, "For our part, brethren, we receive both Peter and the other apostles as Christ, but the writings which falsely bear their names we reject, as men of experience, knowing that such were not handed down to us."[63] Similarly, the Muratorian Canon avers, "There is current also (an epistle) to the Laodiceans, another to the Alexandrians, forged in Paul's name for the sect of Marcion, and several others which cannot be received into the Catholic Church – for it will not do to mix gall with honey."[64]

Second, we must address the existence of falsely ascribed letters. While people of the Greco-Roman world and the early church shared similar concerns about pseudonymity, we must concede pseudony-mous letters falsely ascribed to famous people exist. Within the Greco-Roman World, a group of thirty-five letters are ascribed to Socrates, all of which are generally considered spurious.[65] Similarly within the Church, there were spurious *Letters of Christ and Abgarus* (*ca.* 325 CE), the *Correspondence of Paul and Seneca* (*ca.* 4th century CE), and the *Epistle to the Laodiceans* (*ca.* late 3rd century CE), just to name a few. "These pseudepigraphal writings," according to Wilder, "do not closely re-

---

62. Ptolemy Philadelphus (283–246 BCE) founded the library at Alexandria, and Eumenes II (197–159 BCE) founded the library at Pergamum. These libraries also protected their literary collections. For instance, Diogenes Laertius, the Roman author of *Lives of Philosophers* (3rd century CE) reveals that Athenodoros Cordylion (or Atheneodorus), a first-century BCE Stoic and keeper of the library at Pergamum, was known to cut out passages from books on Stoic philosophy if he disagreed with them (Diogenes Laertius, 7.3). When he was caught, he was punished and the writings were restored in a timely manner to their original status. Compare Wilder, *Pseudonymity, the New Testament, and Deception,* 42–43.

63. See Eusebius, *Ecclesiastical History,* 6.12.3 (trans. J. Oulton in Loeb Classical Library). Similar feelings for apostolic authority are evident in 1 Clement 42:1–2. See Wilder, *Pseudonymity, the New Testament, and Deception,* 135–39.

64. Muratoran Canon, 63–67. Wilhelm Schneemelcher, "The History of New Testament Canon" translated by George Ogg in *New Testament Apocrypha,* vol. 1, Wilhelm Schneemelcher, ed. (Philadelphia: PA: Westminister, 1963). 44.

65. Wilder, *Pseudonymity* 94–100. Other pseudonymous letters are ascribed to Anacharsis, a sixth-century Scythian prince; Crates and Diogenes, Cynic philosophers; and Plato, the Greek philosopher. Whereas the spurious letters of Socrates may have been written out of respect for him, many Cynic letters were written as propaganda for Cynic Philosophy. Yet, "it is not enough," muses Guthrie concerning the disputed New Testament works like the Petrine letters, James, and Jude, "to cite the widespread secular use of the device without producing evidence to show why Christian writers should conform to non-Christian and in fact non-religious patterns in their approach to the highly significant matter of their own religious writings." See Donald Guthrie's reasoning in "Epistolary Pseudepigraphy" in *New Testament Introduction Revised Edition* (Downers Grove, IL: InterVarsity, 1990), 1017–22.

semble the disputed New Testament Letters, were written fairly late, and are not all marked with the name of an apostle as a pseudonymous letter . . ."[66] Furthermore, Jewish authors who falsely ascribed a work to another individual credited it to a person who had been dead for hundreds of years (e.g., 1 Enoch, Psalms of Solomon, etc.). As a result, no Jewish reader would mistake the work as an authentic work by the falsely ascribed named individual. Finally, Jewish pseudonymity is evident predominately in apocalyptic writings and not letters. This conclusion does not deny that some Jewish works are entitled *Letter of Aristeas*[67] or the *Letter of Jeremiah*.[68] Yet the nomenclature "letter" for these works is misleading. They are "letters" in name only and not in format. Nor do they exhibit any features common to an epistle. "The absence of any close contemporary epistolary parallels," avers Guthrie, "must put the investigator on his guard against a too facile admittance of the practices in New Testament criticism."[69] Although much more can be said here, space demands a conclusion.

In summary then, what have we learned about ancient letter-writers, and how does what we now know about these trained letter-writers affect how we study, interpret, and teach the General Letters? First, letter writing was a learned skill of a learned person. Second, letter writing was a time-honored profession whereby amanuenses were part of an upper-class occupation due to the high rate of illiteracy throughout

---

66. Wilder, "Pseudonymity and the New Testament," 301; idem, *Pseudonymity, the New Testament, and Deception*, 77. For a more detailed discussion see Wilder's chapter four, "Responses of Early Christian Leaders to Apostolic Pseudepigrapha," in *Pseudonymity, the New Testament, and Deception*, 123–63.

67. The *Letter of Aristeas* (*ca.* second century BCE) is an alleged history and validation of the Septuagint text as well as an apologetic and self-defense about the Jewish people living in Egypt. In the alleged letter, Ptolemy II Philadephus via Demetrios of Phaleron makes a request of the High Priest in Jerusalem to send translators to translate the Hebrew Bible into Greek. The High Priest sends seventy-two men to Alexandria and in seventy-two days translates the Law into Greek. Throughout the work the author presents Jewish beliefs and lifestyles as favorable and it seems to do so in an attempt to make the strict observance of the Law to be rational. See R. J. H. Shutt, "Letter of Aristeas" in *The Old Testament Pseudepigrapha*, 2 vols., James H. Charlesworthed ed. (New York: Doubleday, 1985), 1:7–34.

68. The *Letter of Jeremiah* (*ca.* 300 BCE) is a polemic against idolatry. The author writes a passionate and sarcastic sermon based on Jeremiah 10 that identifies idols as helpless (vv. 8–16, 57–59), useless (vv. 17–23), lifeless (vv. 24–29), powerless (vv. 30–40a, 53–56), worthless (vv. 45–52), and empty show-offs (vv. 70–73). Idol worshipers are described as foolish and shameful (vv. 40b–44). "Therefore" the author concludes, "one must not think that they are gods nor call them gods, for they are not able either to decide a case or to do good to men or women" (v. 64). "Better is the just person who has no idols" (v. 73b). See *The New Oxford Annotated Apocrypha* (Oxford: University Press, 3rd ed., 2001), 184–87; and David deSilva, *Introducing the Apocrypha: Message, Context, and Significance* (Grand Rapids: Baker, 2001), 214–221, 237–43.

69. Guthrie, "Epistolary Pseudepigriphy," 1017; Wilder, *Pseudonymity, the New Testament, and Deception*, 77.

the Greco-Roman world. Third, the employment of trained letter-writers was a common custom in the ancient Greco-Roman world due to the high rate of illiteracy. Finally, safeguards established in the Greco-Roman world to control and minimize pseudepigraphic productions, the rejection of pseudepigraphic writings in the early church, the distancing of a person falsely ascribed work to Jewish works, and the lack of Jewish pseudepigraphic letters would appear to argue against pseudepigraphic works among the General Letters.[70] So how does what we now know about ancient letter-writers affect how we might study, interpret, and teach the General Letters?

Several presuppositions may be drawn from this section on trained letter-writers that affect our study of the General Letters. First and foremost, in light of the low rate of literacy during the first century, it is conceivable that Peter, James, and Jude may have been illiterate or at least limited in their literary abilities. Granted, Jesus was able to stand in the synagogue and read a passage from an Isaiah scroll (Luke 4:16–20), but was Jesus a learned writer? Perhaps, but we can only surmise of Peter, James, and Jude's literary abilities.[71] Second, it is plausible that Peter, James, and Jude—whether literate or not—used a professional amanuensis.[72] Employing a skilled letter-writer was a customary practice during the first century. Furthermore, who better to communicate important church and theological matters than a person trained in the how-to of letter writing? Finally, the lack of falsely ascribed letters to a dead person among well-known Jewish Pseudepigrapha appears to support our assumption that Peter, James, and Jude are indeed the senders

---

70. We must concede, however, that the evidence to resolve *definitively* the question of authorship of the Petrine Letters, James and Jude remains elusive. Conclusions presented by Evangelicals on both sides of the issue are based upon circumstantial reasoning. Metzger, "Literary Forgeries and Canonical Pseudepigrapha," n. 67.

71. Nevertheless, many commentators argue that Peter and James, and Jude were more than capable in writing their own letters. For example, Davids, *Commentary on James*, 2–22; Jobes, *1 Peter*, 1–19; I. Howard Marshall, *1 Peter* in IVP New Testament Commentary Series (Downers Grove, IL: InterVarsity, 1991), 19–24; Bo Reicke, *The Epistles of James, Peter, and Jude* AB (New York: Doubleday, 1964), 146–47; Carson and Moo, *An Introduction to the New Testament*, 641–46, 659–63, 690–92; Guthrie, *New Testament Introduction*, 762–81, 820–42, 902–05.

72. Other commentators argue that Peter, James, and Jude employed an amanuensis. For example, Dan McCartney, *James*, BECNT (Grand Rapids: Baker, 2009), 28–29; C. E. B. Cranfield, *First and Second Peter* (London, England: SCM, 1958), 7–8; Green, *Jude and 2 Peter*, 18; Carson and Moo, *An Introduction to the New Testament*, 641–46. Although Richards muses, "through Silvanus . . . I wrote briefly" (διὰ . . . δι' ὀλίγων ἔγραψα) suggests Silvanus to be the letter carrier only, he does not exclude the possibility that he is both Peter's amanuensis and carrier. After a lengthy discussion Randoph concludes, "academic integrity prevents me from appealing to 1 Peter 5:12 as support for the use of a secretary in 1 Peter. Silvanus certainly *could* have been the secretary." Compare E. Randolph Richards, "Silvanus was not Peter's Secretary: Theological Bias in Interpreting διὰ Σιλουνοῦ . . . ἔγραψα in 1 Peter 5:12," *JETS* 43 no. 3 (September 2000): 417–432.

of their respective letters and perhaps authored during the mid-to-late 60s. Thus, differences in style and vocabulary between 1 and 2 Peter, and the sophisticated caliber of writing skills within the Petrine Letters, James, and Jude are easily explained via an employed or perhaps even a Christian amanuensis willing to serve Jesus via the donation of his skilled writing services.

Chapter in Review

We began by stating the obvious: Hebrews, James, 1–2 Peter, 1–3 John, and Jude are all deemed canonical letters.

We then learned that ancient non-canonical Greco-Roman and Jewish letters tend to follow a threefold structure; they tend to be short; their opening salutations tend to be brief and to the point; they are purposeful in that they tend to reflect different types of letters; and it was not unusual to hire an amanuensis to compose a letter for another person.

We ended by suggesting that such knowledge affects how we go about studying, interpreting, and teaching the General Letters.

- First, the threefold salutation of an epistle should be both recognized and respected. Although two letters, Hebrews and 1 John, do not fit the pattern of ancient letter writing, the letters written by James, Peter, John, and Jude do.

- Second, the expansions evident in the opening salutations should be acknowledged for their possible contribution to the letter in that they may serve to disclose an attitude (Peter, James, and Jude) or reinforce a relationship in the hope for some sort of compliance (2 John, 3 John, and Jude).

- Third, though challenging, attempts to isolate the letter's type will prove extremely helpful in steering your study, influencing your interpretation, and focusing your teaching of the text.

- Finally, the ancient custom of training and hiring amanuenses to write letters enabled us to conclude that the authors of the General Letters (e.g., Peter, James, and Jude) are indeed the senders of their respectively ascribed letters, even if an amanuensis was hired.

2

THE BACKGROUND OF THE GENERAL LETTERS

The Chapter at a Glance

Greco-Roman World
- Alexander the Great (356 –323 BCE)
- Caesar Augustus (63 BCE –14 CE)

The Judean–Roman Relationship
- Initiation of the Judean-Roman Relationship
- Toleration of the Judean-Roman Relationship
- Insurrection against the Judean-Roman Relationship

Implications for Interpretation
- Wisdom in James (mid 40s)
- Household Codes in 1 Peter
- Rebellion in Jude (mid 60s)

AS WE BEGIN THIS CHAPTER ABOUT "The Background of the General Letters," it is helpful to bear in mind that we are talking about letters written during a definite time in history, to specific groups of people, about particular challenges they faced as followers of Jesus. As presented in chapter 1, nearly all the General Letters reveal a tripartite format of a Greco-Roman letter (opening salutation, body, closing salutation) and address a specific life situation. Thus every letter preserved in the New Testament reveals a human experience rooted in ancient history reflecting a culture different from our own. Consequently, an essential part of interpretation involves being familiar with the historical background of the general letters. This chapter overviews the emerging of the Greco-Roman world, moves to the relations between the Romans and Judeans, and ends with the implications for interpreting the General Letters.

GRECO-ROMAN WORLD

Typically, the nomenclature "Greco-Roman World" draws attention to a geographical area surrounding the Mediterranean Sea and the numerous countries that were influenced by the language, culture, government, and religion of the ancient Greeks and Romans. Two key figures responsible for shaping the Greco-Roman world are Alexander the Great and Caesar Augustus.

Alexander the Great (356–323 BCE)

The personality and military proficiency of Alexander the Great marked the earth-shattering beginning of the Greco-Roman world. He was born a Macedonian in 356, taught by Aristotle, and declared king of Macedonia in 336. He consolidated the city-states and assumed political leadership over Greece in 336–335. Then, in 334, Alexander set out from Pella as Greece's military commander to liberate Sardis, Ephesus, Miletus, and other Ionian city-states from Persia. With several military units (initially 30,000 infantry and archers and 5,000 cavalry), Alexander succeeded in defeating Darius III three times: as liberator at the Granicus River in the geographical region of Troas (May 334), as conqueror at Issus in the southern region of Cilicia (November 333), and finally as avenger at Gaugamela in eastern Assyria (September 331).[1]

With Persian nobility and kingdom under his authority, the expanse of Alexander's kingdom covered the geographical area from Greece in the west, Egypt in the south, and the Indus River in the east. His greater challenge, however, was how to hold this geographically vast, multiethnic, and multicultural kingdom together. In an attempt to organize his empire, Alexander staged a mass wedding at Susa in 324 BCE, whereby his closest

---

1.   For these three battles see Arrian, Anabasis, 1.13.1–16.7; 2.5.6–11.8; 3.9.1–15.7. A. B. Bosworth, *A Historical Commentary on Arrian's History of Alexander*, vol. 1 (Oxford: Clarendon Press, 1980), 114–27, 198–219, 285–313. Peter Green, *Alexander of Macedon 356–323 BC: A Historical Biography* (Berkeley, CA: University of California Press, 1991), 168–81, 224–33, 287–96. Pierre Briant, *From Cyrus to Alexander: A History of the Persian Empire*, translated by Peter T. Daniels (Winona Lake, IN: Eisenbrauns, 2002), 817–52.

officers and friends received a bride from the highest ranks of the Persian nobility. His desire was to create a mixed ruling class of peoples to take over the functions of government in his empire. In areas of government and military, the Macedonians were not to be seen as conquerors but partners, and young Persians were to be trained in the Macedonian fashion to fight alongside Macedonians. At a public banquet, Alexander asked the gods for "many blessings, but especially solidarity [*homonoia*] and community of interest [*koinonia*] in the kingdom between the Macedonians and Persians."[2] Unfortunately, Alexander died in 323 BCE.

After his death, attempts were made to maintain Alexander's kingdom, but those attempts failed. For twenty-two years, three regent rulers strove to hold together Alexander's kingdom: Perdiccas (323–321 BCE), Antipater (321–319 BCE), and Antigonus (321–301 BCE). Regents had divided Alexander's empire into provinces (in keeping with Persia's previous satraps) and appointed military leaders of Alexander's former army to govern them. Yet tensions existed between regent rulers and those who ruled over the provinces. Disagreements led to distrust, distrust led to revolt, and revolt let to a divided empire. Several military leaders joined forces, defeated Antigonus in 301 BCE, and divided Alexander's kingdom into four. Lysimachus controlled Asia Minor as far as Tarsus, Cassander ruled over Macedonia and Greece, Ptolemy dominated Egypt and Cole-Syria (of which Judea was a part), and Seleucid strove to govern Asia Minor to the Indus River.[3] In 198 BCE, Antiochus the Great wrested away Judea from the Ptolemy Empire, and it became part of the Seleucid Empire.

For over one hundred thirty years, from the death of Alexander in 323 BCE until Rome's war with and defeat of the Seleucid King Antiochus the Great in 190 BCE,[4] the Greeks controlled and culturally dominated the Middle East. The Greek city-states established by Alexander (e.g., Alexandria, Samaria), Ptolemies (e.g., Ptolemais, the Decapolis), and Seleucids (e.g., Antioch in Syria, Laodicea SW of Phrygia) introduced Greek education, economics, ethics, politics, recreation, and language to the eastern portion of the Mediterranean world.

---

2. R. Malcolm Errington, *A History of Macedonia* (Berkeley, CA: University of California Press, 1990), 113–15. Briant, *From Cyrus to Alexander: A History of the Persian Empire*, 852–76.

3. Errington, *A History of Macedonia*, 130–147. By 280 BCE, three Greek dynasties remained: Ptolemaic in Egypt, Seleucid from Persia across Syria to Asia, and Antigonid controlling Macedonia. The Attalids of Pergamum overcame Greek rule in Asia Minor.

4. After Antiochus defeated General Scopas of the Ptolemies and Judea became part of the Seleucid kingdom in 198 BCE, Antiochus III turned his attention to the West. He decided to expand into Asia Minor and Thrace with the help of the exiled Hannibal, whom Rome had already defeated once in 202 BCE. Once Antiochus crossed the Hellespont to occupy Thrace in 196 BCE to invade Greece, Rome declared war on Antiochus 192 BCE, defeated him at Thermopylae just north of Athens in 191 BCE, and again at Magnesia just southeast of Ephesus in 190 BCE.

Caesar Augustus (63 BCE–14 CE)

The personality and policies of Caesar Augustus (formerly Gaius Octavius) marked a momentous turning point in the history of the Greco-Roman world. Gaius Octavius (or Caesar Augustus) was born 23 September 63 BCE, and was related to both Pompey and Julius Caesar via his mother, Atia. He was brought into Roman nobility when Atia was remarried to consul Lucius Marcius Philippus in 56 BCE, and he was adopted and made heir of the estate of his great uncle, Julius Caesar in 45 BCE.[5] Yet Roman influence in the Middle East did not begin with Augustus, it began with the coming of Pompey to Syria and Judea in 63 BCE.

Born in 106 BCE, Pompey spent most of his life on military campaigns, and as a result, he was honored with three triumphal processions through the city of Rome. The first was in 81 BCE for his military successes in Gaul and Sicily, the second in 71 BCE for victories in Spain, and the third in September 61 BCE.[6] After his suppression of piracy in the Mediterranean Sea, the restoration of Rome's command of the sea, and his defeat of numerous regions and people groups in the east, namely, Asia Minor, Syria, and Judea; Pompey's third triumph celebrated his victories on three continents: Africa, Spain, and Asia. He was a world conqueror.

Pompey was also a statesman, though deemed a poor one. He had a most notable political agreement with two other significant statesmen: Crassus and Julius Caesar, beginning in 60 BCE and renewed in 56 BCE. After the death of Julia, Pompey's wife and Caesar's daughter (52 BCE), and the death of Crassus (53 BCE), his congenial political relationship with Julius Caesar eroded, and they took up arms against each other. Eventually Pompey fled to Pharsalus in Thessaly with Caesar in pursuit. Pompey was defeated, but he escaped to Alexandria, Egypt in hopes of forming an alliance with the Ptolemies. Unfortunately, he was beheaded in 48 BCE (*History of Rome*, 52.1–53.4). With Pompey dead, Julius Caesar assumed role of dictator over Rome's Republic. Unfortunately, his dictatorship was short-lived, and he was assassinated on 15 March 44 BCE in the Theater of Pompey.[7] Yet his adopted son,

---

5. *History of Rome* (or *Velleius Paterculus*) in Loeb Classical Library, translated by Frederick W. Shipley (New York: G. P. Putnam's Sons, 1924), 177–81. Frédéric Hurlet and Frederik Vervaet, "Augustus, Life and Career," translated by Johanna M. Baboukis in OEAGR, vol. 1 (New York: Oxford University Press, 2010), 332–44.

6. Robin Seager, *Pompey the Great: A Political Biography* (Oxford, UK: Blackwell, 1979, 2002), 28–29, 36–37, 79–80. See also Geoffery S. Sumi, "Pompey" in *The Oxford Encyclopedia of Ancient Greece & Rome*, vol. 5 (New York: Oxford University Press, 2010), 435–38.

7. *History of Rome* (or *Velleius Paterculus*) 56.1–3.

Gaius Octavius, joined forces with Mark Antony, pursued Caesar's assassins (Cassius and Brutus), and avenged Caesar's death in October 42 BCE in the fields of nearby Philippi. As a result of this victory, Octavian refounded Philippi as a military colony, repopulated it with retired veterans, renamed it as Colonia Julia Philippensium, and bestowed upon the people of Philippi Roman citizenship.[8]

After two years of political posturing, Octavian would rule Rome's territory jointly with Antony (40 BCE) until their political relationship eroded (*circa* 37 BCE). Octavian began to present himself as the defender of Rome due to Antony's alleged threats posed by his alliance with Cleopatra VII of the Ptolemy ruling family. Eventually, Octavian and Antony faced off in a naval battle at Actium in September 31 BCE. Antony suffered a humiliating defeat, fled to Egypt, and committed suicide, as did Cleopatra. Octavian discharged veterans of Antony's army and sent them to Philippi, changed the city's name to *Colonia Augusta Julia Philippensium*,[9] and assumed control over all of Rome's conquered territories in both the west and east. When he returned to Rome in August 29 BCE, Octavian celebrated a three-day triumph and took his time in establishing his authority. In January 27 BCE, he presented himself to the senate as having restored

> ### JUDEA NOT PALESTINE
>
> In 539 BCE when the exiles began their returned to Jerusalem (Ezra 1–2), they only occupied the geographical area of Judah.
>
> In 164 BCE when Judas Maccabee re-established religious freedom to Judea, subsequent nephews expanded Judean influence to include Idumean, Samaria, Galilee, the costal plains, and the Transjordan.
>
> In 63 BCE when Pompey brought Judea under Roman control as a client kingdom, it was known as the province of Judea.
>
> In 135 CE when the Romans subdued the Jewish revolts of 66–70 CE and 132–135 CE, Rome renamed Judea to Syria Palestine. Thus Jesus and his disciples lived in the province of Judea, not Palestine.

---

8. This Roman citizenship was a significant event for the Philippians, and Paul contrasts it with a heavenly citizenship in Philippians 3:20.

9. Julius Caesar and Octavian (Augustus) are credited with establishing most of the military colonies for veterans and civilian settlers. Paul visits and establishes churches in five such military colonies: Pisidian Antioch (Acts 13:13–50), Lystra (Acts 14:4–20), and Troas in Asia Minor (Acts 16:8–11; 20:6–12; 2 Tim. 4:13); Corinth in Achaea (Acts 18:1–18); and Philippi in Macedonia (Acts 16:11–40). See A. N. Sherwin–White, *Roman Society and Roman Law in the New Testament* (Grand Rapids: Baker, 1963), 176–78.

the Roman Republic. Augustus recalls the senate's response in this manner, "I received the title Augustus by decree of the senate. . . ."[10] He was also honored as the "first citizen" (*princeps*) of both war and peace. He transformed Rome's political system, repaired the religious institutions, and transformed the social life from a Roman Republic to a Roman Empire with himself as leader.

THE JUDEAN–ROMAN RELATIONSHIP

Rapport between differing ethnic groups living around the Mediterranean arose in one of two ways: military force or international/political posturing. On the one hand, Judea's relationship with the Greeks was by military force. Yet with the exception of Samaria, Alexander did not interfere with the affairs of Jewish life. After the death of Alexander the Great, however, Judea was frequently in the throes of battle between two competing Greek dynasties, the Ptolemies in Egypt and Seleucids in Syria and Asia Minor. On the other hand, Rome did not conquer Judea, but Roman domination over Judea occurred gradually in three phases: the initiation of a Roman relationship resulting from Seleucid interference in Judea, the toleration of the Roman relationship, and the insurrection against the Roman relationship, which escalated into national turmoil that ended in the destruction of Jerusalem and its temple.

Initiation of the Judean–Roman Relationship

Discussion about Judean-Roman relations begins with Judas Maccabee. Judas initiated a relationship with Rome in 160 BCE. At the time, Judas and his entire family had taken a stand against a Greek king of the Seleucid Empire, Antiochus IV. In 167 BCE, Antiochus prohibited people living in Jerusalem from performing all socio-religious practices. Scriptures were destroyed. Sabbath observance and festivals were prohibited. Food laws were abolished. Circumcision was outlawed. Idol worship was mandated. All those who failed to obey, were put to death (1 Macc. 1:41–61; 2 Macc. 6:1–11; cf. Dan. 11:21–35).[11] Thus Judas, along with his brothers Jonathan and Simon,

---

10. *The Acts of Augustus* (or *Res Gestae Divi Augusti*) 34 in Loeb Classical Library, translated by Frederic W. Shipley (New York: G. P. Putnam's Sons, 1924), 399.

11. Discontent with Antiochus first began with his disregard for the hereditary transfer of the high priesthood according to Mosaic Law. Antiochus permitted Jason, the brother of the high priest Onias III, to buy the high priest office for himself in 175 BCE (2 Macc.). Antiochus, however, compounded his disrespect for the office three years later when he accepted even more money from Menelaus, a priest from a differing priestly family, to purchase the office in 172 BCE (2 Macc. 4:29, 39–42). Regardless, both Jason and Menelaus

resisted Antiochus and subsequent Seleucid rulers in order to restore socio-religious practices in Jerusalem. After twenty-four years of war, the people of Judea managed to liberate themselves from the Greeks, but this independence came in incremental stages. First Judas, nick-named "Maccabee" (the "hammer"), cleansed the temple, re-dedicated the temple, and reestablished a degree of religious freedom in 164 BCE (1 Macc. 4:36–61; 2 Macc. 10:1–9).[12] After Judas died in battle, Jonathan assumed leader-ship. In 152 BCE, he estab-lished some semblance of political control as one who judged Judean affairs from Michmash (1 Macc. 9:58–73; Jos *Ant.* 13.1.5–6 §§ 23–34). Yet it was under Simon's leadership, after Jonathan was murdered, that Judea was finally liber-ated from Seleucid control (1 Macc. 12:49–13:42; Jos *Ant.* 13.6.7 §§ 213–15). Thus "the yoke of the Gentiles was removed" in 143 BCE (1 Macc. 13:41). The desire for religious freedom set into motion a movement for complete independence from the Seleucids, and during these conflicts, Judean leaders willingly welcomed, entertained, and maintained a relationship with Rome.

> ## HASMONEAN FAMILY
>
> *Liberators from Seleucid Rule*
>   Judas Maccabee
>   Jonathan
>   Simon
>
> *Expansionists of Judea*
>   John Hyrcanus I (High Priest)
>   Aristobulus I (Royal Priest)
>   Alexander Janneaus (Royal Priest)
>
> *Dynastic Disputers over Judea*
>   John Hyrcanus II
>   Aristobulus II

When Judas learned of the "fame of the Romans"[13] and how they were "well-disposed toward all who made an alliance with them" (1 Macc. 8:1–16),[14] he sent a delegation to Rome to secure an alliance

---

wanted to reform and transform Jerusalem into a Greek city-state (cf. 2 Macc. 4:9), which caused some consternation in Jerusalem among the more conservative religious leaders.

12. On the 25 Chislev 164 BCE, Judeans began the eight day celebration of Hanukkah (1 Macc. 4:59). This holiday is identified as the "Feast of Dedication" in John 10:22 and as the "Feast of Lights" to Josephus (*Ant.* 12.7.6–7 § 316–26). Jewish people continue to celebrate this event every year in December; the Jewish holiday of Hanukkah.

13. The city of Rome, located on the Tiber River in the middle of the Italian peninsula, was originally built on one of seven hills. In 509 BCE, the Romans replaced their monarchy with a republican form of government (*Latin – res publica*) and emphasized military power. Their legions were feared first in Italy and then throughout the world.

14. Rome supported regularly dissention among her enemies. Sicily, Corsica, and Sardinia appealed to Rome to support their rebellion against Carthage, whereby Rome emerged

(1 Macc. 8:17–20). Rome agreed with the proposal, which generated
Rome's blessing for Judea's war effort against the Seleucids (1 Macc.
8:23–32; cf. Jos *Ant.* 12.10.6 §§ 416–19). Jonathan also sent delegations to Rome to renew their friendship and alliance (1 Macc. 12:1–4;
Jos *Ant.* 13.5.8 §§ 163–70), and although Jonathan died, Rome renewed it with his brother Simon (1 Macc. 14:16–24; Jos *Ant.* 13.7.3
§ 227). Thus Judas Maccabee initiated a Judean friendship and alliance with Rome in 160 BCE, which Rome both affirmed and renewed
with Jonathan and Simon. Furthermore, Simon's son John Hyrcanus,
grandsons Aristobulus and Alexander Janneus, and great grandson
John Hyrcanus II continued in this friendship and alliance.[15]

Toleration of the Judean-Roman Relationship

The change in the Judean-Roman relationship from acceptance
to tolerance seems detectable in three significant political shifts:
Pompey's entrance into Jerusalem (63 BCE), Herod's regal appointment over Judea (40 BCE), and the replacement of Archelaus (6 CE).
Yet with each event, the populace's attitude swung from one of toleration to a severe relational deterioration because Rome became
more and more involved in Judean affairs with each political shift.[16]

First, Pompey entered Jerusalem to resolve a dynastic family's
dispute between two brothers: Aristobulus II and John Hyrcanus
II. These two great-great nephews of Judas Maccabee, were unable to settle their mounting differences over who would rule the
expanded Hasmonean kingdom. After Judas and Jonathan secured
freedom from the Seleucid Greeks, their nephew (John Hyrcanus I)
and great nephews (Aristobulus and Alexander Janneaus) expanded
Judea to include other territories. John Hyrcanus I (135–104 BCE)
expanded Judean control into the Transjordan, Samaria, and Idumea.
The temple of the Samaritans was destroyed and the Idumeans were
forced to submit to circumcision and the Jewish law (Jos *Ant.* 13.9.1
§§ 254–58). Aristobulus I (104–103 BCE) expanded Judean con-

---

victorious from her 23-year sea battle with Carthage (264–241 BCE). In 200 BCE, when
Athens, the island of Rhodes, and Pergamum in Asia Minor appealed to Rome for assistance
against Philip V of Macedon, they became friends and allies. So the Judean-Roman
friendship and alliance is in keeping with Roman practice of divide and conquer.

15. When John Hyrcanus renewed his friendship and alliance with Rome, Rome went so far as
to require the Seleucids to return Joppa, Gazara, and other cities taken by Antiocus VII (Jos
Ant. 13.9.2 §§ 259–66).

16. For a more thorough discussion see my chapter about the importance of historical
background: "Obstacles to Overcome" in *Jesus the Messiah: Tracing the Promises, Expectations,
and Coming of Israel's King*, co-authored with Darrell L. Bock and Gordon H. Johnston
(Grand Rapids: Kregel, 2012).

trol into the northern districts of the Galilee region, he too forced them to be circumcised and live according to the Jewish Law (Jos *Ant.* 13.11.3 §§ 318–19). However, most of this region remained predominantly Gentile. Yet the greatest expansion of Judean control came while Alexander Janneaus ruled (103–76 BCE). He nearly doubled the size of the kingdom of Judea. He expanded his kingdom to include the cities of Raphia, Anthedon, and Gaza in the plain of Philistia; the cities of Apollonia and Strato's Tower (the future port city of Caesarea) in the plain of Sharon; the cities of Dora and Geba in the Plain of Dor; the cities of Hippos and Gamala east of the Sea of Galilee; and the cities of Pella, Ephron, Gadara, and Dion in the Decapolis. He also extended his kingdom to include the southeastern area of the Dead Sea (Jos *Ant.* 13.12.2–13.3 §§ 324–65; 13.15.4 §§ 387–97). With each expansion came the enforcing of Judaism. Thus the descendants of Judas Maccabee expanded the Judean territory to nearly the size of that of King Solomon's kingdom. So the settling of the dynastic dispute between Aristobulus II and John Hyrcanus II was of great importance, and each sent delegations to Pompey, who was in the throes of military conquest in Syria. Unfortunately for Aristobulus II, Pompey sided with John Hyrcanus II, entered Jerusalem where Aristobulus II positioned himself militarily against Pompey, defeated and captured Aristobulus, and deemed Judea as a client kingdom dependent on Roman authority (Jos *Ant.* 14.3.1–4.4 §§ 34–76). Although some Jews rejoiced over the new situation (*Pss. Sol.* 17:5b–8), those same individuals were not so thrilled over the fact that the province of Judea was under and even dependent upon Roman authority (*Pss. Sol.* 17:21–25).

The second change in the Judean-Roman relationship from acceptance to tolerance seems detectable in the political posturing of Herod the Great's father, Antipater, which would eventually lead to Octavian, Antony, and the Roman Senate granting Herod kingship over the Hasmonean Kingdom in 37 BCE. After Aristobulus and his family were taken to Rome as Pompey's prisoners,[17] Judea was placed under the authority of a Roman governor in Damascus to whom Syria, Judea, and Egypt were accountable. Nevertheless, John Hyrcanus II was awarded the title High Priest over Judea but without

---

17.   Pompey took Aristobulus as his prisoner to Rome, and when he celebrated his third parade of triumph in Rome, inscriptions listed Judea as one of the nations Pompey had triumphed. The others were Pontus, Armenia, Cappadocia, Paphlogoia, Media, Colchis, Iberia, Albania, Syria, Cilicia, Mesopotamia, Phoenicia, and Arabia and the pirates. Furthermore Aristobulus, king of the Jews, was led captive through the streets of Rome along with the son of Tigranes the Armenian with his wife and daughter, a sister and five children of Mithridates, Scythian women and hostages given by the Iberians, by the Albanians, and by the king of Commagene (*Plu. Pompey* 45. 1–2).

any royal distinction. Because of John Hyrcanus' lack of enthusiasm to lead, Antipater (Idumean by birth; Jew by conversion) became chief advisor to John Hyrcanus. Antipater had the political savvy to position John Hyrcanus, himself, and his sons in ways that ingratiated Judea to numerous Roman leaders who themselves were in the throes of positioning themselves politically in Rome. For instance, after the death of Pompey, Judea fell under the rule of Julius Caesar who once again confirmed John Hyrcanus as High Priest (thanks to Antipater), and Antipater was awarded the role of procurator of Judea (Jos *Ant.* 14.8.1–4 §§ 127–139). As a result, Antipater went throughout the country persuading the Jewish people to submit to the new government headed by John Hyrcanus. Yet in reality, Antipater ruled the government. In 47 BCE, Antipater appointed his eldest son, Phasael governor over Jerusalem and his second eldest son, Herod governor over Galilee (Jos *Ant.* 14.9.1–2 §§ 156–62). With the death of Julius Caesar (44 BCE), Judea came under the auspices of Cassius one of Julius Caesar's assassins. Once again, Antipater and his sons ingratiated themselves to Cassius by raising money for military campaigns. With the defeat and death of Cassius at the hands of Octavian and Antony (42 BCE), Judea was subject to Antony (Jos *Ant.* 14.12.2 § 301). During all these revolutionary exchanges in Rome, Antipater, Phasael, and Herod managed to ingratiate themselves and become faithful allies to whomever Rome placed in charge over Judea.

Roman Alliances with Loyal Judean Leaders		
Roman Leaders	**Jewish Leaders**	**Dates**
Pompey	John Hyrcanus II (High Priest) Antipater (Procurator of Judea)	63–48 BCE
Julius Caesar	John Hyrcanus II (High Priest, ethnarch) Antipater (Procurator of Judea) and his sons 　　　Phasael (Governor of Jerusalem) and 　　　Herod (Governor of Galilee)	48–44 BCE
Cassius	John Hyrcanus II (High Priest, ethnarch) Antipater (Procurator of Judea, d. 43) and his sons 　　　Phasael (Governor of Jerusalem) and 　　　Herod (Governor of Galilee)	48–42 BCE

Roman Alliances with Loyal Judean Leaders		
Roman Leaders	Jewish Leaders	Dates
Mark Antony	John Hyrcanus II (High Priest, ethnarch until 40 BCE) Phasael and Herod (Tetrarchs of Judea until 40 BCE) Herod (designated client king of Judea by Rome in 40 BCE)	42–31 BCE
Octavian (Augustus)	Herod (reaffirmed as Rome's client king over Judea)	31–4 BCE

After Antipater's death in 43 BCE, John Hyrcanus II presented Phasael and Herod to Antony as favorable and competent rulers whom Antony then appointed tetrarchs over Judea (41 BCE; Jos *Ant.* 14.12.2–13.1 §§ 301–27). Later, when the Parthians[18] captured and murdered Phasael in 40 BCE, Herod fled Judea and sought refuge in Rome. It was during this time of refuge that Octavian, Antony, and the Roman senate appointed Herod as a client king over Judea and provided him with military backing to retake Judea from the Parthians (40 BCE).[19] After the demise of Antony, Octavian (who became Augustus after 27 BCE) reaffirmed Herod as a loyal and friendly client king and enlarged his kingdom (31 BCE). Herod was extremely successful in maintaining Judea in a manner that (1) contributed to Augustus' *Pax Romana* ("Peace of Rome"),[20] (2) assisted in the spread of Roman culture by way of comprehensive building projects (e.g.,

---

18. The Parthians are related to the Turanians, entered Iran from Central Asia, and are responsible for preventing Alexander's successors from maintaining and enlarging their eastern territories. From 250 BCE on, the Parthian Kingdom reached from the Indus River to the Euphrates. The Romans and the Parthians became the east's dominant and competing powers. See Mark J. Olson, "Parthians," *ABD*, 170–71; E. E. Carpenter, "Parthians," ISBE, 671)

19. After several battles, the Parthians pretended that they wanted to make peace. Phasael and Hyrcanus went to the Parthian camp in Galilee to make peace only to be captured and placed in irons. When Herod heard the news, he fled Jerusalem with his family to the fortress of Masada and finally to Petra (Jos *Ant.* 14.13.2 §§ 330–64). Herod's appointment was celebrated with a banquet given by Antony (Jos *Ant.* 14.13.10–14 §§ 365–90).

20. The *Pax Romana* began with Augustus from about 27 BCE and lasted until 180 CE when Marcus Aurelius died. Thus the Roman Peace lasted some 207 years. It was a period of relative peace, minimal Roman expansion by military force, and a period of expansion of the arts and architecture.

Caesarea, Sephoris, Jerusalem Temple), (3) provided Rome with a
reliable ally on the eastern fringes of the empire, and (4) prepared his
sons in the ways of Rome with a Roman education. Herod held the
position as client king over Judea for twenty-six years.[21] Thus Judea
was no longer answerable to a Syrian governor; Judea answered only
to Rome's client king, Herod.

The people of Judea, however, merely tolerated Herod's rule.
Although Herod's family was a product of the Jewish proselytization
of John Hyrcanus I when Idumea was subdued and annexed as part
of Judea (Jos *Ant.* 13.9.1 §§ 257–58), the Jewish populace regarded
Herod as a half-Jew and not a true Jew. Furthermore, early in his
career as tetrarch over Galilee, he flaunted his authority before the
Sanhedrin (Jos *Ant.* 14.9.3–5 §§ 162–84). Finally, his ruthless purging of the Hasmonean family, namely, the killing of John Hyrcanus
II, the wife of John Hyrcanus, the daughter of John Hyrcanus, and
some of his own sons, did little to curry favor with the Jewish people.[22] Nevertheless, he was Rome's client king to whom Judea was
to pledge allegiance. Herod, however, was able to placate his Jewish
subjects of Judah, behave like a Hellenistic ruler who was culturally
acceptable to the Greek communities within Northern Galilee and
Decapolis, and appease Caesar Augustus and Rome's senate.

The third and final change in the Judean-Roman relationship
from acceptance to tolerance seems detectable in the replacement of
Archelaus (6 CE), son of Herod the Great to whom Augustus granted rulership over Judah and Samaria. After Herod died (4 BCE), his
kingdom was divided between three sons: Archelaus was granted
the geographical regions of Judah and Samaria, Antipas was granted
the regions of Perea and southern Galilee, while Philip was granted
northern Galilee and the Decapolis. Unfortunately, Archelaus wasted no time in insulting his Jewish subjects. Troubles began when
Archelaus married a divorcee Glaphyra. His marriage not only gave

---

21. Three phases of Herod's rule are the consolidation of his power as king (37–25 BCE), the
prosperity of his kingdom evident in his numerous building projects (25–13 BCE), and the
resolving of family disputes over succession (13–4 BCE). For a more complete history of
Herod, see Peter Richardson's *Herod: King of the Jews and Friend of the Romans* (Columbia, SC:
University of South Carolina Press, 1996).

22. Herod's brother-in-law drowned mysteriously in Jericho (*Ant.* 15.3.3 §50-56), John
Hyrcanus II was executed (*Ant.* 15.6.1–4 §§ 123–60), his wife, the daughter of John Hyrcanus
II, Mariamme was executed (*Ant.* 15.7.4–6 §§218-39), and his mother-in-law, Alexandra,
was executed (*Ant.* 15.7–8 §§ 247–52). There are others. For a good chronological summary
of events see Emil Schürer, *History of the Jewish People in the Age of Jesus Christ* (175 B.C.–A.D.
135), vol. 1 revised and edited by Geza Vermes and Fergus Millar (Edinburgh: T & T Clark,
1973), 287–94.

great offense to those in Judea, it transgressed Jewish Law.[23] His trouble mounted with the brutal treatment of both Jews and Samaritans, which led to a Jewish and Samaritan delegation arriving in Rome, airing their grievances, and denouncing him (Jos *War* 2.7.3 § 111). In response, Caesar August summoned Archelaus to Rome, interrogated, dismissed, and banished him to Vienna in Gaul in 6 CE. (Jos *Ant.* 17.13. 2 §§ 342–45). His territory, Judah and Samaria, was then placed under direct Roman rule and provided with a Roman governor who took up headquarters in the palace built by Herod at Caesarea (Acts 23:33–35). Thus Pompey's entrance into Jerusalem (63 BCE), Herod's regal appointment over Palestine (40 BCE), and the replacement of Archelaus (6 CE) reveals the deterioration of the Judean-Roman relationship. The populace began to swing from toleration to insurrection. In fact, it was during the rule of Archelaus that Jewish insurrection began.

Insurrection against the Judean–Roman Relationship

Discontent over Judean leaders existed long before the coming of Archelaus. The socio-political control of the dynastic family of the Hasmoneans triggered an atmosphere for some Jews to write about a coming messianic figure (125–75 BCE) and continued into Herod's rule (40–4 BCE). This hope resonates clearly in six Dead Sea Scrolls (1Q28, 1Q28a, 1Q28b, 4Q175, 4Q266, 4Q521) written while the Hasmoneans were in power, escalates in seven other texts (4Q161, 4Q382, 4Q458, *Pss. Sol.*, 1QM, 4Q246, 4Q376) composed when Rome was intruding in Jewish affairs (75–30 BCE), and continues in four additional texts (4Q174, 4Q252, 4Q285, *1 Enoch*) composed when Herod ruled over Judea. Thus most extra-biblical material anticipates a regal Messiah figure written within a period of one hundred twenty-five years during the reigns of the Hasmoneans and Herod the Great (125 BCE and 1 BCE). Most people anticipated a human personality, who would be a descendant of David, and a take-charge military man who would be extremely successful in ridding Israel of her enemies.[24]

---

23. Initially, Glaphyra was a widow of Alexander, a half-brother to Archelaus. Through Alexander, she had several children. After Herod had Alexander executed in 7 BCE, she married king Juba. When she divorced King Juba to marry Archelaus, their marriage transgressed ancient law and gave great offense to those in Judea. According to Levirate law, unless the marriage was childless, brothers were prohibited from marrying their sister-in-laws (Lev. 18:1; 20:21) (Jos *Ant.* 17.13.1 §§ 339–41).

24. For a more thorough discussion see "Expectations of Israel's King" in *Jesus the Messiah: Tracing the Promises, Expectations, and Coming of Israel's King*, co-authored with Darrell L. Bock and Gordon H. Johnston (Grand Rapids: Kregel, 2012), 211–29.

Yet the atmosphere always seems to have been ripe to move from merely dreaming of, writing about, and expecting a forthcoming Messiah to actual messianic insurrections.[25] At least three insurrections occurred during the life of Jesus (4 BCE–6 CE)[26] and three after Jesus was crucified and then exalted. On the one hand, at least three messianic insurrections occurred while Jesus was a child. Simon (*circa* 4 BCE), a former slave of King Herod who "dared to place a diadem on his head (διαδημά τε ἐτόλμησε περιθέσθαι) was the first proclaimed king by a group of followers (αὐτὸς Βασιλεὺς ἀναγγελθεὶς), raised an army, and torched the Herodian palace in Jericho and several other royal palaces. Roman officials eventually caught and beheaded him in Perea (Jos *Ant*. 17.10.6 §§ 273–277; *War* 2.56). Archelaus, son of Herod the Great, squelched a second messianic insurrection. While Jesus was still in Egypt with Mary and Joseph (see Matt. 2:13–23), a man named Athronges set himself up as king, placed a diadem on his head, organized a governing council, and slew a great number of Romans (*circa* 4–2 BCE). Within a short period of time, however, Rome along with Herod's son, Archelaus, defeated Athronges (Jos *Ant*. 17.10.7 §§ 278–284; *War* 2.4.3 §§ 60–64). After Ceasar Augustus deposed Archelaus as ruler over Judah and Samaria and replaced him a Roman governor, another insurrection occurred. Jesus was probably around twelve years old at the time. In 6 CE, "Judas the Galilean" rebelled against Rome to reestablish a free nation. He and his followers were religious Jews who resurrected the ideology of freedom that existed during the time of the Maccabees, refused to anyone Lord and ruler over Judea except God, and was to fulfill his own ambitious desire for "royal honor" (Βασιλείου τιμῆς; *Ant*. 17.10.5 §§ 271–72). Gamaliel would later aver, "they were not of God" (Acts 5:37; cf. Jos *Ant*. 18.1.1, 6 §§ 1–10, 23–25; *War* 2.8.1). Thus Messianic rebellions were evident during the early years of Jesus' life. "Anyone might make himself *king* (Βασιλεύς) as the head of a band of rebels," according to Josephus, "and then would press on to the destruction of the community, causing trouble to few Romans . . ." (*Ant*. 17.10.8 § 285, Marcus).[27]

---

25. For a complete survey of Roman Emperors see Chris Scarre, *Chronicle of the Roman Emperors: The Reign-by-Reign Record of the Rulers of Imperial Rome* (London: Thames and Hudson, 1995).

26. For dating of the birth and death of Jesus, see Harold Hoehner, *Chronological Aspects of the Life of Christ* (Grand Rapids: Zondervan, 1977); Ben Witherington III, "The Birth of Jesus" in *Dictionary of Jesus and the Gospels,* edited by J. B. Green and S. McKnight (Downers Grove, IL: IVP Academic, 1997), 60–74.

27. The numerous expectations of Messiah and Jesus' ministry as Messiah were in conflict. See Darrell L. Bock's "The Messiah Preached and Veiled" in *Jesus the Messiah: Tracing the Promises, Expectations, and Coming of Israel's King*, co-authored with Gordon H. Johnston (Grand Rapids: Kregel, 2012).

First Emperors of the Roman Empire	Jewish Rulers and the Wars against Rome	The Rise of the Church in Judea and the Writing of the General Letters
Pompey (63 BCE) Julius Caesar	John Hyrcanus II: High Priest (63–BCE)	
Julio-Claudian Dynasty	**Herodian Dynasty**	**Events of the Early Church**
Augustus (31 BCE–14 CE)		
	Herod the Great (40–4 BCE)	Jesus' Birth (late 5/early 4 BCE)
	Archelaus: Judea (4 BCE – 6 CE)	Jesus' Death & Resurrection (33 CE)
	Philip: Northeast Galilee (4 BCE–37 CE)	Peter at Pentecost (35 CE)
	Antipas: Galilee & Perea (4 BCE–39 CE)	James Leads Jerusalem Church (33–62? CE)
Tiberius (14–37)	Agrippa I (37–44)	General Letters Written
Caligula (37–41)		James (mid 40s CE)
Claudius (41–54)	Agrippa II (50–92??)	
Nero (54–68)		
Roman Civil War (68–69)	**Jewish Wars against Rome (66–73)**	Hebrews, 1 Peter, Jude (mid 60s CE) 2 Peter (67–68 CE)
Flavian Dynasty		
Vespasian (69–79)		
Titus (79–81)		
Domitian (81–96)		1, 2, 3, John (early 90s CE)

On the other hand, after the resurrection and exaltation of Jesus Messiah, three other messianic pretenders arose during the early years of the church. The first occurred sometime after the death of Herod Agrippa I (grandson of Herod the Great). Theudas a magician and self- proclaimed prophet (προφήτεσγὰρ ἔλεγεν εἶναι) gathered a large number of followers at the Jordan River and crossed over into Judea. Taking no chances, the Roman governor, Fadus, killed numerous people and beheaded Theudas (Jos *Ant.* 20.5.1 § 97–98; cf. Acts 5:36). The second came from Egypt. He too claimed to be a prophet (προ-φήτεσεῖναι λέγων), gathered a following on the Mount of Olives, and promised he would destroy the walls of Jerusalem with but a command from his mouth. The Roman governor, Felix, sent troops against the group, but the Egyptian escaped (Jos *Ant.* 20.8.6 §169–72; *War* 2.13.5 §§ 61–63; cf. Acts 21:37–38). The third arose when King Agrippa II (great-grandson of Herod the Great) was granted rule as Rome's client king over Chalcis (*ca.* 50 CE), expanded to include Galilee and Perea (*ca.* 53 CE), and shared political leadership with Festus, Rome's procurator over Judea and Samaria (cf. Acts 25:13–26:32). From 66 to 70 CE, many Zealot-led Judeans rebelled against Rome, which resulted in various active factions among the Jewish leadership. On the one hand, there was a radical faction led by two people: a priest name Eleazar, son of Simon, and the other Menachem from the Sicarii and a descendant of "Judas the Galilean" (see above). There is no need to doubt whether Menahem claimed to be the Messiah. He was a warrior, entered Jerusalem dressed as a king, quarreled with the high priest (who may have entertained some doubts about Menahem's claim), and worshipped God in the Temple (Jos *War* 2.442–448). On the other hand, there was a moderate faction led by the wealthy aristocracy: the Herodian family, the Sadducees, the Boethusians, and those of the priestly tradition who merely wished to work towards accommodation and not confrontation.[28] Hebrews, the Petrine letters, and Jude were written during the mid-60s when Judea's insurrection against Rome was nearing or at its peak. Thus, the upheaval in Judea prior to and during the insurrection of 66 has great implications for the interpretation of the General Letters.

IMPLICATIONS FOR INTERPRETATION

The implications of the Greco-Roman background for interpreting the General Letters vary from book to book. All are written in Greek;[29] all wrestle with how to navigate living as followers of Jesus within a Greco-Roman society; and all the authors lived during a

---

28. Speculations about the war between the Judeans and Romans in Judea are numerous. On the one hand Tacitus, a Roman historian, attributes the war to two cruel and irresponsible Roman governors: Felix and Festus (*Hist* 5.9.3–5; 5.10.1). On the other hand Josephus, the Jewish historian, considers the war to be a Judean civil war that led to Roman intervention. For Josephus, according to Mason, "Jerusalem fell not because of any foreign power, but because *a civil war* provoked divine punishment: the Judaean God's purging of his own house to rid it of the pollution caused by 'tyrants' (BJ 1.9–10)." See Steve Mason, *Josephus, Judea, and Christian Origins: Methods and Categories* (Peabody, MA: Hendrickson, 2009), 78. Yet later rabbinic works attribute the war to moralistic considerations such as social hostility, a breakdown of moral values, and a society overly concerned with materialism (*Tosefta Menahot* 13:22; b. Git 55b–56a). See Marin Hengel, *The Zealots*, trans. by David Smith (Edinburgh: T&T Clark, 1989); L. I. Levine, "Jewish War (66–73 C.E.)" in *The Anchor Bible Dictionary*, Volume 3 H-J (New York: Doubleday, 1992), 3:839–45.

29. See "Genre of the General Letters," page 54 n. "67".

pre-Christian era when distinctions between Jew and Christian were blurred. Attention will be give to three General Letters: wisdom in James, household codes in 1 Peter, and rebellion in Jude.

Wisdom in James (mid 40s)

Although the word "wisdom" (σοφία) or "wise" (σοφός) occurs only five times in James (1:5; 3:13, 15, 17), it is an important concept for James that has direct bearing on other concepts in his letter that are ethical by nature and thereby tied to practical action and a relationship with God. The wisdom theme and proverbial like style, however, does not define the book's genre.[30] As indicated in the previous chapter, James is a Greco-Roman letter.[31] Nevertheless, the letter identifies the values and ethos of a people who are expected to live wisely as community, which are evident in the following chiastic structure for the letter.[32]

A   2:1–11   Violating the Royal Law by speaking and acting inappropriately toward the Poor

B   2:12–13   So speak and so act as one being judged by the law of liberty

C   2:14–3:12   Wrong acting and speaking in community

D   3:13–18   Righteous vs. worldly wisdom

C   4:1–10   Prophetic Rebuke: A call to humility and repentance

B   4:11–12   Do the law, do not judge it

A   4:13–5:6   Twin calls to the arrogant rich

Yet the expectation to live ethically was not unique to followers of Jesus. Greeks, Romans, and Jews emphasized values and an ethos for people living in community.

---

30. There are some, however, who that argue that James is wisdom literature. Ben Witherington, *Jesus the Sage: The Pilgrimage of Wisdom* (Minneapolis: Fortress, 1994), 238–47. Patrick J. Haritin, *James*, SP (Collegeville, MN: Liturgical Press, 2003), 10–16.

31. In his comparisons of wisdom literature, 4Q185, and James, Verseput contends "He [James] shuns the external form of wisdom instruction that was typically spoken by a respected sage to 'my sons,' 'you simple ones,' or even 'my people' and opts, rather, for the formal and substantive features of a 'covenantal diaspora letter." Donald J. Verseput, "Wisdom, 4Q185, and the Epistle of James," *JBL* 117.4 (1998): 691–707, esp. 706.

32. Mark E. Taylor and George H. Guthrie, "The Structure of James" *CBQ* 68 (2006): 681–705.

With the coming of Alexander the Great, the entire Mediterranean world was introduced to the ethical teachings of Epicurus (341–270 BCE) and Zeno of Citium (334–262 BCE). From the teachings of these men arose two philosophical schools: Epicureanism and Stoicism. Both were embraced throughout much of the Greco-Roman world (cf. Acts 17:18). On the one hand, the Epicureans divided their philosophy into ethics and physics. Their goal of life was to pursue a tranquil life and happiness or pleasure in life (not self-indulgent pleasure but pleasure that was free of pain). Good pleasure was attainable and pain was avoided: a maximum on pleasure and a minimum on pain. Attaining tranquility was impossible if someone was involved in political life or if they believed the gods interfered in human affairs. In fact, they had a clear disconnect with divine beings in that they believed there was nothing to fear in the gods. With their emphasis on materialism, they believed once the body died the soul died with it.[33] On the other hand, the Stoics divided their philosophy into logic (e.g., rationalistic), physics (e.g., materialistic), and ethics (e.g., virtuous) though they were closely intertwined. Their goal of life was to be happy. Yet happiness involved living in rational harmony with nature and the cosmic force(s) that controlled the universe. It involved making right rational judgments. So a person who is able to make practical judgments was deemed a wise person.[34] Both sys-

> ## EPICUREAN TEACHINGS REFUTED IN 2 PETER
>
> Peter speaks against the Epicureans teaching to attain a life of pleasure (2:13).
>
> Peter affirms an afterlife and divine judgment (3:10–12) denied within the teachings of the Epicureans.
>
> Peter speaks against the Epicureans rejection of prophecy (1:19–21).

---

33. First Thessalonians 4:9–12 uses wording similar to that of the Epicureans to describe the life of quietness and the withdrawing from public affairs: "But we urge you, brothers and sisters, to do so more and more, to aspire to lead a quiet life, to attend to your own business, and to work with your hands, as we commanded you. In this way you will live a decent life before outsiders and not be in need" (NET). Yet compare Benjamin Fiore's "Passion in Paul and Plutarch: 1 Corinthians 5–6 and the Polemc against Epicureans" in *Greeks, Romans, and Christians: Essays in Honor of Abraham J. Malherbe*, edited by D. L. Balch, E. Ferguson, W. A. Meeks (Minneapolis: Fortress, 1990), 135–43. For more information on the Epicureans see Robert A. Kaster, "Values and Virtues, Roman" in OEAGR, vol. 7 (New York: Oxford University Press, 2010), 148–57. Everett Ferguson, *Backgrounds of Early Christianity* (Grand Rapids: Eerdmans, 3rd ed. 2003), 370–79.

34. A well-known Stoic during the first century was Seneca (*circa* 1–65 CE). J. B. Lightfoot has compiled a list of parallels between Seneca and the New Testament in "St. Paul and Seneca" in *Saint Paul's Epistle to the Philippians* (London, Macmillan, 1873; repr. 1903; repr. Grand Rapids, Kregel, 1953), 270–333. For more information on the Stoics see Richard Bett,

tems flourished during the pre-Christian era of the Greco-Roman World when Christianity began, Paul interacted with both in his letters (e.g., notes 33–34). Some more recent commentators suggest that Peter squares off against Epicurean *teachings* in his final letter.[35] Although this suggestion is true for 2 Peter, it is not the case for James.

When James directed his letter to Jewish Christians of the Diaspora, he did so as a Jewish believer and wrote from a Jewish perspective about living wisely. Judaism had its own set of ethics closely connected with wisdom.[36] Prior to the first temple period (1446–966 BCE), during the first temple period (966–586 BCE), and throughout the second temple period (515 BCE–70 CE), the concept of wisdom had direct connections with living properly within community and with God. First, prior to Solomon's building of the temple, Moses wrote in Deuteronomy, "So be sure to do them [God's decrees], because this will testify of your *wise understanding* to the people who will learn of all these statutes and say, 'Indeed, this great nation is a very *wise people*'" (4:6; NET). Second, during the time of the first temple, the prophet Hosea makes a similar connection between living properly and with God when he asks, "Who is *wise*? Let him discern these things! Who is *discerning*? Let him understand them! For *the ways* of the Lord are right; *the godly walk* in them, but in them the rebellious stumble" (14:9; NET). Third, throughout the second temple period, the Jewish people of Qumran believed the teacher of righteousness "shall give the upright insight into *the knowledge of the Most High* and the *wisdom of the angels*, making *wise those following the perfect way*" (1Q28 4:22).[37] Another Jewish author, one who is not associated with

---

"Stocism" in OEAGR, vol. 6 (New York: Oxford University Press, 2010), 389–94. See also Kaster, "Values and Virtues, Roman," 156. Ferguson, *Backgrounds of Early Christianity*, 354–69.

35. Neyrey appears to be the first to acknowledge that Peter is confronting Epicurean teachings (not necessarily Epicureans), and others appear to concur. Jerome H. Neyrey, "The Form and Background of the Polemic in 2 Peter," *JBL* 99 (1980): 407–31; idem, *2 Peter, Jude*, AB (New York: Doubleday, 1993), 122–28. Richard J. Bauckham, *Jude, 2 Peter*, WBC (Waco, TX: Word Books, 1983), 156. Steven J. Kraftchick, *Jude, 2 Peter*, ANTC (Nashville: Abingdon Press, 2002), 78. Gene L. Green, *Jude & 2 Peter*, BECNT (Grand Rapids: Baker, 2008), 156.

36. Unlike Proverbs 8:27–30 and the Wisdom of Solomon 7:15–26; 9:2–10, "wisdom" is not personified in James.

37. 1Q28 defines the rules for the Qumran community during the pre-messianic age by describing the ritual ceremony for entering the covenant community (1:16–2:18), outlining the annual renewal ceremony, denunciations, and atonement practices (2:19–3:12), providing an exposition of the community's dualistic beliefs (3:13–4:26), supplying rules for life in the community and precepts for punishment (5:1–7:25), issuing a charter for the new congregation (8:1–10:8), and closing with a hymn of praise (10:9–11:22). Officially entitled *Rule of the Community*, 1Q28 is sometimes referred to as *The Manual of Discipline* or 1QS. It is one of three separate works that make up a single scroll discovered in 1947, published in 1951, and enshrined in 1955. For more

the Qumran community wrote, "*Wisdom* is the *knowledge of divine and hu-man matters* and the causes of these. This, in turn, is *education in the law*, by which *we learn divine matters reverently and human affairs to our advantage*" (4 Macc. 1:16–17; NRSV). So when James avers, "Who is *wise* and under-standing among you? *By his good conduct* he should show his works done in the gentleness *that wisdom brings*" (3:13), he does so in a manner that is in keeping with Jewish tradition, a long standing tradition can be seen in a both form and content in at least two other Jewish writings: the Dead Sea Scroll 4QInstruction (4Q416) and the apocryphal book *Sirach*.

Among the Dead Sea Scrolls found in the nearby caves of Qumran was a group of seven manuscripts that contain ethical teachings for an "instruc-tor" to be taught to his disciples called *Instructions*[a-g] (4Q415–418, 423).[38] Lockett identifies several wisdom forms in 4QInstruction (4Q416) that parallel those in James. For instance, he identifies wisdom sayings (twenty-three in 4QInstruction and six in James) that appear as either an admonition (e.g., a warning against taking a given course of action) or an exhortation (e.g., positive command to adopt a given action).[39] For example,

4Q416 2 iii 8b–9a	If you are poor, *do not* long for anything but your inheritance, and *do not* get consumed by it, *lest* you displace your boundary (4Q416 2 iii 8b-–9a).
James 5:9	Beloved, *do not* grumble against one another, *so that* you may not be judged. See, the Judge is standing at the door! (NET).

The document also speaks to poverty and wealth, the socially disadvan-taged and advantaged.

---

information see Michael A. Knibb, "Damascus Document" in *EncDSS*, ed. by Lawrence H. Schiffman and James C. VanderKam (New York: Oxford University Press, 2000), 793–97. Compare Elisha Qimron and James H. Charlesworth, "Rules of the Community" in *The Dead Sea Scrolls*, RCRD vol. 1, James H. Charlesworth, ed. (Tübingen: Mohr Siebeck, 1995), 1–51.

38. According to Puech, the instructions are for a disciple so that he might persevere in doing good and thereby avert the impending and eternal punishment that awaits the sinner on judgment day. The proverbial-like content of these manuscripts resembles that of Ben Sira's apocrypha work, *Sirach*. However, 4Q416 may have been composed *circa* 50–25 BCE during the early reign of Herod the Great. Émile Puech, "Resurrection: The Bible and Qumran" in *The Bible and the Dead Sea Scrolls: The Princeton Symposium on the Dead Sea Scrolls*, 3 vols. ed. James H. Charlesworth (Waco, TX: Baylor University Press, 2006), 3:265–68. For a complete discussion of *Instructions*[a-g] or *Sapiential Works A*[a-g] (4Q415–418, 423) see *Qumran Cave 4.XXIV* (DJD 34; Oxford: Clarendon, 1999). For the dating of *Instructions* (4Q416) see Emanuel Tov, ed. *The Texts from the Judean Desert: Indices and an Introduction* to Discoveries in the Judean Desert *Series* (DJD 39; Oxford: Clarendon, 2002), 405.

39. Darian Lockett, "The Spectrum of Wisdom and Eschatology in the Epistle of James and 4QInstruction" *TynBul* 56.2 (2005): 131–148.

Do not sell your soul for money; it is good for you to be a servant in spirit, and to serve your overseers freely. Do not sell your honor for any price, and do not barter away your inheritance, lest you bring ruin on your body. Do not overindulge yourself with bread when there is no clothing. Do not drink wine when there is no food. Do not seek luxuries when you lack bread. Do not pride yourself on your need when you are poor, lest you despise your life, and more-over, do not disdain your wife, your closest companion. (4Q416 f2ii:17–21, trans. Accordance)

Although similarities between James and Dead Sea Scrolls found among the caves surrounding Qumran are evident elsewhere, there is no in-dication James was part of the Qumran community. It does, however, reinforce the sharing of a Jewish tradition prevalent throughout Judea during the first century reflected in the Hebrew Scriptures, particularly when it concerns the serious social issue of the poor and the wealthy.[40]

"Of all the wisdom books," according to McCartney, "James's clos-est resemblance is to the Jewish Wisdom of Jesus the Son of *Sirach*."[41] Within Sirach, McCartney identifies several conceptual parallels that also appear in James.

Sirach 5:11	Be quick to hear, but deliberate in answering. (NRSV)
James 1:19	Let every person be quick to listen, slow to speak, slow to anger. (NET)
Sirach 29:10	Lose your silver for the sake of a brother or a friend, and do not let it rust under a stone and be lost. (NRSV)

---

40. God is depicted as a just ruler, he is described as "a father to the fatherless and an advocate for widows" (Ps. 68:5; cf. Ex. 22:22–24). Just rulers, in the ancient Near East, were responsible for promoting justice, including caring for the weak and vulnerable (NET n. for Ps. 68:5). Compare Habakkuk where the prophet complains to God for God's seeming toleration of "wrongdoing" or social injustice (1:5). In much the same way God hated the social injustice in Northern Israel (see Amos 2:6–7) and eventually punished them via Assyria (722 BCE), God promised to punish those of Habakkuk's generation via Babylon (605 BCE). Consequently, it should come of no surprise to find similar social concerns in second temple literature. "My child, do not cheat the poor of their living, and do not keep needy eyes waiting. Do not grieve the hungry, or anger one in need. Do not add to the troubles of the desperate, or delay in giving to the needy. Do not reject a suppliant in distress, or turn your face away from the poor" (Sirach 4:1–4; cf. James 1:27; 2:6–7, 15). In James, Jesus Messiah cares for the poor and needy through his followers.

41. Dan G. McCartney, *James*, BECNT (Grand Rapids: Baker, 2009), 45–46.

James 5:3	Your gold and silver have rusted and their rust will be a witness against you. It will consume your flesh like fire. It is in the last days that you have hoarded treasure. (NET)
Sirach 5:13; 19:16	Honor and dishonor come from speaking, and the tongue of mortals may be their downfall. A person may make a slip without intending it. Who has not sinned with his tongue? (NRSV)
James 3:2	If someone does not stumble in what he says, he is a perfect individual, able to control the entire body as well. (NET)

Whereas Sirach's wisdom tradition builds upon material in Proverbs,[42] James recasts the teachings of Jesus. Nevertheless, Sirach differs from Proverbs in two ways. First, Proverbs implies that true wisdom is found in God's revealed law, Sirach explicitly teaches that that is where wisdom is to be found. Second, Sirach's motivation for true wisdom or obedience to Torah is the eschatological hope.[43] In much the same way as Sirach differs from Proverbs and advances the discussion of wisdom tradition eschatological, James does so as well.

James' wisdom tradition, though rooted in Judaism and not Greco-Roman ethics, has a wisdom ethic with a significant caveat. For James, wisdom produces the virtues for living in Diaspora community under the Messiah (1:1; 2:1), and it is a divine gift that produces patience as well as leads to life (1:5). Needless to say, many Judeans (cf. Mark 14:53–65; 15:6–15) and Hellenistic Jews throughout the Diaspora (cf. Acts 13:45, 50; 14:1–2; 17:5, 13) rejected Jesus as Messiah as well as his teachings.

---

42. "He [Sirach] commented on many passages from Proverbs," according to Di Lella, "in order to make them more understandable and more applicable to his own generation of believers." Based on the description of Simon II, a high priest in Jerusalem from 219–196 BCE mentioned in *Sirach* 50:1–24, the book was probably written sometime *circa* 180 BCE. Although *Sirach* is a book of wisdom teachings about proper speech, riches and poverty, honesty, diligence, choice of friends, sin and death, it is not totally proverbial. *Sirach* concludes with a hymn of praise about famous Jewish ancestors (41:1–49:16). "Ben Sira," according to deSilva, "was no reactionary, but he was definitely a conservative voice of the first and second century B.C.E., calling his pupils to seek their fortune, their honor, and their good name through the diligent observance of the demands of the God of Israel first and foremost." See Alexander A. Di Lella, "Ben Sira and His Times" in *The Wisdom of Ben Sira*, AB, trans. by Patrick W. Skehan (New York: Doubleday, 1987), 8–1. David A. deSilva, *Introducing the Apocrypha: Message, Context, and Significance* (Grand Rapids: Baker, 2002), 153.

43. McCartney, *James*, 46. Sirach is a firm believer in divine retribution in that God will reward everyone according to their deeds, punishment is a certainty (Sir 15:11–16:23). See also Lella, "Ben Sira and the Other Books of the Old Testament" in *The Wisdom of Ben Sira*, 40–45.

Nevertheless, James emphasizes the values and ethos of God's kingdom community over which Jesus reigns as Messiah in order to socially orient the Jewish Diaspora community in ways that distinguished them from others and encouraged tranquility.[44] There is no room for greed (1:10; 5:2–3), partiality (2:1–13), and inappropriate speech (3:1–4:12); he expects generosity (1:22–25; 2:14–26), impartiality (2:8–13), and pure speech (3:13–18; 4:11–12). These same themes are evident in the teachings of Jesus.[45]

Theme	Matthew	James
Avoid Greed	And if this is how God clothes the wild grass, which is here today and tomorrow is tossed into the fire to heat the oven, won't he clothe you even more, you people of little faith? (6:30) "Do not accumulate for yourselves treasures on earth, where moth and rust destroy and where thieves break in and steal. (6:19)	But the rich person's pride should be in his humiliation, because he will pass away like a wildflower in the meadow. (1:10) Your riches have rotted and your clothing has become moth-eaten. Your gold and silver have rusted and their rust will be a witness against you . . . you have hoarded treasure! (5:2–3)
Be Generous	"Blessed are the poor in spirit, for the kingdom of heaven belongs to them. . . . Blessed are the meek, for they will inherit the earth." (5:3, 5) "Blessed are the merciful, for they will be shown mercy." (5:7)	Listen, my dear brothers and sisters! Did not God choose the poor in the world to be rich in faith and heirs of the kingdom that he promised to those who love him? (2:5) For judgment is merciless for the one who has shown no mercy. But mercy triumphs over judgment. (2:13)

---

44. Leo G. Perdue, "The Social Character of Paraenesis and Paraenetic Literature," *Semeia* 50 (1950): 23–27.

45. For more exhaustive listings see these commentators who provide a more complete list that identify James's conscious allusions to Jesus' teachings: Peter H. Davids, *The Epistle of James*, NIGTC (Grand Rapids: Eerdmans, 1982), 47–48; D. B. Deppe, *The Sayings of Jesus in the Epistle of James* (Chelsea, MI: Bookcrafters, 1989); McCartney, *James*, 50.

Theme	Matthew	James
Avoid Partiality; Be Impartial	*Love your neighbor as yourself."* The second is like it: *'Love your neighbor as yourself.* (19:19b; 22:39)	My brothers and sisters, do not show prejudice if you possess faith in our glorious Lord Jesus Christ. But if you fulfill the royal law as expressed in this scripture, *"You shall love your neighbor as yourself,"* you are doing well. But if you show prejudice, you are committing sin and are convicted by the law as violators. (2:1, 8–9)
Avoid Inappropriate Speech	But I say to you that anyone who is angry with a brother will be subjected to judgment. And whoever insults a brother will be brought before the council, and whoever says 'Fool' will be sent to fiery hell. (5:22) Do not judge so that you will not be judged. For by the standard you judge you will be judged, and the measure you use will be the measure you receive. (7:1–2)	Do not grumble against one another, brothers and sisters, so that you may not be judged. See, the judge stands before the gates! (5:9) Do not speak against one another, brothers and sisters. He who speaks against a fellow believer or judges a fellow believer speaks against the law and judges the law. But if you judge the law, you are not a doer of the law but its judge. (4:11)
Be Honest in Speech	But I say to you, do not take oaths at all—not by heaven, because it is the throne of God, not by earth, because it is his footstool, and not by Jerusalem, because it is the city of the great King. Let your word be 'Yes, yes' or 'No, no.' More than this is from the evil one. (5:34–35, 37)	And above all, my brothers and sisters, do not swear, either by heaven or by earth or by any other oath. But let your "Yes" be yes and your "No" be no, so that you may not fall into judgment. (5:12)

In summary, it is true that James's wisdom themes and the tie he makes to living ethically resonate with Hebrew Scripture and extra-biblical Jewish literature. James's larger purpose, however, is directing Jewish followers of Jesus to live wisely as directed by their Messiah's "royal law" (James 2:8).

Household Codes and 1 Peter

When Augustus became Emperor of Rome, he rebuilt temples, re-vived historic sacrifices and festivals, and strove to restore old morals of the Republic (see *The Acts of Augustus* 4.20–21). For instance, in 18 BCE, Augustus promoted family values by instituting strict laws applicable to both men and women. He issued laws that gave preferential treatment to women who had three or more children. Inheritance laws were re-written to restrict to whom childless families could leave their estate. Adultery became a criminal offense punishable by exile, confiscation of property, and even execution. It was no longer a private family matter; it was a social one.[46] In fact, the Romans believed that disorder in the home was a threat not only to the Greco-Roman family but also the Greco-Roman society. Plato in his *Republic* (384–370 BCE), Xenophon (430–355 BCE) and Aristotle (384–322 BCE) in their respective works entitled *Discourse on Estate Management* (or *Oeconomica*), Plutarch in his *Advice to Bride and Groom* (46–120 CE), and Seneca in his *Moral Epistles* (40–112 CE) provide instructions concerning slaves to masters, wives to husbands, and children to parents.[47] Yet their emphasis differed. On the one hand, Platonic thought was that "the 'house' is similar to 'the city' in that both," according to Balch, "must have a 'ruler' and those who 'are ruled'."[48] On the other hand, "authority and subordination are necessary for Aristotle," according to Balch, "because the man is the most rational, the woman is less rational, the child immature, and the slave irrational."[49] In Plutarch's *Advice to Bride and Groom*, he avers, "a virtuous household is carried on by both parties (husband and wife) in agreement, but discloses the husband's leadership and preferences"

---

46. Adultery, as defined by Roman law, was extramarital sex that involved a married woman. Suetonius writes, "The existing laws that Augustus revised, and the new ones that he enacted, dealt, among other matters, with extravagance, adultery, unchastity, bribery, and the encouragement of marriage in the Senatorial and Equestrian Orders" (Augustus 34 in *The Twelve Caesars*, trans. Robert Graves [Baltimore: Penguin Books, 1957]). Augustus even exiled his only daughter, Julia, and his granddaughter Julia for adultery. Both were banished into exile. Claudius also banished two of his wives for adultery (Suetonius, *Divus Claudius*, 26).

47. Although Plato and Aristotle may nuance the comparison of rule within a "house" and "city" a bit differently, both agree that the discussion of household begins with marriage. Compare Plato's *Republic* 4.433A, C–D (cf. *Laws* 3.690A–D) with Aristotle's *Oeconomica* 1.1253b 1–14. For a fuller discussion, see David L. Balch, *Let Wives be Submissive: The Domestic Code in 1 Peter* in SBLMS, vol. 26 (Chico, CA: Scholars Press, 1981), 33–34.

48. Balch, *Let Wives be Submissive*, 25.

49. Balch, *Let Wives be Submissive*, 35. Elsewhere Balch also reveals that there were those who refuse to discuss the household codes: Stoic, Ariston and Epicurean, Philodemus. The latter was more concerned about personal happiness. The former due to a concern for individual virtue, not society's. David L. Balch, "Early Christian Criticism of Patriarchal Authority: 1 Peter 2:1–13:12," *USQR* 39 (1984): 161–73, esp. 163–64.

(139.8-11B–D; trans. Frank C. Babbitt; cf. 143.39E). Regardless, all agreed that everyone within the Greco-Roman household was to perform his or her assigned role in order to ensure that society would be orderly, strong, and prosperous.

Yet Greco-Roman household codes are absent from the Hebrew Scriptures and Jewish writings until Judaism had to engage Greco-Roman society. Two Jewish authors, however, did engage the Greco-Roman household codes: Philo of Alexandria (*ca.* 20 BCE–50 CE) and Josephus the historian (*ca.* 37–100 CE). Philo tended to agree with Plato "on the identity of city and house management, against Aristotle's view that a ruler in the state governed differently from the master of a household."[50] In his work entitled *Special Laws*, Philo muses

> Market places, and council chambers, and courts of justice, and large companies and assemblies of numerous crowds, and a life in the open air full of arguments and actions relating to war and peace, are suited to men; but taking care of the house and remaining at home are the proper duties of women . . . for there are two kinds of states, the greater and the smaller. And the larger ones are called really cities; but the smaller ones are called houses. And the superintendence and management of these is allotted to the two sexes separately; the men having the government of the greater . . . and the women that of the smaller, which is called oeconomy (households). Therefore let no woman busy herself about those things, which are beyond the province of oeconomy (household management), but let her cultivate solitude . . . a well-born woman, a real and true citizen, performing her vows and her sacrifices in tranquility, so as to avert evils and to receive blessings (3.169–71, trans. Accordance).

Similarly Josephus, in defense of Judaism's practices contends

> It [the Law] also commands us also, when we marry, not to have regard to portion, nor to take a woman by violence, nor to persuade her deceitfully and knavishly; but demand her in marriage of him who hath power to dispose of her, and is fit to give her away by the nearness of his kindred; for, saith the Scripture, "A woman is inferior to her husband in all things." Let her, therefore, be obedient to him; not so, that he should abuse her, but that she may acknowledge her duty to her husband; for God hath given the authority to the husband (Apion 2.25 §§ 200–01, Accordance).

---

50. Balch, *Let Wives be Submissive*, 52.

> The law ordains also, that parents should be honored immediately after God himself, and delivers that son who does not requite them for the benefits he hath received from them, but is deficient on any such occasion, to be stoned. It also says, that the young men should pay due respect to every elder, since God is the eldest of all beings (Apion 2.28 § 206, Accordance).

Consequently authority in the household during the Greco-Roman period resided in the male. Household codes thereby endorsed a man's rule over his wife, children, and slaves. Both Philo and Josephus strove to align themselves with the Greco-Roman atmosphere of the household codes. They even argued these codes existed prior to the Greeks via Moses.[51] So in what way does Peter align himself and instruct followers of Jesus to align themselves with non-Jewish Greco-Roman household codes?

Using the same categories of those steeped in a predominately Greco-Roman culture in the geographical areas like Pontus, Galatia, Cappadocia, the province of Asia, and Bithynia (1 Peter 1:1), Peter engaged his Greco-Roman culture in ways that both adopted and yet amended the household ethic for wives and slaves in order to transform culture. Not only are wives and slaves elevated, "Peter puts household relationships on an entirely new footing," according to Jobes, "that subverts the moral code as previously taught by Greek Philosophers."[52] On the one hand, Peter alters culture *by elevating the dignity* of both the slave and the wife. He says to all "live as free people, not as a pretext for evil, but as God's slaves" (2:16, NET). Whether a person was a husband/master, wife, or slave all are to subject themselves to God as his slave (cf. James 1:1, Jude v.1).[53] When

---

51. The works of Philo (particularly *Hypothetica*) and Josephus (particularly *Apion*), according to Balch, "were an attempt to persuade them [outsiders] that the Jews' lawgiver and laws do not deserve the censure they have received, but rather should be admired." David L. Balch, "Two Apologetic Encomia: Dionysius on Rome and Josephus on the Jews," *JSJ* 13 (1981): 102–22. For instance, Josephus contends ". . . our nation had not been so thoroughly known among all men as they are, and our voluntary submission to our laws had not been so open and manifest as it is . . . but that somebody had pretended to have written these laws himself, and had read them to the Greeks . . . But even Plato himself, who is so admired by the Greeks on account of that gravity in his manner and force in his words, and that ability he had to persuade men beyond all other philosophers . . . although he that shall diligently peruse his writings, will find his precepts to be somewhat gentle, and pretty near to the customs of the generality of mankind. Nay, Plato himself confesseth that it is not safe to publish the true notion concerning God among the ignorant multitude" (*Apion* 2.32 §§ 220–24, Accordance).

52. Karen H. Jobes, *1 Peter* in BECNT (Grand Rapids: Baker, 2005), 182.

53. Christians, however, were the first to advocate fair treatment of the slave. For Seneca, the Stoic, advised his readers to "Treat your inferiors as you would be treated by your betters. And as often as you reflect how much power you have over a slave, remember that your

addressing the husband, he muses "treat your wives with consideration as the weaker partners and *show them honor* as fellow heirs of
the grace of life" (3:7, NET). On the other hand, the wife is not
expected to worship the gods of the husband or master as expected
among other Greco-Roman households. In his *Advice to Bride and
Groom*, Plutarch muses "it is becoming of a wife to worship and to
know only the gods that her husband believes in, and to shut the
front door tight upon all queer rituals and outlandish superstition"
(140.19, trans. Babbitt). In 1 Peter, the wife was independent enough
from her husband to choose her own God. Peter argues that the way
for her to win over her spouse is to follow the example of women like
Sarah: "holy women *who hoped in God* long ago adorned themselves
by being subject to their husbands" (3:5, NET; cf. 3:1). There is no
worshiping of her husband's gods here. Peter, according to Balch,
"was adopting and modifying the authoritarian Roman household
ethic for wives and slaves in community."[54] Ultimately, Peter perceived a sense of equality within the Messiah's kingdom between
Jesus' followers that was unequaled in Greco-Roman society.

Rebellion in Jude (mid 60s)

Recognizing connections between Jude's theme of rebellion and
the Jewish war of 66–70 CE is seldom considered for interpreting
Jude.[55] Yet if Jude, the brother of Jesus,[56] wrote to Judean believers

---

master has just as much power over you." Seneca, *Ad Lucilium Epistulae Morales* in Loeb
Classical Library trans. By Richard M. Gummere (Cambridge, MA: Harvard University
Press, 1961), 307. A similar concept is found in Tobit's instruction to his son "And what you
hate do not do to anyone" (4:15; NRSV) or Jesus' teaching to his disciples "In everything,
treat others as you would want them to treat you, for this fulfills the law and the prophets"
(Matt. 7:12; cf. Luke 6:31; NET). For Seneca's section depicting the poor treatment of
slaves see "On Master and Slave" 47.1–1. See my previous discussion on the term "slave" in
chapter one, "Genre of the General Letters."

54. Balch, "Early Christian Criticism of Patriarchal Authority: 1 Peter 2:1–13:12," 165. "The
very words which those early slaves and wives understood gave them more independence,
freedom, and power in a repressive, hierarchical, patriarchal Roman society," says Balch later
in the same article, "are now interpreted to mean that Christian women should have less
freedom than their secular counter parts." Ibid., 169.

55. Neyrey comes closest with his evaluation of the social issues of honor and shame in *2 Peter
and Jude*, 46–48, 52–54, 60–61.

56. Jesus had several brothers and sisters (Mark 3:32), some of who are named (Matt. 13:55;
Mark 6:3), and many of who did not believe that Jesus was whom he said he was (John 7:3,
5, 10). Jude was one of them. Mark writes, "Is not this the carpenter, the son of Mary and
brother of James and Joses and Judas and Simon, and are not his sisters here with us?" (6:3;
cf. Matt 13:55). After the death and resurrection of Jesus, his siblings appear to be with Jesus'
disciples before Pentecost (Acts 1:14), at least one sibling, James, saw the resurrected Jesus (1
Cor. 15:7), and James, Simon, and Jude eventually emerged as leaders of the church in Judea

during the mid-60s CE when Jewish relationships with Rome were at the height of deterioration, then it seems more than likely Jude was addressing the issue of Jewish rebellion that permeated all of Judea rather than "false teachers" or subversive "sexual perversions."

First, the decline in Judean-Roman relationship during the 60s affects our definition of "the godless" or "ungodly *people*" (ἀσεβεῖς) who "have secretly slipped in" (παρεισέδυσαν) among you" (v. 4) and to whom Jude references vituperatively throughout his letter as "these *people*" (οὗτοι; vv. 8, 10, 12, 16). To begin with, Jude explains ("for," γάρ) "certain *people*" (τινες ἄνθρωποι) "slipped in secretly" (παρεισέδυσαν). This vague reference is the first of several to a group of people, to whom Jude refers as "certain people" (τινες ἄνθρωποι; more formal "some men").[57] Jude's nebulous references throughout the letter make it difficult to pinpoint exactly who these people were. However, during the Jewish revolt, both men and women took part in the war. It was a cross-generational and cross-gender event evident in the suicides at both Gamala and again at Masada (Jos *War* 4.1.9 §§ 63–83; 7.9.1 §§ 389–406). Thus it seems reasonable to suggest that the less former translation "certain people" best fits Jude's historical context of the Jewish revolt, a revolt underscored with messianic hopes (Jos *War* 2.442–448). Furthermore, the phrase "have secretly slipped in" (παρεισέδυσαν),[58] though unique to Jude in the New Testament, appears in Josephus to speak of people with less than honorable motives. During the time of Herod the Great (40–4 BCE), there were some who acted as friends and endeared themselves to honorable people only to spy on them (Jos *War* 1.24.1 § 468).[59] So despite its infrequent use, the term "have

---

(Acts 15:13; Gal. 2:12; Eusebius *Eccl. Hist.* 4.5.3; Epiphanius *Pan.* 66.20.1–2; Apostolic Constitutions 7.46). See Herbert W. Bateman IV, *2 Peter and Jude*, The Evangelical Exegetical Commentary (Bellingham, WA: Logos, forthcoming).

57. Although some translations render τινες ἄνθρωποι as "certain men" (KJV, ASV, NIV, NET, AB, WEB), others favor "certain people" (ESV, TNIV, CEB; cf. NAB, NASB, NRSV, NLT-SE). The latter translation is a less formal rendering for the more former "certain men." Subsequent references are simply "these people" (οὗτοί; vv. 8, 10, 12 and perhaps 19; cf. 1 Tim. 5:24). Yet unlike Peter who also uses οὗτοί (2 Peter 2:12), Peter's prophecy is about explicitly stated false teachers, identifiable teachings that resemble those of the Epicureans, and more than likely men due to the historical and cultural setting (see NET note for Jude v.4).

58. Although translated as "have secretly slipped in" (NET, CEB; cf. NIV), various renderings exist for παρεισέδυσαν: "have secretly stolen in" (NRSV), "have crept in" (KJV, ASV. ESV), "to sneak in secretly" (BDAG 774c παρεισέδυνω), and even "have wormed their way into your churches" (NLT-SE). Rendered as a consummative aorist, the translation implies an act was already in progress (cf. NRSV, ESV, NIV, NET, CEB, NLT-SE). See Buist Fanning, *Verbal Aspect*, 263–64 (cf. BDF §§76.2). Thus, some people have already slipped in and are mingling among believers.

59. The term is also used in a third-century papyri: "you cannot creep in (παρεισέδυσιν), for the woman has been in possession for a long time." Here there seems to be the idea of secrecy *Griechische Papyrus su Strassburg* I, II [ed. F. Preisigke; Leipzig, 1912–1920], I.22:30. Another

slipped in secretly" (παρεισέδυσαν) appears to communicate that "certain people" (τινες ἄνθρωποι) managed to intermingle among followers of Jesus in a manner that was at first unnoticed but now gaining an influential voice within the community. Perhaps Judean followers of Jesus were being coerced, pressured, perhaps even explicitly threatened to join the national revolt against Rome that may have been inspired by messianic hopes and aspirations for the reestablishment of Israel's kingdom.[60] Furthermore, for Jude a revolt against Rome may have been tantamount to a revolt against Jesus and his messianic claims (vv. 1b, 4b) in that these same people denied Jesus. Eventually, Jude will ask his readers to join in the struggle of the apostles (vv. 17–18; 20–23).

Finally, Jude declares, *"they are godless people"* (ἀσεβεῖς). In its broadest sense, "without god" (ἀσεβεῖς) means to violate the norms for a proper relation to deity, which involves being *irreverent, impious, ungodly*.[61] Certainly the Wisdom of Solomon captures this broad sense of meaning and the subsequent consequences for such behavior: "for the ungodly (ἀσεβεῖς), those who refuse (ἀρνούμενοι) to know you [God], were flogged by the strength of your arm, pursued by unusual rains and hail and relentless storms, and utterly consumed by fire" (16:16). Thus refusal to acknowledge God is a form of being "without god" and is judged with numerous physical discomforts. Josephus, however, implies that the mere failure to remember God's exploits on Israel's behalf is a form of godlessness (*Ant.* 2.9.3 § 214). Quite often, both the LXX and Josephus employ ἀσεβεῖς to describe Jews and Gentiles. It describes Gentiles living in Sodom (Gen. 18:23, 25; cf. Jos *Ant.* 1.11.1 § 194), as well as to describe Egyptians (Ex. 9:27; ἀσεβεῖς for Hebrew: רשע, "wicked") and the Seleucids (LXX 1 Macc. 3:8). Yet the term also describes God's chosen people, the Israelites, during the times of Eli, of Jeroboam, of Habakkuk, of Isaiah, of Jeremiah, of Ezekiel, and of Judas Maccabee.[62] In

---

later usage occurs in the letter of *Barnabas*. It speaks of the devil's activities (2:10; 4:9).

60. For a Judean to honor Rome's sovereignty during this period of time while living in Judea might be likened to being a Tory and honoring British rule during the American revolution (March 23, 1775–Sept. 3, 1783), or to honor Lincoln's desire to free slaves while living in the south during the early 1860s. It would be a tough road to travel. See Bock's discussion "Coming of Israel's King" in Herbert W. Bateman IV, Darrell L. Bock, and Gordon H. Johnston, *Jesus the Messiah: Tracing the Promises, Expectations, and Coming of Israel's King* (Grand Rapids: Kregel, 2012).

61. For additional uses see BDAG 141c, ἀσεβής; Peter Fiedler in *EDNT* (reprint, 1994), ἀσεβέω.

62. The Greek term is naturally ἀσεβεῖς in Josephus, but the Greek term in the LXX often translates different Hebrew terms as noted here. Concerning Eli (e.g. Eli's sons; Jos *Ant.* 5.10.1§339), of Jeroboam (Jos *Ant.* 8.9.1§243–45), of Habakkuk (LXX 1:4; ἀσεβεῖς for Hebrew: רשע, "wicked"), of Isaiah (LXX 33:14; ἀσεβεῖς for Hebrew חנף, "godless"), of Jeremiah (LXX 5:26; ἀσεβεῖς for Hebrew פשע, "rebellion"; cf. 30:23), of Ezekiel (LXX 33:12; ἀσεβεῖς for Hebrew: רשע, "wicked"), of Judas Maccabee (e.g. Jewish High Priests

fact, Josephus uses the term some sixty times in *Jewish Wars* and *Antiquity of the Jews*, mostly to depict the sort of tyrannical leadership over Israel and Judah, which is in keeping with his overall purpose of the his work, particularly the *Jewish War*. The essential thesis of the *Jewish War* (1.4 § 9–12) is that the Jewish revolt against Rome "was caused by only a few troublemakers among the Jews—power-hungry tyrants and marauders who drove the people to rebel against their will."[63] Furthermore, the sectarian group typically associated with Qumran expected all members to confess "*We have committed evil* (הרשענו or ἀσεβεῖς; "ungodliness")—we and our fathers before us" (1QS 21–25; cf. 1QS 4:10). Finally, both Jew and Gentile are taken into consideration when Paul asserts, "For while we were still helpless, at the right time Christ died for the ungodly (ἀσεβεῖς; Rom. 5:6). So Jude's reference to the Judean people of his day as godless is of no surprise. The term "without God" (ἀσεβεῖς), according to Bauckham "may be almost said to give the keynote to the Epistle (cf. vv. 15, 18) as it does to the Book of Enoch"[64] and we might add the *Jewish War* of Josephus. So the terminology in Jude 4, as vague as it may appear, fits the historical context of the Jewish Zealots promoting and pursuing revolt throughout Judea before a full-scale insurrection against Rome took place in 66 CE. More will be said in my exposition of Jude vv.5–7 in chapter 7. In the meantime, as the national insurgence against Rome was gaining momentum in order to reestablish the kingdom of Israel, Jude was well aware of Judea's placement in Roman society, their need to keep their proper station in society, the disruption of the "Peace of Rome" (*Pax Romana*) the revolt would cause, and how such a revolt was counter to the apostolic teachings of Jesus, who is Messiah.[65] Furthermore, placing Jude within the historical context just prior to the Jewish insurrection against Rome (66–70 CE) has significant implication for the theology of Jude.

Menaleus and Alcimus, Jos *Ant.* 12.9.7§385 and 1 Macc. 7:5, 9; 9:26.

63. Steve Mason, *Josephus and the New Testament* (Peabody, MA: Hendrickson, 1992), 60. For a few examples from *Antiquities* of ungodly tyrants over Israel are Jeroboam (8.9.1§§243–45), Baasha (8.12.3 § 299), Ahab (9.1.1§1), Pekah (9.11.1 § 234), etc. For a few examples of tyrants over Judah are Rehoboam (8.10.2 §§ 251, 256), Ahaz (9.12.1 § 243), Manasseh (10.3.1 § 37), etc.

64. Bauckham, *Jude, 2 Peter*, 37. Perhaps we might even contend that Jude denounces them as people of "low character" (G. Green, *Jude, & 2 Peter*, 59).

65. "Legal position and status lay at the root of Roman social organization," muses Craige B. Champion, "which at all levels was formally hierarchical." "Rome exercised a quasi-paternal authority in its foreign policy and expected other states to behave as dutiful clients. In all such cases, Roman authority was paramount and subordinates were hierarchically graded." (*The Oxford Encyclopedia of Ancient Greece & Rome* (2010), Social Organization, Roman"). See also Everett Ferguson, *Backgrounds of Early Christianity* (Grand Rapids: Eerdmans, 3rd edition, 2003), 48–69.

Chapter in Review

In this chapter we learned that the General Letters reveal a human experience rooted in the Greco-Roman world, involve relationships between the Judeans and the Romans, and interact with a pre-Christian culture different from our own. Consequently, familiarity with the historical background of the General Letters had explicit implications for three General Letters.

- For James, the wisdom theme and proverbial style parallels that of his Jewish culture with a single caveat. His values and ethos are directed to followers of Jesus, the Messiah, and his royal law (2:8) whereby he gives instructions to persevere in living wisely as community that involved generosity (1:22–25; 2:14–26), impartiality (2:8–13), and honesty (3:13–18; 4:11–12). Yet unlike James who evidences little connection with governing ethos of the Greco-Roman culture, 2 Peter appears to counter several teachings of the Epicureans.

- For 1 Peter, the Greco-Roman household codes were given a Christian nuance that equalized followers of Jesus (2:16; 3:7) while still teaching the importance of submission within the Greco-Roman household.

- For Jude, the Jewish insurrection of 66 CE provides a historical event that crystallizes the theological theme of rebellion and thereby counters previous suggestions the Jude combats false teachers and their antinomian teachings. Jude's descriptive terminology ("without god" and "secretly slipped in") in verse 4 appears more clearly defined when connected with the Jewish revolt.

Similarities between the first-century Greco-Roman society and ours are growing in our post-Christian culture and thereby make the General Letters relevant today.

3

THE THEOLOGY OF THE GENERAL LETTERS[1]

The Chapter at a Glance

Era of Promise in the Hebrew Scriptures
- God's Strategic Plan
- God's Covenants

Era of Fulfillment in the General Letters
- God's Strategic Plan Inaugurated
- God's Strategic Plan Consummated
- God's Expectations

The Individual Theologies of the General Letters
- The Letter to the Hebrews
- The Petrine Letters
- The Johannine Letters
- The Letters of James and Jude

---

1. This chapter was initially titled "A Biblical Theology of the General Epistles: Development from Promise to Fulfillment" presented at the Southwest Regional Meeting of the Evangelical Theological Society (Southwestern Baptist Theological Seminary, March 10, 2012).

AS WE BEGIN THIS CHAPTER ABOUT "The Theology of the General
Letters," it is helpful to bear in mind that we are talking about a biblical
theology for the General Letters and its specific canonical contributions.[2]
In chapters one and two, in order to lay a foundation for interpreting the
General Letters, we strove to visualize and capture a glimpse into history
past by wearing the glasses worn by the human authors who wrote the
General Letters, namely, the Jewish authors who lived during the Greco-
Roman period. In this chapter, we change our lenses in order to isolate
the divine author's predominate theologies in each General Letter as well
as tackle how they contribute to the canonical whole. The considerable
number of Old Testament quotations and allusions in the General Letters
testify to the importance of continuity between the Hebrew Scriptures
(or Old Testament) and the New Testament. Thus, any theology of the
General Letters must begin with the Hebrew Scriptures where the theme
of promise is introduced and then turn to the General Letters where the
theme of fulfillment is presented. Both theological themes are ultimately
linked together through the person of Jesus. So as we move to discuss the
theology of the General Letters, we trace briefly a theological–canonical
framework of promise introduced during a previous era. We then address
fulfillment during the present era as it is evident in the General Letters.
Finally, we conclude with a portrayal of the predominate theologies presented in the individual General Letters.

ERA OF PROMISE IN THE HEBREW SCRIPTURES

The purpose of this section is to answer this question: What in the
world is God doing anyway? The Hebrew Scriptures reveal over and over
again God's ongoing interrelationship with people: his love for people,
his compassion for people, his longsuffering for people, and his judgment
and restoration of people.[3] Our modest goal is to sketch ever-so-briefly

---

2.   The biblical theology of the General Letters parallels a combination of a canonical and biblical
      theological approach. Köstenberger surveys the present state of Biblical Theology, gauged by
      a selective survey of evangelical works produced during the past decade or so, and discusses
      ramifications of this survey for the future of the discipline. See Andreas J. Köstenberger,
      "The Present and Future of Biblical Theology," *SWTJ*, 56.1 (Fall 2013).

3.   The Hebrew Scriptures distinguish God's love for people in terms of loyal or steadfast love
      (*hesed*, חֶסֶד). Divine love saves people from disaster (Gen. 19:19), sustains life (Pss. 6:5 [6];
      119:88), counteracts God's wrath (Isa. 54:8; Lam. 3:31–32; Micah 7:18), serves as the basis
      for petition or approach to God (Num. 1:17–19; Pss. 25:7; 51:1[3]), and characterizes God's
      rule and establishes his kingdom (Ps. 89:14 [15]; 2 Sam. 7:15–16). Furthermore, God's
      steadfast love is abundant in that it fills the earth (Pss. 33:5; 119:64; cf. Ps. 106:7, 45; Lam.
      3:32; Neh. 13:22) and extends to large numbers of people (Ex. 20:6; Deut. 5:10; 7:9; 32:18;
      Pss. 86:15; 103:8; 145:8; Joel 2:13; Jonah 4:2). Portions of the Dead Sea Scrolls present God
      as the agent who executes his covenantal faithfulness to the community (1QS 2:1; 1QM
      12:3). See D. A. Baer and R. P. Gordon in *NIDOTTE*, 1997 ed., חֶסֶד

God's strategic plan of promise developed during two time periods in the Hebrew Scriptures and summarize God's covenants of promise.

God's Strategic Plan

When we read the Hebrew Scriptures, God's twofold strategic program seems clear: *to reestablish his kingdom* rule on earth and *to redeem a people* to enter into that kingdom.[4] This divine strategy seems evident in the opening and closing chapters of the Bible. Whereas the opening chapters of Genesis introduce God's creation of all things, the closing chapters of Revelation look forward to God's creation of a new heaven and a new earth. Thus, there is linear movement in the canon of Scripture whereby God is advancing from an old created order (Gen. 1–2; cf. Isa. 66:22–23) to a new one (Rev. 21:1–7; 22:1–4; cf. Rom. 8:18–24; 2 Peter 3:13).

God's Strategic Plan Unfolds Linearly through Human History

The need for God's kingdom-redemption program is evident in Genesis. After God created the heavens, the earth, and all that was in them, he declared that his creation was good (Gen. 1:4, 10, 12, 21, 25, 31). Unfortunately with the disobedience (rebellion) of Adam and Eve, God's authority (or "kingship") on earth was challenged—some may say thwarted—divine judgment was pronounced, and the things on earth were not good due to the *coup d'état* in the Garden (Gen. 3; cf. Rom. 1:25). Thus, a need emerged to set right the estranged relationship between God and his now contaminated created order as well as to reestablish his au-

---

4.   Where Merrill contends that "Kingship was part and parcel of God's program to demonstrate and effect his sovereign rule over creation" and eventually uses a Davidic king to represent God on the earth and to establish a human dynasty over which Jesus would reign, Dempster argues in a similar manner that "the Old Testament ends with the prophets looking forward to the coming kingdom of God, while the New Testament begins with John the Baptist and Jesus proclaiming this kingdom." Eugene H. Merrill, *Kingdom of Priests: A History of Old Testament Israel* (Grand Rapids: Baker, 1987), 208–09; Stephen G. Dempster, "The Prophets, the Canon and a Canonical Approach" in *Canon and Biblical Interpretation*, ed. by Graig G. Bartholomew (Gloucestershire, UK: University of Gloucestershire, 2006), 293–329. See also Geerharder Vos, *Biblical Theology: Old and New Testaments* (Grand Rapids: Eerdmans, 1948), and Willem A. VanGemeran, *The Progress of Redemption: The Story of Salvation from Creation to the New Jerusalem* (Grand Rapid: Academie, 1988).

thority (or his kingship) on earth. Rather than annihilate his creation and begin again, God, in divine compassion and love, sets out to remedy the enmity with his creation, which he does eventually through Jesus.

God, however, does not reveal all the details of his kingdom-redemptive program in Genesis immediately after Adam and Eve's rebellion in the Garden. Abraham certainly scratches his head from time to time concerning God's promise to him (Gen. 15:2–3; 16:1–4, 15–19). Even the prophets did not have all the puzzle pieces (Dan. 12:8–9; Eph. 3:9).[5] Each canonical book contributes to revealing God's strategically planned desires in a progressive manner through the various stages of human history. So as we read the Hebrew Scriptures, God is clearly active in administrating his strategically planned desire, which is evident in a series of at least two stages or time periods: Pre-Mosaic and Mosaic periods (or dispensations).[6]

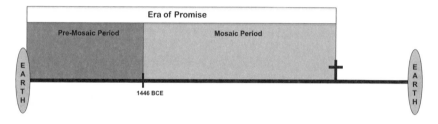

The pre-Mosaic period or the patriarchal period begins with creation and ends with the events of Sinai (creation to 1446 BCE).[7] It reveals a

5. For my fuller discussion about the progressive manner by which God reveal his program, see my introduction to *Jesus the Messiah: Promises, Expectations, and Coming of Israel's King* (Grand Rapids: Kregel, 2011), 19–38.

6. The word "dispensation" is the anglicized form of *dispensatio*, the Latin Vulgate rendering of οἰκονομία. The term, οἰκονομία, "relates primarily to household administration and applies generally to 'direction,' 'administration,' 'provision.'" Otto Michel, *TDNT*, 1967 ed., "οἰκονομία." See also BAGD, 559c 1. Thus, the English translation of οἰκονομί speaks primarily of "household administration" (cf. Luke 16:2–4). Theologically, the word speaks of (1) how God sovereignly and progressively reveals his salvation–history program in stages throughout human history (Heb. 1:1–2) and (2) how human beings are to relate to God as he administers his program in various dispensations (John 1:17). The New Testament clearly speaks of a previous dispensation (Eph. 3:8–9, Col. 1:25–26), a present dispensation (Eph. 3:2–3), and an anticipated or future dispensation (Eph. 1:9–10; 2 Tim. 3:1; 2 Peter 3:3).

7. In the past, some have subdivided the pre-Mosaic period into various periods: (1) *Innocence*, from creation to fall (Gen. 1:28–3:6); (2) *Conscience*, from the fall to the flood (Gen. 3:7–8:14; cf. Rom. 2:15; 13:5); (3) *Human Government*, from the flood to the return of Jesus (Gen. 8:15–11:32; cf. 13:1–7; Rev. 11:15; 19:11–21); (4) *Promise*, from Abram's call to Mosaic Law (Gen. 12:1–Ex. 18:27). See C. I. Scofield, ed., *The Scofield Reference Bible* (New York: Oxford University Press, 1909), 5–6, 10, 16, 20 with the *The New Scofield Reference Bible* (New York: Oxford University Press, 1967), 4, 7, 13, 19. Although the *Scofield Reference Bible* is appealed to on more than one occasion this chapter is not a Scofieldian view that emphasizes the failure of men and women to be

time when there were seemingly few "righteous" people who "walked with God." Nevertheless, God entered into relationship with a number of well-known people and their respective families. Sometimes that relationship is one of favor as in the case of Abel (Gen. 4:4; cf. Heb. 11:4; 1 John 3:12b) and Enoch (Gen. 5:22–24; cf. Heb. 11:5); or blessing as in the case of Noah (Gen. 6:8–9; cf. Heb. 11:7a; 1 Peter 3:20b; 2 Peter 2:5a), Abram and Sarai (Gen. 17:1–8, 15–19; cf. Heb. 11:8, 11; James 2:23; 1 Peter 3:16). Other times God's relationship is severed, and divine judgment occurs as in the case of Cain (Gen. 4:11; cf. 1 John 3:12), angelic beings (Gen. 6:1–4; cf. Jude v.5; 2 Peter 2:4), the people of Noah's generation (Gen. 7:11–24; cf. Heb. 11:7b; 2 Peter 2:5b), and the Gentile cities of Sodom and Gomorrah (Gen. 19:1–29; cf. Jude v.7; 2 Peter 2:6).

Less often, God's relationship with people included a unilateral (or "unconditional") covenant of promise as in the case of Noah and his descendants: Shem, Ham, and Japheth (Gen. 9:8–19). Much later, he made covenantal promises with Abraham, Sarah and their descendants Isaac, Jacob, and his twelve sons (Isaac: Gen. 26:1–5, 24; Jacob: 27:26–29, 33; 28:13–14; 35:11–12; sons: 49:1–28; cf. Heb. 2:16; 11:20–22). Relationship with God during this time involved *trusting* God, namely, believing what God promised (though the content of promise differed from one person to another), and thereby living and acting in light of that promise (cf. Noah in Gen. 6:13–22; with Abram in Gen. 12:1–9; 21:1–8). More will be said about these two diverse promises below when we discuss God's covenantal promises.

The Mosaic period is a time in which God chose an ethnic group of people, namely, the descendants of Jacob, and entered into a theocratic relationship with them. Granted, it could be said that God chose this ethnic group of people during the pre-Mosaic period through the call of Abram. It was after the sojourn to Egypt that Jacob's family grew from seventy into a nation of people so numerous they outnumbered the Egyptians (Ex. 1:5–6; 19:5–9). Unlike the patriarchal period, during the Mosaic period God related to all of humanity through this group of chosen people: the physical and political entity of national Israel (e.g., Solomon's Temple Dedication: 1 Kings 8:41–42; The Syrian Naaman's Healing: 2 Kings 5:1–14; Deliverance of Nineveh: Jonah 3:1–5, 9–10; 4:1–2, 11). This shift occurred at Mount Sinai when God entered into a bilateral (or "conditional") covenantal relationship with Israel via the faithful leadership of Moses (Ex. 2:11–15; 7:1–6; 12:1–42; 14:13–31; cf. Heb. 3:5; 11:24–29). Even though God was enthroned as King reigning from heaven (Pss. 24,

---

the basis for transitioning from one period to another and thereby anthropomorphically centered. This presentation recognizes a greater continuity between the periods and a developing kingdom-redemptive story in Scripture. For a history of Dispensationalism see Craig Blaising, "Development of Dispensationalism by Contemporary Dispensationalists," *BSac* 145 (1988): 254–80.

47, 68, 93, 96, 97, 98, 99, 132; 1 Sam. 2:10; 2 Sam. 22), God's relationship with the nation of Israel was one in which he was to be Israel's King (Ex. 19:1–8; Deut. 33:2–5), and Israel was to be God's "kingdom of priests and holy nation" (Ex. 19:6). Israel was expected to place their *trust* solely in their divine King, which in turn was to affect how they lived. They were to obey the God-given and unanimously agreed-upon Mosaic Law.

Unfortunately, disbelief and rebellion occurred repeatedly. Throughout the entire Exodus journey Israel struggled with rebellion.[8] The ultimate act occurred when they were camped at Kadesh-Barnea with the promised land of Canaan before them (Deut. 12:9–10; Josh. 21:44). They rebelled against God's leading (Num. 14:2b–4; NET). As a result of their rebellion, God judged them with forty years of wandering in the wilderness until an entire generation died (Num. 13–14; cf. Heb. 3:7–11, 15–19; Jude 5). At the end of forty years, God victoriously led a new generation of Israelites into Canaan under the leadership of Joshua (6:1–25; 11:16–23; cf. Heb. 11:30–31).

After the conquest of Canaan, Israel exhibited both excitement and commitment to live as God's people (Josh. 24:14–28). Consequently, the period known as the Judges began with great expectations. God's choice of Israel as his own people was so that Israel might be a model for all other nations to look upon and thereby be drawn to God. Unfortunately, as the Israelites settled in the land, they continued to struggle with disobedience and rebellion, which resulted in a repeated cycle of judgment, repentance, and restoration.[9] The absence of a visible king deluded people into believing they could live in reckless self-centered freedom (Judges 17:6; 18:1; 19:1; 21:25). Eventually, a generation of Israelites arose who desired a human king in order that their nation might be like the other nations (1 Sam. 8:4–22; cf. Gen. 17:6, 16; Deut. 17:14–15). So, God directed the prophet Samuel to appoint a divinely chosen king.

Although Israel's first king, Saul, failed miserably (1 Sam. 13:9–14; 15:1–26), God later appointed David king (1 Sam. 16:1, 7, 10–13) and entered into a unilateral (or "unconditional") covenantal relationship with him

---

8. There is no shortage of rebellion in the wilderness. The Book of Numbers abounds in rebellion: Miriam and Aaron rebelled against Moses and his choice of an Ethiopian wife (12:1–16); Korah, along with Dathan and Abiram rebelled against Moses' leadership (16:1–35); and people rebelled against Moses by way of their perpetual complaints about their circumstances (11:1–15). Each was divinely judged. The first judgment was by way of leprosy (12:10, 13–16), and the latter two by death (16:20–35; 11:3, 31–34).

9. The Book of Judges reveals this cycle of rebellion, judgment, repentance, and restoration. There were six regional apostasies (3:7; 3:12; 4:1; 6:1a; 10:6, and 13:1a), followed by six divine judgments and human repentances (3:3:8–9; 3:12–15; 4:2–3; 6:1b–10; 10:7–16, and 13:1b; 16:28), followed by God appointed deliverers to restore the people: Ehud (3:12–13); Shamgar (3:31); Jael and Barak (4:18–23; cf. Heb. 11:32); Gideon (7:1–23; cf. Heb 11:32); Jephthah (10:1–12:7; cf. Heb. 11:32), Samson (16:27–30; cf. Heb. 11:32).

(2 Sam. 7:4–17). God promised David that his son would have a unique "father-son" relationship with God (2 Sam. 7:14; Ps. 2:7; 110:1[10]), but yet David's son Solomon and subsequent heirs to the throne were still expected to lead the people of Israel to *trust* God and obey the nation's Mosaic Law (Deut. 17:14–15, 18–20; 18:15). Unfortunately, time-and-time again David's enthroned descendents failed to *trust* God, rebelled against God, and disobeyed God's Law (e.g., 1 Sam. 16; 2 Sam. 11–12; 1 Kings 11).

Eventually, God punished the nation. He deported his chosen people to foreign lands, destroyed their temple in Jerusalem, and dismantled the Davidic monarchy.[11] Yet, God gave Israel a hope for national restoration by making a new unilateral (or "unconditional") covenant of promise with the nation (e.g., Isa. 59; Jer. 31; Ezek. 36). Regardless of Israel's failures during this Mosaic period, God continued to relate to all humanity via the nation of Israel and the Mosaic Law. Nevertheless, all that was about to change with the coming of Jesus. Thus, the Mosaic period began in the Sinai with Moses and the law (1446 BCE)—after the redeeming acts of Passover and the crossing of the Red Sea—and ended with the ascension of Jesus (33 CE).[12] It was during these two time periods that God made several covenants of promise.

God's Covenants[13]

Usually in the ancient world, covenants were agreements that served as a form of legal accountability between two or more people in order that each

---

10. See Herbert W. Bateman IV, "The Use of Psalm 110:1 in the New Testament," *BibSac* 149 (1992): 438–53; *idem*. "Psalm 110: A Psalm of Assurance in the Midst of Change" in *Interpreting the Psalms for Preaching and Teaching*, Herbert W. Bateman IV and D. Brent Sandy eds. (St. Louis, MO: Chalice, 2010), 150–61.

11. The deportations and dismantling of the Davidic dynasty occurred in stages. The first occurred in 605 BCE when Nebuchadnezzar deported Daniel and others and placed Jehoiakim on the throne (see Dan. 1:1–2; Jer. 25:1, 3, 8–12; 46:2; Jos *Ant.* 10. 11. 1 § 222–23; cf. Jer. 36:1–4, 21–24, 27–32; Jos *Ant.* 10.6.2 § 88). The second occurred in 597 BCE when Nebuchadnezzar reacted to Judah's revolt, deported Jehoiachin and Ezekiel, and placed Zedekiah on the throne (2 Kings 24:8–14; 2 Chron. 36:9–10; Jos *Ant.* 10.6.3 § 98; *ANET*, 203, Fig. 58). The final occurred in 597 BCE when Nebuchadnezzar deported more people, destroyed the temple, and dethroned David's family (2 Kings 25:112; Jer. 52:4–16; Ezek. 24:1–21; Jos *Ant.* 10.8.1–5 §§ 131–150).

12. Obviously, the 1446 BCE dating of the exodus is an early dating, though some may argue for a twelfth century date as well. See David E. Aune, *ISBE* (1982), "Exodus, Date of the." Argument for the 33 CE dating of Jesus may be found in Harold W. Hoehner, *Chronological Aspects of the Life of Christ* (Grand Rapids: Zondervan, 1977).

13. The approach taken here *differs* from covenant or federal theology, namely theologically constructed covenants into which the biblical covenants are categorized. Most covenant theologians propose two theological covenants: the Covenant of Works (or of law) and the Covenant of Grace. For an introduction to covenant theology see Michael Horton, *God of Promise: Introducing Covenant Theology* (Grand Rapids: Baker, 2006).

party would respectfully fulfill their stated obligations toward each other (see footnote #18). The Hebrew Scriptures reveal that God made covenantal promises too. He did so with a select number of people throughout history. During the pre-Mosaic and Mosaic periods, God made five covenantal promises. They are the Noahic, Abrahamic, Mosaic, Davidic, and new covenants. These covenants consist of sovereign pronouncements of divine promise. Whereas the Noahic covenant is a universal promise for all people,[14] the other four are directed to God's chosen people. Only three, however, are unilateral (or "unconditional") covenants whereby God obligates himself with an "I will do" statement that is not dependent upon the success of the persons with whom he covenants. They are irrevocable. As we shall see below, the one and only exception is the Mosaic covenant.

Unconditional Universal Covenants	Unconditional Covenants of Promise to the Nation Israel	Conditional Covenant to the Nation Israel
Noahic Gen. 6:8; 9:8–17 Consummated in Gen. 7:8–28; 9:12–16	**Abrahamic** Gen. 12:1–4; 13:14–17; 15:1–7; 17:1–8 Confirmed in Gen. 21:2–7 (cf. Heb. 6:13–15)	**Mosaic** Ex. 20:1–26 Confirmed in Ex. 24:1–18; Deut. 28:1–62; 29:2–15
	Davidic Sam. 7:4–17 Confirmed in 1 Kings 1:28–30, 39–40, 45–48; 2:10–12; 1 Chron. 23:1	
	New Jer. 31:31–34; 33:33–34; Ezek 36:24–37:14 Confirmed in Daniel 9:20–27; Ezra 1:1–8; 2 Chron. 36:22–23; Haggai 2:1–9	

The Noahic covenant may be described as a two-part irrevocable (or "unilateral") promise, the ultimate fulfillment of which rests upon God alone. On the one hand, there is the promise to spare ("save"

---

14. Some may argue there are three universal and general covenants. They are the Edenic (Gen. 2:16), the Adamic (Gen. 3:15), and the Noahic (Gen. 9:16) in that the whole human race is represented as present in Adam in his failure. All other covenants are made with Israel or Israelites and apply primarily to the Jewish people through whom God's ultimate blessing to the whole world is made available. Scofield, ed., *The Scofield Reference Bible,* 5–6, 9; idem, *The New Scofield Reference Bible,* 5, 7.

or "redeem") Noah and his immediate family from an impending judgment of a flood (Gen. 6:17–18). This covenant is established in the obedient faith or *trust* of Noah in what God promised him (Gen. 6:22; 7:5, 9). So based upon his *trust* or belief in God and what he promised, Noah built an ark (Gen. 6:14–15; cf. Heb. 11:7a). He and his family then entered the ark for safety so that once the rains came and the great flood rose to destroy all living things on earth, Noah and his family would be delivered (Gen. 7:11–24; cf. Heb. 11:7a; 1 Peter 3:20b; 2 Peter 2:5a). What Noah believed about God's promise affected how he lived. On the other hand, there is God's everlasting and universal promise whereby he promises never again to destroy life on earth by floodwaters (Gen. 9:8–17). Thus, God reveals very early on that despite the *coup d'état* in the Garden and humanity's repeated and escalated rebellion, (Gen. 6:5–6), he desires the earth to be inhabited by life and that he is willing to rescue (e.g. "redeem") people from impending and warranted judgment.[15]

The Abrahamic covenant is a multifaceted irrevocable covenant of promise whereby once again the ultimate fulfillment rests upon God alone. Ultimately, God promises to bless Abraham as well as mediate blessings to other people through him in the following manner:

> *a land* in which Abraham's descendants will dwell (Gen. 13:14–15, 17; 15:18–21; 17:8),

> *innumerable descendants* (Gen. 13:16; 15:5; 22:17; 32:12) who will grow into a nation (Gen. 12:2; 18:18a) with a royal line (Gen. 17:6),

> *descendents who follow God* (Gen. 17:7–8),

> *material and spiritual blessings* (Gen. 12:2; 15:6; 17:16; 24:34–35),

> *mediate blessings* to other nations through his descendents, namely the nation of Israel (Gen. 12:2–3; 18:18b; 22:18a),

> *pronounced curse* on those who persecute Abraham's descendents (Gen. 12:3).[16]

---

15. This point may factor into how a person understands the eternal state. Do believers live eternally on a material new heaven and earth or something totally spiritual in nature? See Steven James, "The Eternal State and Israel: Ambiguities within the History of Dispensational Theology" presented at the Southwest Regional Meeting of the Evangelical Theological Society (Southwestern Baptist Theological Seminary, TX: March 9, 2012).

16. Scofield, ed., *The Scofield Reference Bible*, 20, 24; idem, *The New Scofield Reference Bible*, 19; cf. Henry W. Holloman, *Kregel Dictionary of the Bible and Theology* (Grand Rapids: Kregel, 2005), 86; Craig A. Blaising, "The Structure of the Biblical Covenant: The Covenants Prior to

The Abrahamic covenant of promise is confirmed in the birth of Isaac (Gen. 21:2–7). Abraham obviously lived by faith or *trusted* God (Gen. 17:1–22). He left Ur when called to do so (Gen. 12:1, 4; cf. Heb. 11:8), he had relations with Sarah though barren (Gen. 11:10–11; 21:2–3; cf. Heb. 11:11–12), and he was willing to sacrifice his only son (Gen. 22:1–14; cf. Heb. 11:17–19). Based upon his *trust* or belief in what God promised, Abraham acted accordingly. Like Noah, what Abraham believed about God and his promise affected how he lived. Thus, the stress is not upon Abraham's obedience but rather upon God's unconditional and intentional promise to bless Abraham (Gen. 12:7; 13:14–17; 15:1–7; 17:18–22; 21:1–5; cf. Heb. 6:13–15) in an everlasting manner (Gen. 1:15; 17:7, 13, 19). And though Isaac's birth set into motion the fulfillment of promise, how exactly Abraham and his descendents would be a blessing to other nations, among other things, remained a mystery (cf. Heb. 11:13) until the later revelation via Jesus.

The Mosaic covenant, unlike the unilateral Abrahamic covenant, is a covenant of promise between God and a "kingdom of priests" (Ex. 19:6; Deut. 5:2–3; cf. 1 Peter 2:9–10), namely, Israel, whereby they have a conditional (or "bilateral") agreement with God. If they obey God's delineated expectations on a multitude of levels (e.g., the tabernacle: Ex. 26:1–27:20; cf. Heb. 5:1–4; 9:1–10; 10:1–3),[17] then God would bless them as a nation (cf. Deut. 27:15–28:14). Elements of continuity exist with the Abrahamic covenant in that *as a nation*:

> God will bless them *provided they obey his Law* (Lev. 26:4–12; Deut. 7:13–15; 28:3–12),

> God will multiply them *provided they obey his Law* (Lev. 26:9; Deut. 6:3; 8:1; 28:11),

> God will make them a great nation *provided they obey his Law* (Deut. 7:14; 28:1, 3),

Christ" in *Progressive Dispensationalism: An Up-to-date Handbook of Contemporary Dispensational Thought* by Craig A. Blaising and Darrell L. Bock (Wheaton, IL: Bridgepoint, 1993), 130–40; Darrell L. Bock, "The Covenants in Progressive Dispensationalism" in *Three Central Issues in Contemporary Dispensationalism: A Comparison of Traditional and Progressive Views*, ed. by Herbert W. Bateman IV (Grand Rapids: Kregel, 1999), 172–77.

17. Scofield divided the Mosaic covenant: the commandments that express the righteous will of God (Ex. 20:1–26), the judgments that govern the social life of Israel (Ex. 21:1–24:31), and the ordinances that govern the religious life of Israel (Ex. 24:12–31:18). Scofield, ed., *The Scofield Reference Bible, 95; idem, The New Scofield Reference Bible*, 95; cf. Holloman, *Kregel Dictionary of the Bible and Theology*, 86–87. The threefold division of the Mosaic Law and what was annulled is discussed in footnote #s 19 and 53.

> God will be their God and they will be his people *provided they obey his Law* (Lev. 26:11–12; Deut. 7:6–10; 28:9–10),

> God will confirm his covenant with Abraham's descendants *provided they obey his Law* (Lev. 26:6).[18]

Thus with a bit more specificity given to the Abrahamic covenant, God founded the nation of Israel through Moses (Ex. 3:1–20; cf. Heb. 3:5). God promised to be Israel's God (Ex. 19:1–20:17), and they promised to be his people (Ex. 19:5–8; Deut. 5:27–28). Consequently, the covenant is a bilateral (or "conditional") agreement: "if you obey, you will be blessed" (Deut. 28:1–14) and "if you disobey, you will be cursed" (Deut. 27:15–26; cf. James 2:8–11).

Although the Mosaic covenant was built upon God's promise to Abraham, Israel's disobedience never nullified God's promise to Abraham. Israel's disobedience merely impinged on the physical and political fortunes of the nation during the time of the Mosaic period. The Mosaic Law is Israel's national covenant with God whereby obedience of the nation is expected in exchange for God's provision of physical prosperity and political security. Thus, *God's promise of national blessing was contingent upon obedience.* Again, the Mosaic covenant differs from the other four divine covenants of promise in the Hebrew Scriptures because it is not irrevocable. Eventually, the Mosaic covenant would be replaced with a new covenant of promise (Jer. 31:33; 32:39–40; cf. Heb. 8:7–13; 9:4, 8–10, 18; 10:1, 9).[19]

The Davidic covenant also builds upon the Abrahamic covenant, namely, that a royal line would arise from Abraham's seed (Gen. 17:6; 49:10; cf.

---

18. This sort of bilateral covenant follows the form of an Ancient Near Eastern Suzerain-vassal treaty. For a discussion of the Suzerain-vassal treaty as it parallels the Mosaic covenant see Bock, "The Structure of the Biblical Covenants," 140–51; M. Weinfeld, "The Covenant of Grant in the Old Testament and in the Ancient Near East," *JAOS* 90 (1970): 368–81; Gordon Johnston, "A Critical Evaluation of Moshe Weinfelds' Approach to the Davidic Covenant in the Light of Ancient Near Eastern Royal Grants: What Did He Get Right & What Did He Get Wrong?" presented to The Old Testament and Ancient Near East Study Group at the Annual Meeting of the Evangelical Theological Society (San Francisco: November 2011); Meredith G. Kline, *The Treaty of the Great King: The Covenant Structure of Deuteronomy* (Grand Rapids: Eerdmans, 1963).

19. The point of Hebrews is that Jesus' death inaugurated the new covenant. Thus, there is no longer a need for the Mosaic Law (Heb. 10:1–4, 18; see footnote #43). See David Peterson, "The Prophecy of the New Covenant in the Argument of Hebrews 8:1–10:18," *RTR* 38 (1979): 74–81; Roger L. Omanson, "A Superior Covenant: Hebrews 8:1–10:18," *RevExp* 82 (1985): 361–73. If someone believes the Mosaic Law has a threefold division: moral law, civil law, and ceremonial law, one might argue that Hebrews addresses only the ceremonial portion of the Mosaic Law (see footnote #17). Yet Paul argues the end of the entire law. See David K. Lowery, "Christ, and the End of the Law" in *Dispensationalism, Israel and the Church: The Search for Definition*, ed. Craig A. Blaising and Darrell L. Bock (Grand Rapids: Zondervan, 1992), 230–47.

Deut. 17:14–15). God, however, expands and clarifies his intentions about Abraham's royal line (e.g., Gen. 17:6; cf. 49:8–10) with an irrevocable (or "unilateral") promise to David whereby the ultimate fulfillment once again rests upon God alone. God's straightforward promise is fourfold:

> God would build a Davidic "house" (i.e., posterity, family; 2 Sam. 7:11, 16)

> God would establish a Davidic "throne" (i.e., royal authority; 2 Sam. 7:13, 16).

> God would establish a "kingdom" (i.e., a sphere of rule; 2 Sam. 7:12, 16)

> God would always have a descendant of David rule the kingdom (2 Sam. 7:8–17; cf. 1 Chron. 17:4–27; Ps. 89:20–37).[20]

Solomon was the first within the line of Davidic sons to set into motion God's promise to David (see the prediction of the birth of the Davidic heir in 2 Sam. 7:12; cf. 1 Kings 1:28–30, 39–40, 45–48; 2:10–12; 1 Chron. 23:1). Although God's promise to David was irrevocable (2 Sam. 7:16, 18–19, 25–29; Ps. 89:24, 28–29, 33–37; cf. *Pss. Sol.* 17), the Mosaic covenant demanded national obedience. All Davidic kings were to obey and mediate the Law. Although disobedience of the Law on the part of any one Davidic king could result in Israel's divine chastisement as a nation, it would never result in God annulling the covenant he made with David (1 Kings 11:35–39; Ps. 89:2–3, 28). If physical and political fortunes were to occur for the Jewish people of Israel, it was expected that God's people would, under the leadership and example of the Davidic king, honor the Mosaic covenant (2 Sam. 7:14; Pss. 45:1–7; 89:31–33; Isa. 54:3–8).

Unfortunately, punishment of the nation (Northern Israel and Judah) and David's royal descendents came as a result of their deliberate and repeated disobedience of the Mosaic law (e.g., Solomon: 1 Kings 11:27–39; Jeroboam II: 2 Kings 23–26; Amos 7:10–17; Manasseh: 2 Kings 21:11–15; 23:26–27). Punishment and the promise of restoration led to the anticipation of another Davidite or an idealized Davidic king to rule over the kingdom of Israel (Amos 9:11–12; Isa. 11:1; Jer. 23:5; 33:15; Zech. 3:8; 6:11–13). Thus, it would be through David's Judean family that God would eventually establish another king as well as restore the kingdom of Israel that would endure in perpetuity (2 Sam. 7:12–16;

---

20. Scofield, ed., *The Scofield Reference Bible*, 362; idem, *The New Scofield Reference Bible*, 365; cf. Holloman, *Kregel Dictionary of the Bible and Theology*, 87. Blaising, "The Structure of the Biblical Covenants," 159–71; Bock, "The Covenants in Progressive Dispensationalism," 177–89.

cf. Heb. 1:5–13; 7:14).[21] After the destruction of the temple and dismantling of David's dynasty, however, the identity of that Davidite
and when he would come and restore the nation remained a mystery
throughout the majority of the second temple period (515 BCE–70 CE)
until the subsequent revelation of Jesus.[22]

The new covenant is, like the Mosaic covenant, another promise
to the physical and political nation of Israel. More specifically, it was
God's promise to the Jewish people just prior to Nebuchadnezzar's final military invasion of Jerusalem in 586 BCE (Jer. 31:31–34; 32:37–40;
Ezek. 36:26–36; 37:1–28). Yet unlike the Mosaic covenant, the new
covenant is not contingent upon obedience (Ezek. 36:36), but rather
the ultimate fulfillment of this new covenant of promise rests upon God
alone and thereby irrevocable. Nevertheless, like the Mosaic covenant,
this multifaceted new covenant has continuity with the Abrahamic
covenant in that God would do the following:

> God will bless his people, *specifically with peace and prosperity* (Jer.
> 32:42–44; Ezek. 34:36–39; 36:8–9, 29–36),

> God will multiply his people's descendants (Jer. 31:27; Ezek. 36:10–
> 12, 37–38; 36:26),

> God will make his people a great nation (Jer. 31:36),

> God will be their God and they will be his people (Jer. 31:33; 32:38;
> Ezek. 34:24, 30–31; 36–28; 37:23, 27),

> God will give his people the land promised to Abraham, Isaac, and
> Jacob (Jer. 32:37; Ezek. 34:27; 36:24, 28; 37:12, 14, 21, 25–26).[23]

---

21. For a more complete development of Messianic promise in Hebrew Scriptures, see Gordon
Johnston, "Promise of Israel's King" in *Jesus the Messiah: Tracing the Promises, Expectations,
and Coming of Israel's King*, by Herbert W. Bateman IV, Darrell L. Bock, Gordon Johnston
(Grand Rapids: Kregel, 2012), 39–206.

22. See my discussion concerning the later second temple "Expectations of Israel's King" in *Jesus
the Messiah: Tracing the Promises and Expectations of Israel's* King by Herbert W. Bateman IV,
Darrell L. Bock, and Gordon Johnston (Grand Rapids: Kregel, 2012), 207–320.

23. Scofield, ed., *The Scofield Reference Bible, 807, 881; idem, The New Scofield Reference Bible*, 804,
880; cf. Henry W. Holloman, *Kregel Dictionary of the Bible and Theology*, 87–88; Blaising,
"The Structure of the Biblical Covenants," 151–59; Bock, "The Covenants in Progressive
Dispensationalism," 189–94. Ware describes the New Covenant as "*a new mode* of
implementation, namely the internalization of the law, *a new result*, namely, faithfulness to God;
a new basis, namely, full and final forgiveness; and *a new scope* of inclusion, namely, covenant
faithfulness characteristic of all covenant participants." Bruce A. Ware, "The New Covenant
and the People(s) of God" in *Dispensationalism, Israel ad the Church: The Search for Definition*, ed.
Craig A. Blaising and Darrell L. Bock (Grand Rapids: Zondervan 1992), 68–97.

The emphasis of this multifaceted covenant, however, is that God's promise expands the Abrahamic covenant in various ways. First, his people would have an enduring relationship with God via the indwelling of God's spirit (Ezek. 36:26–27; cf. 1 John 2:20, 27).[24] Jeremiah, however, articulates this aspect of promise differently in that God's expectations would not be externally written on stone but rather internalized and written on the hearts of both men and women (Jer. 31:33; 32:39–40; cf. Heb. 8:10–11, 13; 10:16). Second, God's people would have forgiveness of sin (Jer. 31:34; Ezek. 36:25; cf. Heb. 8:12; 10:14–18; 1 John 1:9–10).[25] Third, there would be an everlasting faithfulness to God and his expectations (Jer. 32:39–40; Ezek. 11:19–20; cf. 1 John 2:29; 3:10). Finally, God's people would experience a national resurrection or restoration (Ezek. 37:1–23). The divided nation of Israel (North and South) would once again be united (cf. Isa. 11:10–16). Like the expected Davidic king, the fulfillment of new covenant promises remained a mystery throughout the second temple period (515 BCE – 70 CE). Although the returnees from exile set into motion God's promise of restoration, people continually looked for the restoration of national Israel (Zech. 6:11–13; Hag. 2:6; cf. Heb. 12:26–27).[26] So as we continue, our focus will be the three covenants Jesus inaugurated during his earthly ministry and the one that was annulled as a result of his sacrificial death.

---

24. Spiritual indwelling of people in the OT did occur, but it was selective and temporal (Moses, Num. 11:25; Azariah, 2 Chron. 15:1–7), task-oriented indwelling (Bezalel for building the tabernacle, Ex. 31:3; cf. 35:31), and temporary indwelling of leaders (seventy elders, Num. 11:336; Othniel, Judg. 3:10; Gideon, Judg. 6:34; Samson, Judg. 13:25; 14:19; 15:14; 16:20; Saul and David, 1 Sam. 16:14; Ps. 51:11). See Leon J. Wood, *The Holy Spirit in the Old Testament* (Grand Rapids: Zondervan, 1976), 39–52.

25. Forgiveness does occur in the OT because it appears for those at Kadesh-Barnea (Num. 14:18–19, 39–40), David's sin of adultery and murder (2 Sam. 11:2–5, 14–17; 12:13; Ps. 32), Ninevah's sin (Jonah 3:1–10), and Manasseh's sin of idolatry (2 Kings 21:1–9, 16) just to name a few. Yet, each suffered sin's consequences (death in the desert, Num. 14:34–35: death of a child and a dysfunctional family, 2 Sam. 12:14; 16–19; 13:1–21; etc.; personal and national captivity, 2 Chron. 33:1–15; cf. *Prayer of Manasseh*). The Hebrew sacrificial system did not allow sacrifices for deliberate sin (Num. 15:30–31; cf. Heb. 9:7). God avers through Samuel, "Does the Lord take pleasure in burnt offerings and sacrifices as much as he does in obedience? Certainly, obedience is better than sacrifice; paying attention is better than the fat of rams. For rebellion is like the sin of divination, and presumption is like the evil of idolatry" (15:22–23a, NET; cf. Heb. 10:26–31; 1 John 5:21).

26. The belief that Israel's national restoration was yet to come even during the time of Jesus is evident in Apocrypha literature (Tobit 14:5–7; Baruch 3:6–8; 2 Macc. 1:27–29), Qumran literature (CD 1.3–11), and the New Testament (Matt. 24–26; Acts 1:6). See N. T. Wright, *The New Testament and the People of God* (Minneapolis: Fortress, 1992), 259–62, 268–79.

ERA OF FULFILLMENT IN THE GENERAL LETTERS

The purpose of this section is to answer this question: Is there evidence in the General Letters that God's kingdom-redemption program has been fulfilled? Generally, discussions of promise-fulfillment focus attention in the Gospels and Paul. Yet the General Letters reveal fulfillment as well. Like all New Testament books, the focal point of the General Letters is Jesus. Furthermore, the authors of the General Letters present God's kingdom-redemption program as having been initiated by God in the historical events of Jesus (Heb. 1:2; 1 Peter 1:20) and later consummated at the subsequent return of Jesus (παρουσία: James 5:7–8; 2 Peter 1:16; 3:2, cf. Jude 20). Jesus is the one through whom God has spoken (Heb. 1:2a; 12:25), and the one whom God sent into the world to carry out God's plan (Heb. 3:1b; 1 Peter 1:20; 1 John 4:9–10, 14; cf. Acts 3:18–20).[27] It is clear that God's kingdom-redemption program is anchored in the life, death, and resurrection of Jesus. God inaugurates the fulfillment of Abrahamic, Davidic, and New covenants during the church period. Yet it appears that God annuls the Mosaic covenant (see note #s 19, 53). So, we will first focus attention on God's inauguration of his strategic plan and then advance to the millennial period where God's plan is consummated. Thus like the era of promise, the era of fulfillment has two stages or time periods (or "dispensations"): the church period where God's promises are inaugurated and the millennial period where God's promises are consummated and may in fact continue into the eternal state.

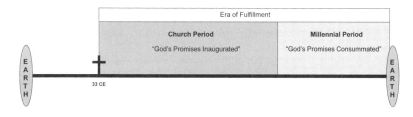

---

27. In fact, similar pictures of Jesus exist in the Gospel of John. Jesus is sent by the Father (5:23–24, 36–38; 6:29, 44, 57; 7:27–29; 8:16, 18, 26, 29, 42; 9:4; 11:42; 12:44–45; 20:21; 13:20; 14:24; 15:21; 16:5, 17:3, 8, 18, 21, 25; 20:21; cf. 16:27–28; cf. Heb. 3:1). As one who is Spirit-led without measure (3:34), Jesus knows things that others do not (1:48; 2:24–25; 5:52; 6:6, 61, 64; 7:29; 8:14, 55; 11:42; 12:50). Jesus' authority and power (5:17–23, 10:37–38, 14:10–11, 17:4–8) over temporal or physical needs (2:1–11, 6:3–15), nature (6:16–20), sickness (4:46–54, 6:1–2, 9:1–34), and death (11:1–47) serve to testify of or witness to Jesus' having been sent by the Father. As one sent by the Father, it is Jesus that the Father has given the authority to judge all things (5:22–23, 26–27, 30; 8:14–18, 26; 12:47–48). Together, these pictures serve to testify of or witness to his oneness of mission with the Father (5:16–23; 10:30, 38; cf. 14:10–11, 20; perhaps 8:19).

God's Strategic Plan Inaugurated

The church period is a time in which God relates with all people through Jesus because God inaugurates his kingdom-redemption promises through him. God makes it perfectly clear in the General Letters that the kingdom portion of his program has been activated through Jesus. In fact, the theological theme about the kingdom appears in several General Letters (Heb. 2:5–10; 10:12–13; 12:28; James 2:5; 1 Peter 1:10–11). Jesus began to reign over his kingdom after he was exalted (Heb. 1:8–9, 2:8; 5:9–10) and sat at the right hand of God.[28] Jesus sits as one who has completed his redemption mission as king-priest or royal priest (Heb. 1:3, 13; 8:1–2; 10:12; cf. 1 John 2:1b–2).[29] Unlike Judean Davidites of the past (Heb. 7:14), however, Jesus rules over an invisible kingdom (or "spiritual kingdom"; cf. Heb. 12:22–23; 2 Peter 1:11) while waiting in anticipation of his future rule over his yet to come visible kingdom (Heb. 2:5–8; 12:25–28; cf. Col. 1:13; see millennial discussion below). Thus, Jesus presently rules over an invisible kingdom and has inaugurated the Davidic covenant of promise.

Furthermore, the fact that Jesus is King appears in every General Letter except 3 John. The letters refer to "Jesus" ('Ιησοῦς) regularly along with his title "Christ" (Χριστός).[30] The epithet "Christ"

---

28. Jesus sitting at the right hand of God is significant (Heb. 1:3, 13; 8:1; 10:12–13; 1 Peter 3:22). In the ancient Near East, depictions of a king sitting at the right hand of a god symbolized the king's honored position and his divine right to rule. In Canaanite literature King Keret sits at the right hand of Baal in "The Palace of Baal" (J. C. L. Gibson, *Canaanite Myths an Legends* [Edinburgh: T&T Clark, 1977], 61–62). In Egyptian literature Pharaoh Horemheb sits at the right hand of Horus (Othmar Keel, *The Symbolism of the Biblical World* translated by Timothy J. Hallett [New York: Seabury, 1978], 263). Similar symbolism is used of a Davidite's honored position and divine right to rule (Pss. 2, 72, 110; cf. 1 Chron. 17:4, 28:5; 2 Chron. 9:8, 13:8). Whereas Yahweh was literally enthroned in heaven (Pss. 2:4, 9:7, 29:10; Isa. 6:1), the depiction of a Davidite sitting at Yahweh's right hand in Hebrew Scriptures served as a *symbol* of honor and rulership (Pss. 80:17, 89:21). In the General Letters, the *literal presence* of Jesus in heaven at God's right hand describes his honored position with God and authority to rule as royal priest (cf. Acts 2:24–33, 5:31, 7:55–56; Eph. 1:20–21; Col. 3:1).

29. The inauguration of the Davidic covenant also appears in Luke 1:31–33 but ultimately in Acts 2:30–36. The angel Gabriel announced to Mary that Jesus will be given "the throne of his ancestor David. And he will reign over Israel forever; his Kingdom will never end!'" (Luke 1:31–33, NLTSE). Jesus received this royal authority at his exaltation (Acts 2:30, 36). See Darrell L. Bock, "The Reign of the Lord Christ" in *Dispensationalism, Israel and the Church: The Search for Definition* (Grand Rapids: Zondervan, 1992), 37–67; idem, "The Covenants in Progressive Dispensationalism," 177–89; idem. "Current Messianic Activity and OT Davidic Promise: Dispensationalism, Hermeneutics and NT Fulfillment" *TrinJ* 15NS (1994): 55–87.

30. Referring to Jesus as "Christ" (Χριστός) is not unique to the General Letters (see footnote #33). Bock identifies 529 occurrences of the epithet "Christ" (Χριστός) in the New

(Χριστός) is favored in the General Letters and is the Greek equivalent of the Hebrew term "Messiah" (היטמ). Simply defined, "Messiah" (היטמ) means, "anointed" (with oil) or "Anointed One." In the Hebrew Scriptures, prophets, priests, and kings were all "anointed" figures. The prophet Elijah anointed his successor, Elisha (1 Kings 19:15–16). Moses anointed Aaron as High Priest (Ex. 40:13; Lev. 7:36) and subsequent priests and High Priests were to be anointed (Ex. 40:14–15; Lev. 16:32; *Sir* 45:15). Kings were also presented as anointed figures. Samuel anointed Saul (1 Sam. 10:1; 15:10) and David (1 Sam. 16:12–13; *Sir* 46:13); Nathan the prophet and Zadok the priest anointed Solomon (1 Kings 1:45; 1 Chron. 29:22), and Elijah anointed Hazael over Syria and Jehu over Israel (1 Kings 19:15–16). Furthermore, it was not unusual for Israel's kings of history past to be called "the Lord's anointed" as in the case of Saul (1 Sam. 26:9, 11, 23), of David and his descendants (2 Sam. 22:51; Pss. 2:2; 18:50; Lam. 4:20), and the psalmist's appeal to God for help on behalf of the Davidic king (Pss. 84:9; 89:38, 51; 132:10, 17). Thus when the authors of the General Letters say "Jesus Christ" (Ἰησοῦ Χριστοῦ), they identify Jesus as God's anointed one and should be understood as "Jesus, *who is the* Christ" (or "who is the Messiah").[31]

Another epithet used to describe Jesus as Messiah is "son" or "son of God." In Hebrews 4:14, it is "Jesus (Ἰησοῦν), *who is* the "son of God" (τὸν υἱὸν τοῦ θεοῦ). Needless to say, Jesus has already been described as the Divine Davidic royal priest in Hebrews 1:2–14.[32] The use of "son" in 1 John 1:7 ("the blood of Jesus, *who is* his son," τὸ αἱμα Ἰησοῦ τοῦ υἱοῦ αὐτοῦ), and "son of God" in 1 John 4:15; 5:5 (Ἰησοῦς ἐστιν ὁ υἱὸς τοῦ θεοῦ) may also be synonmous for the title "Messiah." Certainly, 1 John 2:22 (Ἰησοῦς ἔστιν ὁ Χριστός) and 4:15 (Ἰησοῦς ἐστιν ὁ υἱὸς τοῦ θεοῦ) are parallel expressions emphasizing Jesus' kingship.[33]

Testament. Seventy-two percent of the time the term is used in Paul. Darrell L. Bock, "Coming of Israel's King" in *Jesus the Messiah: Tracing the Promises, Expectations, and Coming of Israel's King*, by Herbert W. Bateman IV, Darrell L. Bock, Gordon Johnston (Grand Rapids: Kregel, 2012).

31. Most of the time the authors of the General Letters "Christ" (Χριστοῦ) employ a genitive in simple apposition to "Jesus" (Ἰησοῦ). See Hebrews 10:10; 13:21; James 1:1; 2:1; 1 Peter 1:1, 2, 3, 7, 13; 2:5; 3:21; 4:11; 2 Peter 1:2, 8, 11, 16; 2:20; 3:18; 1 John 1:3; 3:23; 2 John v.3; Jude vv.1, 21, 25. Less frequently, the title "Christ" (Χριστόν) is an accusative in apposition to the name Jesus (Ἰησοῦν). See 1 John 2:1; 4:2; 5:6; 2 John v.7; Jude v.4.

32. The son's designation as "king-priest" is in keeping with the theological contribution of Hebrews more explicitly spoken of later in Hebrews, namely, that Jesus is a king-priest in the order of Melchizedek (5:5–6, 7:1–28). See also chapter five "Interpreting the General Letters," 190, n. # 20.

33. Yet there are other epithets for Messiah evident in the New Testament, particularly in Mark: Son (1:9–11; 9:7), Son of David (10:47), Holy one of God (1:24), Son of the Most High (5:7), and Son of the Blessed One (14:61). All of these epithets are used in Mark to identify

Naturally, this recognition of Jesus as "Christ" is in keeping with other New Testament texts where Jesus says he came as Messiah to usher in God's kingdom (Mark 1:14–15; cf. Matt. 2:2–11, 4:17; Luke 4:43–44; 10:9–11). Although Solomon was viewed as the initial royal priest of promise who set into motion God's promise to David (1 Kings 1:30, 38–40, 48; cf. Ps. 110), the ultimate king of promise is Jesus who as a divine royal priest far greater than Solomon (Heb. 1:1–13; cf. Matt. 12:42b).[34] God thereby has blessed David's royal line through Jesus and has inaugurated the Davidic covenant. In fact, to deny that Jesus is Messiah is to deny having a relationship with God (1 John 2:22–23; 5:1; cf. 2 John v.7; Jude v.4). Furthermore, Jesus' messiahship is linked closely with his humanity, which in turn fulfills God's plan of redemption.

God makes it perfectly clear in the General Letters that the redemptive portion of his program has been achieved in the humanity of Jesus. In fact, to deny that Jesus came in the flesh is once again to deny having a relationship with God (1 John 4:2–3; 2 John vv.7, 9). Thus, the incarnation of Jesus is an important element in God' kingdom-redemption program. Jesus, in his coming and sharing in our humanity, established solidarity with all people (Heb. 2:10–18; 10:5–10) and "inaugurated" (ἐνεκαίνιζω) the new covenant.[35] Of particular importance is the human suffering and sacrificial death of Jesus, which appears in four of the General Letters.

Jesus as Messiah and are also used in second temple literature in anticipation of a human messianic figure. See Bateman, "Defining the Titles 'Christ' and 'Son of God' in Mark's Narrative Presentation of Jesus" in *JETS*; idem, "Expectations of Israel's King" in *Jesus the Messiah*, 245–320.

34. Herbert W. Bateman IV, "The Use of Psalm 110:1 in the New Testament," *BibSac* 149 (1992): 438–53; idem, "Psalm 45:6–7 and Its Christological Contributions to Hebrews," *TJ* 22NS (2001): 3–21.

35. The verb "inaugurate" (ἐγκαίνιζω) occurs only in Hebrews 9:18; 10:20. In the LXX, it might signify "to give newness to something," and thereby translated "renew" (of the kingdom: 1 Kgdm. [1 Sam.] 11:14; of the temple: 2 Chron. 15:8; 1 Macc. 4:36, 54, 57; 5:1; of people: Ps. 50:12 [51:10]; Isa. 41:1). It might also signify "to bring about the beginning of something" implying that something is newly established and means "dedicate" (of the temple: Deut. 20:5; 3 Kgdm. [1 Kings] 8:63; 2 Chron. 7:5). In Hebrews 9:18, it refers to the ratification of the first covenant by the blood sacrifices of animals (9:19–20) in order to enter the "earthly sanctuary." In Hebrews 10:20, it refers to the ratification of the new covenant by the blood of Jesus. Although sometimes translated as "dedicated" (KJV) or "ratified" (RSV), the better English rendering is "inaugurated" (NASB, ESV, NRSV, NET) or "put into effect" (NIV). Thus, the Mosaic and New covenants were put into effect or inaugurated by blood sacrifices (cf. BDAG 272c, ἐγκαίνιζω; Ceslas Spicq, *TLNT*, 1994 ed., ἐγκαίνιζω).

General Letter	Humanity	Suffering	Sacrifice
Hebrews	2:5–18; 4:14–16; 5:5–10; 10:5–10	2:9–10, 14–15; 4:14–16; 5:8; 10:7, 9–10	1:3; 2:9–10, 17; 5:3, 7–10; 7:26–28; 10:18, 26
1 Peter	5:1	1:11; 2:21–25; 4:1; 5:1	1:2, 18–21; 2:21–25; 3:18
2 Peter	1:16	2:22–23	
1 John	1:1–4; 4:2–3		2:2; 3:16; 4:10

On the one hand, the human suffering and sacrificial death of Jesus serves as a *means* to "redeem" people. First Peter's use of the verb form of "redeem" (λυτρόω), which can also be rendered "set free," is significant (1:18–19). The Septuagint's translation of Hebrew Scriptures uses the verb to speak of God's setting Israel free from Egyptian slavery (Ex. 6:6, 15:13; cf. Deut. 15:15). Hebrews, however, favors the use of the nouns "redeem" (λύτρωσιω; 9:12; cf. Luke 2:28) and "set free" (ἀπολύτρωσις; 9:15).[36] Thus, Jesus has set free all those who follow him. Whereas in the Hebrew Scriptures the Passover lamb was the initial means for redemption (Ex. 12:1–28; cf. Deut. 16:1–8), in the New Testament it is the blood of Jesus and thereby the ultimate *means* of redemption (Heb. 10:1; 9:15). First Peter and Hebrews share a similar emphasis, namely, that the effectiveness of the shed blood of Jesus is better than that of gold, silver, and the blood of bulls and goats. Hebrews, however, also speaks of the eternality of redemption (9:9).

Similarly, 1 John speaks of the redeeming blood of Jesus but in terms of an atoning sacrifice that cleanses sin and subsequently reveals God's love

---

36. Although rare, "set free" (ἀπολύτρωσις) has a consistent meaning: "setting free for a ransom." In Greek literature, captors exact a ransom fee for freedom of an individual (Plut *Pomp* 24; cf. ἀπολυτρόω: D. 12.3; Pl *Lg* 919a). In Josephus, King Aristaeus "sets free" (ἀπολύτρωσις) a group of slaves, who were captured in war and sold into slavery (*Ant.* 12.2.3 § 27), which is how Hebrews 11:35 uses the term. However in Hebrews 9:15, the theological sense is that people are "set free" from sin due to the shed blood of Jesus (cf. Heb. 1:3). Thus, the idea is one of "cancellation" or "remission" of sins that could not be expiated completely under the first covenant (10:1–3, 11; cf. Col 1:14; Eph 1:7). The theological sense of "set free" (ἀπολύτρωσις) also occurs in Luke 21:28; Rom. 3:24, 8:23; 1 Cor. 1:30; Eph. 1:7, 14; 4:30; Col. 1:14. BDAG 117b ἀπολύτρωσις.

for all people of the world (1 John 2:2; 4:10, 14; cf. Heb. 2:17).[37] In the
Hebrew Scriptures, the Day of Atonement (also referred to as *Yom Kippur*)
was an event repeated annually in the life of a Jew (10th Tishri = Sept/Oct;
cf. Ex. 30:10; Lev. 16:34; cf. Philo *Legat* 306–07; Jos *Ant.* 3.10.3 § 240).
Once a year the high priest entered the holy of holies (3 Macc. 1:11).
Although it was the only day he entered the "inner tent" of the tabernacle or "the heart of the sanctuary" (Philo *Ebr* 135–36), he did so three
times that day. The first two times he sought propitiation (to be purged of
guilt) for himself and his priestly family (Lev. 16:6, 11; himself alone: Jos
Ant. 3.10.3 § 243). The third time he entered he sought propitiation for
the entire community (Lev. 16:34; Jos *Ant.* 3.10.3 § 241; cf. Heb. 5:1–3;
9:7). One of many important *symbols* of the Day of Atonement was the
scapegoat that was sent into the wilderness, and with it, the sins of the
community (Lev. 16:7–10, 20–22; Jos *Ant.* 3.10.3 § 241). God's loving
compassion must have appeared larger than life on this day, yet everyone
knew the event needed repeating year after year (cf. Heb. 10:1–4). Annual
sacrifice is no longer the case, with the sacrifice of Jesus.

   First John, 1 Peter, and Hebrews make it clear that Jesus died as a sub-
stitutionary sacrifice and was the ultimate atoning sacrifice for sin (1 John
2:2; cf. 1 Peter 2:22–23; 3:18; Heb. 9:11–12). In Hebrews, Jesus is the pre-
requisite for or the factor that provides a person's inner cleansing (9:13–15;
cf. 1 Peter 1:2; 1 John 2:2). Through his sacrifice there is an eradication
of sin's power (Heb. 2:14; cf. 1 John 3:19–20) and the purging of sin itself
(Heb. 9:26; cf. 1 John 3:3). The human heart is brought into conformity
with God's desires (Heb. 10:16; cf. 1 John 2:29; 3:9–10), and there is a
complete "forgiveness" (ἄφεσις) for sin (Heb. 10:17–18; cf. 1 John 1:9;
3:20). In fact, the book of Hebrews uses the word "forgiveness" (ἄφεσις) in
an absolute sense to highlight the "release" or "pardon" of a community's
offenses. Consequently, a person's pardon is dependent on blood because
without the shedding of blood there is no forgiveness (Heb. 9:22; 10:18).[38]

---

37. Although ἡμέρα τοῦ ἱλασμοῦ may be translated "expiation" (BDAG 474b 1, ἱλασμος),
     propitiation" (KJV, NASB), or "the day of atonement" (NRSV, NIV, NET; cf. BDAG 374b 2,
     ἱλασμος), Origen recognized that the ritual of the Day of Atonement played a significant role
     in interpreting 1 John 2:1–2 because the LXX rendering of ἡμέρα τοῦ ἱλασμοῦ in Lev. 25:9
     is "Day of Atonement." Similarly, in Hebrews atonement is interpreted as completed in Jesus
     (Heb. 2:17). Thus, Brown recognizes that Hebrews 7–10 and 1 John 2:2 share the concepts
     of ἱλασμος namely, blood, cleansing, the innocent victim, and the idea that the one who
     atones is himself in heaven continuing to cleanse, thus offering a basis of confidence for sinners.
     Raymond E. Brown, *The Epistles of John*, AB (Garden City, NY: Doubleday, 1982), 220–22.

38. The noun "forgiveness" (ἄφεσις) in the LXX is used in connection with the sabbatical year
     for the "release" or "liberation" of *Israelite slaves* (Lev. 25:10, 41; Jer. 41[34]: 8, 15, 17; cf. Plb
     1.79.12; 1 Macc. 10:34; Jos *Ant.* 17.7.1 § 185), the "release" or "return" of *property* held for
     debt (Lev. 25:13, 28, 31, 33), and the "release," "remittance," or "discharge" of a *debt* (Deut.
     15:1–2; 31:10; cf. D *CDionys* 26, 28, 34), and the "release" of the land from harvesting
     (translated "jubilee": Lev. 25:11–12; cf. Ex. 23:11). It is rarely used in the LXX and secular

Even if the efficacy of an animal sacrifice was limited and perhaps superficial (Heb. 9:23; 10:1–8, 11), it was God's requirement until the coming of Jesus. Today, God *forgives sin due to the human sacrificial sufferings of Jesus* (Heb. 10:18; cf. 1 John 1:9–10) who offered himself as a sacrifice "once *for all*" (Heb. 9:28; 10:10; 13:20; 1 Peter 3:18).[39] Thus, God's point is simply that He has inaugurated his redemption program through the blood of Jesus.[40] It is no longer necessary for people to present any sort of animal blood offerings for sin because the human suffering of Jesus and his sacrificial shedding of his blood has been declared sufficient for the forgiveness of sin.

On the other hand, the human suffering and sacrificial death of Jesus serves as a *means* of peace between God and humanity (Heb. 12:14; 13:20; James 3:18; 1 Peter 3:11; 2 Peter 3:14; 1 John 1:3).[41] Jesus is the mediator of that peace (perhaps 1 Peter 1:2b; 2 Peter 1:2a; Jude v.2). Thus, the estranged relationship between God and humanity that began in the Garden of Eden is gone (Heb. 3:14; 6:4; 12:8; 1 John 1:4, 7). So too is the hostility between Jew and Gentile. God's people are no longer limited to the physical and political entity of national Israel but rather the kingdom expanded into a transnational and apolitical entity made up of both Jew and Gentile who are being built together (1 Peter 1:1; 2:9; cf. Heb. 3:1). Although not as clearly defined as in Paul,[42] the General Letters reveal that

---

Greek to speak of the "forgiveness" of an offense (cf. "forgiven his guilt": *Her* 6.30; "acquit": Pl *Leg* 9.869; Jos *Ant.* 14.9.5 § 182, *War* 1.9.9 § 214; "pardon": Jos. *War* 1. 24. 4 § 481). Yet the distinctive feature of NT usage is that God *forgives sins due to the sufferings of Jesus* (Matt. 26:28; Mark 1:4; Luke 3:3, 12:47; Acts 5:31, 10:43, 13:38, 26:18; Col. 1:14; cf. Luke 1:77; Acts 2:38; Eph. 1:7; Heb. 10:18).

39. The term "once" (ἅπαξ) in Hebrews 9:28 and 10:10 emphasizes something that is unique. It underscores the inability to repeat an event, namely, the human sacrificial life and death of Jesus. Hebrews further punctuates the unique death of Jesus "to bear the sins of many" with a proverbial wisdom statement that people are "appointed to die once" (9:27). Obviously, verse 26b intends to contrast the absurd idea that Jesus' self–sacrifice would need repeating ("many times"; vv. 25–26a). Consequently, some English translations add *"for all"* to "once" (RSV, NRSV, NIV, ESV, NET). Hebrews 9:28 also underscore the point with an OT text: "Christ was offered once *to bear the sins of many*" (Isa. 53:12; cf. 1 Peter 3:18). Thus, the death of Jesus was unique in that "he put away sin."

40. Jesus coming as a "ransom" (λύτρον) for sinners occurs in Mark 10:45 (cf. Matt. 20:28). Mark's predominate theme is the presentation of Jesus as a suffering Messiah who brings redemption with divinely given authority to forgive sin (12:1–12). The theme of messiahship is evident in most of the titles ascribed to Jesus throughout Mark's narrative story and serve to present Jesus to be "the Christ." See Herbert W. Bateman IV, "Defining the Titles 'Christ' and 'Son of God' in Mark's Narrative Presentation of Jesus," *JETS* 50 (2007): 537–59.

41. The NT frequently speaks of the peace between God and humanity due to the work of Jesus (Luke 2:14; John 14:27; Acts 10:36; Rom. 5:1; 14:17; 15:13; 16:20; Gal. 5:22; 6:16; Eph. 1:2; 2:14, 15, 17; 4:3; 6:15, 23; Phil. 4:7; Col. 3:15; 1 Thess. 5:23; 2 Thess. 3:16; 2 Tim. 2:22).

42. Paul more pointedly speaks of the Jew-Gentile relationship with numerous συν prefixed verbs in Ephesians: "fellow citizens" (συμπολῖται; 2:19); "joined together" (συναρμολογουμένη; 2:21); "built together" (συνοικοδομεῖσθε; 2:22); "heirs together" (συγκληρονόμα; 3:6); "members

Jesus mediates for all believers (Jew or Gentile) a common salvation (Heb. 1:4; cf. 1 John 2:1b–2), eternal life (1 Peter 3:7; cf. 1 John 5:12–13), blessings (1 Peter 3:9), the promises (Heb. 6:12; cf. 10:36; 2 Peter 1:4; 3:13), and the kingdom of God (James 2:5; 2 Peter 1:11). Thus, the human suffering and sacrificial death of Jesus inaugurated the new covenant.

In summary then, Jesus is the means by which God has inaugurated his kingdom-redemption program. Jesus is the Christ who presently rules at the right hand of God over an invisible kingdom. Followers of Jesus have been redeemed (Heb. 2:28; 9:15; 1 Peter 1:18–19; cf. 1 John 2:2; 4:10; Heb. 2:17) and experience the forgiveness of sin (Heb. 10:18) or cleansing from sins (1 John 1:9–10). They have peace or fellowship with God, as well as fellowship with other followers of Jesus whether they be Jew or Gentile (Heb. 12:22–24; 1 Peter 2:9).[43] With the inauguration of the fulfillment of the Davidic and New covenants through Jesus comes the inauguration of the fulfillment of the Abrahamic covenant as well. Whereas the new covenant is *the form* by which God has inaugurated the Abrahamic blessings, the Davidic covenant represents one part of the Abrahamic blessing (the royal line) as well as *the means* by which the blessings of the new covenant are bestowed, namely, through Jesus. Consequently, the descendants of Abraham are a transnational group of people who follow or believe in Jesus, the Messiah. Although Isaac was viewed as the initial child of promise who confirmed God's promise to Abraham (Gen. 21:2–3), the ultimate child of promise through whom God would mediate all of God's covenantal blessings to all people as promised to Abraham is Jesus (compare Heb. 11:2, 14–17 with Gal. 3:16).[44] God, however, is not yet through with Israel (Rom. 9–11).

---

together of one body" (σύσσωμα; 3:6); "sharers together" (συμμέτοχα; 3:6). See Carl B. Hoch, Jr., "The Significance of the Syn Compounds for Jew-Gentile Relationships in the Body of Christ," *JETS* 25 (1982): 175–83; idem, "The New Man of Ephesians 2" in *Dispensationalism, Israel and the Church: The Search for Definition* (Grand Rapids: Zondervan, 1992), 99–126.

43. The new covenant is also evident in Luke 22:20, 1 Corinthians 11:25, and 2 Corinthians 3:6. Through it, God lavishes spiritual blessings upon believers (Eph. 1:3; Titus 3:4–7). All believers have an enduring relationship with God as "his people" (Rom. 9:24–29), are part of God's new creation (2 Cor. 5:17; Gal. 6:15; cf. 2 Cor. 4:16; Eph. 4:23–24; Col. 3:10), are oriented to God through a "new heart" (Rom. 5:5; Gal. 4:6; cf. Acts 2:16, 11:1–18; Eph. 1:13) and thereby a lifestyle of obedience (John 16:12–15; Rom. 6:17–18, 22; 1 Cor. 2:9–16), are forgiven (Rom. 3:22–26; Eph. 1:7; Col. 1:14), and are resurrected (Eph. 2:6). Ware, "The New Covenant and the Peoples of God," 68–97.

44. The inauguration of the fulfillment of the Abrahamic covenant is most clearly seen in Galatians 3 where Paul declares "In the same way, 'Abraham believed God, and God counted him as righteous because of his faith.' The real children of Abraham, then, are those who put their faith in God" (vv. 6–7, NLTSE; cf. Rom. 4:3, 9, 20–22). Paul continues, "So all who put their faith in Christ share the same blessing Abraham received because of his faith" (v. 9, NLTSE). Darrell L. Bock, "The Covenants in Progressive Dispensationalism," 172–77.

Whereas the Hebrew Scriptures reveal the development between each divine promise, the New Testament discloses the fulfillment and escalation of the promises when Jesus came and inaugurated them.[45] God moves the human authors of the General Letters to draw contrasts between the past and the present (Heb. 1:1–2), a distinction between how God operates in this present dispensation and that of the previous two periods evident below.

Development Stated	Era of Promise (particularly Mosaic Period)	Era of Fulfillment (Church Period)
Escalation of the royal priest concerning his person.	The Davidic royal priest had many limitations in that all Davidites were solely human.	Jesus as royal priest expands all royal priestly functions in that as royal priest Jesus is a divine Davidite (Heb. 1:1–15).
Escalation of the royal priest concerning his priestly activities.	The Davidic royal priest had many limitations in that Davidites had limited priestly tabernacle/temple functions as intercessor and offering of sacrifices outside of the holy place (2 Sam. 6:12–13; 24:21–25; 1 Kings 3:4; 8:22–25, 62–64; 12:32–33; Ezek. 45:17–46:17).	Jesus as royal priest expands all royal priestly functions in that as royal priest Jesus intercedes for people (Heb. 2:14–18; 4:14–16; 1 John 2:1–2) in the holy place behind the veil (7:24–25; 9:12b, 24–28).
Escalation of the royal priest concerning his extent of his rule.	The Davidic royal priest had many limitations in that Davidic royal priests were limited to a geographical area to rule.	Jesus as royal priest expands all royal priestly functions in that as royal priest Jesus rules over a cosmic kingdom (Heb. 1:1–14).
Escalation of the royal priest concerning his duration of rule.	The Davidic royal priest had many limitations in that Davidic royal priests duration of rule was limited by human life expectancy (cf. 1 Kings 2:10; 11:43; 14:31; 15:18, 24; 22:50; 2 Kings 8:24; 9:27–28;; 12:21; 14:20; 15:7– 28; 16:20; 20:21; 21:18, 26; 23:30; 34; 24:6)	Jesus as royal priest expands all royal priestly functions in that as royal priest The duration of Jesus is quite literally eternal due to God's resurrection of Jesus from the dead (Heb. 7:3, 15–17, 23–24; 1 Peter 1:3, 21; 3:18, 21–22; 2 Peter 1:16–18).

---

45. See Craig A. Blaising, "Fulfilling the Biblical Covenants through Jesus Christ," 174–211; Bock, "The Covenants in Progressive Dispensationalism," 172–77.

Development Stated	Era of Promise (particularly Mosaic Period)	Era of Fulfillment (Church Period)
Escalation of blessings to God's people are priesthood of God's people expanded to include Gentiles.	Blessings were mediated via the physical and political nation of Israel but limited to ethnic Israel (Ex. 19:6).	Blessings are mediated to a transnational apolitical group of people via Jesus who expands the promises to Jews and Gentiles (1 John 1:2; 1 Peter 2:4–10).
Escalation of blessings to God's people are permanent spiritual indwelling.	Blessings were mediated via the physical and political nation of Israel but spiritual indwelling was selective: Moses (Num. 11:25), Gideon (Judg. 6:34), etc., see note #25.	Blessings are mediated to a transnational apolitical group of people via Jesus who God's spirit dwells in all followers of Jesus permanently (Heb. 5:12–6:1; 8:10; 1 Peter 1:3; 2 Peter 1:3–4; 1 John 2:20, 27; 3:24b).
Escalation of blessings to God's people are forgiveness of sins is unlimited.	Blessings were mediated via the physical and political nation of Israel but the Mosaic Law did not provide sacrifice for intentional sins (Num. (15:30–35; cf. Heb. 9:7), see note #26.	Blessings are mediated to a transnational apolitical group of people via Jesus who and all those who sinned during the previous eras are granted redemption though Jesus (cf. Heb. 10:1; 9:15).
Replacement of Aaronic Priesthood	The Aaronic priesthood and the Davidic royal priest mediated the old covenant. Aaronic priesthood were appointed priests (Lev. 9:1–24; cf. Heb. 5:1–4; 8:3–5).	Jesus as royal priest is the sole mediator of the new covenant (Heb. 8:6; 9:5; 12:24). Aaronic priesthood replaced by a better priesthood, an appointed royal priesthood (Heb. 5:4; 7:11–17).
Replacement of Sacrificial System	The sacrificial system, like atonement, was merely external (Heb. 9:13), repeated annually (Heb. 10:11), and ineffective for any length of time (Heb. 8:7; 9:7).	Sacrificial systems are unnecessary due the "better" sacrificial death of Jesus (Heb. 9:9; 10:11; cf. 1 John 2:1–2; 1 Peter 1:18).

Development Stated	Era of Promise (particularly Mosaic Period)	Era of Fulfillment (Church Period)
Replacement of Old Covenant	The Mosaic Covenant was conditional (Ex. 24:1–8; Deut. 29:2–15).	Davidic priesthood escalated: Old covenant is a shadow (Heb. 10:1–4) and annulled with the implementation of the New covenant (Heb. 8:1–10:25; esp. 10:9–10; 10:12–18).

Although all the General Letters recognize Jesus has already inaugurated God's unilateral covenants of promise, the covenants have not been consummated.

God's Strategic Plan Consummated

The millennial period is a time in which God will continue to relate to all people through Jesus. Unlike the church period, however, Jesus will return to the earth, consummate his covenantal promises with ethnic or national Israel, and execute complete victory over his enemies (Rom. 11:1–6, 17–24, 28–28; cf. Ezek. 33:23–26).[46] More specifically, Jesus will reign as King in space-time history, reestablish the physical and political ethnic nation of Israel, and reign from Jerusalem over a visible transnational and political kingdom for a thousand years (Rev. 20:2–7; cf. Matt. 24:1–25:46; Acts 1:6–7; 3:19–21; Rev. 19:11–20:6), which may extend into the eternal state. By transnational, I mean Jesus will rule over Jew and Gentile nations alike (Rev. 7:9–10; 20:7–10; cf. Dan. 7:13–14; Zech. 14:9–11, 16–17).[47] His rule will manifest both

---

46. Burns develops the thesis that Romans 11 denies that God had rejected ethnic Israel because of their unbelief (vv. 1, 5, 7–10), teaches a future for ethnic Israel because the unbelief of the majority of Israelites will not last forever (vv. 11–24), and finally the mystery and mercy of the divine plan will result in salvation of the elect fullness for Gentiles and Jews (vv. 25–32). See J. Lanier Burns, "The Future of Ethnic Israel in Romans 11" in *Dispensationalism, Israel ad the Church: The Search for Definition*, Craig A. Blaising and Darrell L. Bock eds. (Grand Rapids: Zondervan, 1992), 188–29; idem, "Israel and the Church of a Progressive Dispensationalist" in *Three Central Issues in Contemporary Dispensationalism: A Comparison of Traditional and Progressive Views*, ed. by Herbert W. Bateman IV (Grand Rapids: Kregel, 1999), 263–91.

47. Paul speaks regularly of the people of God as two distinct ethnic groups: Jews and Gentiles (Rom. 1:16; 9:24; 11:1, 11; 1 Cor. 1:24; 12:13; Gal. 2:14, 15). Furthermore, Jew and Gentile share in the same promises (Rom. 4:13; Gal. 3:28–29; Eph. 2:12–22; Col. 2:24–29). Both become partakers of the inheritance together with Israel. Yet Gentiles were never grafted into national Israel. Jews remain Jews, Gentiles remain Gentiles, men remain men, masters

power and righteousness as God had always intended via previous Davidic king-priests (Rev. 5:10, 7:9–10; cf. Pss. 2; 45:1–9; 110; Isa. 32:1–2). People will live in abundant peace (Ps. 72:7; Isa. 2:4; 9:6–7; Micah 4:1–3). People will experience remarkable health (Rev. 7:16–17; cf. Isa. 65:20–23), will live much longer (Isa. 65:20), and will reap enormous physical blessings (Isa. 29:18–19; 32:3; 33:24; 35:5–6) under the rule of Jesus. Yet as it was for Abraham and the prophets, we must admit that God has not completely revealed very much about the millennial period. In fact, details about the millennial rule of Jesus in the General Letters are scant.

We do know, however, that the consummation of God's kingdom-redemption program will begin with the return of Jesus (Heb. 9:28; 10:37; 1 Peter 1:7, 13; 4:13; 5:4; 2 Peter 3:4, 10; 1 John 3:2; Jude vv.20). Clearly, Jesus is waiting in God's presence for the day when his kingdom rule will be fully realized, namely, the subjection of all his enemies (Heb. 1:3,13; 8:1; 10:12–13; 1 Peter 3:22; see footnote #29). Where will Jesus establish his rule? As stated in the opening paragraph of this chapter, the theological background for the General Letters is the Hebrew Scriptures. They make it clear that though God gave the city of Jerusalem over to Babylon in 586 BCE (Jer. 39:1–10; Lam. 1:1–2:22, 5:1–20), God promised to bring ethnic Israel back to Jerusalem (Jer. 31:21–40; 33:1–9; Lam. 3:22–24; 5:21–22; Ezek. 37:1–28) as well as bless both the city and the Jewish people in the land (Jer. 33:10–13; Ezek. 39:21–48:35) over which a forthcoming Davidic King would reign (Jer. 33:14–17).[48] Jesus' royal rule on earth has yet to occur. Abraham looked forward to a physical-earthly city (Heb. 11:10) and followers of Jesus continue to look forward to a city yet to come (Heb. 13:14; cf. Acts 1:6–8) from where Jesus will rule as king over the earth. Consequently, the consummated kingdom will be God's promised kingdom (James 2:5) that is unshakable (Heb. 12:28) and eternal (2 Peter 1:11). Furthermore, there is an anticipation of future blessings and realized inheritance (Heb. 9:15; 10:36; 11:14, 16; 13:14; James 2:5; 1 Peter 1:4). Unfortunately, the millennial period will end in God's final judgment of all people (Heb. 10:25; 1 Peter 4:5, 17–18; 2 Peter 3:10; Jude vv.11–16) before entering into the eternal state (2 Peter 3:12–13; cf. Rev. 20).

---

remain masters, women remain women, and slaves remain slaves (Gal. 5:22–6:9). For further discussion see Robert L. Saucy, "The Church as a Mystery of God" in *Dispensationalism, Israel and the Church: The Search for Definition*, Craig A. Blaising and Darrell L. Bock, eds. (Grand Rapids: Zondervan, 1992), 127–55.

48. David L. Turner, "The New Jerusalem in Revelation 21:1–22:5: Consummation of a Biblical Continuum" in *Dispensationalism, Israel and the Church: The Search for Definition*, Craig A. Blaising and Darrell L. Bock, eds. (Grand Rapids: Zondervan, 1992), 264–92.

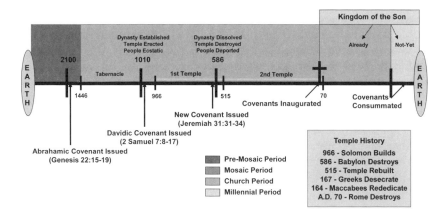

Since specifics about the return and millennial rule of Jesus are vague, not all scholars agree on the four divisions (or dispensations): Pre-Mosaic, Mosaic, Church, and Millennial periods. Some who believe in an earthly millennial period following the return of Jesus (i.e., premillennialists) may differ among themselves concerning some finer nuances,[49] as do those who argue that the Kingdom has come and is fully realized (i.e., amillennialists).[50] Nevertheless, few would argue that dividing salvation-historical events into dispensations is a recent phenomenon.[51] Furthermore, *there is throughout every period* (dispensation) *the expectation to trust God.* Yet within each di-

---

49. See Craig A. Blaising, "The Extent and Varieties of Dispensationalism" in *Progressive Dispensationalism: An Up–to-date Handbook of Contemporary Dispensational Thought* by Craig A. Blaising and Darrell L. Bock (Wheaton, IL: Bridgepoint, 1993), 9–56; Bateman, ed., *Three Central Issues in Contemporary Dispensationalism.* For a historical premillennial view see George E. Ladd, *A Theology of the New Testament*, rev. and ed. Donald A. Hagner ed. (Grand Rapids: Eerdmans, 1993). What distinguishes dispensationalism from historical premillennialism is the stress placed on the visible reign of Jesus over ethnic Israel during the millennial period (Rom. 9–11).

50. See Alan Hultberg, Craig A. Blaising, and Douglas J. Moo, *Three Views of the Rapture: Pretribulation, Prewrath, or Posttribulation* (Grand Rapids: Zondervan, 2010); Darrell L. Bock, *Three Views on the Millennium and Beyond* (Grand Rapids: Zondervan, 1999); Robert G. Clouse, ed. *The Meaning of the Millennium: Four Views* (Downers Grove, IL: Inter-Varsity Press, 1977).

51. Although Ehlert appeals to Jonathan Edwards' (1637–1716) "three great 'Catholic and Grand Oeceonomies'" as "the beginnings of dispensationalism in its larger sense," Poythress correctly argues that an individual who evidences a "sensitivity to the topic of redemptive epochs" (dispensations) is not necessarily a dispensationalist. Like Edwards, Poythress—a modified amillennial covenant theologian—acknowledges the existence of dispensations and yet neither he nor Edwards—an amillennial covenant theologian—are dispensationalists. Arnold D. Ehlert, *A Bibliographic History of Dispensationalism* (Grand Rapids: Baker, 1965), 36–38. Vern S. Poythress, *Understanding Dispensationalists* (Grand Rapids: Zondervan, 1987), 10–13.

vinely administrated period the manner by which God relates with people varied, as is evident in the variety of covenants God extended to various people throughout history. In fact, many recognize that God disclosed his kingdom-redemption program bit-by-bit (progressively) in Scripture, namely, that many elements remained hidden in God's revelatory word until the life, death, and resurrection of Jesus.[52] Thus in the progress of revelation, faith in God is consistent (Heb. 11:1–40), but the focus of that faith changed due to the progressive manner by which God entered into covenant relationships with people and ultimately fulfilled them in Jesus. Today, the focus of faith or *trust* in God is on the person of Jesus who inaugurated God's kingdom-redemptive program and should in turn affect the way we live day-by-day.

God's Expectations

Naturally, a person who wishes to have a relationship with God no longer does so through the physical and political entity of Israel and the Mosaic Law.[53] Today, relationships with God involve a confession about Jesus (1 John 5:12–13; cf. John 14:6; Rom. 10:10), namely, God's promised Messiah (1 John 2:22–23; 2 John 1:7; cf. Mark 8:29; Matt. 16:15; Luke 9:20; John 6:67–71).[54] It is a confes-

---

52. Saucy addresses the hiddenness and revelation as presented in Ephesians 3 as a mystery. "First," he avers, "it is hidden and revealed with regard to its realization in God's historical plan of salvation. It may have been a part of previous prophecy, but it was hidden until the time came for its actualization." Saucy continues, "it is hidden and revealed even then in relation to the reception of the Spirit's enlightening ministry to human hearts. Even in this last instance, the full knowledge of the mystery awaits the final day of the believer's perfection . . ." Thus, "it is the gospel events, the life, death, resurrection and ascension of Jesus Christ, that the mystery was manifested decisively." Saucy, "The Church as a Mystery of God," 146.

53. The noun ἀθέτησις that occurs only in Hebrews 7:18, 9:26 is translated as "set aside" (ESV), "setting aside" (RSV, NIV, NLT, NET), "abrogation" (NRSV; Christian Maurer, *TDNT*, 1972 ed., ἀθετέω, ἀθέτησις), "annulling" (KJV; BDAG 24c ἀθέτησις), or "abolished" (Ceslas Spicq, *TLNT*, 1994 ed., ἀθέτησις). Often suffused with a legal sense, the noun and verbal form express a judicial and official rejecting, canceling, or annulling of political agreements (2 Macc. 14:28, 13:25), of a woman's settlement of claims (*PTebt* 397.13), of a person's will (*POxy* 16:1901.43; Gal. 3:15), or of God's commands (Mark 7:9, perhaps Luke 7:30). In Hebrews 7:18, the annulment of the Mosaic Law has occurred in a judicial and officiating sense. In other words, the Law and the Aaronic priesthood is set aside in light of Jesus' royal–priesthood (see Heb. 7:11–12, 15–17, 19b, 21–22, 24–25, 27). Thus, the inaugurated new covenant in Jesus terminated the old Mosaic covenant (cf. Gal. 2:21; 3:23–24; 5:1–4) as prophesied by several prophets (Jer. 31:31–34; Ezek. 36:26–30; 37:12–14). See also footnote #20

54. See Darrell L. Bock, "Coming of Israel's King" in *Jesus the Messiah: Tracing the Promises, Expectations, and Coming of Israel's King*, by Herbert W. Bateman IV, Darrell L. Bock, Gordon Johnston (Grand Rapids: Kregel, 2012).

sion that involves trusting God when he says he has inaugurated his
kingdom rule—whether that kingdom is believed to be in a mystery,
intermediate, invisible, or spiritual form—through Jesus (Heb. 1:1–
2; cf. Mark 1:15) and through whom God has redeemed a people
to enter into that kingdom. It is a confession that recognizes that all
followers of Jesus will experience human suffering due to the example of Jesus (1 Peter 2:15, 19–25; 3:17–18; 4:14–19). Consequently,
those who profess to follow Christ Jesus are expected to *trust* God
and live as though they are kingdom saints, namely, to live what they
believe. Jesus' followers are chosen to live in righteousness (1 Peter
1:2; 2:24b; cf. Heb. 10:38; 1 John 3:7, 10), in purity just as Jesus is
pure (1 John 3:3; cf. 1 Peter 1:22–23), in holiness (1 Peter 1:15–16; 2
Peter 3:11), and with mercy (Jude vv.22–23). More specifically, God
expects his people to persevere in their belief and act differently than
those who are not kingdom-bound.

General Letter	Perseverance		Conduct	
	Believe in Jesus, who is the Christ	Endure suffering and trials	Avoid sins of . . .	Exhibit love, kindness, mercy, etc. to others
Hebrews	2:1	10:36; 11:1–40; 12:1	3:12; 6:6 (apostasy)	10:24–25 13:15–16
James	2:1	1:2–4, 12–15; 5:7–11	1:21 (vices); 1:26; 3:5–8 (speech) 2:9 (favoritism) 4:17 (evil deeds) 5:9 (gossip) 5:12 (lying)	1:27; 2:8, 15–18; 3:1; 5:14–15, 19–20
1 Peter	1:21	1:6–7 5:12	2:11 (fleshly desires) 5:5a (insubordination)	1:22–23; 3:8–10; 4:7–11; 5:5b–7
2 Peter	1:3, 8		2:1–2 (indulgent immorality) 1:16; 3:10 (denying Jesus kingship and 2nd coming)	2:3–4 3:10

General Letter	Perseverance		Conduct	
	Believe in Jesus, who is the Christ	Endure suffering and trials	Avoid sins of . . .	Exhibit love, kindness, mercy, etc. to others
1 John	2:21–25; 3:23; 4:2, 9–10, 15; 5:1, 5, 10–13, 20		1:9, 11; 3:10, 15; 4:20–21 (hate) 2:15–17 (worldly) 2:4; 3:4–10 (rebellion) 5:21 (idols)	3:16–17, 36; 5:2–9 2:7–8; 3:23; 4:21 (obey God's command to love)
2 John	vv.7, 9		vv.9–10 (denying Jesus)	vv.5–6
3 John	v.3		v.11 (denying God's servants support)	vv.6b–8
Jude	v.4		vv.5–7 (rebellion)	vv.22–237-23

In short, the corporate followers of Jesus, have been transferred into the kingdom, live on earth as God's redeemed community in anticipation of Jesus' return and rule on earth, and model kingdom living for all other people so that they will be drawn to God.

THE INDIVIDUAL THEOLOGIES
OF THE GENERAL EPISTLES

The purpose of this section is to identify the *predominant* theological theme for each of the General Letters. Biblical letters, like our contemporary letters (or emails), are examples of occasional letter writing that address one or two themes (or "subjects"). Often the authors explicitly express their intentions with "I write this . . . " or "I have written . . ." to exhort (Heb. 13:22; Jude v.3), to encourage (1 Peter 5:12), to remind (2 Peter 3:1), and to affirm and warn (1 John 2:12–14, 21, 27). Other times the author has more to say but chooses to wait until he can discuss things face-to-face (2 John v.12; 3 John v.13). Although God and Jesus are the common theological thread that unites all the General Letters, ultimately the General Letters differ in their theological emphasis.

Our goal is to isolate the prevailing theological theme for each General Letter recognizing, however, that every dominating theme is undergirded with several other theological themes.[55] Thus, our discussion presents only the *prevailing* theological themes evident in the letter to the Hebrews, the Petrine letters, the Johannine letters, and the letters of James and Jude.

Letter to the Hebrews

The predominate theological theme of Hebrews is interwoven in the exposition (1:1–14; 2:5–3:6; 4:14–5:10; 6:13–10:28; 10:19–12:13; 13:1–25) and the emotive exhortation (2:1–4; 3:7–4:13; 5:11–6:12; 10:29–39; 12:14–29) sections of Hebrews. Essentially, the theological emphasis is *apostasy versus perseverance* in order to encourage readers to remain in Jesus and avoid God's wrath. God, through the author of Hebrews, provides a clear presentation about the activities of Jesus as God's divine Davidic royal priest along with several emotive and somewhat urgent appeals to Jewish believers to maintain their belief in Jesus.[56]

The letter opens with an unmistakable presentation about Jesus as God's divine Davidic royal priest. As Davidic son, he is an heir (v. 2), he has a unique relationship with God through divine activities (v. 2–3), and after making purification he sat at the right hand of God (v. 3). These descriptions are heightened in Hebrews 1:5–13 by way of several Old Testament texts. Some texts point to his Davidic kingship (2 Sam. 7:14; Pss. 2:7; 110:1), while other texts point to his divine activities (Deut. 32:43; Pss. 104:4; 102:26–27). Yet one Old Testament text merges these two concepts (Ps. 45:6–7). Thus, Hebrews 1 presents the son (i.e., Jesus) as a divine Davidic royal priest. Although the Davidic royal priest's divinity is established very early in Hebrews, Jesus' human activities as royal priest are the focal point throughout the remainder of Hebrews. The repeated linking of Psalm 2:7 with Psalm 110:4 (Heb. 1:5, 13; 5:5–6) and later the linking of Psalm 110:4 with Genesis 14:17–20 (Heb. 7:1–2, 8:1) draw unique attention to Jesus' role as royal priest after the order of Melchizedek. Jesus, the King-Priest is exalted in heaven (Heb. 1:5; 3:6; 5:5–6; 8:1), enthroned in heaven (1:3,

---

55. Many other works exist that identify theological themes in the General Letters. See Roy B. Zuck and Darrell L. Bock, ed., *A Biblical Theology of the New Testament* (Chicago: Moody, 1994), 369–71; Marshall, I. Howard, *New Testament Theology: Many Witnesses, One Gospel* (Downers Grove, IL: InterVarsity Press, 2004), 239–79.

56. The concept of a combined office of king-priest was unmistakably evident beginning with Aristobulus and subsequent Hasmoneans and the subsequent replacement of that system of High Priests with the coming of Jesus as divine King-Priest after the order of Melchizedek. For a historical overview of the significance of that transition see Bateman "Expectations of Israel's King" in *Jesus the Messiah*, 207–44.

13; 8:1), and presently interceding on the behalf of believers in heaven
(4:14–16; 8:1–2; 10:19–22) because of the success of his earthly ministry whereby he inaugurated God's covenantal promises made with
Abraham, David, and the new covenant. Thus, we live in a new era
unlike the previous one; there is a new royal priest unlike any previous
Davidic king-priest; and God's inaugurated kingdom reaches into the
heavens, over which God rules through Jesus (Heb. 1:8–9).

Therefore, there are repeated and urgent appeals not to "turn away"
(ἀφίστημι, 3:12; παραπίπτω, 6:6) from following this Jesus through whom
God has inaugurated his kingdom-redemption program. Historically,
God's people have always wrestled with leaving the God they claim to
love. Ezekiel parallels the wilderness community's *turning away* from
God with that of the first temple (966–586 BCE) Jewish community's
departure from the living God (Ezek. 20:8, 38; cf. Jer. 2:5; Dan. 9:5, 9;
Bar. 3:8). Likewise, second temple (514 BCE–70 CE) Jewish communities depart from God through "abandoning the religion of their fathers"
(1 Macc. 2:19) and through the actions "of the lawless who had rebelled
against God" (1QpHab 8:11, 16). To turn away from God, then, is deliberate rebellion against God: "Far be it from us that we should rebel (ἀπο-
στραφῆναι) against the LORD, and turn away (ἀποστῆναι) this day from
following the LORD. . . ." (LXX Josh. 22:29; cf. Wisd. Sol. 3:10). The
author of Hebrews frequently discusses the heart condition that might
result in forsaking the living God (3:12; cf. Jer. 17:5; Sir. 10:12). Thus,
God has moved the author of Hebrews to weave emotively driven cau-
tions ("take care" or "see to it," Βλέπετε) about a hardened heart (3:8,
15) or evil heart (3:12) that could affect one's relationship with the living
God. But God desires that all followers of Jesus "hold fast" (καύχω 3:6;
4:14; 10:23) to their confession of Jesus as royal priest. [57]

Ultimately, believers are to avoid apostasy, namely, turning away from
Jesus—God's royal priest—through whom God has inaugurated his
kingdom-redemption program. Or we might say it this way: Jesus is the
one through whom God has spoken and through whom God has fulfilled
his promises, so persevere in your confession about Jesus our royal priest.[58]

---

57. "Hold fast" (καύχω) when used in the context of received teachings, takes on a technical
sense: "remember what you have been taught." Paul commends believers when he says,
"you hold firmly the traditions" of the faith and later confirms their salvation "if they hold
firmly to the message" (1 Cor. 11:2, 15:1–2). In Hebrews, "hold fast" speaks of the teachings
about the Jesus' role as royal priest (3:2, 6; 4:14; 10:23). His appointment to exercise rule over
God's house in 3:6 and reinforces the teachings presented in 1:2, 8–9. Similarly in Hebrews
2:1, the community is exhorted to "pay close attention" to those teachings about Jesus in
chapter one. Thus as members of Christ's house (perhaps Kingdom 1:8–9), the community
is expected to *retain or keep in their memory* what they had been taught about the Son. They are
to persevere in their faith.

58. Concerning both themes, there is a strong typological connection made with the Hebrew

Petrine Letters

Although the two Petrine letters are very different, they share a common theme: live righteously among people who do not follow Jesus (1 Peter) and among those who do not look for his return (2 Peter). Yet they differ. First Peter's predominate theological theme is found interwoven in both the consoling (1:3–5; 4:12–5:11) and the exhortation (1:13–2:10; 2:11–4:11) sections of 1 Peter. Essentially, Peter's theological emphasis is about *maintaining godliness while suffering for being a follower of Jesus*. Peter encourages his readers to exhibit godliness as a follower of Jesus despite suffering harsh and hostile treatment from other people. Although Peter makes strong typological connections with the Old Testament throughout the letter (Isa. 53; etc.),[59] Peter's foremost appeal is to Jesus, the Messiah, who suffered in his life (2:21–25) so anyone who follows Jesus should expect to suffer in this world as well (3:13–17).

Despite ill-treatment by others, the characteristic of a follower of Jesus is to be one of hope (1:3, 13, 21; 3:5, 15), one of faith (1:5, 7, 8, 9, 21; 2:6–7; 5:9, 12), one of love (for God and Jesus: 1:8; for others: 1:22; 2:17; 4:8–9; 5:14), and one of holiness (1:2, 15–16; 2:5, 9; 3:5). Regardless of a believer's social situation, he or she is expected to do acts of kindness in society (2:15, 20; 3:6, 17), be submissive to those in authority (2:13, 18; 3:1; 5:5), and live in humility toward one another within the fellowship of believers (3:8–12, 5:5). For Peter, to live rightly and then suffer for it is commendable to God (2:19–20; 4:13–16). Peter makes it clear, "I have written to you briefly, encouraging you and testifying that this is the true grace of God. Stand fast in it" (5:12b).

Second Peter's predominate theological theme is a contrastive message of *vice versus virtue* in order to warn his readers that God will judge all unbelief.[60] Whereas living righteously while waiting for the return of Jesus will be rewarded eternally, living indulgently will end in eternal judgment. As suggested earlier, 2 Peter is a vituperative or maligning letter that also has advisory features. God, through Peter, assaults with great intensity false teachings (or vice) in order to make his message clear: fol-

---

Scriptures. Typology may be defined in several ways. Most simply, Old Testament institutions, persons, and events through which God redeemed his people and established his kingdom were merely types that provided a historical pattern or structure as well as the revelatory biblical vocabulary to be employed in the anticipated the life and work of Jesus by the divine author. It should be noted, however, that the heroes or witnesses of Hebrews 11:1–40 are not *types* but merely OT *examples* of faith.

59. For an excellent discussion of typology in 1 Peter, see W. Edward Glenny, "The Israelite Imagery of 1 Peter 2" in *Dispensationalism, Israel and the Church: The Search for Definition* (Grand Rapids: Zondervan, 1992), 156–187.

60. See Lewis R. Donelson, *I & II Peter and Jude* in NTL (Louisville: Westminster, 2010), 211–12.

lowers of Jesus have a responsibility to live ethically (or virtuously) while
waiting for Jesus. Throughout the letter, people who deny the authority
of Jesus (1:15–19; 2:1), who lead believers to think they can indulge in
self-centered ungodly freedom (2:2–14, 19), and who fail to recognize
the return of Jesus (3:3–7) are condemned vituperatively. In contrast,
Peter advises followers of Jesus of the necessity to live godly lives (1:3–
11), reminds his readers of Jesus' authority being divinely pronounced
(1:16–19), and defends the teaching about Jesus' return (3:10–13). Thus,
the centrality of Peter's message is one of ethics, vice versus virtue.

Johannine Letters

The Johannine letters share a common theme: a person's relationship
with God is determined by believing "the truth" about Jesus and living
according to God's truth. In fact, a person's relationship with God is
expressed in the correct belief about Jesus, which in turn is to affect
how they live in truth with other believers. Whereas 1 John emphasizes
both equally, 2 John emphasizes believing the truth about Jesus while
3 John emphasizes living the truth according to God's expectations.

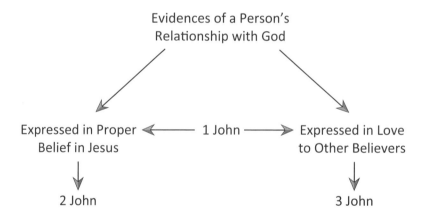

Third John's predominant theological theme is *living the truth,* namely,
providing for those who preach the truth about Jesus. *God expects all believers to provide for his vocationally called servants.* This personal letter of commendation from an unnamed "elder" (presumably John) is addressed to
a beloved fellow believer and friend named Gaius. It begins with a commendation to Gaius for his support of God's vocationally called servants.
Then, through a mitigated exhortation, John commands this same follower of Jesus to continue in his support of God's servants with multiple
forms of provisions (v.6b, cf. 8). John also condemns a sister church's
refusal to support God's pastor-missionary (vv.9–10), but ends positively

with a magnanimous recommendation for another of God's vocationally called servants who is both a worthy model and worthy of support
(vv.11–12). In essence, how one responds to God's truth, namely, the
expectation to support his called servants demonstrates one's commitment to the truth (more specifically, Jesus). Therefore, God expects his
vocationally called servants to be supported lavishly (vv.5–6, 8, 10, 12).

Second John's predominate theological theme is *the truth about Jesus.*
More specifically, it is about the person and mission of Jesus. This type of
advisory letter is also from an unnamed "elder" (again presumably John)
addressed to a sister church.[61] The theological truth of utmost concern is
that Jesus, who is Messiah, was human (v.7). John does not address nor is
he concerned about the deity of Jesus but rather focuses attention on his
humanity. Theologically, anyone who does not confess the humanity of
Jesus and his messiahship is condemned (v.7). In fact, a warning or a sum-
mons ("Watch yourselves," βλέπετε ἑαυτούς; cf. Mark 13:23) is issued
to readers to hold firm the teaching about the humanity of Christ Jesus
(v.8). Affirmation or rejection of this teaching indicates whether or not a
person has a relationship with God and his anointed one (v. 9). Naturally,
concern for "truth" is woven throughout the letter (vv.1a, 1b, 2, 3, 4) but
ends with how to relate with people who reject the truth (vv.10–11).

First John's predominate theological theme is twofold: *the person and
mission of Jesus and living as a loving community.* Both themes are litmus tests
for determining a person's relationship with God. The first addresses
the person and mission of Jesus, namely, his life as a living breathing
human person as well as his coming as the Messiah. The humanity of
Jesus is introduced early in the prologue, which is essentially a "proclamation" (ἀπαγγέλλομεν) about the humanity of Jesus (1:1–2). This
prominent opening proclamation provides the platform that undergirds
John's later and more pointed proclamation that Jesus is the Christ (1:3;
2:22) who came in human flesh (4:2; cf. 2 John 1:7). Belief in the humanity of Jesus makes it possible for a person to have a relationship with
God (2:22–25). It also underscores and foreshadows the importance
of the eyewitness testimony about Jesus (4:14; 5:6–12). Acceptance of
Jesus' humanity and his coming as Messiah is tantamount to one's "relationship" (ἡ κοινωνία) with Jesus and God (1:3; 2:23, 24; 4:15; 5:1,
20) and who is one's real daddy (3:4–12).

---

61. Second John is addressed to the "Elect Lady" (ἐκλεκτῇ κυρίᾳ) and "to the children with her"
    (τοῖς τέκνοις αὐτῆς). Naturally, this could be a real person. She could be a Christian lady
    named "Electa," a Christian lady named "Kyria," or an unnamed Christian lady and means
    "Dear Lady." Arguments against a real person abound (see Brown, *The Epistles of John*, 652–
    53). It is more commonly held that the "Elect Lady" is a metaphor. Perhaps it refers to the
    Universal Church. See Judith M. Lieu, *I, II, III John* in NTL (Louisville: Westminster, 2008),
    244–46. Perhaps it refers to a specific church located at some distance from where John lives.
    See John R. W. Stott, *The Letters of John* in TNTC (Grand Rapids: Eerdmans, 1988), 203–04.

The second litmus test concerns living as community, namely loving other believers. Those who share in the life from God are brought into a relationship with one another, which then becomes the basis for and obligation of mutual love for one another (2:10; 3:10, 11, 14, 18, 23; 4:7, 11, 12, 20, 21). One's relationship with God is demonstrated through obedience to God's command to love other believers, which in turn distinguishes a person's membership within God's community of true believers (2:3–11).

The Letters of James and Jude

James and Jude, brothers of Jesus,[62] wrote letters that are unique in that neither letter says anything about the incarnation, suffering, death, and resurrection of Jesus. Rather than presenting abstract theology, both portray practical theology. They are straightforward down-to-earth letters encouraging people to live what they believe about God (James) and recalling the consequences for all those who do not (Jude).

James's predominate theological theme is the expectation to *live wisely and impartially with other people*.[63] Although allusions to Jesus occur only four times in the letter (2:1; 4:12; 5:7–8, 14–15), James appears to mirror Jesus' sermon on the mount in Matthew and in doing so perhaps indicates the Law's applicability to the church.[64] Nevertheless, the teaching also appears to be qualified by speaking about the Law as "the law of liberty" (1:25; 2:12) and "the royal law of love" (2:8). Regardless of how we reconcile this tension, it is clear that just as Jesus was concerned with how his followers lived as kingdom saints, so too is James.

Believers are expected to grow in God's wisdom (1:2–8, 12–18) when dealing with wealth and poverty (1:9–11; 2:1–13; 48–10, 13–16; 5:1–6), when statements of faith do not measure up with how one lives (1:19–25; 2:14–26; 3:13–18; 4:1–7, 17), when struggling to control slanderous comments about or harmful comments directly spoken

---

62. Although James and Jude state clearly their slave relationship with Jesus (for a discussion about "slave," δοῦλος see p. 124), neither specifies their family tie with Jesus. Nevertheless, both are listed as brothers of Jesus in the Gospels and Acts (Matthew 13:55; Mark 3:32; 6:3; John 7:3, 5, 10; Acts 1:14). Jude most certainly identifies James to be his brother (Jude v.1).

63. It has been suggested that the structure of James is a chiasm that centers on righteous versus worldly wisdom. See Mark E. Taylor and George H. Guthrie, "The Structure of James," *CBQ* 68 (2006): 681–705.

64. While he lived, Jesus clearly taught in his sermon on the Mount (Matt. 5:1–7:29) that he fulfilled the law by reiterating a believers' ethic for his contemporary audience, an ethic that was not new but rather "it was prophetic in that it explained the demands of a righteous and moral God in the context of the Mosaic law." See John A. Martin, Christ, the Fulfillment of the Law in the Sermon on the Mount" in *Dispensationalism, Israel and the Church: The Search for Definition*, ed. Craig A. Blaising and Darrell L. Bock (Grand Rapids: Zondervan 1992), 248–63.

toward other people (1:26–27; 3:1–12; 4:11–12; 5:12), and when considering the importance of patience with and prayer for others (5:7–11, 13–20). In essence, God expects believers to live what they believe. In echoing the teachings of Jesus, there is the expectation that a believer live wisely and impartially with other people.

Jude's predominate theological theme is *rebellion, namely, not to succumb to it but overcome it with mercy*. First, followers of Jesus need to remember God's impartial dealings with rebellion in the past (vv.5–7) and realize that divine and impartial condemnation awaits anyone who presently rebels against God (vv.8–16). Second, followers of Jesus, those who are called and kept by God for Jesus (vv.1–2) are expected to stand against the non-believing rebellious (vv.3–4) and yet extend mercy to them in the hope that they may come to accept and even follow Jesus, who is the Messiah (vv.22–23). In essence, Jude is concerned with the believer's refraining from joining with rebellious people and their subsequent reaction of mercy extended to them.

Chapter in Review

We began our theology of the General Letters by tracing the theme of promise in the Hebrew Scriptures and saw how Jesus links the theme of promise to the theme of fulfillment in the General Letters. Although God created people to rule over his creation (cf. Gen. 2:15 with Psalm 8:5–8), a *coup d'état* in the Garden (Gen. 3) disrupted that plan. Yet the General Letters addresses how God rectified the situation when Jesus completed God's kingdom-redemption plan (Heb. 2:5–9; 10:12–13; cf. 1 Peter 1:18–21; 3:20–22; 4:19; Jude vv.5–6, 14–15, 24–25; 2 Peter 1:3–4; 2:4–10a; 3:5–13).

- First, the theme of promise in the Hebrew Scriptures is about God's kingdom-redemption strategy that has its roots in covenantal promises, particularly the Abrahamic, Davidic, and new covenants.

- Second, the theme of fulfillment concerning God's kingdom-redemption strategy is clearly evident in the General Letters and affirms that Jesus has not only inaugurated God's program, he will also consummate it in the future.

- Finally, the General Letters appear to agree theologically on the importance of perseverance and conduct. Believers are to persevere in their faith about Jesus and they are to conduct themselves differently from those who do not profess Jesus.

4

PREPARING TO INTERPRET THE GENERAL LETTERS

AS WE BEGIN THIS CHAPTER "Preparing to Interpret the General Letters," it is helpful to bear in mind that this chapter is merely the beginning of a step-by-step approach for interpreting the General Letters.

Three chapters, chapters 4–6, provide nine necessary steps to follow when preparing to teach and/or preach from the General Letters. Several tools will be helpful for all three chapters. First, you may wish to consider using a computer program like Accordance,[1] BibleWorks,[2] Logos,[3] or another program to help make the task of interpretation less time-consuming. Second, the following three books (electronic format is also available) may also assist your interpretive endeavors of the Greek text:

Walter Bauer, Frederick W. Danker, William F. Arndt, and F. Wilbur Gingrich. *A Greek–English Lexicon of the New Testament and Other Early Christian Literature*. 3rd ed. Chicago and London: University of Chicago Press, 2000.

Wallace, Daniel B. *Greek Grammar Beyond the Basics: An Exegetical Syntax of the New Testament*. Grand Rapids: Zondervan, 1996.

Metzger, Bruce M. *A Textual Commentary on the Greek New Testament*. 2nd ed. New York: United Bible Society, 1994.

With these tools in hand, we are ready to begin. The purpose of this chapter is both to describe and demonstrate three preliminary steps necessary for preparing to explain the General Letters for teaching and preaching. They are: the initiation of a translation of the Greek text, the identification of interpretive issues, and the isolation of major textual issues. We begin with the easiest step, translation.

STEP ONE: INITIATE A TRANSLATION

The purpose of this section is to introduce the first step for preparing

---

1   **Accordance**: First released in 1994, Accordance is an excellent computer program for doing Biblical exegesis and Biblical studies. Its features and focus are graphical searching, statistical analysis of search results, instant parsing, and diagramming. Accordance offers grammatically tagged editions of the Dead Sea Scrolls, Septuagint, and other Ancient Near Eastern texts. Of the three programs listed, Accordance is by far the best and the most user-friendly, and truly geared for easy and efficient working in the biblical text.

2   **BibleWorks**: BibleWorks is a Bible software program for Biblical exegesis and research. It comes with Greek, Hebrew, and Septuagint Bibles for your computer, as well as translations in English, German, Spanish, Chinese, Korean, and more. Despite its exegetical and research abilities, simple tasks are at times difficult to complete.

3   **Logos**: Logos Bible study software boasts of providing access to almost 10,000 titles, including commentaries, dictionaries and original language texts. They claim to partner with more than 100 publishers to make more than 9,000 electronic Bible study resources available to customers. Unfortunately, many of their titles are public domain works, or out-of-date critical works of minimal value today. Quantity of secondary material is their boast, not necessarily quality. Thus their focus is *not strictly* exegesis in the original languages but rather a collection of sources.

to interpret the General Letters, which is to create a simple translation of a select number of verses from the Greek text. My personal approach is a threefold process that first involves confronting the Greek verbs, then grappling with the Greek clauses, and finally transforming the Greek text into a simple English translation of my own.

Confronting Greek Verbs

Naturally, we start by choosing the verses to study. The passage chosen for this section is 1 John 1:1–4 because the Greek is relatively easy and most people who have taken elementary Greek can readily translate 1 John 1:1–2:10. Obviously, if you were working on a passage of your own you would open your language software program then copy, cut, and paste the selected verses from the Greek text into a Microsoft Word document.

---

1 JOHN 1:1–4

1 Ὃ ἦν ἀπ' ἀρχῆς, ὃ ἀκηκόαμεν, ὃ ἑωράκαμεν τοῖς ὀφθαλμοῖς ἡμῶν, ὃ ἐθεασάμεθα καὶ αἱ χεῖρες ἡμῶν ἐψηλάφησαν περὶ τοῦ λόγου τῆς ζωῆς – 2 καὶ ἡ ζωὴ ἐφανερώθη, καὶ ἑωράκαμεν καὶ μαρτυροῦμεν καὶ ἀπαγγέλλομεν ὑμῖν τὴν ζωὴν τὴν αἰώνιον ἥτις ἦν πρὸς τὸν πατέρα καὶ ἐφανερώθη ἡμῖν – 3 ὃ ἑωράκαμεν καὶ ἀκηκόαμεν, ἀπαγγέλλομεν καὶ ὑμῖν, ἵνα καὶ ὑμεῖς κοινωνίαν ἔχητε μεθ' ἡμῶν. καὶ ἡ κοινωνία δὲ ἡ ἡμετέρα μετὰ τοῦ πατρὸς καὶ μετὰ τοῦ υἱοῦ αὐτοῦ Ἰησοῦ Χριστοῦ. 4 καὶ ταῦτα γράφομεν ἡμεῖς, ἵνα ἡ χαρὰ ἡμῶν ᾖ πεπληρωμένη.

To make the translation process easier, isolate all the verbs and verbals (i.e., participles and infinitives) in the passage. Rather than parse them immediately (the act of parsing occurs later), focus on determining the tense of a verb or verbal and prepare to color-code all of them in the passage. The intention is twofold. First, it creates a visual that differentiates immediately one verb tense from another. Second, it turns the Greek text into a user-friendly tool that can be used time and again as you study. If tense recognition is difficult to recall, use the charts entitled "Indicatives: Distinguishing Tenses." The chart will steer you to recognize the tense of any given indicative verb by isolating a tense formative Greek letter or letters.[4] If all else fails, you can double check yourself via the parsing tool

---

4   A tense formative is a Greek letter or couple of letters inserted between a tense stem and the connecting vowel. For instance, the stem for λυω is λυ. Insert the tense formative letter σ between the stem λυ and the vowel ω or ομεν and you create a future tense verb meaning "I will loose" or "we will loose." Naturally, the charts provided in this chapter identify the tense

that comes with most computer software (e.g., Accordance, BibleWorks, Logos). For the sake of this chapter, I have listed the verbs for 1 John 1:1–4. The chart below lists the variety of verb tenses to be colored so that you can see the immediate benefits of the coloring exercise. Notice there is but one verbal, a participle in verse 4, "complete" (πεπληρωμένη) with an adjoining "to be" verb (ᾖ), which together would be rendered "may be complete" (ᾖ πεπληρωμένη).

INDICATIVES: DISTINGUISHING TENSE[5]

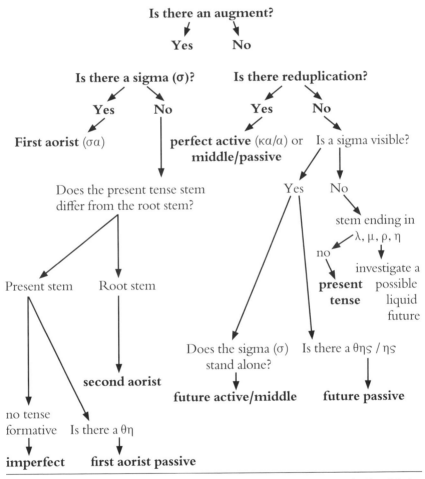

---

formative letters for you. Yet, a "Master Verb Chart" and "Master Participle Chart" listing tense formatives may be found in William D. Mounce, *Basics of Biblical Greek Grammar*, 3rd ed. (Grand Rapids: Zondervan, 2010), 354–56.

5   This chart was first published in Herbert W. Bateman IV, *A Workbook for Intermediate Greek: Grammar, Exegesis, and Commentary on 1–3 John* (Grand Rapids: Kregel, 2008), 589.

1 John 1:1–4			
Verse 1 Verbs	Verse 2 Verbs	Verse 3 Verbs	Verse 4 Verbs
ἦν = imperfect	ἐφανερώθη = aorist	ἑωράκαμεν = perfect	γράφομεν = present
ἀκηκόαμεν = perfect	ἑωράκαμεν = perfect	ἀκηκόαμεν = perfect	ᾖ = imperfect
ἑωράκαμεν = perfect	μαρτυροῦμεν = present	ἀπαγγέλλομεν = present	πεπληρωμένη = perfect
ἐθεασάμεθα = aorist	ἀπαγγέλλομεν = present	ἔχητε = present	
ἐψηλάφησαν= aorist	ἦν = imperfect		
	ἐφανερώθη = aorist		

Using colored pencils (or using your computer software), color (or highlight) all present tense verbs and verbals yellow, aorist verbs light blue, imperfect verbs light green, perfect verbs light red, pluperfect verbs orange, and future verbs light brown. You may create other clues for distinguishing indicatives from verbals. For instance, adverbial participles may be colored to identify tense but then circled with a black pen for quick recognition, infinitives might be colored to identify tense and then underlined, and imperatives might be colored to identify tense and then placed in [brackets]. Once again, the intention is to make the initial translation process a bit easier as well as to create a user-friendly visual tool that differentiates one tense from another. You will use it time and again as you study.

Grappling with Greek Clauses

After confronting the Greek verbs and verbals in a passage, we advance to grappling with the Greek clauses. Once again, our goal is to make the translation process easier. To do so, look for manageable units of thought by isolating the clauses of any given passage, or in our case 1 John 1:1–4. As you know, *a clause contains a subject and a predicate*, which may be a verb, a participle, or an infinitive. Furthermore, clauses may be categorized as either independent or dependent. Distinguishing independent clauses from dependent clauses is part of the grappling process. Whereas independent clauses can stand alone, dependent clauses tend to have a subordinate relationship to another clause. In our grappling with Greek clauses at this point, we wish to merely distinguish independent clauses from the four types of dependent clauses: (1) relative clauses introduced by a relative pronoun (ὅς), relative adjective (οἷος, such as; ὅσος, as much/many as), or relative adverb (ὅπου, *where*; ὅτε, *when*), (2) conjunctive clauses introduced by a subordinate conjunction (ἵνα, ὅτι, καλῶς, εἰ, ἐάν, etc.), (3) participial clauses introduced by a participle, and (4) infinitival clauses introduced by certain infinitives.[6] So for instance, 1 John 1:1–4 has three sentences: verses 1–3a is one sentence with an inserted parenthetical statement (indented below);[7] the second sentence is found at the end of verse three, though the "to be" verb (ἔστιν) needs to be added;[8] and verse 4 is the other. These three sentences, however, consist of sixteen clauses: seven independent clauses with the main verb of the sentence clearly underlined, and nine dependent clauses with their connectors and their verbs clearly underlined. Following the order they appear in the Greek text, we list and distinguish them in this manner:

Dependent Clause	ὃ ἦν ἀπ' ἀρχῆς
Dependent Clause	ὃ ἀκηκόαμεν
Dependent Clause	ὃ ἑωράκαμεν τοῖς ὀφθαλμοῖς ἡμῶν
Dependent Clause	ὃ ἐθεασάμεθα
Dependent Clause	(ὃ) καὶ αἱ χεῖρες ἡμῶν ἐψηλάφησαν, περὶ τοῦ λόγου τῆς ζωῆ
Independent Clause	καὶ ἡ ζωὴ ἐφανερώθη,
Independent Clause	καὶ ἑωράκαμεν
Independent Clause	καὶ μαρτυροῦμεν
Independent Clause	καὶ ἀπαγγέλλομεν ὑμῖν τὴν ζωὴν τὴν αἰώνιον

---

6   A chart exemplifying the types of Greek clauses can be found in chapter five. See also Daniel B. Wallace, *Greek Grammar Beyond the Basics* (Grand Rapids: Zondervan, 1996), 656–65. For other discussions about clauses see James A. Brooks and Carlton L. Winbery, *Syntax of New Testament Greek* (Lanham, MD: University Press of America, 1979, reprint 1988), 154–86.

7   1 John 1:1–3a is one long sentence. Such a sentence in Greek is known as a period (BDF § 458). Similar constructions exist in other General Letters: Heb. 1:1–3; 1 Peter 1:3–5, 6–9; and Jude vv.5–7. When a period exists, it is important to identify the main verb first. In 1 John 1:1–3, the main verb appears in verse 3, "we announce" (ἀπαγγέλλομεν).

8   Why is ἔστιν absent from the Greek text? The verb ἔστιν is frequently omitted in Greek sentences, and this sort of omission occurs often in 1 John. Such omissions are called an "ellipsis," which by definition is the omission of any element of language that technically renders a sentence to be "ungrammatical," yet the sentence is usually understood in context. So it is not unusual to inserted ἔστιν in parentheses as it is done in my listing of the clause.

Dependent Clause	ἥτις ἦν πρὸς τὸν πατέρα
Dependent Clause	καὶ (ἥτις) ἐφανερώθη ἡμῖν
Independent Clause	**ἀπαγγέλλομεν** καὶ ὑμῖν (verb of the independent clause is bold)
Dependent Clause	ἵνα καὶ ὑμεῖς κοινωνίαν ἔχητε μεθ᾽ ἡμῶν.
Independent Clause	καὶ (ἔστιν) ἡ κοινωνία δὲ ἡ ἡμετέρα μετὰ τοῦ πατρὸς καὶ μετὰ τοῦ υἱοῦ αὐτοῦ Ἰησοῦ Χριστοῦ.
Independent Clause	καὶ ταῦτα **γράφομεν** ἡμεῖς (verb of the independent clause is bold)
Dependent Clause	ἵνα ἡ χαρὰ ἡμῶν ᾖ πεπληρωμένη.

Not only does listing clauses make translating easier, this catalog of clauses will be helpful in our next chapter "Interpreting the General Letters" when we discuss structural markers and structural outlines. In the meantime, we are ready to offer a simple translation for 1 John 1:1–4.

Translating the Greek

When translating a passage, my preference is to place all the verbs in parenthesis. Now is the time to execute your parsing skills. Placing the verbs in parenthesis at this time will prove helpful in our second step in preparing to interpret the General Letters. Furthermore, it is visually helpful to *indent the parenthetical statement* in the middle of the first sentence. So my simple translation for 1 John 1:1–4 looks like this:

> ¹What was (ἦν) from the beginning, what we have heard (ἀκηκόαμεν), what we have seen (ἑωράκαμεν) with our eyes, what we have looked at (ἐθεασάμεθα) and our hands have touched (ἐψηλάφησαν) concerning the word of life
> —²the life was revealed (ἐφανερώθη), and we have seen (ἑωράκαμεν) it, and we testify (μαρτυροῦμεν) to it, and we announce (ἀπαγγέλλομεν) to you the eternal life, which was (ἦν) with the Father and was revealed to us—
> ³what we have seen (ἑωράκαμεν) and we have heard (ἀκηκόαμεν), we proclaim (ἀπαγγέλλομεν) also to you, in order that you may have (ἔχητε) fellowship with us. And indeed our fellowship is (ellipsis) with the Father and with his Son, Jesus, who is the Christ. ⁴And we write (γράφομεν) these things so that our joy may be complete (ᾖ πεπληρωμένη).

From this simple translation, the following observation might be offered. John's prologue opens with a progressive pattern of word choices

that builds momentum and ends in some form of eyewitness proclamation. With pristine precision, John provides a personal testimony
about the humanity of Jesus through the elicitation of several significant
verbs: "hear" (ἀκουω), "see" (ὁράω), "look" (θεάομαι), and "touch" (φα-
νερόω).[9] In essence, the prologue provides the platform that will undergird John's later and more pointed proclamation that Jesus is the Christ
(1:3; 2:22) who came in human flesh (4:2; cf., 2 John v.7) as well as
underscores the importance of the eyewitness testimony about Jesus
(4:14, 5:6–12). Thus, the prologue introduces John's "proclamation"
(ἀπαγγέλλομεν) about the humanity of Jesus (1:1–2). John's intention
(ἵνα, "in order that") for proclaiming Jesus' humanity is in order that
mutual fellowship might exist with John and other eyewitnesses, Jesus,
and God (1:3).[10] There is yet another point in verse 4 of the prologue:
John's desired result (ἵνα) for writing, namely joy (1:4). Having con-
fronted the verbs, grappled with the clauses, and our simple translation
before us, we are now ready to move forward to our second step.

STEP TWO: IDENTIFY INTERPRETIVE ISSUES

The purpose of this section is to introduce the second step for interpreting the General Letters, which is identifying interpretive issues within a passage. Needless to say, some concerns will become known while
creating a translation. Yet another profitable path for pinpointing possible
problems (as well as clearing up those surfaced during the translation process) is to compare English translations. In fact, conferring with several
English translations is the most resourceful way to major on the majors
and to stay focused in the text. So the goal is to discover an efficient and
effective use of various English Bibles available today that best prepares
us to explain the General Letters. Yet the numerous Bible options can be
staggering. Why do so many English translations exist? How different
can one Bible be from another? Does the choice of one English Bible
over another matter for comparing a passage for possible interpretive is-

---

9   Although the "we" suffix (μεν, μεθα) or "our" suffix on these verbs may be considered
    a "debatable example," it seems the context throughout all of 1 John 1:1–4 may favor an
    exclusive "we" and "our" because the author appears to speak as an authoritative figure on
    behalf of an entire group of eyewitnesses to the life and ministry of Jesus, which thereby
    distinguishes them from the readers to whom the epistle is being addressed.

10 In the NT, ἡ κοινωνία frequently describes relationships between people (Acts 2:42) and
    people with God (Phil. 2:1, 1 Cor. 1:9, 2 Cor. 6:14, Heb. 13:16). Yet here when joined
    with the preposition "with" (μετὰ), the emphasis is on the *mutual action* between the
    author and the readers (1 John 3:16), which involves a mutual relationship with Jesus and
    God as well (cf. 1 John 2:23, 24; 4:15; 5:1, 20). Thus, those who share in the life from
    God are brought into a relationship with one another, which then becomes the basis for
    and obligation of mutual love for one another, which is a major emphasis of 1 John 2:10;
    3:10, 11, 14, 18, 23; 4:7, 11, 12, 20, 21.

sues? To answer these questions we must first trace ever so briefly the history of the English Bible and then talk about differing theories behind English translations. Most significantly, however, we will illustrate how to use an assortment of English Bibles in preparation for interpretation of the General Letters by way of three exegetical shortcuts. So, we begin with a brief history of the English Bible.

Brief History of the English Bible[11]

The history of the English Bible begins in England around the time of the Protestant Reformation. In 1526, William Tyndale[12] produced the first *printed* English translation of the New Testament based on Erasmus's 1522 New Testament Greek text.[13] It was Tyndale's New Testament translation, along with his translations of the Pentateuch (1530), Jonah (1531), and unpublished portions of the Old Testament from Hebrew, that became the basis for several subsequent English translations. The most notable is the 1611 King James Version.

The King James Version (KJV) was first conceived during a conference initiated by King James VI of Scotland at Hampton Court in 1604 in an attempt to create religious tolerance between English bishops and Puritan clergy. Within seven years, the King James Version was published. Metzger points out, "it is in fact merely a *revision* of the Bishop's Bible, as this itself was a revision of the Great Bible, and the Great Bible a revision of the Coverdale and Tyndale."[14] Nevertheless, several New Testament Greek texts were used for the 1611 King James Version.[15]

---

11 For a more extensive treatment concerning the history of the English Bible see Bruce M. Metzger, *The Bible in Translation: Ancient and English Versions* (Grand Rapids: Baker, 2001).

12 William Tyndale (1494–1536) was an English Biblical scholar, reformer, and martyr. He devoted himself to the study and creating a translation of the Bible in English from the original languages. Unfortunately, he was arrested, imprisoned, and eventually tried for heresy and treason. On October 6, 1536 he was strangled then his body burnt at the stake in the prison yard of the castle of Vilvoorden, just outside Brussels.

13 Erasmuas (1494–1536) was a Dutch humanist scholar who published five Greek texts (1516; 1519; 1522; 1527; 1535). See Metzger, *The Bible in Translation*, 98–103.

14 Metzger, *The Bible in Translation*, 76. In fact, Tyndale's work became the foundation for several English versions: Coverdale, 1535; Thomas Matthew 1537 (probably a pseudonym for John Rogers); the Great Bible, 1539; the Geneva Bible, 1560; and the Bishop's Bible, 1568. Compare *The Holy Bible: Revised Standard Version* (New York: Thomas Nelson, 1952, 1953), vii.

15 Several NT Greek texts served as the basis of the KJV. The KJV of 1611 used Stephanus' 1550 and Beza's 1588–1589 and 1598 editions of the Greek NT, all of which relied upon Erasmus' 1522 edition. Robert Stephanus published 4 Greek texts (1546, 1549, 1550, 1551) and was the first to have a critical apparatus (1550), and the first to divide the text into numbered chapters and verses (1551). Likewise, Theodore Beza published nine Greek texts (1565–1604) and popularized a text that differed little from Stephanus' 1551 edition. See Bruce M. Metzger, *The Text of the New Testament: Its Translation, Corruption, and Restoration* (New York: Oxford University Press, 1992), 95–118.

Surprisingly, the King James Version withstood any serious discussion of a revision for 259 years. Eventually, in 1870, the Church of England commissioned a group of English and American translators to revise the King James Bible. After twenty-five years of work, the English Revised Version (RV) of the Bible was published with an accompanying apocrypha in 1895, and six years later (1901) the American Standard Version (ASV) was published.[16] But these "self-professed" revisions of the King James Version did not end with the RV and ASV. Numerous contemporary English translations are updated English Bible revisions of the 1611 King James Version. The following "Family Tree of the King James Version" traces seven English Bibles that claim to have their origins in the King James Version.

Family Tree of the King James Version

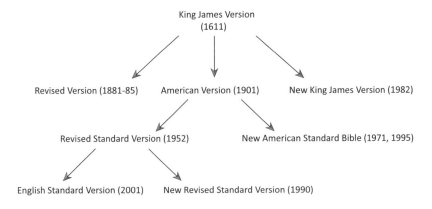

Though certainly not exhaustive, this "Family Tree of the King James Version" points out that seven popular English translations claim to have ancestral roots to King James' translation of 1611. The preface for each of these translations generally recognized two reasons for updating the English Bible: distinctive changes in the English language as well as the mounting discoveries of Hebrew and Greek manuscripts of the Bible. First, consider the changes in the English language for James 4:7–8.

> Submit your selues therefore to God: resist the deuill, and hee will flee from you. Draw nigh to God, and hee will draw nigh to you: cleanse your hands ye sinners, and purifie your hearts yee double minded. (KJV, 1611)

> Be subject therefore unto God; but resist the devil, and he will

---

16   The RV's NT was published in 1881 and the complete OT and NT Bible was available in 1885.

flee from you. Draw nigh to God, and he will draw nigh to you. Cleanse your hands, ye sinners; and purify your hearts, ye double minded. (RV, 1881)

Be subject therefore unto God; but resist the devil, and he will flee from you. Draw nigh to God, and he will draw nigh to you. Cleanse your hands, ye sinners; and purify your hearts ye double minded. (ASV, 1901)

Submit therefore to God. Resist the devil and he will flee from you. Draw near to God and He will draw near to you. Cleanse your hands, you sinners; and purify your hearts you double-minded. (NKJV, 1979)

Submit yourselves therefore to God. Resist the devil, and he will flee from you. Draw near to God, and he will draw near to you. Cleanse your hands, you sinners, and purify your hearts, you double-minded. (NASV, 1989; ESV, 2001)

Obviously, the antiquated English of 1611 is changed. Eventually, pronouns like *thee*, *thou*, and *ye* were replaced with *you* while *thy* and *thine* are replaced with *your* and *yours*. Similarly, though not evident in James 4:7–8 above, there was the elimination of the obsolete seventeenth century verb endings *-eth* and *-est*. So *loveth* or *lovest* was merely translated *love*, and *doeth* or *doest* was rendered *do*, and *hath* or *hast* was converted to *have*. Likewise, English words that had developed different meanings were changed. For instance, the word "let" at one time meant "hinder" or "prevent" but came to mean, "precede" or "allow."[17] In James 2:2–3, the rich person is described in the King James Version as wearing "goodly apparel" and "gay clothing," but it is best rendered today as "fine apparel" and "fine clothes" (NKJV).

Now consider the numerous manuscript discoveries since the 1611 King James Version. The King James Version had at its foundation only a half a dozen Greek manuscripts, the earliest is a tenth-century minuscule (Codex 1). Thirteen years after the publication of the King James Version (1624), the patriarch of Constantinople, gave King James the Codex Alexandrinus.[18] In 1853, Tischendorf discovered Codex

---

17 Other modifications evident in English translations due to a word's shift in meaning is the use of "spirit" rather than "ghost"; "well-being" rather than "wealth"; "ask" rather than "demand"; "be not anxious" rather than "take no thought"; and "immediately" rather than "anon" or "by and by." These are just a few examples generally cited.

18 The Codex Alexandrinus (A) is a 5th century Greek manuscript that contains the majority of the LXX and the NT. It received its name from Alexandria, Egypt where it resided for several years until the Eastern Orthodox Patriarch, Cyril Lucaris, brought the manuscript

Sinaiticus at St. Catherine's Monastery.[19] In fact, a large number of Greek manuscripts discovered during the nineteenth and twentieth centuries contribute to several New Testament Greek texts, which we will list later in step three. In 1948, the discovery of the Dead Sea Scrolls advanced text critical studies of the Old Testament.[20] Thus, today's English translations avail themselves of numerous Hebrew, Greek, and Septuagint texts that were not available in 1611. Yet these discoveries are just two reasons for the continual publications and revisions of previously published English Bibles.

Until now, our focus has been upon the King James Version and several subsequent revisions and updates. Nevertheless, some English translations make absolutely no connection with the 1611 King James Version. In fact, two present themselves as a totally new English translation and thereby not a revision of any previous English version: the New International Version (NIV) and the New English Translation (NET). The first to break away from revising or updating a previous translation was the New International Version (NIV). For thirteen years, hundreds of scholars worked from the best available Hebrew, Aramaic, and Greek texts[21] until the full Bible was released in 1978 with three revisions (NIV[84], NIV[11]; TNIV).[22] Eighteen years later (1996), the New

---

to Constantinople in 1621. Three years later (1624) he gave the codex to James I of England (formerly James IV of Scotland), but due to his death the gift was transferred to King Charles I in 1627 and placed in the British Museum in London, England. Metzger, *The Text of the New Testament*, 46–47.

19   Tischendorf (1815–1874) was a German biblical scholar who is best known for his discovery of the Codex Sinaiticus, a fourth-century manuscript of the NT and portions of the OT, which he discovered in 1859 at St. Catherine's Monastery, Sinai, Egypt. Tischendorf devoted his entire life to text critical study of the NT and published eight critical editions of the Greek NT. His *magnum opus*, however, was his 8th critical ed. (1869–72). See also Metzger, *The Text of the New Testament*, 42–46.

20   Between 1947 and 1956, over 900 texts from the Hebrew Bible, LXX, and other non-biblical documents were found at several locations West of the Dead Sea. These biblical and non-biblical texts date between 150 BCE and 70 CE and have greatly impacted our textual understanding of the OT. See also James VanderKam and Peter Flint, *The Meaning of the Dead Sea Scrolls: Their Significance for Understanding the Bible, Judaism, Jesus, and Christianity* (New York: HarperSanFrancisco, 2002) and Edward D. Herbert and Emanuel Tov, *The Bible as Book: The Hebrew Bible and the Judaean Desert Discoveries* (Grand Haven, MI: British Library & Oak Knoll Press, 2002).

21   Translators used *Biblia Hebraica Stuttgartensia Masoretic Hebrew Text*, the DSS, the Samaritan Pentateuch, the Aquila, Symachus, and Theodotion texts, the Latin Vulgate, the Syriac Peshitta, the Aramaic Targum, and the Juxta Hebraica of Jerome, and Nestle-Aland's *Novum Testamentum Graece* (26th & 27th edition).

22   "The chief goal of every revision to the NIV text" according to the Committee on Bible Translation, "is to bring the translation into line both with contemporary biblical scholarship and with shifts in English idiom and usage. In 1984, various corrections and revisions to the NIV text were made. A lengthy revision process was completed in 2005, resulting in the separately published *Today's New International Version* (TNIV)." The NIV published in

English Translation (NET) presented itself as a completely new translation with no connection with the King James Version. It was placed on the Internet for people to download for free, available to anyone around the world. The editors aver, "The Bible is God's gift to humanity—it should be free."[23] Like the New International Version (NIV), the New English Translation (NET) worked from the best available Hebrew, Aramaic, and Greek texts; and the detailed translational notes are exceptional.

In conclusion, this brief history of the English Bible uncovered the historical linage of several English Bibles. While some claim to be revisions and updates of the King James Version (RV, ASV, RSV, NRSV, NKJV, NRSV, ESV), others do not (NIV[84], NIV[11], TNIV, NET). Although much more could be said here, we must move on to the theories behind these various English Bibles, which is even more relevant in our preparing to study the General Letters.

Theories Behind the Translations

Beyond the unquestionable changes in the English language and the valuable manuscript discoveries of the nineteenth and twentieth centuries, every English Bible committee prepares its translation for a predetermined marketed audience. Thus, they have a prepared purpose that is not always apparent to the average consumer (or member of your church or Sunday school class). For instance, there are competing text critical theories and translational theories behind every English Bible. The self-proclaimed differences, located in the preface of every English Bible are important to be familiar with before comparing English Bibles. While we will examine competing text critical theories in "Step Three: Isolate Major Textual Issues," our focused attention here is on competing translational theories.

Essentially, there are two theories of Bible translation employed today. Some English Bibles purport to practice the formal-equivalence (complete equivalence) method of translating whereby earnest attempts are made to translate word-for-word the original language into English as well as maintain the original word order and sentence structure. Although many English Bibles claim to follow a formal-equivalence

---

2011, "builds on both the original NIV and the TNIV and represents the latest effort of the Committee on Bible Translation (CBT) to articulate God's unchanging Word . . ." The Committee on Bible Translation's "Updating the New International Version of the Bible: Notes from the Committee on Bible Translation" (August 2010), 2.

23   The NET Bible Society provided the NET Bible (with all the translators' notes) to Wycliffe Bible Translators to assist their field translators and works with other groups and Bible Societies to promote fresh translations in other languages. For example, a Chinese translation team has worked on a new translation, which incorporates the NET Bible translators' notes in Chinese, making them available to an additional 1.5 billion people. You may go to www. bible.org and download your free copy.

theory, the New American Standard Bible is generally regarded as the most "complete equivalent" or "formal-equivalent" translation of the twentieth century. In 1995, the text of the NASB was updated to reflect the most recent Greek and Hebrew texts as well as to provide greater understanding and smoother readability.[24] In fact, the ultimate purpose of both the ASV and NASB has always been to provide "the most literally accurate English translation" from the original languages.[25] Other translations that also purport to practice the formal-equivalence (complete equivalence) theory are the Revised Version (RV), the New Revised Standard Version (NRSV), the English Standard Version (ESV), and the New King James Version (NKJV).

In contrast, other Bibles practice a dynamic-equivalence (functional equivalence) theory whereby attempts are made to translate the ancient authors "thought-for-thought." This translation theory begins with an exegetical translation of the original language and then, based upon interpretations, creates a contemporary vernacular English translation that best conveys the ideas and connotations of the ancient authors. The New Living Translation (NLT[SE]), a revision of the Living Bible (LB) is "based upon the most recent scholarship in the theory of translation."[26] It proudly proclaims to be "a thought-for-thought translation" that "seeks to be both exegetically accurate and idiomatically powerful" and that "is to be both reliable and eminently readable."[27] Thus, the emphasis is on being a functional-equivalent translation.

In reality, there are no completely word-for-word, formal-equivalent English translations because they would be unreadable. There are no perfect translations, which is why there are so many Bibles on the market. All translations are, in different and varying degrees, interpretations; all translations have limitations; and all translations have strengths and weaknesses. Our purpose here, however, is not to pit one Bible translation against another. It is our goal to point out how different Bible translations can assist us in our preparation for interpreting the General Letters. As we advance, it may be helpful to identify, on a sliding scale, the degree of differences between those more formal ("for-

---

24 The NASB (1995) uses the 26th & 27th editions of *Nestle-Aland's Novum Testamentum Graece* is closely followed as well as the *Biblia Hebraica Stuttgartensia*, which sheds the most recent light from lexicography, cognate languages, and the *Dead Sea Scrolls*.

25 The preface of the NASB has a clearly stated purpose: "The Editorial Board had a two-fold purpose in making this translation: to adhere as closely as possible to the original languages of the Holy Scriptures and to make the translation in a fluent and readable style according to current English usage. (This translation follows the principles used in the American Standard Version 1901 known as the Rock of Biblical Honesty.)"

26 *New Living Translation: Easy to Understand Relevant for Today* (Wheaton, IL: Tyndale House, 1996),

27 *New Living Translation*, xli-xlii.

mal-equivalent") English Bibles to the more functional ("functional-equivalent").[28]

More Formal								More Functional			
ASV NASB[95]	KJV	NKJV	RSV	ESV	NRSV	NET	NIV[85/11]	TNIV	NLT[SE]	LB

Translations to the right tend to translate English into a more readable contemporary vernacular than those to the left. Consequently with these degrees of difference in mind, we will discover how comparing English translation can provide several efficient and effective shortcuts in preparing to interpret the General Letters.

Number One: Resolving Open-ended Statements

The first shortcut is that English translations sometimes surface unclear and open-ended statements in the text. Take for instance, the various translations of Hebrews 11:5.

Πίστει Ἐνὼχ <u>μετετέθη</u> τοῦ μὴ ἰδεῖν θάνατον, καὶ οὐχ ηὑρίσκετο διότι <u>μετέθηκεν</u> αὐτὸν ὁ θεός (Nestle-Aland 27th, 28th editions)

By faith *Enoch <u>was translated</u>* (μετετέθη) that he should not see death; and *was not found*, because *God <u>had translated</u>* (μετέθηκεν) *him*. (KJV, NKJV)

By faith *Enoch <u>was taken</u>* (μετετέθη) so that he would not see death; and *he was not found*, because *God <u>took</u>* (μετέθηκεν) him up. (NASB, cf. ESV)

By faith *Enoch <u>was taken</u>* (μετετέθη) so that he did not experience death; and *he was not found*, because *God* had *<u>taken</u>* (μετέθηκεν) *him*." (NRSV; cf. NET)

By faith *Enoch <u>was taken</u> **from this life*** (μετέθηκεν) so that he did not experience death; *he could not be found*, because *God had taken* (μετέθηκεν) *him away*. (NIV)

---

28 While writing an initial draft of this chapter, I discovered Carson had a similar sliding scale. His arrangement of English Bibles looks like this: ASV NASB KJV NKJV RSV NRV NJB NIV NIVI NLT CEV LB. Whereas the NIVI (2001) is the International Bible Society's revision of the NIV, the TNIV is a revision of the NIV published by Zondervan (2005). For debates over these revisions see D. A. Carson, *The Inclusive Language Debate: A Plea for Realism* (Grand Rapids: Baker, 1988), 28–37, 69.

"It was by faith that Enoch <u>was taken</u> **up to heaven** (μετετέθη) without dying—"*he disappeared*, because God <u>took</u> (μετέθηκεν) him." (NLT[SE])

Although the KJV, NKJV, NASB[95], ESV, NRSV, and NET provide a somewhat similar rendering for Hebrews 11:5, we should stop and ask ourselves several questions: Where exactly was Enoch taken? Obviously, some Bibles provide more information than the Greek text formally states: "from this life" (NIV[85]) and "up to heaven" (NLT[SE]). In fact, the difference should give us reason to pause and ponder the possible interpretive point these translations offer. What did the author mean when he wrote, "Enoch was taken"? Do the additions help us? Are they right? These are good exegetical questions to pose due to these translational options.

As we prepare to interpret Hebrews 11:5, it seems exegetically sound to conclude that the author of Hebrews simply meant that Enoch no longer lived on earth. Yet is there any foundation for including information not explicitly stated in the Greek text? Let's consider 2 Kings 2:1, 11. It says, "And it came to pass, when the Lord was about to take up Elijah into heaven by a whirlwind . . . Then it happened . . . that suddenly a chariot of fire appeared with horses of fire, and separated the two of them; and Elijah went up by a whirlwind into heaven" (NKJV). It seems 2 Kings about Elijah validates the NIV[85] and NLT[SE] additions about Enoch. Was not Enoch taken "from this life" as rendered by the NIV[85]? Did Enoch go to heaven as translated by the NLT[SE]? Is it true that Enoch disappeared? Thus, the reality and ultimately the point of Hebrews 11:5 is that God took Enoch from this earthly life to heaven; he just disappeared. So, comparing these English translations assist in pinpointing an unclear and open-ended statement in the text, provided a reasonable interpretive addition, and ultimately saved me time.

Number Two: Rendering Greek Idioms

Even the most formal of translations must succumb to translating Greek into something readable. "An attempt has been made," admits the editorial board of the ASV, "to render the grammar and terminology of the ASV in contemporary English. When it was felt that the word-for-word literalness of the ASV was unacceptable to the modern reader, a change was made in the direction of a more current English idiom."[29] Consequently, the second exegetical shortcut is that comparing English translations may help us pinpoint efficiently the transformation of Greek idiomatic expressions and thereby effectively deepen our understanding of the text.

---

29   The quote is cited in the "Preface to the New American Standard Bible AD 1963," *New American Standard Bible* (Carol Stream, IL: Creation House, 1971), vii.

Needless to say, all sorts of Greek grammatical idioms have been converted into good English.[30] So, where does one begin? Are there any translated grammatical idioms that deepen our understanding of the General Letters? Let's consider an easy idiomatic Greek grammatical construction like the singular noun + singular article for a plural number of people in 1 John. The informal Greek construction "everyone" (πᾶς) + the article (ὁ) + a participle frequently speaks of one of two contrasting groups or classes of people.[31] All English translations recognize this idiomatic construction, which then enables us to both recognize and to track two people groups in 1 John. Thus, John's fondness of πᾶς ὁ plus the participle serves to divide people into one of two categories: "everyone who does this" as opposed to "everyone who does the opposite."

Another idiomatic Greek grammatical construction is the back-to-back placement of two negative Greek particles: "not" (οὐ) and "not" (μή) followed by an aorist subjunctive. While this double negative construction may be good Greek, it is bad English and difficult to translate. Nevertheless, this construction is the Greek way to strengthen a negative and thereby makes for a strong emphatic statement.[32] Consider the translations for Hebrews 13:5. I suspect most of us have memorized this more familiar translation: "I will never leave you nor forsake you" (NKJV, cf. NRSV, NIV[85]). Now consider these two renderings: "Never will I leave you; never will I forsake you" (NIV[85]), and "I will never fail you. I will never abandon you" (NLT[SE], cf. NET). Yet despite the punctuation separating the two clauses, and the English rendering "never" for the Greek idiomatic "not" (οὐ) and "not" (μή), neither appear to be very emphatic. So, I created my own translation: "I will *never, no never* (οὐ μή) fail (ἀνῶ) you, neither (οὐδ') will I ever, ever (οὐ μή) abandon (ἐγκαταλίπω) you."

What's the author's point? It appears the original readers of Hebrews were subjected to public abuse, confiscation of property, and imprisonment (10:32–34). Furthermore, their future was bleak due to the prospect of further suffering (12:1–3). Here in Hebrews 13:5, the author

---

30   Two helpful books for addressing idiomatic grammar issues are C. F. D. Moule, *An Idiom Book of New Testament Greek*, 2nd ed. (Cambridge, England: Cambridge University Press, 1959, reprint, 1982) and Stanley E. Porter, *Idioms of the Greek New Testament* (Sheffield: JSOT Press, 1992).

31   This construction, where the singular neuter πᾶς is followed by an articular participle occurs 14 times in 1 John (2:23, 29; 3:3, 4, 6 [2 times], 9, 10, 15; 4:7; 5:1 [2 times], 18; cf. also 2 John v.9). See Bateman, *A Workbook for Intermediate Greek*, 289, 315, 329, 334, 341, 351, 357, 376, 451, 512, 514, and 574. James 3:19 where "every man" (πᾶς ἄνθρωπος) may more correctly be rendered "every person" (ESV, NET) or "everyone" (NRSV, NIV).

32   The Greek idiomatic construction, "not" (οὐ) and "not" (μή), occurs six times in the General Letters: Heb. 8:11, 12, 10:17 (quotes from Jer. 31:31–34); 13:5 (quote from perhaps Deut. 31:6–7); 1 Peter 2:6 (quote from Isa. 28:6); 2 Peter 2:10. As you can see, the emphatic negation occurs predominately in quotations from the LXX. For further discussion, see Wallace, *Greek Grammar Beyond the Basics*, 468.

begins with two exhortations: do not love money (negative) and be content with what you have (positive). Why? Because God promised in the sacred Hebrew Scriptures (Deut. 31:6, 8), "I will *never, no never* (οὐ μή) fail (ἀνῶ) you, neither (οὐδ᾽) will I *ever, ever* (οὐ μή) abandon (ἐγκαταλίπω) you." Thus, God emphatically assures both his provision and his presence. So the point is simply: be content with the possessions you have because GOD WILL (emphatic) provide, and by the way, do not forget to help others who are in need (Heb. 13:16; cf. James 2:15–16; 1 John 3:17).

Let's consider one final idiomatic Greek grammatical construction in 2 Peter 1:1b. Most translations read: "through the righteousness of *our* God and Savior, Jesus Christ." Yet following more closely the Greek word order, the KJV reads: "through the righteousness of God and *our* Savior, Jesus Christ" (ἐν δικαιοσύνῃ τοῦ θεοῦ *ἡμῶν* καὶ σωτῆρος Ἰησοῦ Χριστοῦ). On the one hand, the KJV appears to indicate that two persons are in view—God (the Father) and our Savior Jesus—because of the occurrence of the Greek pronoun "our" (ἡμῶν) immediately after "God" (θεοῦ). On the other hand, most render rightly the pronoun "our" as though it governed both nouns "God and Savior" and thereby the referent is one person, Jesus whom Peter also considers to be the Christ (see Ἰησοῦ Χριστοῦ discussion chapter 1).

You may recall from your Greek grammar courses the Granville Sharp rule[33] whereby the article "the" (τοῦ) + the noun "God" (θεοῦ) + the conjunction "and" (καὶ) + the noun "Savior" (σωτῆρος) always has the same referent (in this case "Jesus"). Furthermore, the nouns "God" and "Savior" are singular, personal, and not proper names. This same Greek idiomatic construction appears elsewhere in 2 Peter where we read on three separate occasions "our Lord and Savior, Jesus Christ" (τοῦ κυρίου ἡμῶν καὶ σωτῆρος Ἰησοῦ Χριστοῦ, 1:11; 2:20; 3:18).[34] Thus, the idiomatic Greek construction in 2 Peter 1:11 conveys to us that Jesus is both our "God" and "Savior." It provides a strong affirmation of Jesus' deity that corresponds with other similar statements expressed

---

33   The Granville Sharp rule is named after an English philanthropist-abolitionist-linguist. For more information about Granville Sharp see Daniel B. Wallace, *Granville Sharp's Canon and Its Kin: Semantics and Significance* (New York: Peter Lang, 2009), 31–44. For an abbreviated discussion see Wallace, *Greek Grammar Beyond the Basics*, 270–71.

34   There are many examples of Granville Sharp's construction (noun + καὶ + noun) in the General Letters: Heb. 3:1 (Jesus, the apostle and high priest of our confession); Heb 12:2 (Jesus, the founder and perfecter of our faith); James 1:27; 3:9 (God and Father); 1 Peter 1:3 (the God and Father of our Lord Jesus Christ); 1 Peter 5:1 (elder and witness of Christ's suffering); Jude v.5 (Master and Lord, Jesus Christ). Yet, the Granville Sharp construction occurs with substantival participles (ptc + καὶ + ptc) in the General Letters: Heb. 7:1; James 1:25; 1 John 2:4, 9; 2 John v.9. The point to keep in mind is simply that each construction speaks of one referent. In other words, two nouns or two participles are used when only one person is in view.

elsewhere (Phil. 2:5–8; Titus 2:13; Heb. 1:5–13).[35] Consequently, pin-pointing and comparing idiomatic Greek grammatical constructions and their subsequent conversions into English have effectively enriched our understanding of the text.

Number Three: Recognizing English Sensitivities

Our third exegetical shortcut centers on pinpointing idiomatic English renderings that exist due to cultural sensitivities of an English reader. English translations often soften Greek expressions due to Christian sensitivities to "coarse words" (though what may be considered a coarse expression for one person may not be for another). Take for instance Jude 11 when Jude condemns a group of "godless" (ἀσεβεῖς) intruders who have infiltrated Christian communities in Judea during the 60s (see chapter 2). Jude avers, "Woe to them" (οὐαὶ αὐτοῖς)! The idiomatic English expression "woe" is reminiscent of the King James era and yet maintained by many translations (ASB, NASB[95], RSV, ESV, NRSV, NET, NIV[85]). Only the NLT[SE] breaks away from the English idiomatic expression with "What sorrow awaits them!"

Perhaps an even more appropriate contemporary English idiom is "They are damned!" or "Damn them!" Jude's expression is a prophetic pronouncement of judgment on a group of people who have forsaken God similar to those of Old Testament prophets (cf. Isa. 5:1–30; Jer. 22:13–17; 23:1–4; Amos 6:1–3; Hab. 2:6–20), the author of 1 Enoch (94:6–8; 95:4–7; 96:4–8; 97:7–8; 98:9–16; 99:11–15; 100:7–9), and Jesus (e.g., Matt. 11:21; 18:7; 23:13–16, 23, 25, 27, 29; cf. Peter's statement in Acts 8:20).[36] So comparing English translations may draw attention to a word or group of words that are harsh emotive expressions that we may miss because of our Christian cultural sensitivities. In fact, even American cultural sensitivities sometimes generate poor English renderings as is the case for the Greek word "slave" (δοῦλος) in several opening salutations that causes us to under-emphasize the point of the text (James 1:1; 2 Peter 1:2; Jude v.1; see p. 145).

---

35 We see the same construction in Titus 2:13. Wallace deals with both Titus 2:13 and 2 Peter 1:11 extensively in *Granville Sharp's Cannon and Its Kin*, 241–72; idem, *Greek Grammar Beyond the Basics*, 276–77.

36 An English idiomatic rendering offered for Matthew 11:21 reads, "Damn you Chorazin! Damn you Bethsaida! If the miracles done in you had been done in Tyre and Sidon, they would have (sat) in sackcloth and ashes and changed their ways long ago." In fact, Jesus tells Capernaum "you'll go to hell" (11:23). See Robert J. Miller, ed., *The Gospels* (New York: Harper San Francisco, 1994). Carson avers, "May your money perish with you" in Acts 8:20 could be rendered idiomatically as "to hell with you and your money." D. A. Carson, *The Inclusive Language Debate: A Plea for Realism* (Grand Rapids: Baker, 1988), 64. Granted, we may not approve of the coarse language, but it catches our attention and moves us away from the softened idioms of a long gone King James era.

Another example worth highlighting is gender-inclusive or gender-neutral Greek words. Many formal-equivalent translations reveal
an ultra-conservative form of translating gender-neutral Greek words
(NASB[95], NKJV). Yet "many churches," avers the NRSV, "have become sensitive to the danger of linguistic sexism arising from the in-
herent bias of the English language towards the masculine gender, a
bias that in the case of the Bible has often restricted or obscured the
meaning of the original text."[37] Consequently, some formal-equivalent
translations like the NRSV reveal gender inclusive renderings of certain Greek words. Although a potentially sensitive issue, our goal is
not to debate the validity of gender-inclusive translations, but rather
to probe how comparing Bible translations helps us to efficiently and
effectively identify three Greek words that may be gender-neutral in
James and thereby deepen our understanding of James.

We begin with the least controversial of Greek terms, "brothers"
(ἀδελφοί). The Greek word "brothers" (ἀδελφοί) could reference a literal
blood-related sibling. James, for instance, is the "brother" (ἀδελφός) of
Jude (Jude v.1). "Brother" (ἀδελφός), however, may be used in terms of
a close relationship with another person or persons (*brother, fellow member,
member, associate*) and thereby "used by Christians in their relations with
each other."[38] So when James writes, "consider it all joy, my brothers"
(Πᾶσαν χαρὰν ἡγήσασθε, ἀδελφοί μου), he is not writing to his blood-
related siblings, nor does he appear to be limiting his comment to the
male readers of his letter. James, in keeping with the Greek term's more
inclusive nuance, refers to both men and women as "brothers" (ἀδελφοί).
Consequently, the twelve occurrences of ἀδελφοί in James are readily
rendered in idiomatic English as "brothers *and sisters*" in several English
translations (NRSV, NET, NIV[11], NLT[SE]).[39] So then, the supplement

---

37   *The New Revised Version Bible with Apocryphal/Deuterocanonical Books*, preface. According to
      Carson, "Bible Rage" may have erupted due to the publication of the NIVI and subsequent
      TNIV. Yet Carson strives to demonstrate the exegetical relevance for gender-neutral
      language as well as cautions us to avoid any assertion that suggests gender-inclusive or
      gender-neutral language promotes feminism. Carson, *The Inclusive Language Debate*, 37.

38   BDAG 18, ἀδελφός 2a. The Colorado Springs policy for translating ἀδελφός says, "Brother"
      should not be changed to "brothers or sisters," but the plural can be translated "brothers and
      sisters" where the context makes clear that the author is referring to both men and women.
      For the entire statement and his subsequent argument, see Carson, *The Inclusive Language
      Debate*, 44–46, 120–29.

39   See James 1:2; 2:1, 5, 14; 3:1, 10; 4:11; 5:7, 9, 10, 12, 19. Taking into consideration the
      occurrences in James, the Greek noun ἀδελφός occurs at least thirty-five times in the
      General Letters for both men and women. Many translations render ἀδελφός as "brothers
      and sisters" (e.g., Heb. 2:11, 17; 3:1, 12; 7:5; 10:19; 13:22, 23; 2 Peter 1:10; 1 John 3:13;
      NRSV, NET, NLT[SE]). "Fellow Christian" (NET) or "brothers and sisters" (NRSV) is a
      suitable rendering evident for 1 John 2:9, 10, 11; 3:10, 13, 14, 15; 4:20, 21; 5:16 (NET).
      Gender neutral renderings like "traveling missionaries" (NLT[SE]) or "friends" (NRSV) occur
      in 3 John vv.3, 5, 10. In fact, the English Standard Version (ESV) translates ἀδελφοί as

"and sisters" to "brothers" serves to recognize explicitly an assumed segment of people in James' purview, namely women.

Similarly, the Greek term "man" (ἄνθρωπος), even more so than "brothers" (ἀδελφοί), tends to be an inclusive expression for "a person of either sex, with a focus on participation in the human race, *a human being*" as well as "a member of the human race, with a focus on limitations and weaknesses, *a human being*."[40] Although one lexical meaning for ἄνθρωπος is "man," it is more commonly employed as a gender-neutral expression that refers to people or humanity in general. Most certainly, James 5:17 illustrates this wider nuance and more inclusive sense of meaning: "Elijah was ***human*** (ἄνθρωπος) just like us" (NET) or Elijah was a ***human being*** (ἄνθρωπος) like us (NLT[SE]). No one would deny that Elijah was male, but it seems James' point is that comparatively speaking he was *human* just like other *human beings*. Another example of an inclusive rendering of "man" (ἄνθρωπος) occurs in James 2:20.

θέλεις δὲ γνῶναι, ὦ ἄνθρωπε κενέ, ὅτι ἡ πίστις χωρὶς τῶν ἔργων ἀργή ἐστιν; (Nestle-Aland 27th, 28th editions)

You foolish ***man*** (ἄνθρωπε), do you want evidence that faith without deeds is useless? (NIV[84])

Do you want to be shown, you foolish ***person*** (ἄνθρωπε), that faith apart from works is useless? (ESV)

But would you like evidence, you empty ***fellow*** (ἄνθρωπε), that faith without works is useless? (NET)

As you might suspect, Bibles that tend to be more formal maintain a more formal-equivalent meaning (NIV[84]; cf. ASV, NKJV), while others allow the more inclusive expression to be rendered idiomatically as "person" (ESV, NASV; cf. NLT[SE]) and "fellow" (NET; cf. NASB[95]). Thus, comparing several English translations cause us to stop and ponder this question: Is James speaking exclusively to the men of his congregation or inclusively to both men and women?

The last Greek term to consider is "man" (ἀνήρ). Although it tends to be much more gender specific to "an adult human male, *man, husband*," a subsequent nuance is equivalent to the Greek term "someone" (τις) or to "a person"[41] James employs "man" (ἀνήρ) several times and is

---

"brothers" with an ★ to point out that "brothers and sisters" is an alternative rendering.

40 BDAG 81, ἄνθρωπος.

41 BDAG 79, ἀνήρ, ἀνδρός, ὁ, 1a and 2. For instance, "Do not praise ***anyone*** (ἄνδρα) before he speaks" (*Sirach* 27:7).

rendered both in a formal-equivalent sense as well as a gender-inclusive English vernacular sense.

James	Various Renderings of "Man" (ἀνήρ)
1:12	Μακάριος ἀνὴρ ὃς ὑπομένει πειρασμόν (NA 27th, 28th editions) Blessed is the man (ἀνήρ) who perseveres under trial (NASB95, NIV84) Blessed is the man (ἀνήρ) who remains steadfast under trial (ESV) Happy is the one (ἀνήρ) who endures testing (NET) Blessed is anyone (ἀνήρ) who endures temptation (NRSV) God blesses those (ἀνήρ) who patiently endure testing and temptation (NIV11, NLTSE)
1:20	ὀργὴ γὰρ ἀνδρὸς δικαιοσύνην θεοῦ οὐκ ἐργάζεται (NA 27th, 28th editions) for man's (ἀνδρός) anger does not bring about the righteous life that God desires (NIV) for the anger of man (ἀνδρός) does not produce the righteousness of God (ESV) for human (ἀνδρός) anger does not accomplish God's righteousness (NET; NLTSE)
3:2	εἴ τις ἐν λόγῳ οὐ πταίει, οὗτος τέλειος ἀνήρ (NA 27th, 28th editions) If anyone is never at fault in what he says, he is a perfect man (ἀνήρ) (NIV; cf. NASB95) And if anyone does not stumble in what he says, he is a perfect man (ἀνήρ) (ESV) Anyone who makes no mistakes in speaking is perfect (NRSV) If someone does not stumble in what he says, he is a perfect individual (ἀνήρ) (NET)

Naturally, the more formal translations tend to render "man" (ἀνήρ) literally (NASB95, ESV, NIV84). Yet as we consider the options, we need to pause to ponder three interpretive questions. Does James limit God's blessing in 1:12 to male Christians who endure trials? Does James limit tackling anger and its effects on righteousness to men alone in 1:20? Does James believe that only men can achieve perfection in 3:2? It appears instead that the two Greek terms for "man" (ἀνήρ and ἄνθρωπος) are synonymous for both men and women throughout the Book of James and are part of James' linguistic and literary style. In all likelihood, it may be an idiolect of James. In summary then, our goal has been to discover then demonstrate an efficient and effective use of various English Bibles. Having focused on the theories of translation employed in several English Bibles and demonstrated how an effective comparison aids in our preparation to interpret the General Letters, we are now ready to tackle competing textual theories of translation.

STEP THREE: ISOLATE MAJOR TEXTUAL PROBLEMS

The purpose of this section is to introduce the third step for interpreting the General Letters, which is to isolate major textual problems.

There are over 5,500 extant manuscripts of the New Testament written on either papyrus or vellum material in either carefully transcribed capital Greek letters called uncials or in rapidly written Greek cursive script called minuscules. In fact, numerous scribes copied the New Testament by hand for nearly 1,500 years. Consequently, they tended to make mistakes as well as pass along another person's scribal errors. Sometimes changes are unintentional; other times the scribe deliberately changed, or attempted to correct a previous scribe. So, no two manuscripts are exactly alike in every detail, and errors exist. Yet of the 7,947 verses in the New Testament, 4,999 verses are free of variant readings. Thus, it has been estimated that 62.9% of the verses in the New Testament are free of any variant. The chart to the right sets out the specifics for the General Letters.[42]

General Epistle	Number of Verses	Error-Free Verses	Percentage of Verses Error-Free
Hebrews	303	234	77.2%
James	108	66	61.1%
1 Peter	105	70	66.6%
2 Peter	61	32	52.5%
1 John	105	76	72.4%
2 John	13	8	61.5%
3 John	15	11	73.3%
Jude	25	18	72%

While some errors are of minimal consequence, others may be more significant. The following chart isolates a sampling with a brief discussion of the variety of textual problems in Hebrews chapter one: grammatical (v. 3), stylistic (v. 4), theological (v. 8), and exegetical (v. 12). The variant as it appears in the *Novum Testamentum Graecae* (NA[27, 28]) is presented first then the subsequent variant (*var*) is cited.

---

42 Kurt Aland and Barbara Aland, *The Text of The New Testament* (Grand Rapids: Eerdmans, 1987), 100–01. For a most recent discussion concerning the reliability of the NT see Robert B. Stewart, ed. *The Reliability of the New Testament: Bart D. Ehrman & Daniel B. Wallace in Dialogue* (Minneapolis: Fortress, 2011).

Ref.	Conflicting Readings	Significance & Explanation
1:3	*txt* καθαρισμὸν τῶν ἁμαρτιῶν ποιησάμενος he made purification for sin (cf. ASV, ESV, NASB, NET, NIV, NRSV) *var* **δι' ἑαυτοῦ** καθαρισμὸν τῶν ἁμαρτιῶν ποιησάμενος **through himself** he made purification for sins (cf. KJV)	Grammatical Issue: The phrase δι' ἑαυτοῦ (or δι' αὐτοῦ) appears to have been added to clarify the meaning of the ambiguous middle voice of ποιησάμενος. *Txt* is preferred (Metzger, *A Textual Commentary*, 592).
1:4	*txt* τοσούτῳ κρείττων γενόμενος τῶν ἀγγέλων by becoming so much better than the angels (cf. ASV, KJV, NET, NIV, NRSV) *var* τοσούτῳ κρείττων γενόμενος ἀγγέλων by becoming so much better than angels (cf. ESV NRSV)	Stylistic Issue: Although the *var* has minimal manuscript support (p⁴⁶ B), whenever ἄγγελος is used in the body of the text, it is anarthrous (2:2, 5, 16; 12:22; 13:2). Only when introducing OT quotes does the author use an article (1:5, 7, 13). It seems a scribe added the article due to the similar appearances in the immediate context. *Var* is preferred (Bateman, *Jewish Hermeneutic*, 215–16)
1:8	*txt* καὶ ἡ ῥάβδος τῆς εὐθύτητος ῥάβδος τῆς βασιλείας σου and the righteous scepter is the scepter of your kingdom (cf. ASV, ESV, KJV, NET, NIV, NRSV) *var* καὶ ἡ ῥάβδος τῆς εὐθύτητος ῥάβδος τῆς βασιλείας αὐτοῦ and the righteous scepter is the scepter of his kingdom (cf. NASB)	Theological/Exegetical Issue: Moving beyond the manuscript support (p⁴⁶ ℵ B), αὐτοῦ appears to be the last of several deliberate interpretive changes to Ps. 44:8 (LXX) by the author of Hebrews, and it is the more difficult reading (Bateman, *Jewish Hermeneutic*, 130–35). Furthermore in Heb. 2:7, 3:2, 8:11, 9:19, a scribe appears to have altered the text to bring it into conformity with the LXX. Although most translations prefer the *txt*, as it is with Heb. 11:4 and 12:3, there is strong evidence for questioning the decision and for favoring the *var*.

Ref.	Conflicting Readings	Significance & Explanation
1:12	txt ὡς ἱμάτιον καὶ ἀλλαγήσονται and like clothing they will be changed (cf. ASV, ESV, KJV, NASB, NET, NIV, NRSV) var καὶ ἀλλαγήσονται and they will be changed	Exegetical Issue: As in verse 8, the author made interpretive change to Ps. 44:8 (LXX) to both balance and heighten the transitory character of creation in contrast to the son. *Txt* is preferred (Metzger, *A Textual Commentary*, 593).

As manuscripts were discovered, they were grouped into one of three family text-types: Alexandrian, Western, or Byzantine;[43] they were systematized according to their uncial or minuscule script;[44] and they were compared and evaluated by way of specific scientific methods known as textual criticism.[45] Textual criticism is both a science as well as an art in that there needs to be sensitivity to both the original biblical author and the subsequent copyist. Realizing that all original manuscripts of the New Testament are lost, textual criticism facilitates discovering, as nearly as possible, the original wording of the New Testament text. Consequently, textual criticism (lower criticism) compares all known extant copies (*manuscripts*) of any given text in an effort to determine the original wording of a document (*an original autograph*) no longer available to twenty-first century readers.[46] So the purpose of this third step involves how to isolate textual problems and supporting evidence in the Greek New Testament, how the

---

43 J. A. Bengel (1687–1752) was the first to (1) classify mss into text-types or as he called them, "nations" (Asiatic nation = the texts developed around Constantinople; African nation = the texts in the Alexandrinus manuscripts and the Old Latin version) and (2) devise a system to evaluate variants (a = genuine reading; b = better reading; g = good reading; d = inferior reading; e = spurious reading). Building upon Bengel's classification of "nations," J. J. Griesbach (1745–1812) developed the three text-types employed today: Alexandrian, Western, and Byzantine.

44 J. J. Wettstein (1693–1754) devised the system that distinguished uncial by employing capital Roman letters (for example: A B C) from minuscules by Arabic numerals (for example: 33 81 322 323 436 1067 1735 1739 1846 1881). As more uncials were discovered and the English letters exhausted, Greek capitals letters were employed. Eventually in 1890, Casper René Gregory created a new system for identifying Uncial texts whereby all uncial manuscripts are designated with a numerical number prefixed with a zero (A=01 B=02 C=03, etc.).

45 Whereas Bengel developed an internal criticism canon, whereby the more difficult reading is preferable to the easier reading, Griesbach attempted to develop a historical foundation in the genealogical relations of extant external evidence (this effort was furthered by Westcott and Hort).

46 Although "all participating scholars [of the NKJV] have signed a document of subscription to the plenary and verbal inspiration of the original autographs of the Bible," no translator of the New King James Version actually worked with the original autographs because they are lost and unavailable. *The New King James Version*, iv.

evidence is grouped, and how to evaluate the evidence. So, we begin with discovering how to isolate textual problems in a Greek New Testament text.

Isolating Textual Problems

Isolating significant textual problems generally occurs one of two ways, either through a note in an English translation or by reading a New Testament Greek text. For instance, the New English Translation (NET) both identifies and then provides extensive discussions of textual variants, but many English translations selectively point out significant problems in the margins. In either case, the ability to interact with a textual problem involves knowing something about New Testament Greek texts. So we begin with how to isolate a textual problem in a New Testament Greek text as well as locating its supporting evidence found in the textual apparatus.

Most of us probably began with *The Greek New Testament* published by the United Bible Society (UBS⁴), which has as its basis the *Novum Testamentum Graecae* (NA²⁷). Whereas the latter is the foundational tool for research and study upon which many of our English translations are based, the former is published, "to meet the growing need for an edition of the Greek New Testament specially adapted to the requirements of the Bible translators throughout the world." As a result, it has several special features:

- a critical apparatus restricted to variant readings significant for translators,

- an indication of the relative degree of certainty for each variant adopted as the text,

- a full citation of representative evidence for each variant selected,

- a second apparatus giving meaningful differences of punctuation.[47]

These special features, particularly the first three that isolate *major* text critical problems, are why we will use the UBS⁴ *Greek New Testament* for isolating textual problems. Furthermore, there is a supplementary volume that provides the rational for adopting one variant reading over another: Bruce Metzger in *A Textual Commentary on the Greek New Testament* (2ⁿᵈ edition).

47   Barbara Aland, Kurt Aland, Johannes Karavidopoulos, Carlo M. Martini, and Bruce M. Metzger, eds. *The Greek New Testament*, 4ᵗʰ rev. ed. (Stuttgart, Germany: United Bible Societies, 2010), viii.

Naturally, we start by isolating a text critical problem in the Greek text. We will focus on the textual problems in Jude vv.3–4. As noted in chapter one, Jude's letter divides into three parts: opening salutation (vv.1–2), body (vv.3–23), and doxology (vv.24–25). Jude vv.3–4 moves us from salutation to full disclosure explaining the reason why Jude is writing his letter. The following is (1) a reproduction of the UBS[4] Greek text with superscript numerals and letters in the text that are referenced in the critical apparatus (verbs and verbals are underlined), (2) my interpretative translation of the text with Greek verbs and verbals placed in parentheses and superscript numerals and letters in the text that are referenced in the critical apparatus, and (3) a reproduction of the apparatus for verses 3 and 4 typically located at the bottom of the UBS[4] *Greek New Testament.*

Jude vv.3–4

3 Ἀγαπητοί, πᾶσαν σπουδὴν ποιούμενος γράφειν ὑμῖν περὶ τῆς κοινῆς ἡμῶν[3] σωτηρίας ἀνάγκην ἔσχον γράψαι ὑμῖν παρακαλῶν ἐπαγωνίζεσθαι τῇ ἅπαξ παραδοθείσῃ τοῖς ἁγίοις πίστει.

4 παρεισέδυσαν γάρ τινες ἄνθρωποι, οἱ πάλαι προγεγραμμένοι εἰς τοῦτο τὸ κρίμα, ἀσεβεῖς, τὴν τοῦ θεοῦ ἡμῶν χάριτα μετατιθέντες εἰς ἀσέλγειαν καὶ τὸν μόνον δεσπότην[4] καὶ κύριον ἡμῶν[e] Ἰησοῦν Χριστὸν[5] ἀρνούμενοι.

Translation

3 Dear friends, *although* I was making (ποιούμενος) every effort to write (γράφειν) to you about our[3] common salvation, I have (ἔσχον) a necessity to write (γράψαι) to you *in order to* urge (παρακαλῶν) *you* to contend (ἐπαγωνίζεσθαι) earnestly for the faith that was entrusted once to the saints.

4 For certain *people* have slipped in secretly (παρεισέδυσαν) *among you* those who long ago have been written (οἱ . . . προγεγραμμένοι) about for this judgment. *They are* godless *people* who have turned (τὴν . . . μετατιθέντες) the grace of our God into immoral *behavior* and who even deny (καὶ . . . ἀρνούμενοι)[4] our only Master and our Lord, Jesus, *who is* our [5] Christ.

Textual Apparatus

[3]**3** {A} ἡμῶν 𝔓[72] ℵ A B Ψ 81 322 323 436 1067 1243
1292 1409 1611 1735 1729 1846 2138 *l* 596 (*l* 422
ἡμετέρας) (*l* 884 σωτηρίας ἡμῶν) vg[mss] syr[ph, h] cop[sa] arm
eth geo slav Cyril; Lucifer // ὑμῶν 1505 1844 1881
2298 it[ar] vg cop[bo] // *omit* 945 1175 *Byz* [K L P] *Lect*

[4]**4** {A} δεσπότην 𝔓[72, 78] ℵ A B C 0251 33 81 322 323
436 1067 1241 1243 1409 1739 1846 1881 2344 *Lect*[pt]
it[ar] vg cop[sa bo] arm eth geo Didymus Didymus[dub] Cyril;
Lucifer // δεσπότην θεόν Ψ 945 1175 1292 1505 1611
1735 1844 2138 2298 *Byz* [K L P] *Lect*[pt AD] (*l* 592[1/2] δεσπότην καὶ θεόν) syr[ph, h] slav // θεόν *l* 593

[5]**4** {A} ἡμῶν Ἰησοῦν Χριστόν (𝔓[72] ἡμῶν *after* Χριστόν)
𝔓[78] ℵ A B C Ψ 0251[vid] 33 81 322 323 436 945 1067
1175 (1241 ὑμῶν *for* ἡμῶν) 1243 1292 1409 1505 1611
1735 1739 1844 1846 2138 2298 2344 *Byz* [K L]
Lect it[ar] vg syr[ph, h] cop[sa bo (bomss)] arm eth geo Didymus
Didymus[dub] Cyril; (Lucifer) // Ἰησοῦν Χριστὸν 1881 *l*
422 *l* 593 vg[mss]

As you look at the Greek text and my translation, can you isolate
the three superscripted numerical signs [3, 4, 5]? One is in verse 3 ([3]) and
two are in verse 4 ([4, 5]). They are intended to show the location of a
textual problem. Now look at the corresponding numerical signs in
the critical apparatus: [3] **3**, [4] **4**, [5] **4**. The information to the right of each
verse notation reveals three things about the textual variant. First, the
bracketed letter {A} immediately follows the verse number in all three-
verse notations. There are, however, other possible options such as {B},
{C}, or {D}. Each letter identifies how the editors of the UBS[4] Greek
text evaluated the degree of certainty for the reading that appears in
the Greek text: {A} indicates virtual certainty, {B} only some degree of
doubt, {C} a considerable degree of doubt, and {D} a very high degree
of doubt. For each variant reading in Jude vv.3–4, the editors are con-
vinced that the variant they placed in the Greek text was the original
word Jude wrote.[48]

Second, after the letter {A}, the manuscript evidence supporting
the editors' choice appears in the following order: papyri codices (or
"manuscripts"), uncial codices, minuscule codices, followed by lec-

48   The explanation of symbols A B C D appears in the introduction for the UBS[4] Greek Text
      (p. 3), and discussions about the decision appear in Metzger, *A Textual Commentary on the
      Greek New Testament* (2nd edition, 1994).

tionaries, versions, and church fathers. First are the three types of codices: papyrus, uncials, and minuscules. On the one hand, the papyri of the New Testament are our earliest manuscript evidence that date as early as 125 CE ($\mathfrak{P}^{52}$ fragment) to the eighth century ($\mathfrak{P}^{41}$ $\mathfrak{P}^{60}$ $\mathfrak{P}^{61}$). Most papyri, however, are from the third and fourth centuries.[49] On the other hand, the uncial codices are written on vellum (prepared animal skins also referred to as parchment), designated with a numerical number prefixed with a zero (e.g., B or 02; K or 018; 0251), and like the papyri are written in uncial script but date later, from 325 CE (B) to the 9th century (e.g., K L P Ψ).[50] Unlike the papyrus and uncials, minuscule codices are written in small letters in a running hand or "cursive" script. This sort of hand-written manuscript is designated with an Arabic numeral (e.g., 33, 1739, 2143). Although the earliest minuscule of the New Testament dates around the ninth century (33), many minuscules are from the fourteenth century (1409 1881).[51] Minuscules, however, may have been the preferred form of correspondence. "It seems likely," according to Greenlee, "that the originals of the letters of St. Paul were written in a cursive hand, since they were written as personal letters and not as formal literature."[52] If Greenlee's speculation is correct, then it stands to reason the same is true for the General Letters. The following chart lists all the papyrus, uncial, and minuscule codices from the textual apparatus for Jude vv.3–4.

49   Of particular significance is $\mathfrak{P}^{72}$ (a Bodmer Papyrus VII-VIII) for the General Letters because it is the earliest known copy of 1 Peter 1:1–5:14; 2 Peter 1:1–3:18 and Jude vv.1–25 dated *ca.* third or fourth century. Another significant papyrus, though it is not listed above, is $\mathfrak{P}^{74}$ (Bodmer Papyrus XVII) dating from the seventh century and contains portions from James, Petrine letters, Johannine letters, and Jude. The papyrus $\mathfrak{P}^{78}$ contains Jude vv.4–5 and vv.7–8 and dated *circa* third or fourth century. All three texts are significant Alexandrian text types.

50   Although not the earliest, codex Sinaiticus (א 01) is most certainly of primary importance. Positioned at the head of the list of Uncials, it is the only codex that preserves the entire NT and dated around 350. Equally valued is codex Vaticanus (B 03) dated to be a few years older than codex Sinaiticus. It lacks some of Hebrews, the Pastoral Letters, and Revelation. With the exception of 31 vss., the entire NT is represented in codex Alexandrinus (A 02), which is dated *circa* fifth century. All three texts are significant Alexandrian text types. Metzger, *Text of the New Testament*, 42–48; Aland and Aland, *Text of The New Testament*, 106–07.

51   Readily described as the Queen of the cursives, codex 33 contains the entire NT except Revelation and dates to the ninth century and is extremely important for Pauline and General letters. Metzger, *Text of the New Testament*, 62; Aland and Aland, *Text of The New Testament*, 129.

52   J. Harold Greenlee, *Introduction to New Testament Textual Criticism* (Grand Rapids: Eerdmans, 1964, repr 1984), 29. Scanning the numerous volumes of *The Oxyrhynchus Papyri* (London: Oxford University Press) may support Greenlee's statement. See also Metzger, *The Text of the New Testament*, 8–9; and M. David and B. A. Van Groningen, *Papyrological Primer* (Leyden, Netherlands: Brill, 1952), 11–14.

PAPYRI:	$\mathfrak{P}^{72}$	$\mathfrak{P}^{78}$							
UNCIALS:	א	A	B	C	K	L	P	Ψ	0251
MINUSCULES:	33	81	322	323	422	436	593	945	1067
	1175	1241	1243	1292	1409	1505	1611	1729	1735
	1739	1844	1846	1881	2138	2144	2298	2344	*Byz*
LECTIONARIES:	*Lect*	*l*422	*l*592	*l*593	*l*884				
VERSIONS:	it	syr	cop	vg	arm	eth	slav		
FATHERS:	Cyril	Lucifer	Didymus						

Resuming our discussion of the textual apparatus, lectionaries are designated daily and weekly lessons for church worship and instruction. They are identified in the apparatus with the letter "*l*" or by the abbreviation "*Lect.*" They date as early as the sixth century (fragments) to the eighth century (complete) and onward. Next listed are the versions. Because of the broad missionary outreach of the early church, most of the New Testament was translated into Latin (abbreviation = it, *ca.* 200), Syriac (abbreviation = syr, *ca.* 400), and Coptic (abbreviation = cop, *ca.* 200). Eventually Jerome took the best of the available Latin texts and created the Latin Vulgate (abbreviation = vg, *ca.* 386) of which there are some eight thousand manuscripts. Finally, there is the listing of church father citations. Since the fathers often cited the New Testament from memory, no one can be sure that their memory reflects the actual wording of their Greek text.

Before we move on, we need to stop and explain the superscriptions that accompany the manuscript evidence. Some superscriptions are evident in the apparatus for Jude vv.3–4, and others will appear in subsequent variant listings for Jude. Regardless, these sorts of symbols are also explained in the introduction of the UBS[4] Greek Text (pp. 18–19).

A*	*	= original hand
B[vid]	vid	= most probable reading (complete verification is impossible)
C[c]	c	= corrected reading
K[1 or 2]	1 or 2	= 1st or 2nd hand has corrected reading
Byz		= reading of a great number of Byzantine witnesses
Byz [ ]	[ ]	= brackets enclose certain selected Byzantine manuscripts immediately following the symbol Byz.
Byz[pt]	pt	= one part of the Byzantine text when its witness is divided and appears twice in a given set of variants
Lect		= reading of a great number of Lectionaries with the lectionary text of the Greek Church published by Apostoliki Diakoni, Athens.
Lect[pt]	pt	= a part of the lectionary manuscript tradition (at least ten manuscripts) that differ from the other lectionaries.

Finally, after all the evidence for the chosen reading has been listed, comes the rejected variant readings, which are generally separated by a pair of vertical lines //. So for instance, look at the textual apparatus for Jude v.3. The textual problem in verse three has two variant readings that are separated clearly from the favored reading with //.

> Text   ἡμῶν³ σωτηρίας ἀνάγκην ("our³ common salvation")
> Variant #1 // ὑμῶν σωτηρίας ἀνάγκην ("your common salvation")
> Variant #2 // σωτηρίας ἀνάγκην ("common salvation")

Did you notice the two minor variations of the chosen textual reading? One lectionary (*l* 422) adds a synonymous form of "our" (ἡμετε-ρας). Another lectionary (*l* 884) places "our" (ὑμῶν) after "salvation" (σωτηρίας) rather than before it. These two variants might be a single lector's intentional transcriptional altercation. Thus, the presence of these parentheses indicates a slight difference in word choice or word order, but they are not considered significant variants. In conclusion, we have learned how to isolate a textual problem in the Greek text, how to locate the evidence in the textual apparatus, and then how to read the evidence. The information, however, as presented in the textual apparatus, is merely raw manuscript data or external evidence. In order to evaluate this external manuscript evidence, we need first to group data into family text-types.

Grouping the External Evidence

As we mentioned earlier, all manuscripts are grouped into one of three text-types or manuscript families: Alexandrian, Western, or Byzantine. They tend to represent three geographical regions where New Testament manuscripts have been discovered. Yet the placement of a single codex into a manuscript family is based upon a text-critical expert's recognition of common elements within a manuscript family after critically evaluating large numbers of variant readings. Thus, the placement of a manuscript into a family is predetermined for us. We merely need to familiarize ourselves with their respective placements determined for us in the UBS⁴ introduction or from Aland's book *The Text of the New Testament*.

Although we have chosen Jude vv.3–4 to exemplify how to isolate and resolve a textual problem, we will group all the papyri, uncials, and miniscules cited in the textual apparatus for the entire Book of Jude.[53] Of

---

53 Similar charts exist for the Book of Hebrews and the Johannine Letters are available in Bateman, "Classification & Dates of Manuscript Evident in Hebrews" in *Charts on the Book of Hebrews*; idem, "Classification & Dates of Manuscript Evident in Johannine Literature" in *A Workbook*

the twenty-six manuscripts cited in UBS⁴ nineteen are grouped within the Alexandrian family from the geographical areas of Alexandria, the Nile Delta of Egypt, and the Sinai Peninsula. They tend to be far older manuscripts, they tend to have the shortest interval of time from the original autography, and they tend to have a greater potential to reflect the text of the original due to the limited intervening copies. While some are considered to be of a very early period and highly valued, other valued texts have some non-Alexandrian influences.

Alexandrian Family		
These manuscripts represent an Alexandrian text of an early period and considered very reliable texts		
Papyri	Uncials	Minuscules
$\mathfrak{P}^{72}$ (3ʳᵈ 4ᵗʰ century)	ℵ 01 (4ᵗʰ century)	1241 (12ᵗʰ century)
$\mathfrak{P}^{78}$ (3ʳᵈ 4ᵗʰ century)	A 02 (5ᵗʰ century)	1243 (11ᵗʰ century)
$\mathfrak{P}^{74}$ (7ᵗʰ century)	B 03 (4ᵗʰ century)	1739 (10ᵗʰ century)
These manuscripts, though predominately Alexandrian, evidence some non-Alexandrian influences.		
Papyri	Uncials	Minuscules
	C 04 (5th century)	33 (9ᵗʰ century)
	Ψ 044 (8th–9th century)	81 (1044)
		1292 (13ᵗʰ century)
		1409 (14ᵗʰ century)
		1735 (11ᵗʰ/12ᵗʰ century)
		1881 (14ᵗʰ century)
		1852 (13ᵗʰ century)
		2344 (11ᵗʰ century)

The other significant family of manuscripts is the Byzantine family (or "Syrian text"). They tend to be preserved in geographical areas of the old Byzantine Empire (324–634), namely present-day Turkey, Bulgaria, Greece, Macedonia, Albania, and former Yugoslavia. Most are from a later period, and they are far greater in number. Despite the large number of manuscripts, the UBS⁴ selectively lists Byzantine texts. So if a text is cited, it is probably an important one.

for Intermediate Greek: Grammar, Exegesis, and Commentary on 1–3 John, appendix 3.

Byzantine Family		
Most Important Uncials	**Minuscules**	
K (018) (9th century) L (020) (9th century) P (025) (6th century)	18 (1364) 596 (11th century) 1175 (11th century) 2144 (11th century) *Byz* is group symbol for less important Byzantine Uncials and all other Byzantine manuscripts of which there are many.	

"Numerous theories have thus been proposed to explain the origin of the Western text," according to Greenlee, "but the final answer seems to be as much shrouded in mystery as ever."[54] Despite this mystery, the term is used to represent manuscripts developed on the western edge of the Mediterranean: Italy, Spain, and Carthage. What is certain, however, is that there are no Western papyri, uncials, or minuscule witnesses listed for Jude. There are, however, a large group of manuscripts, predominately minuscules in Jude that do not fit a specific family text-type. They are classified as having an independent character.

Independent Character					
The following manuscripts are of a distinctive character with an independent text.					
Uncials	**Minuscules**				
0251 (6th century)	6 (13th century) 436 (11th century) 1241 (12th century) 1844 (15th century) 2298 (11th century)	322 (15th century) 945 (11th century) 1505 (1084) 1846 (11th century)	323 (12th century) 1067 (14th century) 1611 (12th century) 2138 (1072)		

---

54 Greenlee believes, "The Western text may be divided into three sub-groups, with Codex D representing one group, the Old Latin mss. *k* and *e* a second group, and the Old Syriac a third group." Naturally, Old Syriac representation are Syr^s = *Sinaitic* and Syr^c = *Curetonian* (UBS[4], 2). Yet, these two texts do not appear in Jude. The two Syriac texts in Jude are Byzantine. Compare Greenlee, *Introduction to New Testament Textual Criticism*, 89 and Wasserman, *The Epistle of Jude: Its Text and Transmission*, 19.

Having grouped all the papyri, uncials, and miniscules cited in the textual apparatus for the entire Book of Jude, it is time to address the lectionary, versions, and fathers. They too are grouped according to families. However, they are not so easily identified. The following chart is a modest attempt at classifying them.[55]

Alexandrian Family	
Versions	**Church Fathers**
Cop = represents all Coptic versions extant for a particular Greek reading (3rd to 5th centuries). Bohariric[bo] is a dialect variations of Coptic Sahidic[sa] is a dialect variations of Coptic	Didymus of Alexandria (398) Clement of Alexander (215) Clement[lat] Latin translation (540) Cyril of Alexander (d. 444) Origen[lat], Latin translation (???)

Western Family	
Versions	**Church Fathers**

it = Itala represents the majority of Old Latin witnesses as a group.
  it[ar] (9th century)
  it[t] (11th century)
 	
vg = Vulgata represents agreement of the most important editions of the Vulgate in support of the same Greek reading.
  vg[cl] Editio Clementina (1592)
  vg[ms] indicates individual Vulgate mss with independent readings
  vg[ww] Wordsworth and White (1889–1954)
	Augustine (430)
	Jerome (420)
	Lucifer, of Calaris (370/371)
	Priscillian (385))

---

55   The dating of all the manuscripts is based upon Tommy Wasserman, *The Epistle of Jude: Its Text and Transmission*, CBNTS 43 (Stockholm, Sweden: Almqvist & Wiksell International, 2006), 106–17. Generally, Wasserman (W) and Aland/Aland's (AA) manuscript dates are in agreement with eleven (11) exceptions: 18 (W 1364; AA 14th), 323 (W 12th; AA 11th), 326 (W 10th; AA 12th), 431 (W 12th; AA 11th), 436 (W 11th/12th; AA 11th), 621 (W 11th; AA 14th), 630 (W 12th/13th; AA 14th), 1175 (W 10th; AA 10th), 1735 (W 10th; AA 11th/12th), 2374 (W 13th/14th; AA 13th).   Compare the manuscript dating in Aland and Aland, *The Text of The New Testament* (1987), 96–159.

Byzantine Family	
Versions	**Church Fathers**

Syr = Syriac Version (These Syriac texts are Byzantine)
    Syr^h = *Harklensis* (version made by Thomas of Harkel
        in 615/616)
    Syr^{ph} = Philoxeniana (507/508)
arm = Armenian (5th century)
eth = Ethiopic (5th century)
geo = Georgian (5th century)
slav = Old Church Slavonic (9th century)
	Fulgentius (532)
	Eusebius (339–40)
	Chrysostom (407)
	Cyril of Jerusalem (386)

We need to pause for a moment to consider the Alexandrian family and the Byzantine family of manuscripts. As mentioned under "Step Two: Identifying Interpretive Issues," English Bibles identify competing text critical theories along with their competing translational theories. These competing theories center on how to weigh the external evidence from the Alexandrian and Byzantine families. The *Greek New Testament* (UBS^4) and the *Novum Tetamentum Greaece* (NA$^{27, 28}$) editions tend to favor the older Alexandrian manuscripts. As already mentioned, most English Bibles claim in their respective prefaces a dependence on *Novum Tetamentum Graece* (e.g., NASB, EVS, NASV, NIV, NET, NLT).

The New King James Version (NKJV), however, tends to favor Byzantine readings typically found in New Testament Greek texts that rely heavily on the Byzantine family text-types: *The Greek New Testament According to the Majority Text* (MTGNT) and *The New Testament in the Original Greek* (OGNT). Editors of the *Majority Text* are persuaded that the transmission history has been both stable and regular, and thus, the best guide for determining with greater precision a Greek New Testament text is through "the great mass of surviving Greek documents." Thus "any reading overwhelmingly attested by the manuscript tradition is more likely to be original than its rival."[56] Editors of the *Original Greek* "reflect a dominant consensus pattern of readings that is maintained throughout most of the New Testament."[57] In essence, both prioritize via the many—majority rules. Consequently, how to weigh external manuscript evidence from these two families is an essential part of evaluating the evidence.

---

56   Zane C. Hodges and Arthur L. Farstad, *The Greek New Testament According to the Majority Text* (Nashville: Thomas Nelson, 1985).

57   Compiled and Arranged by Marice A. Robinson and William G. Pierpont, *The New Testament in the Original Greek: Byzantine Textform* 2005 (Southborough, MA: Chilton, 2005), ix.

Evaluating the Evidence

Evaluating any textual decision involves a two-part examination. Part one examines the external manuscript evidence, and part two examines the internal evidence of the scribe and biblical author.[58] The external evidence, concerns the information found in the textual apparatus. We will describe and demonstrate issues about internal evidence after examining the manuscript evidence. The goal in examining both, however, is to determine which reading is most likely to have been the original reading when penned by its inspired author, in our case Jude v.4 and the problem labeled #4 in the text. We begin with part one: the external evidence.

Entry Level: My personal approach for evaluating the external evidence begins with the creation of a chart that (1) identifies the options, (2) groups evidence according to family text-type, (3) lists evidence according to text-type (e.g., papyri are grouped, uncials are grouped, minuscules are grouped), (4) dates evidence for easy recognition and eventual evaluation, and (5) identifies manuscripts of exceptionally good quality within a family with an asterisk (★).[59]

UBS[4th] καὶ τὸν μόνον δεσπότην[4] καὶ κύριον ἡμῶν ε Ἰησοῦν Χριστὸν[5] ἀρνούμενοι "And deny our only Master and Lord, Jesus Christ" NASB[95], ESV, NRSV; cf. NET, NLT[SE]			
Alexandrian	Western	Byzantine	Independent
𝔓[72] (3rd 4th century) 𝔓[78] (3rd 4th century)	No papyri	No papyri	
ℵ 01 (4th century)★ A 02 (5th century)★ B 03 (4th century)★ C 04 (5th century)	No uncials	No uncials	0251 (6th century)

---

58   My approach to textual criticism, like that of many other people, is reasoned eclecticism. I do not limit myself to the external manuscript evidence to make a decision (Majority Text or Byzantine Priority), nor do I limit myself to internal evidence (Thoroughgoing Eclecticism). Rather, I consider both external and internal evidence. For a thorough discussion on these approaches see David Alan Black, ed. *Rethinking New Testament Textual Criticism* (Grand Rapids: Baker, 2002).

59   For a selection of charts for evaluating text critical problems, see "A Worksheet for Textual Criticism" in David Allen Black's *New Testament Textual Criticism: A Concise Guide* (Grand Rapids: Baker, 1994), 67–71.

UBS[4th] καὶ τὸν μόνον δεσπότην[4] καὶ κύριον ἡμῶνε
Ἰησοῦν Χριστὸν[5] ἀρνούμενοι
"And deny our only Master and Lord, Jesus Christ"
NASB[95], ESV, NRSV; cf. NET, NLT[SE]

Alexandrian	Western	Byzantine	Independent
1241 (12th century)★	No miniscules	596 (11th century)	322 (15th century)
1243 (11th century)★		2144 (11th century)	323 (12th century)
1739 (10th century)★			436 (11th century)
33 (9th century)			1067 (14th century)
81 (1044)			1846 (11th century)
1409 (14th century)		Lect[pt]	
1881 (14th century)			
cop[sa] (3–5th century)	it[ar] (9th century)★	arm (5th century)	
cop[bo] (3–5th century)	vg (4th/5th century)	eth (5th century)	
		geo (5th century)	
Didymus (398)	Lucifer (370/371)		
Cyril (444)			

Variant καὶ τὸν μόνον δεσπότην θεόν καὶ κύριον ἡμῶν[e]
Ἰησοῦν Χριστὸν ἀρνούμενοι
"And deny the only Lord God and our Lord Jesus Christ"
NKJV (cf. KJV)

Alexandrian	Western	Byzantine	Independent
No papyri	No papyri	No papyri	
Ψ 044 (8th–9th century)	No uncials	K (9th century)★	
		L (9th century)★	
		P (9th century)★	
		1175 (11th century)★	
1292 (13th century)★	No miniscules	Byz★	195 (11th century)
1735 (11th century)			1611 (12th century)
No versions		Lect[pt]	1844 (15th century)
No fathers			1505 (1084)
	vg[mss] (9th century)	syr[ph] (615/616)	2138 (1072)
		syr[h] (507/508)	2298 (11th century)

Advanced Level: From this chart, we now apply three criteria for *judging the external evidence*: (1) date and character, (2) geographical distribution, and (3) genealogical solidarity. First, we evaluate **the date and character of the external evidence**. We ask two questions of the evidence: How old are the readings of the supporting manuscript witnesses, and what is the character (very good vs. good representation) of these witnesses? Concerning the UBS[4] reading to omit "God" (θεόν), it has the oldest papyri and uncial manuscripts from the third ($\mathfrak{P}^{72}$ $\mathfrak{P}^{78}$), fourth (א B) and fifth centuries (A C) as well as a few Coptic versions from around the same time frame (cop$^{sa\ bo}$). The minuscule evidence is also impressive beginning with the ninth century (33) through the tenth (1739), eleventh (596 1243 2144), twelfth (1241 1244), and fourteenth centuries (1409 1881). Of these, eight manuscripts are considered to be good representatives from the Alexandrian family ($\mathfrak{P}^{72}$ $\mathfrak{P}^{78}$ א A B 1241 1243 1739). So the variant reading that omits "God" (θεόν) has continuous representation from the third to fourteenth centuries but also very good representation from the Alexandrian family.

Concerning the variant reading that includes "God" (θεόν), it does not have any manuscript evidence prior to the ninth century. Yet one uncial from the Alexandrian family (Ψ) and three significant uncials from the Byzantine family (K L P 1175) support the inclusion "God" (θεόν). The minuscule evidence is also impressive with two Alexandrian texts from the eleventh and thirteenth centuries (1292 1735), one of which is a fairly good representative of the Alexandrian family (1292), and a multitude of Byzantine manuscripts (*Byz*).[60]

In conclusion, the Alexandrian family's representation to omit "God" (θεόν) is both early ($\mathfrak{P}^{72}$ $\mathfrak{P}^{78}$ א A B) and of good quality ($\mathfrak{P}^{72}$ $\mathfrak{P}^{78}$ א B 1241 1243 1739). Yet, the evidence from the Byzantine family to include "God" (θεόν) is also pretty good (K L P 1175) and well represented (*Byz*). Thus, the date and character for both readings appear good. So, we move on to the next criterion.

Second, we evaluate **the geographical distribution of the external evidence**. How widespread is the geographical distribution of the manuscript witnesses? A reading from all three geographical areas is more likely to be original than if a reading is supported from only one region. Geographically, the UBS[4] reading to omit "God" (θεόν) exists in all three families: Alexandrian ($\mathfrak{P}^{72}$ $\mathfrak{P}^{78}$ א B 1241 1243 1739 etc.), Western (it^{ar}, vg),

---

60   The abbreviation Byz include three Byzantine Uncials: 049 (9th), 056 (10th), 0142 (10th) not cited individually in UBS[4th]; and numerous minuscules: 1 (12th), 3 (12th), 18 (14th), 57 (12th), 76 (12th), 82 (10th), 97 (12th), 105 (12th), 110 (12th), 133 (11th), 141 (13th), 201 (14th), 203 (12th), 204 (13th), 221 (10th), 226 (12t[h]), 302 (11th), etc. For a complete listing of all the manuscript evidence that includes "God" (θεόν), see Wasserman, *The Epistle of Jude*, 146–47. Then compare it with Byzantine type minuscules identified in Aland and Aland, *The Text of the New Testament*, 152–55.

and Byzantine (596 2144). In a similar way, the variant reading to include "God" (θεόν), exists in all three families: Alexandrian (Ψ), Western (vg^mss), and Byzantine (K L P 1175 *Byz* etc.). Thus, the readings for both options are geographically widespread. So, we move on to the next criteria.

Third, we evaluate *the genealogical solidarity of the external evidence*. How solidly attested (united vs. split) is a particular reading *within* each text type? Most manuscripts were written in locales in which certain traditional variants were copied repeatedly and thereby find their roots in a local ancestor. When all or almost all of the external evidence of a family agree on a reading, one could say that that reading is considered genealogically solid. Naturally, the ideal would be that there is no split reading or disagreement within a family. In our case, however, there is a clear disagreement in all three families. So then, how does one weigh the evidence?

Concerning the UBS⁴ reading to *omit* "God" (θεόν), the large number of manuscript agreement (𝔓⁷² 𝔓⁷⁸ ℵ A B C 1241 1243 1739) suggests a possible original reading for the Alexandrian family. In fact, the two primary uncials (ℵ B) along with the two primary papyri (𝔓⁷² 𝔓⁷⁸) weigh very heavily in favor of an original reading. Yet the variant reading that *includes* "God" (θεόν) has substantial manuscript support from the Byzantine family (K L P 1175 *Byz*), which suggests a possible original reading. Thus, genealogical solidarity appears good for both readings. So in summary, the external evidence seems less than helpful at this point. Manuscripts of good quality from both the Alexandrian and Byzantine families represent both readings; both reveal widespread geographical distribution as well as genealogical solidarity. With the external evidence evaluated, we now press on to investigate part two: the internal evidence.

Internal evidence is the examination of the actual wording of the variants. Essentially there are two criteria for judging internal evidence: transcriptional probability of the scribes and intrinsic likelihood of the biblical authors. As we make our way through the internal evidence, there are four principles that guide and direct us as we weigh the internal evidence. We will

> give preference to the shorter reading,
> give preference to the more difficult reading,
> give preference to the reading that best fits the author's style and/or vocabulary,
> give preference to the reading that best fits the author' context and/or theology.

Entry Level: Let's begin by *evaluating the transcriptional probability of the scribes* whereby we ask this question: How might a scribe intentionally or unintentionally affect the preserved reading? Consequently, we begin with a re-creation of the text in upper case uncial lettering, with words run together, without accents, and within the middle of the text. Can you see how it is that the variant occurs somewhere in the midst of the reproduction. Needless to say, the reproduction is not perfect and yet it does provide some scribal perspective.[61]

UBS⁴ θεόν Omitted	
τὸ κρίμα, ἀσεβεῖς, τὴν τοῦ θεοῦ ἡμῶν χάριτα μετατιθέντες εἰς ἀσέλγειαν καὶ τὸν μόνον δεσπότην καὶ κύριον ἡμῶν Ἰησοῦν Χριστὸν ἀρνούμενοι. 5 Ὑπομνῆσαι δὲ ὑμᾶς ἀρνούμενοι	ΤΟΚΡΙΜΑΑΣΕΒΕΙΣΤΗΝΤΟΥΘΕΟΥΗΜΩΝΧΑΡΙΤΑ ΜΕΤΑΤΙΘΕΝΤΕΣΕΙΣΑΣΕΛΓΕΙΑΝΚΑΙΤΟΝΜΟΝΟΝ ΔΕΣΠΟΤΗΝΚΑΙΚΥΡΙΟΝΗΜΩΝΙΗΣΟΥΝΧΡΙΣΤΟΝ ΑΡΝΟΥΜΕΝΟΙΥΠΟΜΝΗΣΑΙΔΕΥΜΑΣΑΡΝΟΥΜΕ ΝΟΙ
Variant θεόν Added	
τὸ κρίμα, ἀσεβεῖς, τὴν τοῦ θεοῦ ἡμῶν χάριτα μετατιθέντες εἰς ἀσέλγειαν **θεόν** καὶ τὸν μόνον δεσπότην καὶ κύριον ἡμῶν Ἰησοῦν Χριστὸν ἀρνούμενοι. 5 Ὑπομνῆσαι δὲ ὑμᾶς	ΤΟΚΡΙΜΑΑΣΕΒΕΙΣΤΗΝΤΟΥΘΕΟΥΗΜΩΝΧΑΡΙΤΑ ΜΕΤΑΤΙΘΕΝΤΕΣΕΙΣΑΣΕΛΓΕΙΑΝ**ΘΕΟΝ**ΚΑΙΤΟΝ ΜΟΝΟΝΔΕΣΠΟΤΗΝΚΑΙΚΥΡΙΟΝΗΜΩΝΙΗΣΟΥΝ ΧΡΙΣΤΟΝΑΡΝΟΥΜΕΝΟΙΥΠΟΜΝΗΣΑΙΔΕΥΜΑΣ

From this modest reproduction, *is it possible that a scribe may have unintentionally changed the text*? Could the addition or the omission of "God" (θεόν) have emerged as a result of problems of sight,[62] hearing,[63]

---

61 The example does not include contracted abbreviations for sacred names (*nomina sacra*), "God" (θεος) would be abbreviate as θσ; "lord" (κύριος) would be abbreviated κσ; "Jesus" (Ἰησοῦν) would be abbreviated ιϛ; "Christ" (Χριστὸν) would be abbreviated Cϛ; etc. These at times could be cause for an unintentional scribal error as in 2 Peter 1:2 where it appears a scribe confused "God" (θσ) for "lord" (κσ). For a more complete listing of abbreviations, see Greenlee, *Introduction to New Testament Textual Criticism*, 30.

62 One potential error of sight is confusion over lettering. Several groups of letters are similar and could readily be confused: ΑΔΛ, and ΕΣ, and ΟΘ, and ΗΝ, and Π/ ΙΤ / ΓΤ. For example, in 2 Peter 2:13 the letter gamma (Γ) in "love feasts" (ΑΓΑΠΑΙΣ, ἀγάπαις) may have been confused with pi (Π) of "deceptions" (ΑΠΑΤΑΙΣ, ἀπάταις). Another potential error of sight could be over "similar ending" (*homoioteleuton*). For instance in 1 John 2:23 many scribes skip from the first occurrence of τὸν πατέρα ἔχει in the middle of verse 23 to the second τὸν πατέρα ἔχει found at the verse's conclusion. Compare Metzger, *The Text of the New Testament*, 186–90 with Greenlee, *Introduction to New Testament Textual Criticism*, 63–64.

63 Copyists were often part of a scriptorium where a person might read a NT manuscript

fatigue, or some other unintentional error? Scribes often changed the text accidentally. It seems unlikely that a scribe would unintentionally add "God" (θεόν) as a result of sight, hearing, or fatigue, though he could inadvertently delete "God" (θεόν) if fatigued. So, it seems more difficult to explain an accidental addition of "God" (θεόν) than an omission.

Is it possible that a scribe intentionally changed the text? Could the addition or the omission of "God" (θεόν) emerge to correct grammar, endorse a theological perspective,[64] or to correct an apparent discrepancy?[65] Granted, evaluating scribal motivations involves a degree of subjectivity. Nevertheless because other New Testament references (Luke 2:29; Acts 4:24; Rev 6:10) specify God as Master, copyists may have inserted "God" (θεόν) for theological reasons, either to distinguish God from Jesus or perhaps it was added to enhance the Christological standing of Jesus as God.[66] In some sense, we might surmise a scribe inserted a personal interpretation similar to the one we examined previously in some English translations for Hebrews 11:5 (NIV, NLT[SE]).

Advanced Level: Examination of internal evidence continues by **evaluating the intrinsic likelihood of the biblical author** whereby we ask this question: What was the biblical author most likely to have written? Knowing an author, the theological emphasis of his work, and his writing style is helpful here. In Jude's opening salutation, he

---

to a group of scribes. So one potential error of hearing could be confusion over letters or diphthongs that sound alike. For instance, A and O may have been pronounced alike; or perhaps O and Ω were pronounced alike. Similarly H and EI sound very similar. So for instance in Heb. 4:11 the scribe of Codex Claromontanus wrote "truth" (ἀληθείας) rather than "disobedience" (ἀπειθείας). Compare Metzger, *The Text of the New Testament*, 190–92 with Greenlee, *Introduction to New Testament Textual Criticism*, 64–65.

64 A blatant example of an intentional alteration for theological reasons among the General Letters exists in the 1522 edition of Erasmus, KJV, and NKJV. In 1 John 5:7–8a, we read: "For there are three who bear witness in heaven: The Father, the Word, and the Holy Spirit; and these three are one and there are three that testify on earth . . ." (5:7 ὅτι τρεῖς εἰσιν οἱ μαρτυροῦντες, ἐν τῷ οὐρανῷ, ὁ πατὴρ, ὁ λόγος, καὶ τὸ ἅγιον, πνεῦμά, καὶ αὐτοι οἱ τρεῖς ἐν εἰσι. 5:8 καὶ τρεῖς εἰσιν οἱ μαρτυροῦντες ἐν τ τῇ γη). Since this passage was in the Vulgate, someone protested its omission from Erasmus' Greek text. Unfortunately, Erasmus promised to include it in a later edition if it could be found in a single Greek manuscript. Miraculously, the reading appeared in a manuscript (Codex 61) and very possibly was prepared for the sole purpose to endorse the trinity. Consequently, Erasmus kept his promise and placed the reading in his 1522 edition. Although he omitted it from subsequent editions, it was the 1522 edition that primarily influenced the textual tradition of the King James Version and some subsequent editions.

65 There are times when a scribe may correct apparent historical facts. For instance, in Hebrews 9:4 the author of Hebrews places the golden altar of incense in the Holy of Holies contrary to Ex. 30:1–6. So, a scribe of codex Vaticanus (B 02) corrects the placement of the golden altar to agree with the Old Testament account.

66 See Metzger, *Textual Commentary*, 656 and Wasserman, *The Epistle of Jude*, 253.

refers to himself as a "slave" (δοῦλος) to Jesus (v.1). The noun "slave" (δοῦλος) typically referred to the legal status of a person in the Roman Empire. Jesus is not described as a related sibling, but rather Jude presents himself as one who is "duty-bound" to Jesus, a slave (NET, NLT^SE) who is in servitude to and thereby labors for Jesus his master; he is attached to his lord. Thus, the idea of "slave" (δοῦλος) in verse 1 has some correlation with "master" (δεσπότην) here in verse 4 and thereby the reading of UBS⁴ is more than likely the original.[67] So in summary, the internal evidence seems to support the UBS⁴ Greek text or the omission of "God" (θεόν). First, it is the shorter reading. It seems more than reasonable to suspect that "God" was added either to distinguish God from Jesus or to enhance the Christological standing of Jesus. Second, it is more difficult to explain a scribe's unintentional adding of the variant "God" (θεόν). Third, it is more than likely that the correlation of "slave" (δοῦλος; v.1) and "master" (δεσπότην; v.4) best fits Jude's context and/or theology.

Conclusion of External & Internal Evidence: In drawing some sort of conclusion concerning both the external and internal evidence, it seems clear the internal evidence is particularly strong. Our inability to describe a scribe's unintentional adding of "God" (θεόν) together with early external evidence (𝔓⁷² 𝔓⁷⁸ ℵ B 1241 1243 1739) is solid for the UBS⁴ reading. Moreover, Jude appears to make some correlation between "slave" (δοῦλος; v.1) and "master" (δεσπότην; v.4). Thus, Jude's stated purpose (v.3) and explanation (v.4) expands from his personal commitment to Jesus to include a commitment of all the Judeans to whom he writes. Thus rather than write about their *common deliverances* (τῆς κοινῆς ἡμῶν σωτηρίας) that all Judean Christians experienced during the beginnings of the church in Judea (v.3a), Jude changes his mind and *urges* (παρακαλῶν) Judean Christians to *fight* (ἐπαγωνίζεσθαι) for their faith in Jesus, who is their Messiah, a belief that was *handed down* (παραδοθείσῃ) to them from the very beginnings of the church (v.3b). Jude then explains (γάρ) that godless *people* have maneuvered (παρεισέδυσαν) in among them (v.4a), who behave immorally and reject the true King over Israel, Jesus who is in fact their master, their Lord, their Messiah (v.4b). Thus, these godless people are really rebels in that they have denied Jesus as sovereign Messiah. The focus here is upon people who have rebelled and rejected Jesus. From this clearly expressed purpose statement, Jude will leave no stone unturned in his forthcoming scathing descriptions of these godless people (vv.5–16).

---

67   A defense for the longer variant reading has been argued by Charles H. Landon, "The Text of Jude 4," *Hervormde Teologiese Studies* 49 (1993): 823–43 as well as in *A Text-Critical Study of the Epistle of Jude*, JSNTSup 135 (Sheffield: Academic Press, 1996), 63–67.

Chapter in Review

"Preparing to Interpret the General Letters" served as a beginning of our step-by-step approach for interpreting the General Letters. This chapter both described and demonstrated three preliminary steps necessary for interpreting the General Letters.

- Step one demonstrated in 1 John 1:1–4 how to initiate a translation of a passage of the Greek text by way of confronting the verbs of the passage, grappling with the clauses of the text, and finally translating the text.

- Step two demonstrated how to identify interpretive issues of a given passage by way of comparing English translations, by talking about differing theories behind English translations, and by illustrating how different English Bibles provides helpful insights for resolving open-ended statements (e.g., Enoch taken to heaven in Heb. 11:5), for rendering Greek idioms (e.g., πᾶς ὁ + ptc in 1 John; οὐ μή in Heb. 13:5; Granville Sharp rule in 2 Peter 1:1), and for revealing our Christian cultural sensitivities (e.g., "they are damned" in Jude v.11; gender inclusive language in James).

- Step three demonstrated how to isolate and even resolve major textual issues in Jude vv.3–4.

INTERPRETING PASSAGES IN THE GENERAL LETTERS

AS WE BEGIN THIS CHAPTER ON "Interpreting Passages in the General Letters," it is helpful to bear in mind that we are merely continuing our step-by-step approach to studying the General Letters. We began this step-by-step process in the previous chapter when in step one we

initiated a simple translation of the Greek text, in step two we identified interpretive issues by way of comparing English translations, in
step three we isolated and even resolved a major textual issue evident
in the UBS[4] Greek text's apparatus. We advance now with three additional steps: step four interpreting structure, step five interpreting style,
syntax, and semantics, and step six interpreting Greek words. We begin, however, with the most important, interpreting structure.

STEP FOUR: INTERPRETING STRUCTURE

The purpose of this section is to introduce the fourth step for interpreting the General Letters, which is to interpret structure by way of creating a structural outline. Yet, step four is a continuation of our grappling
with Greek clauses. So we begin with a simple definition of a structural
outline, advance to preparation for doing a structural outline, and conclude with a "how to" demonstration for creating a structural outline.

Defining Structural Outlines

Creating a structural outline[1] is an important step for interpreting any
passage in a General Letter because it is the foundation upon which we
will eventually build an exegetical outline (step 7), which in turn is the
basis for a homiletical outline (step 9). In fact, the structural outline process begins with a list of independent and dependent clauses whereby all
independent clauses have their main verbs underlined and dependent
clauses have connectors and respective verbs underlined. We demonstrated this process in step one when we grappled with clauses prior to creating
a simple translation for 1 John 1:1–4. Consequently, steps one, four, sev-
en, and nine are essential for teaching what a biblical author of a General
Letter actually wrote and thereby follow a natural sequential order.)

Preparing to Interpret (Chapter 4)	Interpreting (Chapter 5)	Communicating (Chapter 6)	
Step One	*Step Four*	*Step Seven*	*Step Nine*
Simple Listing of Clauses →	Structural Outline of Clauses →	Exegetical Outline Based on Structural Outline →	Homiletical Outline Based on Exegetical Outline

---

1   Although my preference is to describe this process by means of a "structural outline," other
terminology exists. Mounce calls it "phrasing," Guthrie calls it "grammatical diagram," and
MacDonald calls it "textual transcription." I also concentrate on the clause level whereas the
others will tend to break sentences into smaller units. William D. Mounce, *A Graded Reader
of Biblical Greek* (Grand Rapids: Zondervan, 1996), xvi–xxiii; George H. Guthrie and J. Scott
Duvall, *Biblical Greek Exegesis: A Guided Approach to Learning Intermediate and Advanced Greek*
(Grand Rapids: Zondervan, 1988), 27–42; William G. MacDonald, *Greek Enchiridion: A Concise
Handbook of Grammar for Translation and Exegesis* (Peabody, MA: Hendrickson, 1979), 145–52.

So what is a structural outline? A structural outline is an exegetical tool that assists interpreters to identify and *visualize* the biblical author's flow of thought, clause-by-clause. When clauses are isolated and structurally outlined, interpreters are able to see the basic grammatical and syntactical associations, parallelisms, and emphases of the text. Once clauses are positioned in a structural format, *they portray subordination and coordination of thought*, and as a result we are more apt to recognize the main point of any verse or group of verses. Although we began with listing Greek clauses in step one from 1 John 1:1–4, we will tackle 2 Peter 1:3–11 in order to illustrate the structural outlining process. You can return to 1 John later to practice and develop your structural outlining skills.[2]

Preparing for the Structural Outline

Like textual criticism, creating a structural outline for any New Testament letter is both a science and an art. In other words, there is a great deal of objectivity in the process as well as a bit of subjectivity. So we begin with this question: What are the objective elements in creating a structural outline? The objective elements are isolating and listing the clauses, determining their type, and underlining their "structural markers." Structural markers are the main verb(s) of an independent clause and the *important* connectors along with the verbs or verbals of a dependent clause. Thus after isolating the clauses, we ask two important questions: What type of clause is this and what are its structural makers? The following chart lists three types of independent clauses (coordinating, prepositional, and asyndeton) and four types of dependent clauses (relative, conjunctive, participial, and infinitival) found in the General Letters.[3]

Types (Classifications) of Independent and Dependent Clauses	
Three Types of Independent Clauses	Four Types of Dependent Clauses
Coordinating conjunctive clauses are introduced by simple connective (καί or δέ), contrastive conjunction (δέ, πλὴν), correlative conjunction (μέν…δέ or καί…καί) explanatory conjunction (γάρ), inferential conjunction (ἄρα, διό, οὖν, γάρ), transitional conjunction (δέ or οὖν).	Relative clauses are introduced by a relative pronoun (ὅς), a relative adjective (οἷος, such as; ὅσος, as much/many as), a relative adverb (ὅπου, where; ὅτε, when).

---

2   For a step-by-step guide through the structure and exegesis of the Johannine letters see Herbert W. Bateman IV, *A Workbook for Intermediate Greek: Grammar, Exegesis, and Commentary on 1–3 John* (Grand Rapids: Kregel, 2008).

3   Daniel B. Wallace, *Greek Grammar Beyond the Basics* (Grand Rapids: Zondervan, 1996), 656–65.

Types (Classifications) of Independent and Dependent Clauses	
Three Types of Independent Clauses	Four Types of Dependent Clauses
Prepositional clauses are introduced by "for this reason" (διὰ τοῦτο) Heb. 2:1; 1 John 3:1 "for this reason" (ἐπὶ τοῦτο) 3 John v.10 "as a result of this" (ἐκ τοῦτο) 1 John 4:6 "why" (εἰς τίνα) 1 Peter 1:11 "in this" (ἐν τοῦτο) 1 John 3:1, 16; 4:13	Conjunctive clauses are introduced by a subordinate conjunction that denotes: time (ὅτε, ὅτον); reason and cause (διό, ὅτι, ἐπεί); purpose and result (ἵνα, ὥστε); comparison (καθώς, ὡς, ὡσεί, ὥσπερ).
	Participial clauses are introduced by a participle
Asyndeton clauses are not introduced by a conjunctive word or phrase. 1 John 2:10, 12–14, 15; 3:1; 2 John vv.4, 8; 3 John vv.4, 9; James 1:26–27; 2 Peter 2:4; 3:1–3	Infinitival clauses are introduced by certain infinitives

So when we list all the clauses in 2 Peter 1:3–11, we can say, with objectivity that there are twenty-one clauses and two phrases (the phrases will be discussed later). Following the order they appear in the Greek text (NA 27th, 28th), we list the clauses, distinguish the independent from the dependent clauses, underline Greek structural markers for each clause, and provide a simple translation for each clause with the translated structural marker also underlined.

Dependent (?) Clause   3a Ὡς πάντα ἡμῖν τῆς θείας δυνάμεως αὐτοῦ τὰ πρὸς ζωὴν καὶ εὐσέβειαν <u>δεδωρημένης</u>
   3a *Because* (lit. "as") his divine power <u>has given</u> us all things for life and duty

★Dependent Phrase   3b διὰ τῆς ἐπιγνώσεως τοῦ καλέσαντος ἡμᾶς ἰδίᾳ δόξῃ καὶ ἀρετῇ,
   3b *through* the knowledge of the one who called us by his own glory and excellence,

★Dependent Phrase   4a <u>δι' ὧν</u> τὰ τίμια καὶ μέγιστα ἡμῖν ἐπαγγέλματα <u>δεδώρηται</u>,
   4a *through which* things he has given us honorable and extraordinary promises,

Dependent Clause   4b <u>ἵνα</u> διὰ τούτων <u>γένησθε</u> θείας κοινωνοὶ φύσεως,
   4b *so that* through these things *you may become* partakers of the divine nature,

Dependent Clause	<u>⁴ᶜ ἀποφυγόντες</u> τῆς ἐν τῷ κόσμῳ ἐν ἐπιθυμίᾳ φθορᾶς. ⁴ᶜ <u>by escaping</u> the corruption in the world, namely worldly desires.
Dependent Clause	⁵ᵃ σπουδὴν πᾶσαν <u>παρεισενέγκαντες</u> ⁵ᵃ <u>by making</u> every effort
Independent Clause	⁵ᵇ καὶ αὐτὸ τοῦτο δὲ . . . <u>ἐπιχορηγήσατε</u> ἐν τῇ πίστει ὑμῶν τὴν ἀρετήν, ⁵ᵇ And also for this reason, . . . <u>add</u> to your faith moral excellence,
Independent Clause	⁵ᶜ (<u>ἐπιχορηγήσατε</u>) ἐν δὲ τῇ ἀρετῇ τὴν γνῶσιν, ⁵ᶜ and (<u>add</u>) to moral excellence knowledge,
Independent Clause	⁶ᵃ (<u>ἐπιχορηγήσατε</u>) ἐν δὲ τῇ γνώσει τὴν ἐγκράτειαν, ⁶ᵃ and (<u>add</u>) to knowledge self-control,
Independent Clause	⁶ᵇ (<u>ἐπιχορηγήσατε</u>) ἐν δὲ τῇ ἐγκρατείᾳ τὴν ὑπομονήν, ⁶ᵇ and (<u>add</u>) to self-control endurance,
Independent Clause	⁶ᶜ (<u>ἐπιχορηγήσατε</u>) ἐν δὲ τῇ ὑπομονῇ τὴν εὐσέβειαν, ⁶ᶜ and (<u>add</u>) to endurance godliness,
Independent Clause	⁷ᵃ (<u>ἐπιχορηγήσατε</u>) ἐν δὲ τῇ εὐσεβείᾳ τὴν φιλαδελφίαν, ⁷ᵃ and (<u>add</u>) to godliness brotherly love,
Independent Clause	⁷ᵇ (<u>ἐπιχορηγήσατε</u>) ἐν δὲ τῇ φιλαδελφίᾳ τὴν ἀγάπην. ⁷ᵇ and (<u>add</u>) to brotherly love *self-denying* love.
Dependent Clause	⁸ᵃ ταῦτα γὰρ ὑμῖν <u>ὑπάρχοντα</u> ⁸ᵃ For *if* these things <u>are *really*</u> yours
Dependent Clause	⁸ᵇ καὶ (ταῦτα) <u>πλεονάζοντα</u> ⁸ᵇ And *if* (*these things*) <u>*continually* increase</u>
Independent Clause	⁸ᶜ οὐκ ἀργοὺς οὐδὲ ἀκάρπους <u>καθίστησιν</u> εἰς τὴν τοῦ κυρίου ἡμῶν Ἰησοῦ Χριστοῦ ἐπίγνωσιν· ⁸ᶜ <u>they will</u> not <u>make</u> you useless or fruitless in the knowledge of Jesus, *who is the* Messiah.
Dependent Clause	⁹ᵃ ᾧ γὰρ <u>μὴ πάρεστιν</u> ταῦτα, ⁹ᵃ For <u>whoever lacks</u> these things

Independent Clause	⁹ᵇ τυφλός ἐστιν μυωπάζων,
	⁹ᵇ He is blind, namely nearsighted,
Dependent Clause	⁹ᶜ λήθην λαβὼν τοῦ καθαρισμοῦ τῶν πάλαι αὐτοῦ ἁμαρτιῶν.
	⁹ᶜ because they have choosen to forget the cleansing of their former sins.
Independent Clause	¹⁰ᵃ διὸ μᾶλλον, ἀδελφοί, σπουδάσατε βεβαίαν ὑμῶν τὴν κλῆσιν καὶ ἐκλογὴν ποιεῖσθαι·
	¹⁰ᵃ Therefore, brothers *and sisters*, make every effort to be certain of your calling and election;
Dependent Clause	¹⁰ᵇ ταῦτα γὰρ ποιοῦντες
	¹⁰ᵇ For *by* doing this
Independent Clause	¹⁰ᶜ οὐ μὴ πταίσητέ ποτε·
	¹⁰ᶜ You will never, never stumble
Independent Clause	¹¹ οὕτως γὰρ πλουσίως ἐπιχορηγηθήσεται ὑμῖν ἡ εἴσοδος εἰς τὴν αἰώνιον βασιλείαν τοῦ κυρίου ἡμῶν καὶ σωτῆρος Ἰησοῦ Χριστοῦ.
	¹¹ For in this way, the entrance into the eternal kingdom of our Lord and Savior, Jesus, who is king, will be richly provided for you.

Of these twenty-one clauses, twelve are independent clauses, nine are dependent clauses, and two are identified as phrases. Let me first describe the twelve independent clauses listed for 2 Peter 1:3–11. Remember, we need to ask ourselves, what type of independent clause is represented here? See the chart that identifies the types of independent clauses. Obviously, eleven reflect *the most common type of independent clause* in the New Testament in that they are *independent clauses introduced by a coordinating conjunction*, "and" (καί or δέ) and "for" (γάρ). Take for instance the clauses from 2 Peter 1:5b–7. Each independent clause is introduced with "and" (καί or δέ) with the main verb assumed in each subsequent clause.

⁵ᵇ καὶ αὐτὸ τοῦτο δὲ . . . ἐπιχορηγήσατε ἐν τῇ πίστει ὑμῶν τὴν ἀρετήν,
⁵ᵇ And also for this reason, . . . add to your faith moral excellence,

⁵ᶜ (ἐπιχορηγήσατε) ἐν δὲ τῇ ἀρετῇ τὴν γνῶσιν,
⁵ᶜ and (add) to moral excellence knowledge,

⁶ᵃ (ἐπιχορηγήσατε) ἐν δὲ τῇ γνώσει τὴν ἐγκράτειαν,
⁶ᵃ and (add) to knowledge self-control,

6b (ἐπιχορηγήσατε) ἐν δὲ τῇ ἐγκρατείᾳ τὴν ὑπομονήν,
6b and (add) to self-control endurance,

6c (ἐπιχορηγήσατε) ἐν δὲ τῇ ὑπομονῇ τὴν εὐσέβειαν,
6c and (add) to endurance godliness,

7a (ἐπιχορηγήσατε) ἐν δὲ τῇ εὐσεβείᾳ τὴν φιλαδελφίαν,
7a and (add) to godliness brotherly love,

7b (ἐπιχορηγήσατε) ἐν δὲ τῇ φιλαδελφίᾳ τὴν ἀγάπην.
7b and (add) to brotherly love self-denying love.

Several figures of speech are worth noting here. The specific repetition and the string of conjunctions "and" (δέ; e.g., figure of speech known as "polysyndeton") along with another figure of speech, an ellipsis whereby I insert the verb "add" (ἐπιχορηγήσατε) has significant rhetorical value. As you reread these clauses, do you sense the gradual increase of emphasis with each successive line? Peter begins with faith (e.g., trust in God) and progressively climbs step-by-step to the climatic crown jewel of the list, love (e.g., self-denying love, ἀγάπη) to be extended toward others.[4] The other four independent clauses of verses 8a, 9b, 10b, and 11 are also introduced by way of a coordinating conjunction. Yet in these verses, Peter employs the conjunction "for" (γάρ). Despite the fact that "for" (γάρ) appears in the dependent clause, the conjunction governs and serves to introduce the entire sentence, which ultimately identifies the type of independent clause as a coordinating conjunctive one.

We now draw attention to the eight dependent clauses listed for 2 Peter 1:3–11. Determining the syntactical relationship of one group of words (dependent clauses) to another group of words (independent clauses) moves us into the subjective aspect behind a structural outline. Thus, we move from isolating and classifying "types of clauses" and advance to raising questions about their "syntactical function." While many decisions about syntax can be answered objectively, many others may be subject to interpretation because of subsequent semantic interpretations.[5] As you might suspect, particular attention is directed at the dependent clauses be-

---

4 A similar progress of thought occurred in 1 John 1:1–14 where John moves from what was heard, what was seen, what was touched. This sort of occurrence is also referred to as an anabasis. See "Johannine Figures of Speech" in Bateman, *A Workbook for Intermediate Greek*, 606–12. For a quick and abbreviated study for the word "love," (ἀγάπη) see my comments under "Opening Salutations" in chapter one on genre.

5 Semantic interpretation involves answering questions about "semantic function" of a given structural marker. Semantic classifications are those defined and nuanced in Daniel B. Wallace, *Greek Grammar Beyond the Basics* (Grand Rapids: Zondervan, 1996) and frequently discussed in critical commentaries, and often evident in English Bible translations.

cause dependent clauses may *function syntactically* in one of three ways:

> *substantively* whereby the dependent clause functions like a sub-
> ject of a verb, predicate nominative, direct object of a verb, or in
> apposition to a noun or pronoun;

> *adjectivally* whereby the dependent clause modifies a noun or
> pronoun, noun phrase, or another substantive;

> *adverbially* whereby the dependent clause modifies a verb.

Thus, the ultimate question we are obligated to ask of all dependent
clauses is simply: *How is the dependent clause functioning syntactically?* What
is the relationship of the dependent clause to the independent clause or
perhaps to another dependent clause? The chart below lists the three
possible syntactical functions of a dependent clause (substantival, adjectival, and adverbial), restates the four types of dependent clauses (relative,
conjunctive,[6] participial and infinitival), and lists some noted examples
that you can expect to appear in the General Letters.[7]

Syntactical Function	Four Types of Dependent Clauses and Selected Examples from the General Letters	
Substantival Clauses	Relative	Subject (1 Peter 1:9; 2 Peter 1:9) Direct Object (1 John 1:1)
	Conjunctive	ὅτι + Indicative Mood (Heb. 3:19; 7:14; 11:6; James 1:13; 2:22; 1 Peter 1:12; 2 Peter 1:20; 3:3, 5; 1 John 1:5; 2:4, 18; 4:15; 3 John v.12; Jude vv.5, 18) ἵνα + Subjunctive Mood (2 Peter 1:4; 1 John 3:11, 23; 4:21; 5:3, 16; 2 John v.6; 3 John v.4)
	Participial	(James 5:4; 1 Peter 3:13; 1 John 2:26; 3:9; 4:2; 2 John v.3)
	Infinitive	Subject (Heb. 2:1; 4:6; 9:27; 10:31; 11:6; 2 Peter 2:21) Direct Object (Heb. 7:25; 1 John 2:6) Indirect Discourse (Heb 3:18; 11:5; James 1:26; 2:14; 1 Peter 2:11; 1 John 2:6, 9; Jude v.3) Appositional (James 1:27); See Robertson for Epexegetical (Heb. 7:9; 2 Peter 3:2)

6   Technically, examples of a conjunctive clause that functions adjectivally do not exist (at least,
     to my knowledge). However, the epexegetical and appositional semantic occurrences of the
     ὅτι and ἵνα appear to be the closest facsimile to an adjectival clause and thereby identified in
     this chart to be *like* an adjective.
7   Compare Wallace, *Greek Grammar Beyond the Basics*, 474–76; 617–40; 656–65.

Syntactical Function	Four Types of Dependent Clauses and Selected Examples from the General Letters	
Adjectival Clauses	Relative	Pronoun (1 John 2:7)
	Conjunctive	ὅτι Epexegetical (Heb. 10:6; 2 Peter 3:1; 1 John 1:5; 3:1; 4:9, 10, 13; 2 John v.6; Jude vv.5, 17) ἵνα Epexegetical (Heb. 5:1; 1 John 2:27a; 3:23; 4:21; 5:3)
	Participial	(Heb. 6:18; 7:9; 10:31; James. 2:15; 1 Peter 1:7, 21; 2 Peter 1:19; 3:2; Jude v.3)
	Infinitive	Epexegetical (James 1:19)
Adverbial Clauses	Relative	Relative Adverb (ὅθεν; Heb. 8:3); relatives tend to be substantival/adjectival
	Conjunctive	ὅτι + Indicative Mood Clauses (James 1:10, 12; 1 Pet. 1:16; 2:15; 3:9, 18; 4:8; 5:5; 1 John 2:11; 3:2, 14, 22; 4:4, 10, 19; 2 John v.4; Jude v.5) ἵνα + Subjunctive Mood Clauses (James 1:4; 1 Peter 1:4; 3:1, 16, 18; 4:11; 5:6; 1 John 1:9; 2:1; 3:8) Conditional: 1st class (Heb. 2:2; 4:8; 12:25; James 1:23, 26; 2:11 4:11; 1 Peter 2:20; 2 Peter 2:4; 1 John 5:9; 2 John v.10); 2nd class (Heb. 4:8; 8:4, 7; 1 John 2:19); 3rd class (Heb. 6:3; 10:38; James 2:14, 15, 17; 5:19; 1 Peter 3:13; 1 John 1:8, 9, 10; 2:15; 4:12; 3 John v.10); 4th class (1 Peter 3:14)
	Participial	Temporal (Heb. 1:3; 11:23) Means (Heb. 2:18; 1 Peter 5:6–7; 2 Peter 1:5; 2:15; 3:6) Manner (Heb. 11:27; 13:17) Cause (Heb. 4:2; 2 Peter 1:9, 14; with wjß prefix: 1 Peter 4:12) Conditional (Heb. 2:3; 7:12; 10:26; 11:32; 1 Pet. 3:6; 2 Pet.1:8, 10) Concession (Heb. 4:3; 5:8; 1 Peter 1:8; 2 Peter 1:12) Result (Heb. 12:3; James 1:4; 2:9; 1 Peter 3:5; 2 Peter 2:1, 6) Complementary (Heb. 10:2; 1 John 4:2; 3 John v.4)
	Infinitive	Purpose (James 3:3; 1 Peter 3:7) Result (Heb. 3:12; 6:10; 11:3, 8; 1 Peter 3:7) Time (Heb. 2:8 [means]; 3:15; 10:15, 26) Cause (Heb. 7:24; James 4:2) Means (Heb. 2:8 [contemporaneous]; 8:13) Complementary (Heb. 1:14; 9:8; James 1:27; 1 Peter 5:1; 1 John 3:9, 16; 3 John v.8)

In determining the syntactical relationship of the dependent clauses to their respective independent clauses for 2 Peter 1:3–11, stylistic prefaces are worth noting. Unlike 1 John 1:1–4 where the type of dependent clause preferred was the relative that began with a relative pronoun "what" (ὅ)[8] or the conjunctive clause that began with the conjunction "that" (ἵνα), Peter prefers the participial dependent clause:

> v 4c "by escaping" (ἀποφυγόντες; ptc of means; or temporal "after" in NET),
> v 5a "by making" (παρεισενέγκαντες; ptc of means),
> v 8a "if are really" (ὑπάρχοντα; conditional ptc; KJV, NASB, ESV, NIV, NET)
> v 8b "if continually increase" (πλεονάζοντα; conditional ptc; KJV, NASB, ESV, NIV, NET)
> v 9c "because they have chosen" (λαβών; causal ptc; or "since" in NET)
> v 10b "by doing" (ποιοῦντες; ptc of means; or conditional "if" in KJV, ESV)

When I ask *how are these dependent participial clauses functioning syntactically*, my response is that they are adverbial because they appear to modify a verb in an independent clause. The italic portion of my translation represents a semantic classification for each adverbial participle.[9] It is not unusual, however, for English translations to limit adverbial participles to "*ing*." For instance, some English Bibles are non-committal in their respective renderings: "having escaped" (1:4c; KJV, NASB, ESV), "giving all diligence" (1:4d; KJV; cf. NASB), "increasing among you" (1:8b; NRSV, NIV), "forgetting" (1:9b; NET[SE]; cf. KJV, NASB, ESV, NIV), and "choosing" (1:10b; NASB). Did you observe that the translations that limited their renderings to "ing" tend to be more formal?

More Formal											More Functional
ASV	NASB[95]	KJV	NKJV	RSV	ESV	NRSV	NET	NIV[85/11]	TNIV	NLT[SE]	LB

On the one hand, it is disappointing when translations refrain from providing an interpretation for us. On the other hand, it is nice because we now can grapple with the text, decide for ourselves what might be the most appropriate semantic rendering according to the author's intention, and thereby teach accordingly. Yet numerous helps exist to

---

8   John loves the relative dependent clause. There are at least twenty-five relative pronoun clauses in the Johannine Epistles. They function either as direct objects of a verb (1 John 1:1; 2:7, 25; 4:16; 3 John v.10), or adjectivally modifying the antecedent (1 John 2:5, 7, 8, 27; 4:2, 3, 16, 20; 5:15). Up for investigation: 1 John 2:5; 4:15; 5:15; 2 John vv.5, 8; 3 John vv.5–6, 10.

9   Semantic classifications for adverbial participles are more clearly defined and nuanced in Wallace, *Greek Grammar Beyond the Basics*, 617–40. Answering questions about "semantic function" concerns your ability to tell how a word functions semantically within a clause.

help direct interpretive decisions: the numerous English translations, the NET Bible's translational notes, Greek grammars, and commentaries (sources are listed in chapter eight).

Finally, there is the conjunctive dependent clause (ὡς . . . δεδωρη-μένης, v. 3a), a conjunctive dependent clause (ἵνα . . . γένησθε, 4b), and a relative dependent clause (ᾧ . . . πάρεστιν, v. 9a). As we did with the participial dependent clauses, we need to ask once again: *How are these dependent clauses functioning syntactically?* First, how is this conjunctive dependent clause (ὡς . . . δεδωρημένης, v. 3a) functioning syntactically? Obviously, the clause is a conjunctive clause that begins with the comparative "as" (ὡς), which I have rendered "because . . . his divine power" (ὡς . . . θείας δυνάμεως αὐτοῦ). It appears the comparative conjunction (ὡς) along with its verbal "has given" (δεδωρημένης; genitive absolute ptc) is a subordinate clause of cause providing the reason or the basis for Peter's prayer in verse 2, "Grace and peace be multiplied to you" (χάρις ὑμῖν καὶ εἰρήνη πληθυνθείη). Furthermore, the presence of the genitive absolute makes for a loose grammatical connection with the independent clause in verse 2.[10] Consequently, this cumbersome Greek construction is rendered one of two ways. Some translations emphasize the adverbial connection to the verb "be multiplied" (πληθυν-θείη; see KJV NASB NKJV). Others emphasize the loose grammatical connection to the verb that is typical of a genitive absolute and thereby render the clause as though it were an independent clause (NIV, NET, NLT). What does this interpretive decision matter to our understanding of the passage? Whereas the former translations consider verse 3 to be an expanded conclusion of the opening salutation, the latter renderings view verse 3 as the opening of the body of Peter's letter. Both are viable options. Thus, your decision whether to divide verse 3 from the salutation or not will affect your subsequent outline of the passage.

The second conjunctive dependent clause "*so that* . . . you may become" (ἵνα . . . γένησθε, 4b) seems straightforward. Nevertheless, we ask: *how is this conjunctive dependent clause functioning syntactically?* Like the participial dependent clauses, this dependent conjunctive clause is functioning adverbially but it specifically modifies the verb "has given" (δεδωρημένης). Semantically, "*so that*" (ἵνα) expresses the result of "God's power given for both life and duty," namely *with the result that* believers become "partakers of the divine nature."

---

10   If "has given" (δεδωρημένης) is a genitive absolute, the Greek then appears to be somewhat idiomatic in that the genitive absolute does not appear to follow exactly what we might expect. Structurally, the genitive absolute is in the genitive (as it is here), anarthrous (as it is here), and placed at the front of a sentence (as it is here). Semantically, the genitive absolute is unconnected with the rest of the sentence (what about ὡς?), always adverbial (is it not governed by ὡς?), and normally temporal (causal or comparative?). Wallace, *Greek Grammar Beyond the Basics*, 654–55.

Finally, we must also ask: *how is the relative dependent clause* "whoever lacks" (ᾧ ... μὴ πάρεστιν) *functioning syntactically?* Unlike the other dependent clauses, this dependent clause is functioning substantively. Actually, it is the subject of the verb "is" (ἐστιν). Consequently, we might visualize this subjunctive dependent clause in this manner: "(For whoever lacks these things) is blind, namely nearsighted." By placing "For whoever lacks these things" in parenthesis, we still recognize the relative clause to be dependent as well as identify it as the subject of the independent clause.

The prepositional phrases are a twofold example of subjectivity on my part. First, because of the length of the previous phrase, I decided to place the phrases on their own lines.

★Dependent Phrase	3b διὰ τῆς ἐπιγνώσεως τοῦ καλέσαντος ἡμᾶς ἰδίᾳ δόξῃ καὶ ἀρετῇ,
	through the knowledge of the one who called us by his own glory and excellence,
★Dependent Phrase	4a <u>δι' ὧν</u> τὰ τίμια καὶ μέγιστα ἡμῖν ἐπαγγέλματα <u>δεδώρηται</u>,
	through which things he has given us honorable and extraordinary promises,

Furthermore, because of my semantic interpretation of "through" (διὰ and δι' ὧν + δεδώρηται), it seems Peter may have chosen these two prepositional phrases to describe the "how to" of his previous clause.[11] Naturally, this decision is the second reason for listing the two phrases on their own lines, I perceive there is a potential interpretive issue looming in the future for me to address. Remember we are now in the interpretive mode, which takes into consideration the semantic function of words. We must now conclude our discussion with a how-to demonstration for creating a structural outline.

Demonstrating Structural Outlines

As we stated above, the basic principle of a structural outline is to recognize *visually* the syntactical relationship of one group of words (dependent clauses) to another group of words (independent clauses). Consequently, in the following structural outline, Peter's flow of thought is represented by reproducing the exact word order of the Greek text according to its major clauses. Three essential steps are taken to *visualize* Peter's structure. First, all independent clauses (the main thought) are placed farthest to the left. Second, dependent clauses that directly modify a word or concept of

---

11   Although a general rule of thumb is to major on the majors (e.g., independent and dependent clauses), there are times when a prepositional phrase may warrant special attention. Herein lies another example of the art of exegesis.

an independent clause are indented and positioned either over or under the modified word for easy identification. The positioning of a Greek clause above or below depends on the Greek word order. For instance, if a dependent clause appears before the independent clause, then the dependent clause will appear above the independent clause and vice versa (cf. 2 Peter 1:8a, b with 1:9b). Finally, all key structural markers that distinguish clauses as well as highlight significant parts of a clause are underlined. (For convenience, verses are grouped into conceptual units followed by explanations and simplistic summaries.)

1. Divine Power Given for Life and Duty (vv. 3–4)

^{3a} Ὡς πάντα ἡμῖν τῆς θείας δυνάμεως αὐτοῦ τὰ πρὸς ζωὴν

καὶ εὐσέβειαν <u>δεδωρημένης</u>

^{3a} His divine power <u>has given</u> us all things for life and duty

^{3b} διὰ τῆς ἐπιγνώσεως τοῦ καλέσαντος ἡμᾶς ἰδίᾳ δόξῃ καὶ ἀρετῇ,

^{3b} *through* the knowledge of the one who called us by his own glory and excellence,

^{4a} δι' <u>ὧν</u> τὰ τίμια καὶ μέγιστα ἡμῖν ἐπαγγέλματα <u>δεδώρηται</u>,

^{4a} *through* <u>which</u> things *<u>he has given</u>* us honorable and extraordinary promises,

^{4b} <u>ἵνα</u> διὰ τούτων <u>γένησθε</u> θείας κοινωνοὶ φύσεως,

^{4b} <u>so that</u> through these things <u>you may become partakers</u> of the divine nature,

^{4c} <u>ἀποφυγόντες</u> τῆς ἐν τῷ κόσμῳ ἐν ἐπιθυμίᾳ φθορᾶς.

^{4c} <u>by</u> <u>escaping</u> the corruption in the world, *namely worldly desires*.

Explanation of the Outline: Whereas 3a is to the extreme left because it has been interpreted to be an independent clause, the two prepositional phrases (3b, 4a) and the "so that" (ἵνα) clause are viewed as modifying the verb "has given" (δεδωρημένης). Because of space issues the dotted line is meant to visulize the suborination of all three. The final dependent participal clause "by escaping" (ἀποφυγόντες) modifies the verb "may become" (γένησθε) in the previous dependent result clause (ἵνα) and is thereby placed under "may become" (γένησθε).

Simplified Train of Thought: Through the clauses and structural markers, we can trace Peter's flow of thought for verses 3–4 in this manner: God has given (δεδωρημένης) divine power to believers for life and duty (how?) by way of (διὰ) knowledge of either God or Jesus that has a rather sgnificant result (ἵνα) that believers may share in God's nature (how?) by escaping (ἀποφυγόντες; ptc of means) the world's corruption.

2. Peter's Appeal (vv. 5–7)

^{5a} σπουδὴν πᾶσαν <u>παρεισενέγκαντες</u>
^{5a} *by* <u>exerting</u> every effort

|

^{5b} καὶ αὐτὸ τοῦτο δὲ . . . <u>ἐπιχορηγήσατε</u> ἐν τῇ πίστει ὑμῶν τὴν ἀρετήν,
^{5b} And also for this reason, . . . <u>add</u> to your faith moral excellence,

^{5c} (<u>ἐπιχορηγήσατε</u>) ἐν δὲ τῇ ἀρετῇ τὴν γνῶσιν,
^{5c} and (<u>add</u>) to moral excellence knowledge,

^{6a} (<u>ἐπιχορηγήσατε</u>) ἐν δὲ τῇ γνώσει τὴν ἐγκράτειαν,
^{6a} and (<u>add</u>) to knowledge self-control,

^{6b} (<u>ἐπιχορηγήσατε</u>) ἐν δὲ τῇ ἐγκρατείᾳ τὴν ὑπομονήν,
^{6b} and (<u>add</u>) to self-control endurance,

^{6c} (<u>ἐπιχορηγήσατε</u>) ἐν δὲ τῇ ὑπομονῇ τὴν εὐσέβειαν,
^{6c} and (<u>add</u>) to endurance godliness,

^{7a} (<u>ἐπιχορηγήσατε</u>) ἐν δὲ τῇ εὐσεβείᾳ τὴν φιλαδελφίαν,
^{7a} and (<u>add</u>) to godliness brotherly love,

^{7b} (<u>ἐπιχορηγήσατε</u>) ἐν δὲ τῇ φιλαδελφίᾳ τὴν ἀγάπην.
^{7b} and (<u>add</u>) to brotherly love *self-denying* love.

Explanation of the Outline: Clauses 5b–7b are to the extreme left because they are all independent clauses. The dependent participial clause ("*by* exerting every effort") modifies the main verb "add" (ἐπιχορηγήσατε) of the independent clause and is placed above it. Because I wish to follow the word order in the Greek as well as strive to show subordination of thought, I have taken the participal clause out of sequence and placed " . . . " where the clause would appear.

Simplified Train of Thought: Through the clauses and structural markers, we can trace Peter's flow of thought for verses 5–7 in this manner: Peter tells how he expects believers to move ("add") from believing faith to moral excellence, self-control, endurance, godliness, brotherly love, and ultimately self-denying love (how?) by taking the initiative (παρεισενέγκαντες ptc of means).

3. Reasons for Peter's Appeal (vv. 8–9)

^{8a} ταῦτα γὰρ ὑμῖν <u>ὑπάρχοντα</u>
^{8a} For *if* these things <u>are *really*</u> yours

^{8b} καὶ (ταῦτα) <u>γένησθε</u>

^{8b} And (*if* these things) *continually* <u>increase</u>

|

^{8c} οὐκ ἀργοὺς οὐδὲ ἀκάρπους <u>καθίστησιν</u> εἰς τὴν τοῦ κυρίου ἡμῶν Ἰησοῦ Χριστοῦ ἐπίγνωσιν·

^{8c} <u>they will</u> not <u>make</u> you useless or fruitless in the knowledge of Jesus, *who is the* Messiah.

^{9a} (ᾧ γὰρ μὴ <u>πάρεστιν</u> ταῦτα) τυφλός <u>ἐστιν</u> μυωπάζων,

^{9a} For (<u>whoever lacks</u> these things) <u>is</u> blind, namely nearsighted,

|

^{9b} λήθην <u>λαβὼν</u> τοῦ καθαρισμοῦ τῶν πάλαι αὐτοῦ ἁμαρτιῶν.

^{9b} <u>because they have choosen</u> to forget the cleansing of their former sins.

Explanation of the Outline: Clauses 8c and 9a are to the extreme left because they are independent clauses. The dependent participial clauses in 8a and 8b are positioned above "they will make" (καθίστησιν) because the two adverbial participles (ὑπάρχοντα and γένησθε) modify the main verb of the first independent clause. As already observed, the relative dependent clause "whoever lacks these things" (ᾧ γὰρ μὴ πάρεστιν ταῦτα) is the subject of "is" (ἐστιν), and thus, it is placed in parenthesis to visualize the fact that the relative clause is functioning substantivally as the subject of the independent clause. Yet the subsequent dependent participial clause is functioning adverbially and thereby is placed under "is" (ἐστιν).

Simplified Train of Thought: Through the clauses and structural markers, we can trace Peter's flow of thought for verses 8–9: based upon a twofold assumption (ὑπάρχοντα and γένησθε conditional ptc) about a believer's progression from faith to love (vv. 5–7), Peter reasons (γὰρ) that believers will be fruitful and concludes those who lack the faith to love are blind (why?) because they have (λαβὼν causal ptc) chosen to forget what God has done for them, namely forgive.

---

4. Conclusion for Peter's Appeal (vv 10–11)

^{10a} <u>διὸ μᾶλλον</u>, ἀδελφοί, <u>σπουδάσατε</u> βεβαίαν ὑμῶν τὴν κλῆσιν καὶ ἐκλογὴν <u>ποιεῖσθαι</u>·

^{10a} Therefore, brothers *and sisters*, <u>make every effort to be certain</u> of your calling and election;

^{10b} ταῦτα γὰρ <u>ποιοῦντες</u>

^{10b} For *by* <u>doing</u> this

|

^{10c} οὐ μὴ <u>πταίσητέ</u> ποτε·

^{10c} You will never, never <u>stumble</u>

¹¹ οὕτως γὰρ πλουσίως <u>ἐπιχορηγηθήσεται</u> ὑμῖν ἡ εἴσοδος εἰς τὴν αἰώνιον βασιλείαν τοῦ κυρίου ἡμῶν καὶ σωτῆρος Ἰησοῦ Χριστοῦ.

> Explanation of the Outline: Clauses 10a, 10c, and 11 are to the extreme left because they are independent clauses. Both the verb "make every effort" (σπουδάσατε) and the infinitive "to be certain" (ποιεῖσθαι) are underlined because the infinitive is a complementary infinitive that completes the main verb. The dependent participial clauses in 10b are positioned above "you will stumble" (πταίσητέ) because it modifies the main verb in the second of three independent clauses.
>
> Simplified Train of Thought: Through the clauses and structural markers, we can trace Peter's flow of thought for verses 10–11 in this manner: Peter draws verses 3–9 to a conclusion (διὸ μᾶλλον) with an expectation: "be certain about your salvation" (σπουδάσατε. . . ποιεῖσθαι), followed by Peter's twofold reasoning (γὰρ): you will never, no never stumble (οὐ μὴ πταίσητέ) and your needs will be provided (ἐπιχορηγηθήσεται).

¹¹ For in this way, the entrance into the eternal kingdom of our Lord and Savior, Jesus, who is king, <u>will</u> be richly <u>provided</u> for you.

Granted, more could be said concerning Peter's train of thought, but we must press on to other issues of interpretation, namely interpreting style, syntax, and semantics. Hopefully you will return to this structural outline and advance your personal study of 2 Peter 1:3–11 at a later time. In the meantime, let me summarize step four. First, we defined a structural outline to be an exegetical tool that assists us in our ability to identify and *visualize* the biblical author's flow of thought via structural markers. We then advanced to preparation, which is by nature, objective in that it entailed isolating, identifying and listing all the clauses of a given passage (in our case 2 Peter 1:3–11). We then ended with a "how to" demonstration for creating a structural outline by way of 2 Peter 1:3–11. We might visualize step four in this manner:

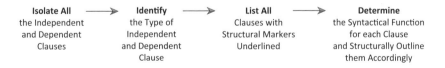

| **Isolate All** | → | **Identify** | → | **List All** | → | **Determine** |
| the Independent and Dependent Clauses | | the Type of Independent and Dependent Clause | | Clauses with Structural Markers Underlined | | the Syntactical Function for each Clause and Structurally Outline them Accordingly |

Ultimately we have asked these three questions: What type of clause is it, what are the *structural markers*, and what is the *syntactical function of* dependent clauses? If you create this pattern of questioning for every passage, you should have no problem interpreting the General Letters for teaching and preaching purposes, particularly as we move into our next chapter.[12] But we must attend to some additional work first: interpreting style, syntax, and semantics.

STEP FIVE: INTERPRETING STYLE, SYNTAX, AND SEMANTICS

The purpose of this section is to introduce the fifth step for interpreting the General Letters, which is the interpretation of style, syntax, and semantics. The multiplicity of authors and the employment of different amanuenses create a divergence of writing styles among the General Letters. Clearly, an author's literary style involves syntactical idiosyncrasies and semantic patterns. So, we pause to paint several portraits of three different author's preferred stylistic, syntactical, and semantic approaches to letter writing. The material will not only distinguish one letter from another, but the conscious awareness of a given literary writing style can pay great dividends for interpreting the General Letters. As we observed in chapter four, James had a stylistic idiosyncrasy concerning his synonymous use of the Greek terms for "man" (ἀνήρ and ἄνθρωπος). Thus, we ask: Are there other examples evident within the General Letters? As a result, step five involves painting a portrait of Hebrews *style*, Johannine *syntax*, and Petrine *semantics* to illustrate how such portraits help us make interpretive decisions. We begin with an examination of several stylistic issues in Hebrews.

Style of Hebrews

Westcott avers, "the language of the Epistle is both in vocabulary and style purer and more vigorous than that of any other book in the N.T. The vocabulary is singularly copious . . ."[13] Elsewhere he contends "The style is even more characteristic of a practiced scholar than the vocabulary . . . the language, the order, the rhythm, the parenthetical involutions, all contribute to the total effect."[14] Characteristic of the author of Hebrews'

---

12 See also Jay E. Smith, "Sentence Diagramming, Clausal Layouts, and Exegetical Outlining" and Herbert W. Bateman, "3 John: Tracing the Flow of Thought" both articles are in *Interpreting the New Testament Text: Introduction to the Art and Science of Exegesis* (Wheaton, IL: Crossway, 2006), 73–134, 449–61.

13 Brooke F. Westcott, *The Epistle to the Hebrews* (London: MacMillan, 1909), xliv. For a listing of words unique to Hebrews see Hebert W. Bateman IV, *Charts on the Book of Hebrews*, Kregel Charts of the Bible and Theology (Grand Rapids: Kregel, 2011), chart #s 100–102.

14 Westcott, *The Epistle to the Hebrews, xliv*. For another more focused look at the style of Hebrews see Niger Turner, *A Grammar of New Testament Greek*, vol. 4, *Style* (Edinburgh: T & T Clark, 1976, 1980), 114–20.

style is his repeated employment of two figures of speech: the inclusio and the chiasmus as well as the Greek grammatical period.

First, the inclusio, a figure of speech that brackets a passage of text with the same set of words at the beginning and end, occurs throughout Hebrews. For example, the author may bracket verses or entire sections by way of an inclusio.

1. Bracketing Verses by way of Inclusio

    Hebrews 1:5 and 1:13   This group of verses begins and ends with the repeated pre-
                            sentation of the Son positioned at the right hand of God.

    Hebrews 3:12 and 3:19   This group of verses begins and ends with the repeated pre-
                            sentation of the unfaithfulness of the wilderness generation.

    Hebrews 4:14 and 5:10   This group of verses begins and ends with the repeated pre-
                            sentation of Jesus as regal priest.

    Heb. 8:7 and 10:16–17   This group of verses begins and ends with the repeated pre-
                            sentation of the new covenant.

2. Bracketing Sections by way of Inclusio

    Hebrews 1:1 and 4:13   This literary section begins and ends with the similar gram-
                            matical period on God's Son and the periodic sentence on
                            God's word.

    Hebrews 4:14 and 10:23 This literary section begins and ends with the repeated ex-
                            hortation to hold fast.

Consequently, an awareness of this sort of literary feature, the inclusio, is helpful when trying to determine where to break verses or sections for teaching and preaching purposes.

Second, the author of Hebrews is partial to the literary chiasmus feature because chiastic structures seem to appear even more often than even the inclusio. A chiasmus is a figure of speech whereby several clauses (or concepts) are related to each other through a reversal of structure in order to make a larger point by way of an inverted parallelism. Often, this literary phenomenon provides balance within a particular text. In fact, there are numerous commentators who consider the entire letter to be chiastic.[15]

---

15 For example see: David Allen, *Hebrews*, NAC (Nashville: Broadman & Holman, 2010),
    Gareth Cockerill, *Hebrews*, NICNT (Grand Rapids: Eerdmans, 2011), Paul Ellingworth, *The
    Epistle to the Hebrews: A Commentary on the Greek Text*, NIGTC (Grand Rapids: Eerdmans,

1. <u>Chiastic Structure via Specific Words within a Verse:</u> Hebrews 1:5

    A   You are my son
          B   today I have become your father
          B' I will be his father
    A' and he will be my son

2. <u>Chiastic Structure via Specific Concepts within an Inclusio</u>: Hebrews 1:5–13

    A   The Son's Status as Davidic King: He is the heir of promise in Ps. 2:7; 2 Sam. 7:14 (1:5)
          B   The Son's Status as Divine: Creation honors him in Deut. 32:43 and serves him in Ps. 104:4 (1:6–7)
                C   The Son's Status as Divine Davidic King: His epithet and rulership are the same as God's in Ps. 45:6–7 (1:8–9)
          B' The Son's Status as Divine: He is Creator-King in Ps. 102:25–27 (1:10–12)
    A' The Son's Status as Davidic King: He is exalted (enthroned) at God's right hand (Ps. 110:1) (1:13)

3. <u>Chiastic Structure via the Intermixing Exhortation – Exposition:</u> Hebrews 12:14–29

    A   Exhortation: Do not fail to obtain the Grace of God (12:14–17)
          B   Exposition: You have not come to Mount Sinai (12:18–21)
          B' Exposition: You have come to Mount Zion (12:22–24)
    A' Exhortation: Do not refuse him who is speaking (12:25–29)

Whereas the first chiastic structure emphasizes the relationship between father (God) and son (Jesus) by way of two Old Testament passages (Ps. 2:7 and 2 Sam. 7:14), the second builds a case for and thereby spotlights the son's status as the divine Davidic king. In reality, Hebrews 1:5–13 is the author's scriptural validation for his prologue (vv. 1–4).[16] The final chiastic structure identifies the parallel units of the thought within chapter twelve. All three spotlight the heart of their respective contexts and

---

1993), Alan C. Mitchell, *Hebrews*, Sacra Pagina, vol. 13 (Collegeville, MN: The Liturgical Press, 2007); cf. Bateman, *Charts on the Book of Hebrews*, chart 20.

16   For a fuller discussion of this chiastic structure see "Psalm 45:6–7 and Its Christological Contributions to Hebrews," *TJ* 22NS (2001): 3–21.

are helpful for interpreting what is important to the author of Hebrews.[17]

Finally, the author of Hebrews favors the use of the Greek grammatical period (1:1–4; 2:2–4; 3:12–15; 4:12–13; 5:1–3, 7–10).[18] Here we wish to pause and pinpoint two particular features of the author's style, namely his propensity for both the chiastic structure and the grammatical period that are combined and thereby contribute to our interpretation of Hebrews 1:1–4. The prologue is an elegantly designed grammatical period and a well-proportioned chiastic that introduces to us the son through whom God has spoken recently (vv. 1–2c), who has exceptional credentials (vv. 2b–3e), and whose inherited name is superior to angelic beings (v. 4).

[1]Πολυμερῶς καὶ πολυτρόπως πάλαι ὁ θεὸς <u>λαλήσας</u> τοῖς πατράσιν ἐν τοῖς προφήταις
[1]Long ago in many and various ways God <u>spoke</u> to our ancestors by the prophets,

[2a]ἐπ᾽ ἐσχάτου τῶν ἡμερῶν τούτων <u>ἐλάλησεν</u> ἡμῖν ἐν υἱῷ,
[2a]but (ellipsis) in these last days, <u>he has spoken</u> to us by a Son

       [2b] <u>ὃν ἔθηκεν</u> κληρονόμον πάντων,
       [2b] <u>whom he appointed</u> heir of all things,

       [2c] <u>δι᾽ οὗ</u> καὶ <u>ἐποίησεν</u> τοὺς αἰῶνας·
       [2c] <u>through whom he</u> also <u>created</u> the ages

       [3a]<u>ὃς ὢν</u> ἀπαύγασμα τῆς δόξης
       [3a] <u>who is</u> the reflection of God's (ellipsis) glory,

       [3b] καὶ χαρακτὴρ τῆς ὑποστάσεως αὐτοῦ,
       [3b] and <u>who is</u> (ὤν, ellipsis) the exact imprint of God's very being,

       [3c] <u>φέρων</u> τε τὰ πάντα τῷ ῥήματι τῆς δυνάμεως αὐτοῦ,
       [3c] and <u>who sustains</u> all things by his powerful word,

   [3d] καθαρισμὸν τῶν ἁμαρτιῶν <u>ποιησάμενος</u>,
   [3d] <u>after he had made</u> purification of sins,

[3e] <u>ἐκάθισεν</u> ἐν δεξιᾷ τῆς μεγαλωσύνης ἐν ὑψηλοῖς,
[3e] <u>he sat</u> down at the right hand of the Majesty on high,

---

17   For a discussion on the chiastic structure of Heb. 15, see Victor Rhee (Sung-Yul), *Faith in Hebrews: Analysis within the Context of Christology, Eschatology, and Ethics*, Studies in Biblical Literature 19 (New York, NY: Peter Lang, 2001).

18   An extremely long sentence in Greek is known as a period (BDF § 458). Although the use of the Greek period is not unique to the Book of Hebrews, it does appear to be favored more so than any other author among General Letters. Greek periods also appear in other General Letters: 1 Peter 1:3–8, 14–16, 17–21; 1 John 1:1–4; Jude 5–7.

^{4a}τοσούτῳ κρείττων <u>γενόμενος</u> τῶν ἀγγέλων
^{4a}<u>he became</u> positionally much more superior to angels

γενόμενος
|
^{4b} <u>ὅσῳ</u> διαφορώτερον παρ᾽ αὐτοὺς <u>κεκληρονόμηκεν</u> ὄνομα.
^{4b} as the name <u>he has inherited</u> is more excellent than their name.

Although Hebrews 1:1–4 is one long sentence, it consists of eleven clauses. There are four independent clauses positioned to the extreme left and seven dependent clauses placed either below or above the word they modify. Notice how the clauses draw attention to the son's credentials, predominantly by way of several relative clauses. The first couple of verses, however, speak about God. During a previous era God revealed himself through prophetic writings (e.g., of dreams, visions, and encounters with angels), but in this new era God has revealed himself through a son (1:1–2a). Who exactly is this son? The subsequent clauses (1:2b–3b) reveal that the son is a king–priest (1:2b, 3d, e) who created and presently sustains the universe as one who is the reflection of God himself (1:2c, 3a, b, c). The prologue closes with a reference about the son's name being superior to the angels (v. 4). Consequently, the thrust of Hebrews 1:1–4 is located in the author's description about the son and underscored in a chiastic presentation. The center of attention in the chiastic structure occurs in Hebrews 1:3a (letter "D"), the relationship between God and son.

A   The son's superiority: The son is superior to former prophets (1:1–2c)
   B   The son's *appointment*: He is heir of all things (1:2b)
      C   The son's *relationship with the universe*: He created the created order (1:3a)
         D   The Son's relationship with God: He is the reflection of God's Glory (1:3b)
      C'   The son's *relationship with the universe*: He sustains the created order (1:3c)
   B'   The son's *appointment*: He is exalted (enthroned) at God's right hand (1:3d, e)
A'   The son's superiority: The son is superior to angels (1:4)

So it would appear teaching Hebrews 1:1–4 should focus upon the son's credentials. Both the structural outline and the chiastic structure drives us visually to focus upon the superiority of the son by way of his divine appointment as king-priest (v.2b), his apparent divinity via his creating and sustaining authority over all creation (vv.3a, b, c), and his self-sacrifice for the purification of sin as king-priest (v.3d, e).[19] Consequently, attention to a biblical author's *stylistic* idiosyncrasies can pay dividends for interpreting the General Letters.

Syntax of Johannine Letters

The syntactical idiosyncrasies of John are readily recognizable. We have already observed John's preference for the relative pronoun in 1 John 1:1–4 (see note #8), the πᾶς ὁ plus the participle construction that serves to divide people into one of two categories, and his prominent use of the asyndeton listed in the chart "Types (Classifications) of Independent and Dependent Clauses" (see above). So here we will focus on one other Johannine syntactical idiosyncrasy, his choice use of the prepositional phrase "in this" (ἐν τοῦτο) that serves to introduce independent clauses.

John loves to use the prepositional phrase "in this" (ἐν τοῦτο), which occurs fourteen times in 1 John (2:3, 4, 5 [2x]; 3:10, 16, 19, 24; 4:2, 9, 10, 13, 17; 5:2). It is, as Raymond Brown declares, "a frequent and most troublesome Johannine idiom."[20] To what does the prepositional phrase refer? Thus, whenever you see this prepositional phrase, you must ask yourself this question: Does "in this" (ἐν τοῦτο) refer to the preceding statement or to the statement that follows? John appears, however, to follow a specific syntactical pattern that helps us answer our question. In cases where a subsequent subordinate clause is introduced by "that" (ὅτι + indicative mood clause), "in order that" (ἵνα + subjunctive mood clause), "if" (ἐαν + subjunctive mood clause), "whenever" (ὅταν), or "from" (ἐκ), then the prepositional phrase "in this" (ἐν τοῦτο) will point to and thereby be defined by what follows in the subordinate clause. For example in 1 John 3:16 we read,

ἐν τούτῳ <u>ἐγνώκαμεν</u> τὴν ἀγάπην,
In this <u>we know</u> love,

---

19   The son's designation as "royal priest" is in keeping with the theological contribution of Hebrews more explicitly spoken of later, namely that Jesus is a royal-priest in the order of Melchizedek (5:5–6, 7:1–28). Prior to 586 BCE, the Davidite function was primarily as King over Israel, though he also did some functions of a priest. See E. H. Merrill, "Royal Priesthood: An Old Testament Messianic Motif," *BSac* 150 (1993): 50–61; idem, *Kingdom of Priests* (Grand Rapids: Baker, 1987), 263–67. Thus, we might say David was KING-priest. In this present age, he is king-PRIEST. This is not to suggest that Jesus has no authority (see Heb. 1:5–14, 3:2–6; cf. Eph. 5:23, Col. 1:18–20). The designation, however, distinguishes the different emphasis between the first temple and this present age. Kurianal argues in *Jesus Our High Priest* that in Heb. 7:26–28 "the two titles of Jesus, High Priest and Son are inseparably connected as the identity of the new High Priest" (New York: Peter Lang, 2000, [p. 158]). Eventually, the Son will rule as KING-PRIEST.

20   "In this" (ἐν τοῦτο) occurs 5 times in John's Gospel (4:37; 9:30; 13:35; 15:8; 16:30), 12 times in 1 John (2:3, 5; 3:10, 16, 19, 24; 4:2, 9, 10, 13, 17; 5:2) without counting 2:4 and 5 because "in this" (ἐν τοῦτο) means "in this person" in those two verses. See Raymond E. Brown, *The Epistles of John*, Anchor Bible (Garden City, NY: Doubleday, 1982), 248.

|ὅτι ἐκεῖνος ὑπὲρ ἡμῶν τὴν ψυχὴν αὐτοῦ <u>ἔθηκεν</u>
<u>that he laid</u> down his own life for us.

The independent clause is "in this <u>we know</u> love" (ἐν τούτῳ <u>ἐγνώκαμεν</u> τὴν ἀγάπην). It is placed at the far left with its main verb "we know" (ἐγνώκαμεν) underlined because it is an independent clause introduced by a prepositional phrase. We now need to ask two questions: How is the dependent conjunctive clause (ὅτι + the indicative clause) functioning syntactically and to what does the prepositional phrase "in this" (ἐν τοῦτο) refer? According to our rule, "in this" (ἐν τοῦτο) points forward to the dependent conjunctive clause (ὅτι + the indicative clause). Thus, the dependent conjunctive clause (ὅτι + the indicative clause) is *like* an adjective modifying or explaining the demonstrative pronoun,[21] "this" (τούτῳ), and the prepositional phrase "in this" (ἐν τοῦτο) points forward telling us a very profound truth: Believers know love (how?) *by means of* (ἐν) Jesus dying for us. A similar straightforward example exists in 1 John 4:9.

Yet there are many other times in 1 John when following this rule can be tricky (2:3, 5; 3:10, 19, 24; 4:2, 10, 13, 17; 5:2). For instance in 1 John 2:2 we read,

Καὶ ἐν τούτῳ <u>γινώσκομεν</u> (<u>ὅτι ἐγνώκαμεν</u> αὐτόν),
And in this <u>we know</u> (<u>that we know</u> him),

|
<u>ἐὰν</u> τὰς ἐντολὰς αὐτοῦ <u>τηρῶμεν</u>.
<u>if we keep</u> his commandments.

The independent clause is "and in this <u>we know</u> (<u>that we know</u> him)." Thus, this independent clause, introduced by a prepositional phrase, is placed to the far left with the main verb "we know" (γινώσκομεν) underlined. On the one hand, there is a dependent "that" (ὅτι) clause following "in this" (ἐν τοῦτο). Yet, when we ask how the dependent conjunctive clause (ὅτι + the indicative clause) is functioning syntactically, we must answer that it is the direct object of the main verb "we know" (γινώσκομεν) and answers what is known, namely we know "him" or we know God. Thus, the ὅτι + the indicative substantival clause is placed within parentheses and appears as part of the independent clause, namely the direct object of "we know" (γινώσκομεν).

On the other hand, there is another dependent clause following "in this" (ἐν τοῦτο). So once again we ask two questions of the third class conditional "if" (ἐὰν) clause: How is this dependent conditional

---

21   The semantic classification of this clause would appear to be appositional in that the conjunctive clause (ὅτι + the indicative clause) is cataphoric revealing the content of "this." Compare Wallace, *Greek Grammar Beyond the Basics*, 458–59.

conjunctive clause (ἐὰν + the subjunctive clause) functioning syntactically, and to what does the prepositional phrase "in this" (ἐν τοῦτο) refer? According to our rule, "in this" (ἐν τοῦτο) points forward to the dependent conditional conjunctive clause (ἐὰν + the subjunctive clause). Thus, the conditional clause (ἐὰν + the subjunctive clause) is like an adjective modifying the demonstrative pronoun, "this" (τούτῳ). The prepositional phrase "in this" (ἐν τοῦτο) points forward to the conditional "if" (ἐὰν) clause affirming truth. Believers know they have a relationship with God (how?) *by means of* (ἐν) keeping his commandments. In fact, the "in this" (ἐν τοῦτο) structure described above is an idiolect of John.[22] Consequently, attention to a biblical author's *syntactical* idiosyncrasies can pay dividends for interpreting the General Letters.

Semantics of Peter

Peter (or his amanuensis) apparently loves the participle. In 1 Peter chapter one alone, Peter employs over twenty-five participles, and of the twenty-five verses in chapter one, eighteen contain at least one participle.[23] The most striking semantic phenomenon of 1 Peter concerns his substituting the Greek participle for the Greek imperative verb. This sort of substitution seldom occurs anywhere in the General Letters. Peter, however, clearly favors formulating exhortations by way of the Greek participle on five different occasions in 1 Peter, upon which we will now focus attention. By way of these participial exhortations, Peter expects followers of Jesus within Greco-Roman society to be like Jesus within the home (2:18; 3:1, 7) and within the community (4:8).[24]

The first three examples concern followers of Jesus within the home:

---

22 A similar idiolect of John is the "this is" (αὕτη ἐστὶν) construction whereby the subsequent "that . . ." (ἵνα + Subjunctive Mood) is in apposition to the demonstrative pronoun (1 John 3:11, 23; 2 John 1:6) "Although not frequent," avers Wallace, "it is almost idiomatic of Johannine literature." Wallace, *Greek Grammar Beyond the Basics*, 475.

23 The participles in 1 Peter 1 may function grammatically in one of four ways: substantival: 1:12, 15; attributive: 1:3, 4, 5, 7 (?), 8, 12, 17, 20, 25; independent verb: 1:14 (?), 18 (?); adverbial: 1:6, 7 (?), 8, 9, 11, 13, 14 (?), 23 (?).

24 Discussions about "household codes" (e.g., *Haustafeln*) emerged among German scholars in order to categorize the duties and responsibilities of a private household. The general consensus about the "household" within Greco-Roman society is that it was *pater familias* (a "father of the family"), which means the father had absolute authority and control over his entire household. A household generally consisted of the wife (or wives and concubines), children (by blood or adopted), close relatives, and slaves. Yet New Testament texts do not give absolute power to men, but rather requires a high degree of responsibility and mutual respect for all members living as a family (see Col. 3:12–4:1; Eph. 5:15–6:9). In 1 Peter 2:18–3:7 the Christlike winsome attitude to be exhibited by all family members while living among those who do not follow Jesus is that of submission.

slaves and wives are to be submissive (2:18; 3:1) and husbands are to be understanding and to show honor to their wives (3:7). Thus, the participles "submitting" (ὑποτασσόμεναι), "understanding" (συνοικοῦντες), and "showing" (ἀπονέμοντες) are all grammatically independent participles expressing an expectation; they serve as the controlling verbs of independent clauses, and they are placed to the extreme left of the structural outlines below.[25] We will skip 1 Peter 2:18 because of limited space, and we will focus attention on the household codes between the wife and husband (see "Household Codes," pp.80–84). Notice how Peter's propensity to use the participle continues in chapter three. These three verses present three participles as independent with imperatival force (3:1a, 7a, 7b) and one as adverbial with temporal force (3:2).

^{3:1a} Ὁμοίως [αἱ] γυναῖκες <u>ὑποτασσόμεναι</u> τοῖς ἰδίοις ἀνδράσιν,

^{3:1a} In the same way, wives, <u>be subject</u> to your own husbands

^{1b} καὶ <u>εἴ</u> τινες ἀπειθοῦσιν τῷ λόγῳ

^{1b} even <u>if</u> some are disobedient to the word

^{1c} <u>ἵνα</u> . . . διὰ τῆς τῶν γυναικῶν ἀναστροφῆς ἄνευ λόγου <u>κερδηθήσονται</u>

^{1c} so that . . . they might be won over without words through the life of the wife

² <u>ἐποπτεύσαντες</u> τὴν ἐν φόβῳ ἁγνὴν ἀναστροφὴν ὑμῶν.

² *when they see* your pure and reverent conduct

^{3:7a} Οἱ ἄνδρες ὁμοίως <u>συνοικοῦντες</u> κατὰ γνῶσιν ὡς ἀσθενεστέρῳ σκεύει τῷ γυναικείῳ

^{3:7a} Husbands, in the same way, <u>be understanding</u> to your wives as to the weaker, female vessel

^{7b} <u>ἀπονέμοντες</u> τιμήν ὡς καὶ συγκληρονόμοις χάριτος ζωῆς,

^{7b} *and* (ellipsis) <u>show</u> them honor

^{7c} <u>εἰς τὸ</u> μὴ <u>ἐγκόπτεσθαι</u> τὰς προσευχὰς ὑμῶν.

^{7c} *so that* nothing <u>will hinder</u> your prayers.

On the one hand, the expectation of the wife anticipates an excuse. Suppose my husband is not following Jesus? Should I still be submissive? Peter's focus "even if" (καὶ εἴ, ascensive conjunction) is precisely

---

25 Although some like Achtemeier may debate whether these participles are independent participles with imperatival force, most acknowledge commentators and translations recognize their syntactical independence as the main structural marker of their respective clauses. Compare Paul J. Achtemeier, *1 Peter*, Hermeneia (Minneapolis: Fortress, 1996), 205–11 with Karen H. Jobes, *1 Peter*, BECNT (Grand Rapids: Baker, 2001), 202–12.

the point. A wife's readiness to surrender herself to her husband was with the hopeful *result* that (ἵνα) she might be a winsome witness to her husband. On the other hand, the expectation of the husband, who during the first century was considered to have the most power and authority within the household, was to be considerate to his wife (whether a believer or not) with the *result* that (εἰς τὸ . . . ἐγκόπτεσθαι) his prayers would not be hindered.

One final example where Peter substitutes the Greek participle for the Greek imperative verb occurs in 1 Peter 4:8, where Peter focuses attention on an expectation of the followers of Jesus within the community. Once again, the independent participle expressing an expectation serves as the controlling verb of the independent clause, and thus, it is placed to the extreme left of the structural outline.

^{4:8a} πρὸ πάντων τὴν εἰς ἑαυτοὺς ἀγάπην ἐκτενῆ <u>ἔχοντες</u>,

^{4:8a} Above all, <u>maintain constant</u> love for one another,

> ^{8b} <u>ὅτι</u> ἀγάπη <u>καλύπτει</u> πλῆθος ἁμαρτιῶν·
> ^{8b} <u>*because*</u> love <u>covers</u> a multitude of sins (4:8)

Peter's propensity to employ the participle as an independent verb with an unusual imperatival force leads to some situations where similar semantic interpretations of the participle in our English translations conflict with one another. Two examples are worthy of our consideration. One occurs in 1 Peter 1:14–16. While some translations render the participle "conforming" (συσχηματιζόμενοι) as though it were an independent participle of command (RSV, NRSV, NASB, NIV, NET, NLT), others render the participle as though it were adverbial to the imperative verb "be" (γενήθητε), and thereby a dependent clause (KJV, NKJV). After wrestling with 1 Peter 1:14–16, the participle "conforming" (συσχηματιζόμενοι; v 14b) is identified in the structural outline as an independent participle with imperatival force and parallel to the imperative verb "be" (γενήθητε; v 15b) with the subsequent scriptural reasoning for being holy (v 16; cf. Lev. 11:44; 19:2; 20:7–8, 26).[26]

^{14a} ὡς τέκνα ὑπακοῆς,

^{14a} like obedient children,

^{14b} μὴ <u>συσχηματιζόμενοι</u> ταῖς πρότερον ἐν τῇ ἀγνοίᾳ ὑμῶν ἐπιθυμίαις,

^{14b} <u>do</u> not <u>conform</u> to evil desires pursued in your ignorance,

---

26   Because of space limitations, the comparative phrase "like obedient children" (ὡς τέκνα ὑπακοῆς) and the prepositional phrase "according to the holy one who called you" (κατὰ τὸν καλέσαντα ὑμᾶς ἅγιον) are placed on separated lines above the verbal/verb they modify.

^{15a} <u>ἀλλὰ</u> κατὰ τὸν καλέσαντα ὑμᾶς ἅγιον
^{15a} but according to the holy one who called you,

^{15b} καὶ αὐτοὶ ἅγιοι ἐν πάσῃ ἀναστροφῇ <u>γενήθητε</u>,
^{15b} *you* also <u>be holy</u> yourselves in all *your* conduct,

^{16a} <u>διότι γέγραπται</u>, (Ἅγιοι <u>ἔσεσθε</u>),
^{16a} <u>for it is written</u>, (You will be holy)

^{16b} <u>ὅτι</u> ἐγὼ ἅγιος.
^{16b} <u>because</u> I *am* holy.

Another example occurs in 1 Peter 5:6–7. While some translations render the participle "casting" (ἐπιρίψαντες) as though it were an independent imperatival participle of command (RSV, NRSV, NIV, NLT), others render the participle as though it were adverbial to the imperative verb "humble" (ταπεινώθητε). It then is a dependent clause (KJV, NKJV, NASB, NET). As you examine the following structural outline for 1 Peter 5:6–7, notice the following items: the single independent clause governed by the imperative verb "humble yourself" (ταπεινώθητε), the adverbial conjunctive dependent clause "*in order that*" (ἵνα), the adverbial participial dependent clause "*by* casting" (ἐπιρίψαντες), and the adverbial conjunctive dependent clause "because he cares" (ὅτι . . . μέλει).[27]

^{6a} <u>ταπεινώθητε</u> οὖν ὑπὸ τὴν κραταιὰν χεῖρα τοῦ θεοῦ,
^{6a} <u>Humble yourself</u>, therefore, under the mighty hand of God,

^{6b} <u>ἵνα</u> ὑμᾶς <u>ὑψώσῃ</u> ἐν καιρῷ,
^{6b} <u>in order that</u> in due time <u>he may exalt</u> you,

^{7a} πᾶσαν τὴν μέριμναν ὑμῶν <u>ἐπιρίψαντες</u> ἐπ᾿ αὐτόν,
^{7a} <u>*by* casting</u> all your cares upon him.

^{7b} <u>ὅτι</u> αὐτῷ <u>μέλει</u> περὶ ὑμῶν.
^{7b} <u>because he cares</u> for you.

Obviously, the Greek word order as well as syntactical relationships between the clauses in 1 Peter 1:14–16 and 5:6–7 are both complex and cumbersome. So how are we to discern whether the

---

27 We might trace Peter's flow of thought in this manner: Expectation: Humble yourselves (ταπεινώθητε) under his mighty hand; purpose: *in order* that (ἵνα) God might exalt (ὑψώσῃ) believers in due time; how are believers to humble themselves: by casting (ἐπιρίψαντες) all their cares on him; why: *because* God cares (ὅτι . . . μέλει) for believers.

participles "conforming" (συσχηματιζόμενοι) and "casting" (ἐπιρίψαντες) are functioning as independent verbs with imperatival force
or adverbially expressing how to be holy (συσχηματιζόμενοι, "by
conforming"; ptc of means), or how to be humble (ἐπιρίψαντες, "by
casting"; ptc of means)? On the one hand, the use of the participle
with imperatival force is a striking idiomatic semantic phenomenon
of 1 Peter. On the other hand, the occurrence of the participle with
imperatival force is rare.

So then, how might we resolve the interpretive conflict? The fact
that the participle with imperatival force is rare forces me to first look
for a more common possibility. Without a doubt, a more common
phenomenon is the frequent occurrence of adverbial participles, not
the independent participles with imperatival force. Furthermore,
most English translations that render "conforming" (συσχηματιζόμενοι) and "casting" (ἐπιρίψαντες) as imperatives tend to be more concerned with a readable English rendering rather than with semantics.
Nevertheless can we translate the participles in 1 Peter 1:14–16 and
5:6–7 as adverbial in a readable manner? While I was unable to generate a readable rendering for 1 Peter 1:14–16, I was able to do so for 1
Peter 5:6–7. So at this point in my study, 1 Peter 1:14 may be another
example (though debatable) of an imperatival participle, and 5:6 is
not. Therefore, Peter's multifaceted use of the participle suggests that
both renderings appear to be viable options. Consequently, attention
to a biblical author's semantic idiosyncrasies can pay great dividends
for interpreting the General Letters.

Obviously, more could be said concerning interpreting style, syntax, and semantics, but we need to pursue interpreting Greek words
in the General Letters. In summary, we noted the existence of divergent writing styles among the authors who wrote the General Letters.
We then observed the author of Hebrews' *stylistic* use of the inclusio, chiastic structuring, and the period; the *syntactical* idiolect of John
concerning the prepositional phrase "in this" (ἐν τούτῳ); and Peter's
semantic preference for substituting Greek participles for the Greek
imperative. Consequently, attention to a biblical author's stylistic,
syntactical, and semantic idiosyncrasies proved profitable for interpreting the General Letters.

STEP SIX: INTERPRETING GREEK WORDS

The purpose of this section is to introduce the sixth step for interpreting the General Letters, which is the interpretation of Greek
words. As you know, words are essential for communication, whether
we are exchanging facts or expressing emotion. Words, however, are
merely symbols with a variety of meanings. Consequently, words

do not inherently possess meaning; they simply convey meaning. Furthermore, words are shared symbols in that they communicate a variety of meanings and can be easily misinterpreted.[28] For instance, the word "apple" could be a fruit or a computer. Furthermore, words do not have to be logical to communicate meaning. For example, to say 9/11 is literally two numbers, a way to refer to September eleventh as a day in the calendar year, and a coined figure of speech for a "terrorist attack" on America (2001). Thus, words tend to have various levels of meaning.

The goal in studying a Greek word is to determine the biblical author's intended meaning of a symbol in his specific literary context. Consequently, we study words in order to determine the best meaning of a word in a given biblical context because what a word might mean and what it does mean are *not* the same. The challenge, however, is to prevent reading twenty-first century presuppositions and traditional church expressions on the biblical author's intended meaning. So in step six, we learn "how to choose" a Greek word to study, and then advance to studying three Greek words in Jude.

How to Choose a Word

Determining what words are worthy of study is easy. First, study words whose English lexical definition is unclear. In other words, if English translations cannot agree on how to define a word, then study it yourself. Second, study words that have apparent synonyms or antonyms in the text.[29] Are there real synonyms and antonyms in the text? Are they true synonyms and antonyms or is there a nuance difference between the terms? Third, study rarely used Greek words.[30] Are they words that are used only one time in the New Testament

---

28 Carson addresses several "common fallacies that repeatedly crop up when preachers and others attempt word studies of biblical terms." See D. A. Carson, *Exegetical Fallacies*, 2nd ed. (Grand Rapids: Baker, 1996), 27–64.

29 There are many Greek words that have synonyms. In chapter one, we examined four for expressing love: (1) στέργω, (2) ἔρος, (3) φιλέω, and (4) ἀγαπάω. Yet, we render all four of these terms with one word, "love."

30 In Hebrews 2:1, the verb παραρρέω is unique to Hebrews. Defined frequently as "drift away" (NASB, RSV, NIV, ESV, NET, NLT), commentators tend to give *the verb* a nautical nuance (Westcott, 37; Bruce, 27). Yet, an alternative rendering is "slip away" (KJV). In the LXX, Proverbs 3:21 uses the verb to translate the Hebrew word *lavâ* ("lose from sight"). Immediately following twenty verses of instruction (Prov. 3:1–20), the author exhorts: "Son, let not my words of wisdom escape from your sight, but pay attention to my counsel and understanding" or "Son, let not (my words of wisdom) slip away from your eyes" (cf. Prov. 4:21; *TDOT*, 7:478–79). Although both "slip away" and "drift away" are possible, the author's exhortation to pay attention to what was spoken through the Son (1.2a), about the Son (1:2b–4), and to the Son (1:5–13) appears to favor "slip away." Do not let the teachings about the son slip away.

(*hapax legomena*)? Are they unique words used by an author throughout his letter? Fourth, study words that seem to carry conceptual or
theological weight.[31] What is the biblical author's theological point?
How does its contextual use contribute to or challenge our theological presuppositions? Fifth, study words that could be either figurative or literal. Does an author use a Greek term figuratively on more
than one occasion with a different figurative nuance? Finally, study
words whose meaning substantially affects the exegesis of the passage.
Whatever Greek word is chosen for study, there are three objectives,
according to Darrell Bock, for interpreting its meaning.[32]

1. The exegete must initially pursue the meaning intended by the author for the original audience.

2. The exegete must establish the precise meaning of a word by first
   recognizing its possible range of meanings.

3. The exegete must recognize that words operate in a context and
   receive meaning from that context.

In order to execute Bock's three objectives in the subsequent "how-
to" demonstration for studying three Greek words in Jude, certain
steps and resources are essential. Because each word study is presented
in an abbreviated format (as were those in note #s 27–29), the step-
by-step approach followed is provided in the excursus to guide future
Greek word studies.

---

31   The Greek word "I forgive" (ἀφίημι) in 1 John 1:9 rarely occurs in the LXX and secular
      Greek to speak of the "forgiveness" of an offense or "sins" (cf. "forgiven his guilt": *Her.*
      6.30; "acquit": Plato *Leg.* 9.869; Jos *Ant.* 14.9.5 § 185, *War* 1.8.9 § 214; "pardon": Jos *War* 1.
      24. 4 § 481). Yet, Philo employs the term in a religious context to speak of the "liberation"
      of one's soul (*Her.* 273) and the "remission" of sins (*Mos.* 2:147; *Spec.* 1:190, 215). In fact,
      Philo's latter usage is very similar to the NT in that "forgiveness" is almost always qualified
      as "forgiveness *of sins*" (*hamartion*; Matt. 26:28; Mark 1:4; Luke 3:3, 12:47; Acts 5:31, 10:43,
      13:38, 26:18; Col. 1:14; cf. Luke 1:77; Acts 2:38; Eph. 1:7; Heb. 10:18). In 1 John 1:9, it is
      used to highlight the reality that divine "release" or "pardon" of an individual's or perhaps
      a community's offense (or shall we say "sin") *is dependent upon confession:* "assuming ("if"
      1st class condition) we *confess* our sin, *then* God is faithful to pardon our offenses." The
      point is simply this: forgiveness of one's wrong-doing is dependent upon one's confession or
      repentance of it.

32   I am indebted to Darrell Bock for my approach to studying Greek words. For a more
      detailed presentation see Darrel L. Bock, "Lexical Analysis: Studies in Words" in
      Interpreting the New Testament Text: Introduction to the Art and Science of Exegesis (Wheaton,
      IL: Crossway, 2006), 135–53.

Excursus: How to Trace the Range of Meaning for a Greek Word	
Study Classical Greek Usage	First, identify (if any) the classical usage of your chosen Greek word. Search all the definitions that come from 300 BCE and earlier in Liddell-Scott (Classical Greek Lexicon). Then while listing each definition separately, employ the classical author's definition. Using Liddell-Scott's indices, identify the author, the work, and the date for each example. Then group the definitions into categories. Think why the categories differ and be aware of the literal versus figurative uses. Finally in a single paragraph, describe the classical Greek usage of the term.
Study Septuagint Usage	Second, identify all the definitions that come from the LXX. If you own an electronic version of the LXX, this is a simple step. If not, search Hatch-Redpath (concordance to the LXX). Determine different definitional categories, but BE SURE TO GROUP SIMILAR USES TOGETHER because each use is not a separate category. The result should look like the categories one would find in a lexicon. Look for frequent meanings, meanings in relation to classical usage, new meanings, religiously influenced meanings, and figurative meanings. Finally in a single paragraph, summarize what you find. Note any comparisons with Classical usage and include religious or theological significant observations.
Study Koine Usage	Third, identify all the definitions that come from Koine sources (but not the NT). Begin with a search in Moulton-Milligan (extra-biblical Koine Greek sources) and Spicq's *TLNT*. Then search Josephus and Philo (electronic versions of these works make this step extremely easy). Be sure to take into consideration any definitions left over in Liddell-Scott that date 299 BCE to 100 CE. *Do not* use examples if they are later than 100 CE. Then create definitional categories for each distinct kind of meaning. List definitions, examples date for each category. Finally in a single paragraph, summarize the various meanings of the term, particularly, significant examples, comparisons to Classical, LXX, and Koine usage, new meanings, religious meanings, and figurative meanings where applicable.

Excursus: How to Trace the Range of Meaning for a Greek Word	
Study New Testament Usage	Fourth using your Greek software program identify *all* NT occurrences. If you do not have a Greek software program, search Moulton-Geden (concordance of the NT). Then determine different definitional categories, but once again BE SURE TO GROUP SIMILAR USES TOGETHER because each use is not a separate category. In a single paragraph, summarize the various meanings of the term, particularly, significant examples, comparisons to Classical, LXX, and Koine usage. You may decide to divide usage into Synoptics, John and his epistles, Acts, Hebrews, General Epistles, and Revelation. Do not neglect defining the term in the verse you are studying. Ultimately, you want to give a *periphrastic definition for the word as it is used in the passage you are studying*. Then check BDAG, EDNT, and TDNT.

Synonymous Terms

As we have seen, four Greek words (στέργω, ἔρος, φιλέω, ἀγαπάω) are typically translated with one English word, "love" (see pp 32–33). In a similar way, one English word "immorality" that appears in Jude translates two different Greek words (ἀσέλγεια and ἐκπορνεύω). Whereas the noun form of "immorality" (ἀσέλγεια) occurs ten times in the New Testament (Mark 7:22; Rom. 13:13; 2 Cor. 12:21; Gal. 5:19; Eph. 4:19; 1 Peter 4:3; 2 Peter 2:2, 7, 18; Jude v.4), the verbal form used substantivally ("those who are immoral," ἐκπορνεύσασαι) occurs only in Jude v.7. So, not only are these two terms good choices for a word study because they appear to be synonymous terms, the latter occurs only once in the New Testament (i.e., *hapax legomena*). Do they mean the same? Are they true synonyms that have the exact same meaning? Or is there a nuanced difference between the two terms? Consequently, we will focus attention on the noun "immorality" (ἀσέλγεια) and address the verbal "those who are immoral" (ἐκπορνεύσασαι) in our next example for studying a Greek *hapax legomena*.

Although various definitions exist among English translations, the general consensus appears to be that the Greek noun for "immorality" (ἀσέλγεια) speaks of improper behavior in very broad terms: "lasciviousness" (KJV, ASV, NAB, NRSV, NASB, WEB), "sensuality" (ESV), "a license for immorality" (NIV; cf. NLT^SE), and "a license for evil" (NET). "Debauchery" (*Wisdom* 14:26; Mark 7:22 [NET]) is yet another possible rendering because the term simply means a lack of self-constraint involving conduct that violates socially acceptable behavior, namely *self-abandonment*.

When considering extrabiblical sources, we discover a similar broad array of meaning for the Greek noun, "immorality" (ἀσέλγεια). While

Plato uses the term mostly to speak of wanton behavior (*Republica*, fifth and fourth centuries BCE), Josephus specifies immoral conduct to involve inappropriate language, the wickedness of governing officials, the inconsistent behavior of Herod's wife, the imprudent obstinacy of a soldier, and inappropriate sexual behavior.[33] Another first-century writer employs the term to speak of insolence (Philodemus, *Lib.* 42.12). So then, with an understanding that "immorality" (ἀσέλγεια) refers to a wide range of socially unacceptable behavior, we now ask: How does Jude understanding the word?

Jude attributes specific deeds of misconduct to the "godless" (ἀσεβεῖς) people throughout his letter. For instance, they reject authority (vv.8, 11), they slander others (vv.8, 10, 16), they grumble (v.16), they find fault with others (vv.16, 19), and ultimately they are self-seekers (vv.11, 16). Consequently, the Greek noun "immorality" (ἀσέλγεια) in Jude v.4 appears to be defined later in the letter to involve various sorts of wicked activities. The "godless" in Jude appear to be an audacious group of people that Judean believers are to avoid. Perhaps they are the very people who desire to revolt against Rome (see chapter 2). Thus, Jude's immediate context appears to support a broader typological interpretation of immorality, which involves unrestraint and self-indulgent behavior (vv.8, 10–13, 16, 19).[34]

Although the immoral *behavior* to which Jude speaks may include sexual perversion (v.8), it is not limited to it. Thus in contrast to some commentators, we concur with Kraftchick when he concludes, "we cannot say that the opponents were actually engaged in sexual misconduct."[35] Translations like "a license for evil" (NET), "wicked deeds" or "immoral *behavior*" appear to be the best three English ren-

---

33 Josephus' usage of the verb includes "inappropriate" language (*Ant.* 4.6.12§151), following a way of "wickedness" as a reproof to governing officials (*Ant.* 8.10.2§252), the *inconsistency* of Mariamne, which was not sexual (*Ant.* 16.7.1§185), of "wasteful behavior" (*Ant.* 17.5.5§110), of an "impudent obsceneness" of a soldier (*Ant.* 20.5§112), as well as for inappropriate sexual behavior: of a women who falls into "impurity" (*Ant.* 8.13.1§318), of Herod's feelings of "lust" (sexual?) for Cleopatra (*Ant.* 15.4.2§98), of Cleopatra's sexual lust for Anthony (*War,* 1.22.3§439). And yet, he too uses it to speak broadly of "lascivious behavior" of women (*War,* 2.8.2§121) and of "unlawful pleasures" (*War,* 4.9.10§562).

34 BDAG 141, ἀσέλγεια. Bauernfeind considers this self-abandonment to include heresy and apostasy (*TDNT* (1983), ἀσέλγεια). Some view their activities broadly as antinomian (Kelly, *A Commentary on the Epistles of Peter and Jude*, 251; Bauckham, *Jude, 2 Peter*, 38). Reese limit the term to immorality and violence (*2 Peter & Jude*, 40). Moo specifies the meaning to include "sexual misconduct, drunkenness, gluttony, and so on" (*2 Peter, Jude*, 230).

35 Kraftchick, *Jude, 2 Peter*, 33–34. Schriner wrongly limits the term to sexual immorality due to the angels and Sodom and Gomorrah (vv.6–7). They ignore the Jewish rebellion of verse 5 and the comparisons with Cain, Balaam, and Korah in verse 10. Furthermore, in New Testament vice lists, "sexual immorality" stand apart from "immoral behavior" or "licentiousness" (ἀσέλγεια; e.g. Rom. 13:13; 2 Cor. 12:21; and Gal. 5:19). Schreiner, 1, 2 Peter, Jude, 439.

derings. Thus, the Greek noun "immorality" (ἀσέλγεια) in Jude v.4
speaks more of "immoral *behaviors*" or "wicked deeds" that include a
wide range of possibilities (cf. 2 Macc. 2:26). So then, how is the verbal
form "those who are immoral" (ἐκπορνεύσασαι) in Jude v.7 similar to
or different from the noun "immoral *behavior*" (ἀσέλγεια) in Jude v.4?

Hapax Legomena

The Greek word translated "those who practiced immorality" (ἐκπορνεύσασαι) in Jude v.7, occurs only here in the New Testament.
Furthermore, our English translations of the verb cannot agree on
how to define the term. They tend to move from a vague form of
immoral conduct to some gross form of immorality: "immorality"
(NLT^SE), "fornication" (KJV, ASV), "sexual immorality" (ESV, NIV,
NET, WEB), "immoral sexual relations" (CEB), "sexual promiscuity"
(NAB), or "gross immorality" (NASB). So, the Greek word "I live immorally" (ἐκπορνεύω) is a good Greek word to study.

When considering extrabiblical sources, we discover that the verb "I
live immorally" (ἐκπορνεύω) does not appear in Classical or Koine Greek
sources. Nevertheless, it appears in the Septuagint (forty-four times) for
various literal *sexual* sins: premarital sex, whoredom or perhaps adultery,
sexual orgies, cultic prostitution, and marriage to a non-Jew; as well as
figuratively for describing Judah's national whoredom by their worship
of idols, or just a general form of lusting after things.[36] Consequently, this
specific Greek "I live immorally" (ἐκπορνεύω) would appear to take into
consideration an array of socially unacceptable *sexual behaviors that are extramarital.* In other words, they are sexual activities not in accord with God's
marital norm. And yet Jude v.7 expects the readers to remember ("remember" in v.5) the notorious immoral events of Sodom and Gomorrah.[37]

36 Literal Sexual Deviations: of premarital sex (Deut. 22:20–21); of sex with foreigners (Num.
    25:1; Philo, *Somn* 1:89); of Tamar and Gomer playing a whore or perhaps better an adulterer
    in Gomer's case (Gen. 38:24; Hos. 1:2, 5); of Northern Israel's sexual orgies (Hos. 4:18);
    of cultic prostitution (Ex. 34:15–16; Lev. 17:7; 19:9; 20:5; 21:9; Deut. 31:16), of Dan
    committing revolting acts of the Gentiles: chasing after wives of lawless men (T. *Dan* 5:5).
    Figurative Deviations: of worshiping idols (Judg. 8:27; 2 Chron. 21:11; Hos. 4:12–13; 5:3;
    Sir. 46:11); of Judah's national whoredom (Jer. 3:1; Ezek. 6:9; 16:16, 20, 26, 28, 30, 33;
    20:30; 23:3, 5, 30, 43); of general lusting (Num. 15:39; Judg. 2:17).
37 Although Josephus, in his retelling of the events of Sodom and Gomorrah, muses "they
    resolved themselves to enjoy these beautiful boys by force and violence" (*Ant.* 1.11.3–4 §
    200–04; cp Philo, *Abel* 122; *Somn* 1:85), Sodom and Gomorrah came to symbolize the sort
    of divine judgment to expect for any sinful city (Jer. 23:14; 49:18; 50:40): Jew (Amos 4:11;
    T. Levi 14:6) or Gentile (Zeph. 2:9). The DSS declare that "Just as the Sodomites were
    destroyed from the earth, so all who serve idols will be destroyed" (4Q221 f2i:3; cf. 4Q223
    224 f2ii:53). Later, Jesus equates Galilean rejection of him and his ministry in the cities of
    Capernaum as sin whose judgment will be more terrible than that of Sodom and Gomorrah
    (Matt. 10:15; 11:23–24; cf. Luke 10:12; 17:29; Rom. 9:29).

What sort of immorality is Jude actually recalling? In order to answer this question, let me pause and pinpoint a parallel structure within verse 7. (For the fuller discussion of Jude vv.5–7, see chapter seven.)

^{7a} [ὅτι] ὡς Σόδομα καὶ Γόμορρα καὶ αἱ περὶ αὐτὰς πόλεις . . . πρόκεινται δεῖγμα . . .

^{7a} similarly *that* Sodom and Gomorrah and the cities around them . . . are now set as an example . .

    ^{7b} τὸν ὅμοιον τρόπον τούτοις ἐκπορνεύσασαι

    ^{7b} that practiced immorality in the same way as these

        ^{7c} καὶ ἀπελθοῦσαι ὀπίσω σαρκὸς ἑτέρας,

        ^{7c} and that went after different flesh

The parallel of "that practiced immorality" (ἐκπορνεύσασαι) with "that went after different flesh" (ἀπελθοῦσαι ὀπίσω σαρκὸς ἑτέρας) compels me to move to our next word to study,[38] the figure of speech in Jude v.7c "different flesh" (σαρκὸς ἑτέρας) because it plays a noteworthy role in my ability to define the nuanced meaning of our *hapax legomena*.

Figure of Speech

Defining the word "flesh" (σάρξ) is also important because it affects how we understand Jude's nuance of "those who practiced immorality" (ἐκπορνεύσασαι). The challenge in defining "flesh" is heightened, however, because the participle "who went" (ἀπελθοῦσαι)[39] is joined with the subsequent phrase "after different flesh" (ὀπίσω σαρκὸς ἑτέρας). The entire clause is baffling. Thus, English translations offer various and rather negative interpretive possibilities for "different flesh" (σαρκὸς ἑτέρας): "gone after *strange* flesh" (KJV, ASV, WEB), "pursued *unnatural* desire" (ESV, NET), "pursued *unnatural* lust" (NRSV), "pursue *other sexual urges*" (CEB), or they describe the urban centers as being filled with "every kind of sexual *perversion*" (NLT[SE]; cf. NIV). Our question, therefore, is simply: what does "different flesh" (σαρκὸς

---

38   The term "who practiced immorality" (ἐκπορνεύσασαι) is an aorist active participle feminine plural nominative from ἐκπορνεύω that means, "I live immorally." Syntactically, the participle functions adjectivally modifying feminine plural nominative "cities" (πόλεις). Semantically, it is a constative aorist that merely identifies immorality as a whole with no particular emphasis on its beginning, end, or continuation.

39   The term that is translated "who went after" (ἀπελθοῦσαι) is an aorist active participle feminine plural nominative from ἀπέρχομαι that means, "I go after" or "I depart." Syntactically, the participle is functioning adjectivally modifying feminine plural nominative "cities" (πόλεις). Semantically, it is a constative aorist that merely identifies the act of attaining something, in this case man after men, as a whole with no particular emphasis on its beginning, end, or continuation (Wallace, *Greek Grammar Beyond the Basics*, 557–58).

ἑτέρας) really mean, and how might its interpretation contribute to the parallel clause "those who practiced immorality" (ἐκπορνεύσασαι)?

Typically, the word "different" (ἑτέρας) means another of a different kind, and "flesh" in Jude's literary context (σαρκός) is a figure of speech for "a person" or "a living being."[40] When considered in Jude's context about Sodom, Gomorrah, and the other Gentile cities, commentators and English translations are generally predisposed to one of two options. Going after "different (*strange*) flesh" indicate people having sexual desires for angelic beings while the other rendering "*unnatural lust*" is often taken to insinuate people who have homosexual propensities. Both are problematic. First, "different flesh" (σαρκὸς ἑτέρας) *may* support the possibility that people in these Gentile urban centers, specifically Sodom, "solicited sexual relations with transcendent figures" (cf. Gen. 19:1–2, 3–7).[41] Angels most certainly are of "different (*strange*) flesh" (σαρκὸς ἑτέρας).[42] Yet has the term "flesh," as a figure of speech, ever been applied to angelic beings? Furthermore, to limit the sin of these Gentile urbanites to the solicitation of sexual relations with visiting angels appears to contradict God's desire to destroy the cities *prior* to the angelic visitation: "So the LORD said, 'The outcry against Sodom and Gomorrah is so great and their sin so blatant that I must go down and see if they are as wicked as the outcry suggests'" (Gen. 18:20–21, NET), at which point Abram begins pleading with God not to destroy Sodom (18:16–33). Finally, the term "immorality" (ἐκπορνεύω) points to more than one sort of sexual misconduct. It also seems odd that sex with angels is absent from the list. Thus, limiting the figure of speech "different (*strange*) flesh" (σαρκὸς ἑτέρας) to desiring sexual relations with angelic beings seems too narrow in scope.

Second, the option that insinuates *only* homosexual behavior occurring at these Gentiles also appears too limiting.[43] For it seems more probable that "while Jude notes the sexual component of the sin," we

---

40 BDAG defines "different" (ἑτέρος) as "to be dissimilar in kind or class from all other entities" and cites speaking with another language (Acts 2:4; Isa. 28:11; 1QH 4.16) as an example (399d 2, ἑτέρος). The use of the noun "flesh" (σάρξ) for a "whole person" or "living being" is a figure of speech known as a synecdoche where the part is put for the whole (Gen. 6:12; Ps. 56:4(5); Isa. 40:5; Rom. 3:20; 1 Cor. 1:29).

41 See BDAG (102c 4 ἀπέρχομαι). Commentators who favor this view are Bauckham, *Jude and 2 Peter*, 54; Harrington, *Jude and 2 Peter*, 296–97; Hillyer, *1 and 2 Peter, Jude*, 243; Kelly, *Commentary on 1, 2 Peter and Jude*, 258–59; Kraftchick, *Jude, 2 Peter*, 39–40; Richards, *Reading 1 Peter, Jude, and 2 Peter*, 265–66.

42 Many commentators see a reversal of activity between the angels in verse 6 who go after women (human flesh) and the Gentiles in verse 7 who go after transcendent celestial beings. However, Jude v.6 says nothing about the sexual behavior of the angels but rather leaving their residence in heaven.

43 This view may be conveyed in the translation "pursued unnatural lust" (NRSV) or "other sexual urges" (CEB).

concur to some degree with Green's observations that, "he [Jude] high-lights the way such sin is a violation of the order of things."[44] Sexual misconduct is, as Green puts it, "the vehicle by which they had violated the order established by God."[45] What divine order or societal norm was violated? It would appear that the Gentile urbanites rejected God's acceptable practices of sexual intercourse (cf. Rom. 2:14), which most certainly involved more than the execution of sexual relations with someone of the same sex, which leads to my suggestion that "different flesh" (σαρκὸς ἑτέρας) speaks of one's spouse.

Scripture clearly employs the Greek word "flesh" (σάρξ) as a way to refer to a marriage relationship between a man and a woman, a hus-band and wife (Gen. 2:23; cf. Eph. 5:28–31). So, it would appear that rather than sleeping with *only* their wives (spouses), flesh of their flesh (cf. Gen. 2:23), Gentile urbanites went after "different flesh" (woman or man) and thereby practiced various forms of sexual whoredom that spans sexual activities like marriage to foreign women, premarital sex, adultery, prostitution, orgies, cultic prostitution, and homosexuality. Thus in a very broad sense, Jude v.7 draws attention to the sin within these Gentile urban centers that involved seeking sexual intercourse ("immorality," ἐκπορνεύω) with someone other than one's spouse (e.g., "different flesh," σαρκὸς ἑτέρας), which in turn maintains and solidifies the synonymous parallelism of the two clauses. Perhaps we might say Jude draws attention to a society's unhealthy orientation to "free sex."

So it would seem, in defining both the verb "those who practiced immorality" (ἐκπορνεύσασαι) and the figure of speech "different flesh" (σαρκὸς ἑτέρας) Jude speaks of *many sorts of socially unacceptable forms of sex-ual intercourse outside of a marriage relationship*, which includes marriage to a foreigner. Thus, the two synonyms for the one English translation "im-morality" have differently nuanced meanings in Jude. Whereas the noun "immorality" (ἀσέλγεια) is used broadly in Jude v.4 to speak of a group of Judean godless people as audacious, the verbal form of "immorality" (ἐκ-πορνεύω) used in Jude v.7 of Gentile urbanites of Abraham's time is more pointedly a reference to the sexual relations outside of God's marital norm.

---

44 G. Green, *Jude & 2 Peter*, 71–72. Green also muses, "As the angels abandoned their proper station (v. 6), so too, the inhabitants of Sodom, Gomorrah, and the surrounding cities 'indulged in unfaithful acts' . . . in sexual relations (Gen. 38:24; Lev. 19:29; Hos. 2:7; 4:13) or to indulge in acts of unfaithfulness with respect to God (Ex. 34:15; Deut. 31:16; Ezek. 2030; Hos. 1:2; 4:12; 5:3; Sir. 46:11))."

45 Ibid, 71–72. Furthermore, "The rabbis deemed the biblical prohibition against homosexuality to be one of the Seven Noachide Commandments, which apply to all nations of the earth (B. Sanhedrin 57b-58a) . . . the rabbis apparently saw homosexuality and lesbianism as almost unthinkable and only infrequently referred to such practices." *Dictionary of Judaism in the Biblical Period 450 B.C. E. to 600 C.E.*, "homosexuality." *Dictionary of Judaism in the Biblical Period*, 2 volumes edited by Jacob Neusner and William Scott Green (New York: Macmillan, 1996).

In summary, the goal of step six was to learn how to study a Greek word in order to determine the biblical author's intended meaning of a word in his specific literary context. Three well-chosen Greek terms from Jude (σέλγεια, ἐκπορνεύω, and σάρξ) were studied to illustrate how an English translation of two different Greek words (σέλγεια, ἐκπορνεύω) along with a figure of speech (σάρξ) may not necessary have the same nuanced meaning in English and thereby prevented our reading twenty-first-century presuppositions and traditional church interpretations on the biblical author's intended meaning.

Chapter in Review

Chapter five demonstrated that "Interpreting the General Letters" is not for the faint of heart because it is a multifaceted endeavor and demonstrated the hard work of exegesis by adding three additional steps to the three we learned in chapter four.

- In step four, we learned about structural outlines and then traced 2 Peter 1:3–11 flow of thought by transforming a list of independent and dependent clauses into a structural outline.

- In step five, we learned the importance of recognizing an author's style of writing, syntactical preferences, and semantic peculiarities for interpretation and then demonstrated each through the interpretation of *style* in Hebrews 1:1–4, of *syntax* in 1 John (2:2; 3:16), and of *semantics* in 1 Peter (1:14; 2:18; 3:1, 7; 4:8).

- In step six we learned the importance of studying a word in context and then demonstrated how to interpret three well-chosen words from Jude: the synonymous Greek terms typically rendered as "immorality" (ἀσέλγεια, ἐκπορνεύω) in English and a figure of speech "different flesh" (σαρκὸς ἑτέρας) in Jude v.4 and v.7.

COMMUNICATING THE GENERAL LETTERS

As we begin this chapter on "Communicating the General Letters," it is helpful to bear in mind that this chapter will complete our step-by-step approach to studying the General Letters. We began our step-by-step process in chapter four when we initiated a simple translation of the Greek text, identified key structural markers within our translations, and isolated and resolved major textual issues evident in the Greek text's apparatus. We then added three steps in chapter five interpreting structure; interpreting style, syntax, and semantics; and interpreting Greek words. Having done the initial interpretive work, this chapter advances to communicating exegetically, communicating the central idea of a text, and communicating homiletically. Like interpretation, communication is both an art and a science.[1]

As we shall see, communication of the text has the Greek clause at its foundation. As you know, we began grappling with clauses in step one and continued in step four. As we move to communicating exegetically, wrestling with Greek clauses is at the forefront of our discussion and remains an essential element for teaching what the biblical author of a General Letter actually wrote. It is therefore worth reiterating this natural sequential order.

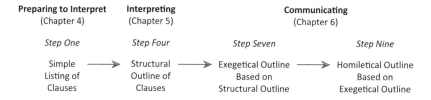

Preparing to Interpret (Chapter 4)	Interpreting (Chapter 5)	Communicating (Chapter 6)	
Step One	Step Four	Step Seven	Step Nine
Simple Listing of Clauses	Structural Outline of Clauses	Exegetical Outline Based on Structural Outline	Homiletical Outline Based on Exegetical Outline

Thus building upon what we have already learned in the previous two chapters, we now move to learning skills for communicating exegetically.

STEP SEVEN: COMMUNICATING EXEGETICALLY

The purpose of this section is to introduce the seventh step for interpreting the General Letters, which is to communicate them exegetically by way of an exegetical outline. We begin, naturally, with our structural outline. After creating a structural outline for a given passage, we take steps to convert it into an exegetical outline. The significance of this process is simply that all exegetical outlines begin at the bottom (i.e., *clause with structural markers underscored*) and work their way up by way of summary statements, grouping summary statements topically, grouping topical summations, and then producing an exegetical outline. Therefore, step seven will pursue four developmental phases:

---

1   Although this chapter's focus is communication not interpretation, interpretive decisions appear in footnotes to avoid scripture-eze (e.g,, restating the words of Scripture in outlines without interpretative understanding). Some examples may be found in footnote #s 6, 11, 13, 15, 18, 24, 25, 26.

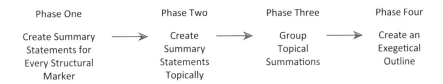

Phase One		Phase Two		Phase Three		Phase Four
Create Summary Statements for Every Structural Marker	→	Create Summary Statements Topically	→	Group Topical Summations	→	Create an Exegetical Outline

The General Letter chosen to demonstrate how to communicate exegetically is 3 John. The Greek of the letter is relatively easy; the structure is straightforward; the letter is short; and we can present an exegetical outline for the entire letter. Although presuppositions about 3 John will be minimal, there may be times of disagreement. Remember, communication is both an art and a science, it involves distinguishing the objective from the subjective, and entails an exercise in humility as we wrestle with the text together.

Creating Summary Statements

The most objective element of interpretation for any biblical passage occurs at the clause level with respective *structural markers clearly underlined* (e.g., the main verb of an independent clause and the *important* connectors along with the verbs or verbals of a dependent clause). When clauses are isolated and structurally outlined, we are able to *visualize* the biblical author's flow of thought, namely the basic grammatical and syntactical associations, parallelisms, as well as coordination and subordination of thought in a biblical text. Thus, we begin with a structural outline for 3 John vv.1–4.

1a ʽΟ πρεσβύτερος Γαΐῳ τῷ ἀγαπητῷ,
1a The Presbyter, to Gaius the beloved

        |

    1b <u>ὃν</u> ἐγὼ <u>ἀγαπῶ</u> ἐν ἀληθείᾳ.
    1b <u>whom I love</u> in truth.

2a Ἀγαπητέ, περὶ πάντων <u>εὔχομαί</u> (σε εὐοδοῦσθαι καὶ ὑγιαίνειν),
2a Beloved, in all respects <u>I pray</u> that you are prospering and that you are well,

           |

      2b <u>καθὼς</u> <u>εὐοδοῦταί</u> σου ἡ ψυχή.
      2b *just as* your soul <u>is prospering</u>.

3a <u>ἐχάρην</u> γὰρ λίαν
3a For <u>I rejoiced</u> greatly

   |

    3b <u>ἐρχομένων</u> ἀδελφῶν καὶ <u>μαρτυρούντων</u> σου τῇ ἀληθείᾳ,
    3b *when* the brothers <u>came</u> and <u>testified</u> to your truth,

³ᶜ <u>καθὼς</u> σὺ ἐν ἀληθείᾳ <u>περιπατεῖς</u>.
³ᶜ *even as* you are <u>walking</u> in truth

|

⁴ᵃ μειζοτέραν τούτων οὐκ <u>ἔχω</u> χαράν,
⁴ᵃ <u>I have</u> no greater joy than this,

|

⁴ᵇ <u>ἵνα ἀκούω</u> τὰ ἐμὰ τέκνα ἐν τῇ ἀληθείᾳ περιπατοῦντα.
⁴ᵇ *namely,* <u>that I hear</u> my children are *continually* walking in the truth.

With the structural outline before us we are ready to set into motion the first phase for creating an exegetical outline for 3 John vv.1–4.[2] We start by listing the structural markers. Because the structural markers were already underlined, listing them is a relatively easy task. We then move to creating a complete declarative statement for each marker that includes a chapter and verse notation at the end of *every* summary statement. Needless to say, we want to create as many individual statements as we need in order to cover the entire passage. Often the statements reflect interpretations, which are either in italic or footnote. Yet it is important that we identify the structural marker to the left of each statement.

Structural Markers	Summary Statements
(ellipsis)	John ***greets*** Gaius in a letter[3] (v.1a).
ὃν ... ἀγαπῶ	John *expresses* his love for Gaius (v.1b).
Ἀγαπητέ ... εὔχομαί	John ***prays*** for Gaius (v.2a).
εὐοδοῦσθαι καὶ ὑγιαίνειν[4]	The *content* of John's prayer is that Gaius <u>may prosper</u> and be physically <u>healthy</u> (v.2b).
καθὼς εὐοδοῦταί	The *content* of John's prayer is that Gaius's physical health

---

2 For my detailed explanation of the structural outline for verses 1–4 see "3 John: Tracing the Flow of Thought" in *Interpreting the New Testament Text: Introduction to the Art and Science of Biblical Study*, Darrell L. Bock and Buist Fanning eds. (Wheaton, IL: Crossway Books, 2006), 449–52.

3 Who is the recipient of the letter, Gaius? He is unknown to us, and yet well-known to the author (vv.1–2) in that he is a valuable ally in providing support for traveling Christian workers (vv.3, 5–8), and an apparent friend. Although the Apostolic Constitutions 7.46.9 (*ca.* 370 CE) states that John the Apostle ordained a person by the name of Gaius as bishop of Pergamum, the connection with the Gaius of 3 John seems dubious.

4 Why are the substantival infinitives (εὐοδοῦσθαι καὶ ὑγιαίνειν) set apart here? Obviously, the main thought of these verses is the prayer (εὔχομαί for Gaius (v.2). The infinitives function as the direct object (indirect discourse) of John's prayer. They also supply the content of the prayer, namely Gaius' financial prosperity (εὐοδοῦσθαι) and physical health (ὑγιαίνειν). Therefore, I have chosen to highlight the infinitives in order to draw attention to the content of John's prayer: that Gaius continues to experience prosperity comparable to his spiritual well being.

	may mirror his spiritual health (v.2c).
ἐχάρην	John *rejoices* (v.3a).
ἐρχομένων. . .	John's *rejoicing* occurred when believers brought news to him and
μαρτυρούντων[5]	his church about Gaius's spiritual lifestyle (v.3b).
ἔχω	John *has* joy (v.4a).
ἵνα ἀκούω	John *explains* that hearing about people's spiritual life always brings great joy to him (v.4b).

Significant features within this listing of structural markers are the summary statements and the corresponding verse notations. Whereas the **bold italic** word identifies the main verb of the independent clause, the plain *italic* word reflects my interpretation of the syntactical and/or semantic relationship of the dependent clause to the independent clause. Each statement is a succinct and accurate declarative statement about the clause. Do you see the three concepts communicated by the main verbs that are in bold italic? They are a greeting (v.1), a prayer (v.2), and two expressions of joy (vv.3–4). We will return to these three concepts below. The other italicized words in the subsequent summary statements reflect my syntactical and/or semantic interpretations because therein lies John's argument. As we shall see, the thrust is not that John prays for Gaius, it is the *content* of his prayer that captures the trained eye of an interpreter.

Grouping Statements Topically

An essential and thought provoking aspect of creating an exegetical outline is the ability to group individual statements topically. We will work in 3 John vv.5–8 to demonstrate this phase of communicating exegetically. So, we start once again with our structural outline. We then list structural markers with a complete declarative sentence that succinctly summarizes each marker with a chapter and verse notation at the end of *every* summary statement.

[5a] Ἀγαπητέ, πιστὸν ποιεῖς

[5a] Beloved, you *continually* demonstrate faithfulness

|

[5b] ὃ ἐὰν ἐργάσῃ εἰς τοὺς ἀδελφοὺς καὶ τοῦτο ξένους,

[5b] in whatever you do for the brothers, and strangers at that,

---

5   Why is "*even as* you are walking" (καθὼς . . . περιπατεῖς) not represented in the above listing of clauses? When I first listed and summarized the clause, it appears to be a mere restatement of the previous clause "when they came . . . testified" (ἐρχομένων . . . μαρτυρούντων). So I decided to subsume the "even as you are walking" (καθὼς . . . περιπατεῖς) clause with "when they came . . . testified" (ἐρχομένων . . . μαρτυρούντων) clause.

τοὺς αδελφοὺς

|

⁶ᵃ οἳ ἐμαρτύρησάν σου τῇ ἀγάπῃ ἐνώπιον ἐκκλησίας,

⁶ᵃ who have testified to your love before the church,

|

⁶ᵇ οὓς καλῶς ποιήσεις προπέμψας ἀξίως τοῦ θεοῦ·

⁶ᵇ whom you will do well to send them on their way in a manner worthy of God;

⁷ᵃ ὑπὲρ γὰρ τοῦ ὀνόματος ἐξῆλθον

⁷ᵃ for they have gone forth on behalf of 'The Name'' (e.g. Jesus)⁶

|

⁷ᵇ μηδὲν λαμβάνοντες ἀπὸ τῶν ἐθνικῶν.

⁷ᵇ while accepting nothing from the pagans.

⁸ᵃ ἡμεῖς οὖν ὀφείλομεν ὑπολαμβάνειν τοὺς τοιούτους,

⁸ᵃ We, therefore, ought to support such people,

|

⁸ᵇ ἵνα συνεργοὶ γινώμεθα τῇ ἀληθείᾳ.

⁸ᵇ in order that we become co-workers in cooperation with the truth (e.g., Jesus).⁷

Structural Markers	Summary Statements
Ἀγαπητέ . . . ποιεῖς	John **commends** Gaius for his habitual support for itinerant preachers and teachers of God's word (v.5).⁸
οἳ ἐμαρτύρησάν	John points out that itinerant preachers and teachers _testify_ of Gaius' faithful support (v.6a).

---

6   What does John mean when he says, "The name" (τό ὄνομα)? First, it is a figure of speech (metonymy of adjunct) whereby τό ὄνομα is used here in place of the subject, which raises another issue. To whom does "of the name" (τοῦ ὀνόματος) refer? Two views exist. On the one hand, the expression could refer to God because it is a frequent substitute for the Tetragrammaton _Yahweh_ (Ps. 124:8; Isa. 30:27). This option would make good sense in 3 John, because in the previous verse the author has instructed Gaius to send the missionaries on their way "in a manner worthy of God." And yet in 1 John 2:12 the author wrote, "your sins are forgiven on account of His (Jesus') name." Furthermore in John's Gospel speaks of believing "in the name of Jesus" (cf. 1:12, 3:18). Here in 3 John v.7, it also seems "the name" is a reference to Jesus. Thus in keeping with Johannine usage, it seems itinerate preachers and teachers have gone out in _the name_ (τό ὄνομα) of Jesus.

7   For an explanation of my interpretation see "co-workers in cooperation with the truth (e.g., Jesus)," see footnote #15 "What does John mean when he says, "co-workers . . . with the truth" (συνεργοὶ . . . τῇ ἀληθείᾳ)?"

8   For the explanations of my interpretation of "habitual demonstrations of support" see footnote #19 "What is the basis of John's commendation?" and for my interpretation of "support of itinerant preachers and teachers," see footnote #11 "And strangers at that" (καὶ τοῦτο ξένους)"

οὓς ... ποιήσεις[9]	John **_exhorts_** Gaius to meet the needs of itinerant preachers and teachers in a manner worthy of God (v.6b).
γὰρ ... ἐξῆλθον	The _reason_ Gaius _is exhorted_ to meet the needs of itinerant preachers and teachers _is because_ they have given their lives to preach about _Jesus_ (v.7a).
(γὰρ) ... λαμβάνοντες[10]	The _reason_ Gaius _is exhorted_ to meet the needs of itinerant preachers and teachers _is because_ they accept nothing from unbelievers (v.7b).
ὀφείλομεν ὑπολαμβάνειν	Christians are **_expected_** to take responsibility for the support of itinerant preachers and teachers of God's word (v.8a).
ἵνα ... γινώμεθα	_The intention for John's expectation_ to support itinerant preachers and teachers _is in order that_ people become co-workers with _Jesus_ (v.8b).

As we ponder this list of succinctly stated summaries, we are about to enter phase two of communicating exegetically. We must pause to determine groups either by subject matter or by structural shifts where structural units of the passages are located. For instance, notice once again the three **_bold italic_** verbs for each of the independent clauses: **_commends_**, **_exhorts_**, and **_expects_**. Thus, there appears to be a commendation, an exhortation, and an expectation with subsequent clauses supporting each topic. With the concepts identified, the grouping process begins.

Two issues are at the forefront here: assemble all clauses that relate to each topic, and summarize clearly the coordination and subordination of thought derived from the dependent clause(s). As we focus attention on John's _commendation_ of Gaius, two statements appear to be associated with it. The latter comment appears to be the basis for John's commendation. So, they are both isolated from the other clauses and a subsequent topical summation is offered with an appropriate chapter and verse. Since John's subsequent comment appears to be an _affirmation_

---

9   For an explanation of my interpretation of this relative clause see footnote #12 "Whom you will do well' (οὓς καλῶς ποιήσεις)."

10 How is the participle "receiving" (λαμβάνοντες) functioning in this clause? At least two options exist. On the one hand, the participle "receiving" (λαμβάνοντες) could be adverbial as it is reflected in the structural outline. Thus, the adverbial force of the participle may be understood as either (1) temporal ("while accepting") or (2) of means ("by accepting"; so John Painter, _1, 2, and 3, John_ in Sacra Pagina Series, ed. by Daniel J. Harrington [Collegeville, MN: Liturgical Press, 2002], 370). On the other hand, it could be functioning as an independent verbal and thereby translated "and they accept" (NLT; Brown, _Johannine Epistles_, 712) and thereby provides a second reason (γὰρ) why traveling Christian workers merit support: they accept nothing "from unbelievers."

about Gaius' faithful support of God's servants (e.g., the thrust of John's commendation), a two-word remark to that regard is also present.

Structural Markers	Summary Statements
ποιεῖς	John **commends** Gaius for his habitual demonstrations of support of itinerant preachers and teachers of God's word[11] (v.5).
οἳ ἐμαρτύρησάν	John points out that itinerant preachers and teachers testify of Gaius' faithful support (v.6a).
Affirming Commendations:	The basis for John's commendation for Gaius is founded upon the testimony of itinerant preachers and teachers of his support (vv5–6a).

As we move to focus on John's *exhortation* (οὓς ... ποιήσεις), three statements appear to be associated with it. So these too are separated and grouped, and a subsequent topical summation is offered with its own appropriate chapter and verse. The latter two statements provide the reasons (γάρ) for John's exhortation. Thus, John's expectation is a *reasoned* one (γάρ; e.g., the thrust of John's exhortation), and a two–word remark once again precedes the summation.

Structural Markers	Summary Statements
οὓς ... ποιήσεις[12]	John **exhorts** Gaius to meet the needs of itinerant preachers and teachers in a manner worthy of God (v.6b).

---

11   "And strangers at that" (καὶ τοῦτο ξένους) is to be itinerant preachers and teachers to whom Gaius offered hospitality (cf. vv.8, 10). Paul and Peter were itinerant servants worthy of support (1 Cor. 9:4–12). The "strangers" appear to be the same people mentioned in v.3, who have brought John a favorable report concerning Gaius' hospitality, a report that is mentioned again in v.8 (cf. Rom. 12:13; 1 Tim. 3:2, 5:10; Titus 1:8, Heb. 13:2). Thus, these strangers appear to be vocational servants of God's word whom Gaius has offered assistance. Identifying who they are in the outline avoids scripture-eze. See B. F. Westcott, *The Epistles of St. John* (Grand Rapids: Eerdmans, 1966), 238; Brown, *Johannine Epistles*, 709; Painter, *1, 2, 3, John*, 369; Judith M. Lieu, *The Second and Third Epistles of John* (Edinburgh: T&T Clark, 1986), 105.

12   "Whom you will do well" (οὓς καλῶς ποιήσεις) is interpreted as an exhortation. Yet when we ask: "How is the relative dependent clause functioning syntactically," our answer is adjectivally modifying "the brothers" (τοὺς ἀδελφοὺς). Nevertheless, this clause is an example of a mitigated exhortation. Brown suggests that the use of καλῶς ποιήσεις ("you will do well") may be a standard way of introducing the whole purpose of the letter. See Raymond Brown, *Johannine Epistles* in AB (Garden City, NY: Doubleday, 1982), 710.

γὰρ . . . ἐξῆλθον	The *reason* Gaius is expected to meet the needs of itinerant preachers and teachers *is because* they have given their lives to preach Jesus (v.7a).
(γὰρ) . . . λαμβάνοντες	The *reason* Gaius is expected to meet the needs of itinerant preachers and teachers *is because* they accept nothing from unbelievers (v.7b).
Reasoned Exhortation:	The *reason* Gaius is **exhorted** to support Christian workers lavishly[13] *is because* they have given their lives to God's service and accept nothing from nonbelievers (vv.6b–7).

As we conclude, only two statements appear to be associated with John's *expectation* (φείλομεν ὑπολαμβάνειν), so these too are grouped together and a third and final topical summation is offered with its appropriate chapter and verse. Here, the latter comment reveals John's intention for his all-inclusive expectation. Since John's exhortation is an *intentional* one (ἵνα; e.g., the thrust of John's expectation), a comment stating intention precedes the summation.

Structural Markers	Summary Statements
ὀφείλομεν ὑπολαμβάνειν	John **expects** believers everywhere[14] to take responsibility for the support of itinerant preachers and teachers of God's word (v.8a).
ἵνα . . . γινώμεθα	The *intention* for John's expectation of all believers to support itinerant preachers and

---

13 The translation "support . . . lavishly" is an interpretation of "by sending them in a manner worthy of God" (προπέμψας ἀξίως τοῦ θεοῦ). The verb προπέμπω has the sense of to "help on one's journey with food, money, by arranging for companions, means of travel, etc., send on one's way" (BDAG 873c 2 προπέμπω). Furthermore it is frequently used in the NT in the sense of providing Christian workers with supplies to enable them to continue their journey to the next stopping place (Acts 15:3, Rom. 15:24, 1 Cor. 16:6, 11; 2 Cor. 1:16, Titus 3:13). Thus the manner by which these workers are to be supported *lavishly* (i.e., "in a manner worthy of God").

14 The universality of John's expectation is clear in his emphasizes "we" (ἡμεῖς) in this clause at the very beginning of the clause. Furthermore, it is a first person plural construction inclusive of all true Christians (see Wallace, *Greek Grammar Beyond the Basics*, 321–23, 393–99). Finally, ὑπολαμβάνειν (a complementary infinitive completing the thought of ὀφείλομεν, "I ought"), according to Delling, is not limited to hospitality but extends to even protecting those who are persecuted (*TDNT* ὑπολαμβάνw; cf. BDAG 1038c 2). Thus, all followers of Jesus are obligated or *expected* to offer various kinds of support to those whose vocation it is to proclaim Jesus, the Messiah.

teachers *is in order that* everyone can become co-workers with Jesus (v.8b).

Intentional Expectation:	John's *intention* for **expecting** all Christians to be in the habit of supporting itinerant preachers and teachers *is in order that* everyone can become co-workers with Jesus[15](v.8).

An evaluation of each topical summation reveals that the thrust of John's argument is found in the dependent clause. As a result, we are able to discern who, what, when, where, why, and the basis of the main verbal idea. Thus, the real subject is **not limited** to merely a commendation, an exhortation, and an expectation, but rather it incorporates the syntactical and semantic contributions the accompanying clauses make to the main verb (or topic). In other words, whereas **the subject** (main verb/topic) is what the text is discussing as *a point of focus*, **the complement** (subsequent clauses) is *what the text says about that subject*.[16]

Subject	The *basis* for John's **commendation** for Gaius . . .
Complement	. . . *is founded* upon the *testimony* of itinerant preachers and teachers of his support (vv.5–6a).
Subject	The *reason* Gaius is **exhorted** to support Christian workers lavishly. . .
Complement	. . . *is because* (γὰρ) they have given their lives to God's service and accept nothing from nonbelievers (vv.6b–7).
Subject	John's *intention* for **expecting** all Christians to be in the habit of supporting lavishly itinerant preachers and teachers . . .
Complement	. . . *is in order that* (ἵνα) everyone can become co-workers with Jesus (v.8).

---

15 "Co-workers . . . with the truth" (συνεργοὶ . . . τῇ ἀληθείᾳ) speaks of a believer. The συν- prefix of the noun modified along with an abstract concept like "truth" is a personification. In John 8:32, "the truth will make you free"; in 1 John 4:6 the Holy Spirit is 'the Spirit of Truth,' a characterization repeated in 1 John 5:6. (NET). Jesus describes himself as "the truth" (John 14:6). Thus, "the truth" (τῇ ἀληθείᾳ) in 3 John could be the Spirit or it could be Jesus. Context would seem to favor Jesus (e.g., "the name"). In order to avoid scripture-eze, Jesus is inserted in the outline. Thus, the author's theological understanding is that support of a traveling Christian worker results in becoming co-workers with Jesus. This conclusion differs from my workbook (*A Workbook for Intermediate Greek*, 54–55).

16 For another discussion about "subject-complement" statements, see Jay Smith's "Sentence Diagramming, Clausal Layouts, and Exegetical Outlining" in *Interpreting the New Testament Text: Introduction to the Art and Science of Exegesis*, ed. Darrell L. Bock and Buist Fanning (Wheaton, IL: Crossway, 200), 106–17.

So then, in this phase of communicating exegetically, we moved from listing summary statements to isolating three distinct topics within 3 John vv.5–8, grouped them accordingly, offered a subsequent topical (subject-complement) summation with appropriate chapter and verse, and underscored the thrust of each summation with a simple word or two. Note that there are no structural markers presented with the subsequent topical (subject-complement) statements, and yet the wording chosen within each coordinates with the subordinate statements with structural markers. Before we can actually create our exegetical outline, however, we need to complete one more preliminary phase: organizing groups of topical (subject-complement) summations.

Grouping Topical Summations

Now that individual statements with identifiable structural markers are grouped according to topic or subject matter, it is time to enter phase three of communicating exegetically, namely, organizing topical (subject-complement) statements into groups. In order to demonstrate how to group topical statements, topical statements for 3 John verses 1–4 have been added to those created for verses 5–8. Furthermore, summary statements with clearly identifiable structural markers are now beneath their respective topical (subject-complement) summations with the underscored thrust of the statement in bold type. Thus, there are listed below six groupings or six separate sets of topical (subject-complement) statements.

1. **Salutation to Gaius:** In typical first century format, John *greets* and *expresses* his love for Gaius in a letter (v.1).

   (ellipsis) John **greets** Gaius in a letter (v.1a).

   (ὃν . . . ἀγαπῶ) John *expresses* his love for Gaius (v.1b).

2. **John's Prayer:** The *content* of John's *prayer is that* Gaius might prosper and experience physical health that mirrors his spiritual health (v.2).

   (Ἀγαπητέ . . . εὔχομαί) John *prays* for Gaius (v.2a).

   (εὐοδοῦσθαι καὶ ὑγιαίνειν) The **content** of John's prayer is that Gaius may prosper (v.2b).

   (καθὼς εὐοδοῦταί) The **content** of John's prayer is that Gaius' physical health may mirror his spiritual health (v.2c).

3. **John's Joy:** The *basis* for John's *joy* about Gaius *is founded* upon *reports* about the manner in which Gaius is living for God (vv.3–4).

   (ἐχάρην) John **rejoiced** when believers brought news to him and his church about Gaius's spiritual lifestyle (v.3).

   (ἔχω) John **experiences great joy** when he hears about people's spiritual life (v.4).

4. **Affirming Commendations:** The *basis* for John's *commendation* of Gaius *is founded* upon the *testimony* of itinerant preachers and teachers of his support (vv.5–6a).

   (Ἀγαπητέ . . . ποιεῖς) John **commends** Gaius for his habitual demonstrations of support of itinerant preachers and teachers of God's word (v.5).

   (οἳ ἐμαρτύρησάν) John points out that itinerant preachers and teachers *testify* of Gaius' faithful support (v.6a).

5. **Reasoned Exhortation:** The *reason* Gaius is **exhorted** to support Christian workers lavishly *is because* they have given their lives to God's service and accept nothing from nonbelievers (vv.6b–7).

   (οὓς . . . ποιήσεις) John **exhorts** Gaius to meet the needs of itinerant preachers and teachers in a manner worthy of God (v.6b).

   (γὰρ . . . ἐξῆλθον) The *reason* Gaius is expected to meet the needs of itinerant preachers and teachers *is because* they have given their lives to preach Jesus (v.7a).

   ([γὰρ] . . . λαμβάνοντες) The *reason* Gaius is expected to meet the needs of itinerant preachers and teachers *is because* they accept nothing from unbelievers (v.7b).

6. **Intentional Expectation:** John's *intention* for *expecting* all Christians to be in the habit of lavishly supporting itinerant preachers and teachers is *in order that* everyone can become co-workers with Jesus (v.8)

   (ὀφείλομεν ὑπολαμβάνειν) John **expects** believers everywhere to take responsibility for the support of itinerant preachers and teachers of God's word (v.8a).

   (ἵνα . . . γινώμεθα) The *intention* for John's expectation of all believers to support itinerant preachers and teachers is *in order that* everyone can become co-workers with Jesus (v.8b).

As we consider grouping these six topical (subject-complement) summations, three details deserve attention. First, consideration should be given to the vocative, "beloved" (Ἀγαπητέ), which is clearly marked with bold type (vv.2a, 5). Second, remember that this letter has an opening salutation, a body, and a closing salutation (see chapter one). Third, be aware that this third phase will pay great dividends for creating our exegetical outline in that these final statements should reflect the author's progression of thought clearly and succinctly (about thirty words).[17] So based upon the vocative, "beloved" (Ἀγαπητέ), the genre, and the reality that whatever statement created here will become Roman numeral points of the exegetical outline, these six separate sets of topical statements (i.e., those without structural markers) are split in half and another summation is created for each new grouping of three. Thus, the first three topical statements may be summarized in this manner:

> In typical first century format, John **greets** his beloved friend, Gaius, and discloses both his **prayer** for and **joy** about Gaius' *faithfulness in supporting God's servants* (vv.1–4).[18]

>> **Salutation to Gaius:** In typical first century format, John *greets* and *expresses* his love for Gaius in a letter (v.1).

>> **John's Prayer:** The *content* of John's **prayer** *is that* Gaius *might prosper and experience physical health* that mirrors his spiritual health (v.2).

>> **John's Joy:** The *basis* for John's **joy** about Gaius is founded upon *reports* about the manner in which Gaius is living for God (vv.3–4).

Evaluating the summarization for the first three topical statements,

---

17   A general rule of thumb concerning the length of any given summary statement is about thirty words. Although there is no set rule, the attempt to limit statements to thirty words forces summary statements to synthesize material, to major on the majors, and avoid complex sentences.

18   *"Faithfulness in supporting God's servants"* is interpretive of the subsequent clauses. John prays for Gaius' physical prosperity and rejoices about reports about how he is living for God (his "spiritual health"). The reports about his manner of living for God (spiritual health) are that Gaius shared his wealth with God's servants ("brothers" and "strangers at that"; v. 5). Gaius faithfully met the needs of those who are preaching and teaching about Jesus.

the **bold italic** words in the summation (*greets, prayer,* and *expresses the joy*) reveal a corresponding coordination and subordination of thought for 3 John vv.1–4. Similarly, the next three statements may be summarized in this manner:

> While **commending**[19] Gaius for his faithful support of God's servants, John **exhorts** him to lavish support upon God's workers *because* their livelihood depends upon God's people, and thereby John's **expectation** is expanded to include all believers (vv.5–8).

> **Affirming Commendations:** *The basis* for John's **commendation** of Gaius *is founded* upon the *testimony* of itinerant preachers and teachers of his support (vv.5–6a).

> **Reasoned Exhortation:** The *reason* Gaius is **exhorted** to support Christian workers lavishly *is because* they have given their lives to God's service and accept nothing from non-believers (vv.6b–7).

> **Intentional Expectation:** John's *intention* for **expecting** all Christians to be in the habit of supporting lavishly itinerant preachers and teachers *is in order that* everyone can become co-workers with Jesus (v.8).

Once again, when evaluating the summarization for this second set of topical statements, the **bold italic** words in the summation (*commend, exhort,* and *expect*) makes plain the coordination and subordination of thought for 3 John vv.5–8. Bear in mind that no structural markers are present in these statements, and yet every summation has emerged from structural markers. In an attempt to stay within a thirty-word limit, the summation is selective and not exhaustive.[20] Thus,

---

19   The basis for John's commendation is in verses 3 and 4. The customary present of "you do" or "you act" (ποιεῖς) communicates a life-style of consistency or a pattern of behavior. Yet does Gaius "act faithfully" (NASB; cf. KJV, NRSV) or does he "demonstrate faithfulness" (NET)? The former considers πιστόν to be an adverbial accusative: "you act loyally" (BDAG 821 1b) or "you act faithfully" (Painter, *1, 2, 3, John*, 369). The latter renders πιστόν as though it were a direct object of ποιεῖς: "you will demonstrate fidelity" or "faithfulness" (Brown, *Johannine Epistles*, 708; or "you are faithful" (cf. Westcott, *Epistles of St. John*, 237). In either case, the absence of any New Testament parallel may be an intentional expansion of a common use of πιστόν, which Lieu describes as "an attribute or epithet of Christians" (*The Second and Third Epistles of John*, 105) and thereby idiomatic (for ποιεῖς itself cf. Matt. 25:21; Luke 12:42, 1 Cor. 4:17, Eph. 6:21, Col. 1:7).

20   Grouping subject-complement statements into larger conceptual units can be a daunting and even humbling task. It is at this point you must think synthetically about textual relationships,

there is no mention of John's stated intention for all believers to support God's vocationally called servants.[21] Yet, it still captures John's flow of thought. So then, after completing three phases of synthesizing 3 John vv.5–8, we are now ready to create an exegetical outline for 3 John.

Exegetical Outline for 3 John

As stated at the beginning of step seven, communicating exegetically begins at the bottom (i.e., clause with structural markers underscored) and works up by way of summary statements, grouping summary statements topically, grouping topical (subject-complement) summations, and then producing an exegetical outline. Can you visualize an exegetical outline unfolding for our summations, grouped topical (subject-complement) statements, and structural markers with summary statements for 3 John 1–4 presented below?

> In typical first century format, John *greets* his beloved friend, Gaius, that discloses both his *prayer* for and *joy* about Gaius's *faithfulness in supporting God's servants* (vv.1–4).

> > **Salutation:** In typical first century format, John *greets* and expresses his love for Gaius in a letter (v.1).

> > > (ellipsis) John *greets* Gaius in a letter (v.1a).

> > > (ὃν . . . ἀγαπῶ) John *expresses* his love for Gaius (v.1b).

> > **John's Prayer:** The *content* of John's *prayer is that* Gaius might prosper and experience physical health that mirrors his spiritual health (v.2).

> > > (Ἀγαπητέ . . . εὔχομαί) John *prays* for Gaius (v.2a).

---

look for changes in John's thought process, and realize there may not always be a single way of dividing the text. This fact will be evident when you consult commentaries. See also Smith's "Sentence Diagramming, Clausal Layouts, and Exegetical Outlining" in *Interpreting the New Testament Text*, 120–24.

21   In keeping with Os Guinness's *The Call: Finding and Fulfilling the Central Purpose of Your Life* (Nashville: Word, 1998), all followers of Jesus are called disciples created to serve God (see Eph. 2:10). Yet, all followers are also called vocationally: plumber, electrician, mechanic, carpenter, computer analysis, medical doctor, lawyer, politician, teachers, preacher/teacher, missionary. Those who are vocationally called preacher/teachers and missionaries are vocational servants worthy of support.

(εὐοδοῦσθαι καὶ ὑγιαίνειν) The **content** of John's prayer is that Gaius may prosper (v.2b).

(καθὼς εὐοδοῦταί) The **content** of John's prayer is that Gaius's physical health may mirror his spiritual health (v.2c).

John's Joy: The *basis* for John's *joy* about Gaius *is founded* upon *reports* about the manner in which Gaius is living for God (vv.3–4).

(ἐχάρην) John **rejoiced** when believers brought news to him and his church about Gaius's spiritual lifestyle (v.3).

(ἔχω) John **experiences great joy** when he hears about people's spiritual life (v.4).

As you examine the exegetical outline below, Roman numeral "I" is our summation for our grouped topical summaries with chapter and verse notation, the Arabic letters "A," "B," and "C" are topic (subject-complement) summaries with chapter and verse notations, and numbers "1" and "2" are structural markers followed by a summary statement with chapter and verse notation. Then examine Roman numeral "II" and compare it to what we suggested above. As you continue to work your way through the subsequent Roman numerals, can you visualize the text of 3 John? Are you able to trace John's train of thought?

I. **Salutation to Gaius:** In typical first century format, John **greets** his beloved friend, Gaius, and discloses both his **prayer** for and **joy** about Gaius' *faithfulness in supporting God's servants* (vv.1–4).

A. **Salutation:** In typical first-century format, John writes a letter to Gaius that expresses his love for him (v.1).

1. (ellipsis) John **greets** Gaius in a letter (v.1a).

2. (ὃν . . . ἀγαπῶ) John expresses his love for Gaius (v.1b).[22]

---

22   All those who share in life from God are brought into a relationship with one another, which then becomes the basis for and obligation of mutual love for one another (2:10; 3:10, 11, 14, 18, 23; 4:7, 11, 12, 20, 21). Thus, John's expectation to support God's vocationally called servants is an obligated act of love (3 John v.8).

B. **John's Prayer:** The *content* of John *prayer is that* Gaius might prosper and experience physical health that mirrors his spiritual health (v.2).

    1. (εὔχομαί) John *prays* for Gaius (v.2a).

    2. (εὐοδοῦσθαι καὶ ὑγιαίνειν) The *content* of John's prayer is that Gaius may prosper (v/2b).

    3. (καθὼς εὐοδοῦταί) The *content* of John's prayer is that Gaius' physical health may mirror his spiritual health (v.2c).

C. **John's Joy:** The *basis* for John's *joy* about Gaius *is founded* upon *reports* about the manner in which Gaius is living for God (vv.3–4).

    1. (ἐχάρην) John *rejoiced* when *believers brought news to him and his church*[23] about Gaius's spiritual lifestyle (v.3).

    2. (ἔχω) John *experiences great joy* when he hears about people's spiritual life (v.4).

II. **Solicitation of All Christians:** While *commending* Gaius for his faithful support of God's servants, John *exhorts* him to lavish support upon God's workers *because* their livelihood depends upon God's people and thereby the *expectation* is expanded to include all believers (vv.5–8).

A. **Affirming Commendations:** *The basis* for John's *commendation* of Gaius *is founded* upon the *testimony* of itinerant preachers and teachers of his support (vv.5–6a).

    1. (ποιεῖς) John commends Gaius for his habitual demonstrations of support of itinerant preachers and teachers of God's word (v.5).

    2. (οἳ ἐμαρτύρησάν) John points out that itinerant preachers and teachers testify of Gaius's faithful support (v.6a).

---

23 Is the church (ἐκκλησίας) (1) the church where Gaius is; (2) the church where John is; or (3) a different local church where the "brothers" worship? Since the "brothers" have come and testified to John (v.6) about what Gaius has done for them (see v.3), it seems most likely that the *church* mentioned in verse 6 is John's church where John worships. Thus, it seems that two churches have been mentioned thus far: Gaius' church seems to be implied (v.1; cf. v.15; ἀσπάζονταί σε οἱ φίλοι) and John's explicitly mentioned church (v.6).

B. **Reasoned Exhortation:** The *reason* Gaius is *exhorted* to support Christian workers lavishly *is because* they have given their lives to God's service and accept nothing from nonbelievers (vv.6b–7).

1. (οὓς . . . ποιήσεις) John *exhorts* Gaius to meet the needs of itinerant preachers and teachers in a manner worthy of God (v.6b).

2. (γὰρ . . . ἐξῆλθον) The *reason* Gaius is exhorted to meet the needs of itinerant preachers and teachers *is because* they have given their lives to preach Jesus (v.7a).

3. ([γὰρ] . . . λαμβάνοντες) The *reason* Gaius is exhorted to meet the needs of itinerant preachers and teachers *is because* they accept nothing from unbelievers (v.7b).

C. **Intentional Expectation:** John's *intention* for all Christians to be in the habit of lavishly supporting itinerant preachers and teachers is *in order that* everyone can become co-workers with them (v.8).

1. (ὀφείλομεν ὑπολαμβάνειν) John *expects* believers everywhere to take responsibility for the lavish support of itinerant preachers and teachers of God's Word (v.8a).

2. (ἵνα . . . γινώμεθα) The *intention* for John's expectation of all believers to support itinerant preachers and teachers lavishly *is in order that* everyone can become co-workers with Jesus (v.8b).

III. **Stubbornness of Diotrephes:** The *basis* for John's *concern* about and the resistance from Diotrephes *is founded* upon Diotrephes' *rejection* of John's authority and *refusal* to support God's workers (vv.9–10).

A. **John's Concern:** The *basis* for John's *concern is founded* upon Diotrephes' rejection of a letter in which John addressed the issue of supporting God's workers (v.9).

1. (Ἔγραψά) John wrote a *similar letter*[24] to a sister church in the area (v.9a).

---

24 John's letter to Diotrephes is surmised from "I wrote" (Ἔγραψά, constative aorist: KJV, NASB, NIV, NET) or "I have written" (epistolary aorist: NRSV) "something (τι) to the church" (τῇ ἐκκλησίᾳ). It seems "something" (τι) may be a lost or a destroyed letter written

2. (ἀλλ᾽ . . . οὐκ ἐπιδέχεται) Diotrephes, a leader in that church, rejected John's expectations to support itinerant preachers and teachers of God's Word (v.9b).

B. **Diotrephes' Stubbornness:** The *basis* for John's charges of Diotrephes' rejection *is founded* in his slander of John, his refusal to support workers, his hindering others who support workers, and his excommunicating people who support God's workers (v.10).

   1. **The Ridicule of Diotrephes:** The *means* by which Diotrephes' *rejects* John's authority and expectation *is by* ridiculing him and others (v.10a–c).

      a. (ὑπομνήσω) John intends to address Diotrephes' rejections (v.10a).

      b. (ἃ ποιεῖ) John points out that Diotrephes rejects his authority and his expectation to support itinerant preachers and teachers of God's Word (v.10b)

      c. (φλυαρῶν) The *means* by which Diotrephes rejects John and others is by talking nonsense about John and others (v.10c). [25]

   2. **The Obstructive Acts of Diotrephes:** The *basis* for John's *concerns* about Diotrephes' behavior *is founded* upon slander, refusal to support God's servants, and the hindering and excommunication of those who want to support God's preachers and teachers (v.10d–g).

      a. (ἀρκούμενος) John notes further that Diotrephes' insubordination is not limited to slanderous talk (v.10d).

---

by John. We can only assume that the content of the letter concerned the expectation to support God's servants due to verse 8 and the list of charges against Diotrephes in verse 10. The insertion of "similar letter" expresses my reasonable interpretation of "something." Thus John appears to have written a letter to a church with similar expectations: Support itinerant teachers and preachers.

25 Diotrephes rejects John, "by talking nonsense" (φλυαρῶ: adverbial participle of means). The verb φλυαρῶ, appears only here in the NT. Yet it may be translated as "talk nonsense about" or "bring unjustified charges against" or to speak of someone as "an idle babbler" (Moulton and Milligan, 673). A related adjective φλύαρος appears in 1 Timothy 5:13 and can be translated "gossipy" or "foolish" (BDAG 1060c). This nonsense is modified with "evil" (πονηρος). Thus, Diotrephes speaks evil nonsense (πονηροῖς φλυαρῶν), he slanders John with false charges.

       b.   (ἐπιδέχεται) John notes that Diotrephes' insubordina-
tion is evident in his refusal to support itinerant preachers and teachers of God's Word (v.10e).

       c.   (κωλύει) John notes that Diotrephes' insubordination is
evident in his hindering others from welcoming itinerant preachers and teachers of God's Word (v.10f).

       d.   (ἐκβάλλει) John notes that Diotrephes' insubordination
is evident in his excommunicating people who welcome
itinerant preachers and teachers of God's Word (v.10g).

IV. **Sponsor for Demetrius, a Good Servant:** The *basis* for John *exhortation* to imitate Demetrius *is founded* on his relationship with God
and John's endorsements of him to both follow and support (vv.11–12).

  A. **Expectation:** The *basis* for John **exhortation** to imitate, like
Demetrius, *is founded* on his relationship with God (v.11).

     1.   (μιμοῦ) John exhorts Gaius not to imitate bad behavior
(v.11a).

     2.   (ellipsis: μιμοῦ) John exhorts Gaius to imitate good behavior
(v.11b).[26]

     3.   (ἐστιν) John declares that people who make it a habit of do-
ing good have a relationship with God (v.11c).

     4.   (ἑώρακεν) John declares that people who make it a habit of
doing evil do not have a relationship with God (v.11d).

  B. **Endorsed Example to Follow and Support:** The *basis* for
John's **endorsement** of Demetrius *is founded* upon the fact that
Demetrius is a *good example* to follow (and support) and is con-
firmed via *good endorsements* from various sources (v.12).

---

26   The verb μιμέομαι occurs only four times in the NT (2 Thess. 3:2, 9; Heb. 13:7; 3 John
v.11). Generally employed in exhortations, μιμέομαι tends to be used when the actions of
a particular model are to be emulated. For instance, Philo held that imitating God's works,
such as kindness, was an act of piety (cf. *Leg* 1:48 w/ *Spec.* 4:73). The author of Hebrews
encourages readers to imitate the faith of their leaders (13:7; cf. BDAG 651d). Here in
3 John, this first and only imperative in the letter issues an expectation of Gaius: imitate
(μιμοῦ) the good. Thus, terms "good" and "evil" appear to reference good and bad behavior
(vv. 8, cf., BDAG 501b 1c; Brown, *Johannine Epistles*, 721).

1. (μεμαρτύρηται) John points out that Demetrius has a good endorsement from others concerning both his belief and his lifestyle (v.12a).

2. (μαρτυροῦμεν) John provides Demetrius with a reliable endorsement as well as for the other itinerant preachers and teachers (v.12b).

V. **Closing Salutation:** The *basis* for John *ending* his letter *is founded* in his expressed need to *discuss* the issue of support, a *desire to visit* Gaius and speak with him in person, and some *closing greetings* (vv.13–15).

    A. **John's Writing:** John has more to write but rather would not write any more (v,13).

        1. (εἶχον γράψαι) John has more to write (v.13a).

        2. (οὐ θέλω . . . γράφειν) John would rather not write anymore (v.13b).

    B. **John's Visit:** John intends to visit Gaius and will speak with him in more detail in person (v.14).

        1. (ἐλπίζω . . . ἰδεῖν) John hopes to visit Gaius soon (v.14a).

        2. (λαλήσομεν) John will speak to Gaius in more detail when he visits (v.14b).

    C. **John's Closing Greetings:** John closes his letter with greetings of peace, greetings from others, and greetings to others (v.15).

        1. (ellipsis) John offers a greeting of peace (v.15a).

        2. (ἀσπάζονταί) John offers greetings to Gaius from those who are with him (v.15b).

        3. (ἀσπάζου) John requests that Gaius extend his greetings to the people at the church (v.15c).

In summary, it is important to state once again that communicating exegetically is both an art and a science. While some aspects are clearly objective, others are not and thereby subject to interpretation. Speaking objectively, declarative statements exist throughout the outline, each statement ends with a chapter and verse notation, the larger headings logically summarize subpoints, subpoints come in pairs (e.g., if there is a Roman numeral "I," there is a "II"; if there is an "A," there is a "B"; if there is a "1," there is a "2"), and structural markers with succinct descriptive statements are plainly evident throughout the outline.

Speaking subjectively, someone may wish to group the topical (subject-complement) statements differently. Someone may wish to emphasize the intention for supporting John's expectation of all believers to support God's workers (v.8), which is left out in Roman numeral "II. Solicitation of All Christians." Needless to say, my outline for 3 John is open for improvement and perhaps even a better interpretation of the particulars, and yet the structure of John's letter has been honored. Naturally, some may address aspects of this process differently. Yet most will agree that creating exegetical outlines always begins with the text, from the bottom (i.e., clause with structural markers underscored) and follows these four phases:

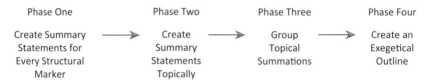

Phase One	Phase Two	Phase Three	Phase Four
Create Summary Statements for Every Structural Marker	Create Summary Statements Topically	Group Topical Summations	Create an Exegetical Outline

With the outline complete we now advance to communicating the big idea of the text.

STEP EIGHT: COMMUNICATING THE CENTRAL IDEA

The purpose of this section is to introduce the eighth step for interpreting the General Letters, which is communicating the central or big idea of a passage. Communicating the big idea of a passage entails the creation of a one-sentence statement that captures what the text says.[27] So then, we need to identify the component parts of a central idea in order to create a big idea (e.g., an exegetical idea) based upon the exegetical outline for 3 John, and then identify other types of outlines with corresponding ideas.

Component Parts of the Central Idea

The component parts of a central idea are simply the subject and

---

27   See Jay E. Smith, "Sentence Diagramming, Clausal Layouts, and Exegetical Outlining" in *Interpreting the New Testament Text: Introduction to the Art and Science of Exegesis*, edited by Darrell L. Bock and Buist M. Fanning (Wheaton, IL: Crossway, 2006), 73–134; and Haddon W. Robinson, *Biblical Preaching: The Development and Delivery of Expository Messages*, 2nd ed. (Grand Rapids: Baker, 2001), 33–50.

complement (similar to those above). Whereas the subject is what the text is discussing as a point of focus, the complement is what the text says about that subject. Communicating the central idea of any given text involves the ability to isolate these two component parts.

Constructing the central idea of a book occurs only after an exegetical outline for a passage has been completed. After an outline is established, constructing the central idea of a given book comes from combining Roman numerals of an outline so that the letter's emphasis is clear. When Roman numerals are inserted for 3 John, the exegetical outline for 3 John has five Roman numerals.

I.   **Salutation to Gaius:** In typical first century format, John **greets** his beloved friend, Gaius, and discloses both his **prayer** for and **joy** about Gaius' *faithfulness in supporting God's servants* (vv.1–4).

II. **Solicitation of All Christians:** While **commending** Gaius for his faithful support of God's servants, John **exhorts** him to lavish support upon God's workers *because* their livelihood depends upon God's people and thereby **expects** all believers to do the same (vv.5–8).

III. **Stubbornness of Diotrephes:** The *basis* for John's **concern** about and the resistance from Diotrephes *is founded* upon Diotrephes' *rejection* of John's authority and *refusal* to support God's workers (vv.9–10).

IV. **Sponsor for Demetrius:** The *basis* for John's **exhortation** to imitate Demetrius *is founded* on his relationship with God and John's endorsements of him to both follow and support (vv.11–12).

V.   **Closing Salutation:** The *basis* for John *ending* his letter *is founded* in his expressed need to *discuss* the issue of support, a *desire to visit* Gaius and speak with him in person, and some *closing greetings* (vv.13–15).

In pondering these five statements, three subject matters catch my attention. First, three people are the subject of his letter: Gaius, Diotrephes, and Demetrius. Second, these three people are described one of three ways: faithful (Gaius), stubborn or rebellious (Diotrephes), and one worthy of imitation and support (Demetrius). Finally, the focus of the letter is an exhortation and expectation for the lavish support of God's vocational servants, namely those who preach and teach about Jesus (vv.5–8). Thus, John paints three separate portraits about individuals and three respective responses about provisions. There is undeniable praise for one who faithfully provides for the livelihood of God's servants (Gaius), notable scorn for one who refuses to provide provisions (Diotrephes), and endorsement of one worthy to receive provision (Demetrius). So it appears to me a clear contrast exists in this letter[28] about supporting God's servants and may be summed up by way of a subject-complement statement in this manner:

Subject: In contrast to John's prayer, love, praise, and reasoned expectation of Gaius to support lavishly *worthy* preachers and teachers . . .

Complement: . . . John sternly scorns Diotrephes' refusal to support God's servants, while endorsing Demetrius as one worthy of support.

OR

Subject: In contrast to John's prayer, love, praise, and reasoned expectation of Gaius to support lavishly *worthy* preachers and teachers (like Demetrius). . .

Complement: . . . John sternly scorns Diotrephes' refusal to support God's servants.

This central idea not only captures the thrust of the letter, namely the contrast between the faithful and the rebellious pertaining to the lavish support of God's endorsed vocational servants, it also captures the subsequent flow of the letter evident sequentially in the Roman numerals. Unfortunately, this outline is not the one from which we would preach. Although there are other types of outlines, the exegetical outline with its central idea expressed is essential for other types of outlines.

Other Types of Outlines

As we have demonstrated, there are various types of outlines. Structural outlines, exemplified in step four, are the cornerstone of all other outlines of a biblical text. Exegetical outlines, like the one illustrated in step seven, essentially are *descriptive* outlines in that they report or reflect the biblical author's concerns as well as the letter's literary structure. Yet, a

---

28   The contrast between Gaius and Diotrephes is both implicit and explicit with the appearance of the verb "I make" (ποιεω). On the one hand, it appears to be used positively for Gaius when John says, "you demonstrate faithfulness" (πιστὸν ποιεῖς 5a). On the other hand, it is use negatively of Diotrephes, namely "which he demonstrates" (ἃ ποιεῖ) by rejecting John's authority and support of itinerant preachers and teachers of God's word is continual (10b). Whereas John makes it clear that one act of compliance has become habitual (πιστὸν ποιεῖς), another act of insubordination has also become habitual (ἃ ποιεῖ) and thereby accentuates two contrasting patterns of behavior.

descriptive outline must be converted into an *interpretive* outline in order to recognize the biblical author's underlying assumptions and logical
development. Thus, the following *interpretive* outline attempts to reflect
John's underlying assumptions and his train-of-thought evident in 3 John
that in essence transcends John's first-century historical-cultural milieu.

1. Believers who support God's vocational servants warrant prayer,
    love, and praise for their faithful support of God's vocational ser-
    vants (vv.1–4).

2. Believers are expected to support God's vocational servants lavishly
    because vocational servants are dependent on believers for their live-
    lihood (vv.5–8).

3. Believers who do not support God's vocational servants warrant
    correction (vv.9–10).

4. Believers are to imitate God's vocational servants as models to mir-
    ror and warrant support (vv.11–12).

5. Believers are to exercise wisdom when discussing the support of
    God's vocational servants (vv.13–15).

The central idea remains the same: the *lavish* (e.g., "in a manner worthy of God") support of God's vocational servants.[29] Yet, the universality of John's message has transcended his historical-cultural milieu
and has penetrated our own. The Apostle John does not suggest that
we pray, "God you keep your vocational servants humble, and we will
keep them poor." In fact, such a contemporary prayer resonates as
though it were a first century sound bite from Diotrephes. John says,
lavish God's preachers, teachers, and missionaries with all sorts of support. Perhaps we could reshape our exegetical idea into an interpretive
one like this one:

Subject	While believers who support lavishly God's vocationally-called servants are to be prayed for, loved, and praised for obeying God's expectation . . .

---

29 During the first century, supporting Christian workers meant providing them with supplies
    to enable them to continue their journey to the next stopping place. Today it involves far
    more. How much more? Providing not just monetary pay for food and shelter, but also for
    all forms of insurance (e.g., car, life, medical insurance). Supplying the needs for today's
    vocational servant warrants support in keeping with the twenty-first-century standards.

Complement	those who do not are to be corrected, and those who are vocational servants worthy to receive lavish support.

Naturally, this *interpretive* outline for 3 John can be converted rather easily into a *theological* outline in order to reflect the theological principles underlying John's words that in turn expresses the main theological idea of John's letter. Thus, the following reshaping of John's message into theological principles should also challenge all twenty-first-century believers.

1. God welcomes the prayer and praise for believers who support his vocational servants (vv.1–4).

2. God expects all believers to lavish support upon all his vocational servants *in order to partner with Jesus* (vv.5–8).

3. God is not pleased with believers who rebel against the lavish support of God's worthy vocationally called servants (vv.9–10).

4. God expects his vocational servants to be models for other believers (vv.11–12).

5. God wants believers to employ wisdom in the manner in which they communicate about their lavish support of his servants (vv.13–15).

The central idea remains the same: the *lavish* (e.g., "in a manner worthy of God") support of God's vocational servants, and yet the emphasis is no longer a human author's perspective, but rather the divine author's perspective. Thus, John's message should penetrate us as sacrosanct.

Subject	While God welcomes prayers and praise for believers, who support lavishly his vocationally called servants . . .
Complement	he is displeased with those who do not support his servants, and he expects worthy vocational servants to be supported and live as models for Jesus.

Regardless of which outline is used, several features are the same: While there are people who deserve prayer, love, and praise for lavishing support on God's vocationally called servants, all followers of Jesus are expected to support preachers/teachers, correct noncompliant supporters of God's servants, imitate God's vocationally called servants, and to exercise wisdom in communicating with one another about God's vocationally called servants. As we move to communicating homiletically, we move to application.[30]

STEP NINE: COMMUNICATING HOMILETICALLY

The purpose of this section is to introduce the ninth step for interpreting the General Letters, which is to communicate homiletically. Sound expositional preaching always begins with a solid exegetical outline. People unable to communicate exegetically risk distorting the message of the biblical text (cf. James 3:1). Needless to say, the General Letters were written for people of a different historical-cultural context than the one in which we live. Furthermore, they address a specific occasion, which often entails some reconstruction of the historical situation. Thus, we must strive to reconstruct cautiously the historical situation, bridge the historical-cultural chasm, strategize to shape a biblical author's message into a sermon that challenges people living in our twenty-first-century historical-cultural milieu,[31] and thereby speak God's word with integrity, sincerity, and yet with a degree of humility. So it is with a sense of humility that the following homily for 3 John is presented.

Some preliminary remarks are necessary before we present the sermon. First, the sermon does not follow 3 John sequentially, verse by verse. Those sorts of expository sermons will be exemplified in chapter seven. Here we want to present an expository sermon that tackles the message of 3 John without necessarily preaching the book in a verse-by-verse sequence. Second, the title of the sermon is "The Good, The Bad, The Faithful." The title echoes Clint Eastwood's *The Good, the Bad, and the Ugly*, and the theme song presently resonates in my head—portions of the song may even serve as a backdrop for the sermon.[32] Third, it is important to point out that *I did not seek first a clever presenta-*

---

30   There is no prayer or praise offered for people who donate money for constructing lavish buildings, ornately furnished rooms, and fancy memorial gardens in 3 John. Not that donations to projects are of *no value*, but too many people are more than willing to donate to buildings and programs at the expense of supporting God's vocationally called. Preachers and teachers live hand-to-mouth while massive building projects are erected because, as it so often is stated, "people are more willing to give support to build a building rather than support a person." Third John is a call to support people, not a building. See Timothy J. Ralston, "Showing the Relevance: Application, Ethics, and Preaching," in *Interpreting the New Testament Text: Introduction to the Art and Science of Exegesis*, edited by Darrell L. Bock and Buist M. Fanning (Wheaton, IL: Crossway, 2006), 293–310.

31   Timothy Warren. "Paradigm for Preachers," *Bibliotheca Sacra* 148 (October–December 1991): 463–90.

32   *The Good, the Bad and the Ugly* is a 1966 Italian western directed by Sergio Leone. Clint Eastwood plays Blondie: *The Good*; Lee Van Cleef plays Angel Eyes: *The Bad*; Eli Wallach as Tuco: *The Ugly*. The movie is set in the West during the Civil War era, and the three men (Blondie, Angel Eyes, Tuco) competitively search for stolen money.

tion for 3 John, but rather I studied the letter then sought something to fit
the message of 3 John.[33] Fourth, it is extremely helpful to have someone
with good reading skills recite 3 John as a whole from beginning to end
from perhaps the NET or NLT in order to introduce and grasp John's
flow of thought. Let congregants *hear* the reading of 3 John from a Bible
different from their own.[34] Reading the entire letter orally is important
because the sermon does not deal with every aspect of 3 John. The following is my translation for 3 John.

> [1]The Presbyter, to Gaius the beloved, whom I love in truth.
>
> [2]Beloved, in all respects I pray that you are prospering and that you are well,
> just as your soul is prospering. [4]For I rejoiced greatly when *our delegation of preachers*
> *and teachers* came and testified to your *faithfulness* to the truth, just as *I know* you are
> *living* with respect to the truth. I have no greater joy than this, namely that I hear
> my children are continually *living* in the truth.
>
> [5]Beloved, you *continually* demonstrate faithfulness, *in* whatever you do for the
> brothers (and strangers at that), [6]who have testified to your love before the church.
> You will do well by sending them on their way in a manner worthy of God, [7]for
> they went out on behalf of 'The Name' *of Jesus* and because they accept nothing
> from pagans.
>
> [9]I wrote *a similar letter* to *a sister* church; but Diotrephes, who loves to be first
> among them, does not acknowledge us. [10]Therefore, if I come, I will bring up his
> deeds, which he is *continually* doing, by talking *slanderous* nonsense about us. And
> because he is not being content with that, he himself *continually* refuses to welcome
> the traveling servants of God, he *continually* hinders the people who want *to welcome*
> *these servants*, and he *continually* throws them out of the church.
>
> [11]Beloved, do not imitate that which is bad *behavior*, but imitate that which is
> good *behavior*. The one who does what is good *has a relationship with God*; the one
> who does what is bad *has no relationship with God*. [12]Demetrius has received *a good*
> *report* by all, even by the truth itself; and we also testify *to him*, and you know that
> our testimony is true.
>
> [13]I have many *more things* to write to you, but I do not wish to write *it out* to
> you by means of ink and pen. [14]Rather, I hope to see you *immediately*, and we will
> speak *face to face*. [15]Peace *be* to you. The friends *here* greet you. Greet the friends
> *there* by name.

---

33   In verse 11, John speaks of good and bad models, namely Demetrius is good and Diotrephes
     is bad. Thus we have the good and the bad. Obviously, there is no ugly in the letter, but there
     is the faithful in 3 John v.4, namely Gaius "demonstrates faithfulness." Finally, we begin at
     the end of the letter and work toward its beginning because the thrust—namely, the focal
     point of the letter—occurs in verses 5–8.

34   For a presentation about the importance of Scripture reading see Timothy J. Ralston,
     "Scripture in Worship: An Indispensable Symbol of Covenant" in *Authentic Worship: Hearing*
     Scripture's Voice, Applying Its Truth, ed. Herbert W. Bateman IV (Grand Rapids: Kregel,
     2002), 195–222.

Fifth, a "Sermon in a Sentence" may be provided for the congregants that summarize your point succinctly. For this sermon we might submit the following: *"Attitudes about giving generously to God's servants distinguish the good, the bad, or the faithful."* Sixth, some people like to take notes. The following is a possible sermon outline to be inserted in a bulletin. The words underlined may be left blank for people to fill-in during the message. Thus, this deductive preaching approach informs the congregants the central idea at the very beginning of the sermon.[35]

The Good, the Bad, the Faithful

3 John

Attitudes about giving generously to God's servants distinguish the *good*, the *bad*, and the *faithful*.

The Good (vv.11–12)

1. The good is a underlined{model}.
2. The good has a relationship with God.
3. The good is a servant who is recommended without reservation.

> *The Good are people who model the Christian life, have a relationship with God, and are highly recommended servants.*

The Bad (vv.9–10)

1. The bad is self-absorbed.
2. The bad ignores leaders who support God's servants.
3. The bad slanders people who support God's servants.
4. The bad refuses and hinders people who support God's servants.

> *The Bad are people who are self-absorbed individuals who ignore, slander, and hinder the support of God's servants.*

The Faithful (vv.1–7)

1. The faithful is prayed for, loved, and praised for supporting God's servants.
2. The faithful brings joy to people who endorse God's servants.
3. The faithful is expected to, and actually supports lavishly, God's servants.

> *The Faithful are people who are prayed for, loved, and praised for their willingness to provide lavishly for God's vocationally called servants.*

Attitudes about giving generously to God's servants distinguish the *good*, the *bad*, and the *faithful*.

Finally, illustrations are sprinkled throughout the sermon because of space limitation. This presentation is meant to exemplify one way to *communicate homiletically* an entire General Letter in one message. Naturally, all technical discussions are missing from the message communicated to the audience. So, we begin the message with an introduction.

---

35 For differentiating between deductive and inductive sermons see Haddon Robinson, *Biblical Preaching: The Development and Delivery of Expositor Messages*, 2nd ed. (Grand Rapids: Baker, 2001), 115–37.

Introduction

Letters of reference or recommendations are important today for nearly everything: for getting a job, for getting into college, for getting into graduate school, and sometimes for even buying a house or renting an apartment. During the first century, it was not unusual for missionary pastors to move around from one house church to another. Churches often sent people to preach about Jesus at sister churches. So, they carried with them letters of reference so that believers in neighboring sister churches might know to provide for their needs. Paul, Barnabas, Silas, and Timothy were sent from the church in Antioch, and although we have no explicit record of their carrying letters of recommendation, Paul writes in a somewhat disappointing manner to the Corinthians in 2 Corinthians 3:1

> Are we beginning to praise ourselves again? Are we like others, who need to bring you letters of recommendation, or who ask you to write such letters on their behalf? Surely not! (NLT^{SE})

People like Paul, Peter, Timothy, Barnabas, and many others would travel from church to church to preach the gospel message to those who did not know Jesus, as well as teach and disciple those who had already made a profession of faith.[36] As you might expect given our understanding of first century letter writing, those who were less famous would carry letters of introduction from their sending churches to receive resources to carry out their ministries. Third John was written to tackle a specific situation in the early church, namely the financial support of God's vocationally-called servants. As we shall see in 3 John, *attitudes about giving generously to God's servants distinguish the good, the bad, or the faithful.* Our manner of giving generously to support God's vocationally called pastor-teachers and missionaries defines us as either good, bad, or faithful.

---

36 Paul sometimes took up manual labor to support himself. For instance, he took up a manual labor job in Thessalonica (1 Thess. 2:8–9; 2 Thess. 3:8), and yet the Philippians sent gifts to Paul while he was in Thessalonica (Phil. 4:6). Luke tells us (Acts 18:2b–3a) that when Paul arrived in Corinth, he went to Aquila and Priscilla, and because he was of the same trade he stayed with them and worked (since no conversion is mentioned and since a work partnership is established, it is probably that Aquila and Priscilla were already Christians). Yet elsewhere, Paul expects support (1 Cor. 9:4–12). John too is not expecting these itinerant preachers and teachers to be bi-vocational, though Paul at times chose to be bi-vocational. It appears John expects vocational servants to receive total support. See footnote #12 "Whom you do well" (οὓς καλῶς ποιήσεις).

The Good (vv.11–12)

The first person we want to introduce is *The Good*[37] spoken of in 3 John. His name is Demetrius, and he is first spoken of directly in 3 John vv.11–12. Who is Demetrius? Unfortunately, we know nothing about the man except what we have in this letter. Demetrius, however, is a *good servant* of God. He is *The Good* in this epic presentation in 3 John. To begin with, John says Demetrius—this good person—is to be imitated. In verse 11, we are told somewhat cryptically that those who exhibit good behavior are to be imitated.[38] What does John mean when he expects good behavior to be imitated? Philo, a Jewish philosopher who lived around the time of Jesus, taught that imitating God's works, such as kindness, was an act of piety. The author of Hebrews encourages readers to imitate the faith of their leaders. Thus, we suggest that imitating good behavior involves both a believing faith in Jesus and performing acts of kindness.[39] So, it seems *The Good* model the Christian life.

John continues to describe Demetrius as a good person who "has God." John's writing style continues to be somewhat cryptic. So, we must ask what does John mean when he says, "the good have God" and the bad "have not seen God"? Simply put, John says those who are vocationally called servants have a relationship with God. So, *The Good* have a relationship with God. In fact, the NLT translates the phrase in 3 John 11 as "those who do evil prove that they do not know God." Behavior determines to whom we are related. Supporting God's vocationally called servants, according to John, is a marked demonstration of one's relationship to God. If we do not support them, our relationship with God may be called into question.[40] Listen to what John says in his first letter, more specifically chapter 3, verse 10:

---

37   For some preachers, they prefer transmitting complete ideas rather than three single words as major points. So "The Good," "The Bad," "The Faithful" could be expanded to "The Good: Worthy servants of worthy support," "The Bad: Avoid self-absorption that dishonors God's servants," "The Faithful: Provide lavishly for God's vocationally called servants."

38   For an interpretation of "do not imitate the bad but the good" see note #25: "The verb μιμέομαι"

39   The clause "*that which is* good" could refer to John or Gaius. Perhaps, Gaius is called to choose between John and Diotrephes (Painter, *1, 2, 3 John*, 377). Perhaps, it is a reference to the reputation or behavior of Demetrius (cf. Lieu, *2 and 3 John*, 115; Stott, *The Johannine Letters*, 232). It seems the latter is true. John exhorts Gaius to follow the example of Demetrius because of a chiastic structure of vv.11 and 12 supporting the contrast (ἀλλά) between the bad behavior of Diotrephes and good of Demetrius (NET).

40   Although this statement appears harsh, remember, we are preaching what the text says, not what our Christian or church culture wants to hear. Johannine usage makes it clear that this idiom is used only of those who are not genuine believers (John 3:17–21; 1 John 3:6, 10; 4:7, 20; cf. NET).

> By this the children of God and the children of the devil are revealed: Everyone who does not practice righteousness—the one who does not love his fellow Christian–is not of God. (NET).

Finally, John tells us that this good person, who we know to be Demetrius, has the highest of commendations.[41] Verse 12 provides for us John's threefold reference. There is the reference given by way of Demetrius' public persona outside the church. There is the reference given by the truth. "Truth" is personified to express Demetrius' ethical behavior. More specifically it speaks on his behalf in the manner in which Demetrius lives life. Then, there is the reference given by John and his church on behalf of Demetrius. This threefold reference—people outside the church, his ethical lifestyle, and people in the church—depict the "good" as people who are to be imitated (v.11) and worthy of a preaching and teaching audience (v.12). So, *The Good* are recommended without reservation for service. We might also add that Demetrius may have been the leader for a delegation of traveling Christian workers and may even have been the bearer of this letter to Gaius. Letter couriers are frequently named in Paul's letters: Epaphroditus, Phoebe, Tychicus, and Onesimus.[42] Demetrius also may have been the letter carrier of his own letter of commendation.

Now let's pause a moment to consider John's central message. *Attitudes about giving generously to God's servants distinguish the good, the bad, or the faithful.* Our manner of giving generously to support God's pastor-teachers and missionaries defines us as good, bad, or faithful. So we might conclude that those who are cast as *The Good* in 3 John are people who are recipients of God's lavish support from believers. *The Good person in 3 John is one who models the Christian life, has a relationship with God, and is highly recommended for God's service.* They are those who are *worthy* to be called our missionaries, our pastors, and our teachers. So then, who are the bad?

The Bad (vv.9–10)

The second person spoken of in 3 John is *The Bad*. His name is Diotrephes, and he is spoken of directly in 3 John vv.9–10. Who is

---

41   Although this letter of commendation is unique to the New Testament, other first-century letters of commendation were presented in chapter one. And though 3 John is the only explicit letter of commendation in the NT, Paul speaks of writing letters of commendation: "When I come, I will write letters of recommendation for the messengers you choose to deliver your gift to Jerusalem" (NLT[SE]).

42   These four letter carriers are mentioned in Paul's letters: Epaphroditus in Philippians 2:25, Phoebe in Romans 16:1–2, Tychicus in Ephesians and Colossians 6:21–22, and Onesimus in Philemon 1:10–17. There is no need to state these citations in the sermon unless you intend to look at each one.

Diotrephes? Like Demetrius, we know nothing about him except what we have here in 3 John. It seems, however, Diotrephes is a leader of a neighboring sister church to the one Gaius attends and perhaps even leads.[43] Furthermore, John describes him as *The Bad* in this epic presentation from 3 John. To begin with John tells us in verse 9 that Diotrephes is one "who loves to be first." This description of Diotrephes is unique in that it occurs nowhere else in the New Testament.[44] Yet a Greek historian uses a similar term to describe a tyrant. Ahab, the king of Northern Israel, is an example of a tyrant. He wanted to buy a vineyard adjacent to his palace but was turned down. Ahab pouted and refused to eat. So, his wife Jezebel had the owner of the vineyard stoned. Then Ahab got up and took the vineyard (1 Kings 21:1–17). Perhaps John is suggesting that Diotrephes' leadership skills are in need of some assistance. Regardless, he appears to be self-absorbed, and perhaps even an arrogant tyrant. So, *The Bad* are self-absorbed.

John continues to describe Diotrephes as a person who received a letter from John but ignored it. As a result, John does not take this rejection well. Look with me at 1 John 4:6. The Apostle John says, "We are from God; the person who knows God listens to us, but whoever is not from God does not listen to us. By this we know the Spirit of truth and the spirit of deceit." John who walked with Jesus, was taught by Jesus, and even sent out by Jesus has been ignored. So, *The Bad* ignore John's expectation to support God's vocationally called servants.

Furthermore, ignoring John's letter was more than a matter of receiving it and throwing it in the trash. During the first century, letters were written to people who led early churches. In turn, these leaders were expected to read the letters publically to the church.[45] For instance,

---

43 The church (τῇ ἐκκλησίᾳ) mentioned in verse 9, which John says he may visit (v. 10), is not the same as the one mentioned in verse 6. It also seems unlikely that Gaius belongs to the church in verse 9 because John uses a third-person pronoun ("of them," αὐτῶν) as a way to refer to the other members of the church. If Gaius were one of these members, it would have been much more natural to use a second person pronoun ("of you," ὑμῶν; cf. Brown, *The Johannine Epistles*, 715; NET). Thus, there appears to be three churches explicitly mentioned in 3 John: John's church (v. 6), Diotrephes's church (v.9), and Gaius's church, which is implied. See footnote #23.

44 This substantival participle "who desires to be first" (ὁ φιλοπρωτεύων) never occurs in Greek literature other than in 3 John and subsequent church literature. Contra Moulton and Milligan's erroneous definition "I love the chief place," Brown suggests John may have coined the participle (ὁ φιλοπρωτεύων) to discredit Diotrephes (Brown, *Johannine Epistles*, 717, 743). Others render the term as though it were a relative pronoun: "wish to be first" or "who loves to be first" (BDAG 1058d: KJV, NASB, NIV, NET, NRSV, NLT). Perhaps John desires to paint Diotrephes to be an arrogant leader, one who was rising to prominence through his own enterprising efforts. Regardless, Diotrephes appears to be in a place of leadership and able to execute resistance against those who wish to support itinerant teachers and preachers (cf. NET).

45 For the public reading of letters, see John Grassmick, "Epistolary Genre: Reading Ancient

when Paul wrote Colossians he expected the church to forward it to the church at Laodicea. When he wrote to Philemon, it was expected that the letter would be read before the church. So, letters like 3 John were read publically. Perhaps a delegation of people arrived from John's church with a letter of commendation, and Diotrephes rejected not only the letter but also the entire delegation. Regardless of the scenario we paint, we know that letters were publically read, and Diotrephes was pretty full of himself. His rebellion against John's request was public knowledge, and he did not seek to hide his contempt for John. The world is full of people who are full of themselves. They tend to have keen appreciation of their own worth, and expect people to share in their inflated view of themselves. They come in many shapes and sizes and in every occupation: They could be performers like Charlie Sheen, they could be business executives like those of Enron, or they could be a boss who promotes people based upon personal relationship rather than performance outlined in policy guides. So, *The Bad* are self-serving people. They publically ignore John's letter to support God's servants.

John also points out in verse 10 that Diotrephes moves from publically refusing to acknowledge John's authority to slandering John.[46] For instance, the NASB translation says, "he unjustly accuses us with wicked words" or the NET says, "he brings unjustified charges against us with evil words." The NIV, however, captures the truest sense with "he is gossiping maliciously about us." So, *The Bad* slander other people. But wait, there's more.

Finally, *the Bad* also refuse to support God's vocationally-called servants in three ways. They themselves "refuse" to help God's servants.[47] Furthermore, they "stop" (NIV) or "forbid" (NASB)[48] other believers from helping to support God's servants to the extent that he even "puts them out" (NIV) or "throws them out" (NET)[49] of the

---

Letters" in *Interpreting the New Testament Text: Introduction to the Art and Science of Exegesis,* (Wheaton, IL: Crossway, 2006), 221–39.

46   For an interpretation of "by talking nonsense" see footnote #25, "Diotrephes rejects John."

47   The first indicator of an overt and aggressive attitudinal problem against John is in v. 9, "he does not receive us" (οὐκ ἐπιδέχεται ἡμᾶς). It defines Diotrephes' rejection of John's authority (BDAG 370c 2). Here in v.10, however, the verb means refusal to "show hospitality to" (BDAG 370c 1) or "to welcome" someone (Brown, *Johannine Epistles,* 719; NET, NLT). The present tense may accentuate a pattern of behavior.

48   The verb "he hinders" (κωλύει) means, "to prevent something from happening" and is often translated as "hinder," "prevent," "refuse" (NIV, NET, NRSV NLT) or "forbid" (KJV, NASB) (BDAG 580a 1). In Acts 8:36 the eunuch asks Philip, "What prevents (κωλύει) me from being baptized?" In Acts 11:17, after the Spirit filled the Gentiles at Caesarea, Peter defends his actions when he asks, "Was I to forbid (κωλύω) God?" Here in 3 John 1:10, Diotrephes hinders people who wish to support itinerant missionaries. The present tense accentuates a pattern of behavior.

49   The verb "he expels" (ἐκβάλλει) is typically used in cases of divorce ("nor to put her away,"

church. These acts do not appear to be one-time events. They are patterns of behavior in desperate need of correction. John makes it perfectly clear that followers of Jesus are to support God's servants. Yet Diotrephes has resisted John's explicit expectation, rejected John's letter (v. 9), ridiculed John, and has led in overt acts of insubordination against John's expectation to support God's servants (v. 10).[50]

So, let's once again pause to consider John's central concern. *Attitudes about giving generously to God's servants distinguish the good, the bad, or the faithful.* Our manner of giving generously to support God's pastor-teachers and missionaries defines us as good, bad, or faithful. It seems John depicts *The Bad* to be people who are self-absorbed, who ignore as well as speak poorly of those who encourage the support of God's vocational servants, and who do all they can to hinder the support of God's vocational servants. Or we might more succinctly say, those who are cast as *The Bad* are people who resist God's expectation to lavish support on his called servants. So far, we've read about *The Good*, people who are worthy of support, and *The Bad*, people who are in need of reproof. It's time to look at *The Faithful*.

The Faithful (vv.1–7)

The third person spoken of in 3 John is *The Faithful*. His name is Gaius, and he is spoken of directly in 3 John vv.1–7. Gaius, like Diotrephes, is a leader of a church. Once again, we know nothing about the man except what we have here in this New Testament letter. He is *The Faithful* in our presentation from 3 John. To begin with, John tells us Gaius is prayed for, loved, and praised for supporting God's vocationally-called servants (vv.1–4). We need to pause, isolate, and interpret the word "truth" in this set of verses because, as we have seen previously, John tends to be cryptic in his letter writing. This step is especially true concerning his use of "truth." The term "truth" could have several different meanings.

Moulton & Milligan, 1050.15), in cases of the Essenes who expelled people from their community ("those who are convicted of serious crimes they *expel* from the order," Jos *War* 2.8.8 § 143), as well as in cases of expulsion from the synagogue (John 9:34–35). In 3 John v.10, it seems that Diotrephes, as a leader in his local church, forbids people from supporting Christian workers and expels those who do. The present tense accentuates a pattern of behavior.

50 Burge believes, "John is confident that he can enter this situation successfully because he is prepared. He has continued to communicate with those in the church; he has counseled with his couriers; he will talk deeply with Gaius when he gets there; and he knows that God is with him and that God's desire is for the truth to win and for his people to walk in its freedom and joy." Gary M. Burge, *Letters of John* in The NIV Application Commentary (Grand Rapids: Zondervan, 1996), 251–54. Although John's point is not to offer advice as to how to confront conflict, John does exemplify that people who do not support God's servants are in need of correction.

If I say, "I was eating an apple while walking the streets of the 'Big Apple,' when suddenly a group of muggers stole my computer bag where I kept my Apple MacBook Pro," we would know that the word "apple" speaks of a literal piece of fruit, the city of New York, and a brand-name computer. Contextually, John is using the word "truth" in a similar manner. On the one hand, "truth" in verse 1 could be another way to speak of Jesus. "I love you in Jesus." In John 14:6, Jesus says of himself "I am the way, the truth and the life, no one goes to God the Father except through me." So John tells Gaius of his love for him because of their mutual love and, might we say, belief in Jesus. On the other hand, "truth" when used in connection with "walking" speaks of living ethically. It speaks of ethical behavior.[51] It seems that what Gaius believes about Jesus is affecting how he lives for Jesus. Perhaps we might say it this way: What we believe affects how we live, how we live reflects what we believe. Such people are to be prayed for, loved, and praised.

John continues to describe Gaius as one who brings joy to other believers. Look at verse 4 once again. Gaius, in his providing for the needs of God's vocationally called servants brought joy to those who benefited from such provisions, brought joy to John, and we might also imagine brought joy to John's entire church. Perhaps those who returned to John's church and praised Gaius were the very same individuals who were turned down by Diotrephes. Perhaps, Gaius was well aware of the nearby sister church's rejection (namely Diotrephes' church) and yet, he stepped in and provided for their needs without any letter of commendation. They were truly strangers.[52] Nevertheless, what is certain is that Gaius provided for the needs of a group of God's called servants, and it brought joy to numerous people.

Finally, John expects Gaius to provide lavishly for God's vocational servants (vv.5–7). As this new delegation of vocationally-called servants arrive, Gaius is "to send them on their way in a manner worthy of God." What does this phrase mean exactly? To begin with, to send someone on a journey involved helping a person on his or her journey with food, money, arranging for companions to travel with them, and helping them with their means of travel to reach their next stopping place.[53] Yet John

---

51   The phrase ἐν ἀληθείᾳ περιπατεῖς in this clause literally means, "walking in truth." "In truth" (ἐν ἀληθείᾳ) occurs twice in 3 John v.3. In Johannine letters ἐν ἀληθείᾳ may refer to Christological belief (1 John 2:21–23, 4:2, 4:6, 5:10, 5:20; 2 John v.7) or ethical behavior (1 John 1:6, 2:4, 3:18–19, 4:20). Here, the emphasis is on behavior because of the verb περιπατεω, which is typically used in the NT for lifestyle (cf. 2 John v.2). It speaks of behavior that is in accordance with God's desire and in close relationship with God (1 John 1:6). Here in 3 John v.3, Christian workers commend Gaius for his actual "living the truth" (v. 3), particularly his faithful work with regard to hospitality on their behalf (v.5). Thus, ἐν ἀληθείᾳ appears to emphasize Gaius' Christian lifestyle or ethical behavior (cf. NET).

52   For an interpretation of "strangers at that" see footnote #11.

53   For an explanation of support for why God's vocationally called should be supported see

heightens the expectation with the added phrase "in a manner worthy of God." John's culture expected some sort of provision; however, when it came to helping God's servants, John expected more than the cultural norm. He expected God's servants to be lavished with support as though they were helping God himself. Why? Why should *The Faithful* support lavishly God's vocationally called servants? John provides two reasons: They've gone out in "the NAME" and "the NAME" is Jesus.[54] Furthermore, they go out in "the NAME" of Jesus and they don't expect unbelievers to feed them.[55] People who go out in "the NAME" of Jesus are totally dependent upon God's people to meet all of their needs.

John's central concern is simply that *Attitudes about giving generously to God's servants distinguish the good, the bad, or the faithful.* Our manner of giving generously to support God's pastor-teachers and missionaries defines us as good, bad, or faithful. Those who are cast as *The Faithful* in 3 John are people who respond obediently to God's expectation to lavish support on his vocationally-called servants. *Thus they are people who are prayed for, loved, and praised for their willingness to provide lavishly for God's vocationally called servants.*

Conclusion

Providing proper or adequate support for those who have been recognized and set apart for God's service as preachers, teachers, and missionaries, has always been a problem for followers of Jesus. We've all heard the saying, "***Do not muzzle an ox while it is treading out the grain***." In contemporary terms, it's like being given a tractor with no gas, or like a hired carpenter with blueprints and all the materials to build a house with no nails or screws to complete the job, a student who is given a computer with no power cord to recharge its battery, or a person asked to make bricks with no straw.

Today's worthy servants of God ***tend*** to have earned an expensive degree that prepared them for vocational service, they have many letters of commendation, and they have been ordained by a group of recognized church leaders. They are tractors in need of gas, carpenters in

---

footnote #12.

54   For an interpretation of "the Name" see footnote #6.

55   Although ἔθνος is used in John to describe the Jewish leaders as unbelievers (11:48, 50–52; 18:35), the word ἐθνικος occurs only four times in the NT (3 John v.7, Matt. 5:47, 6:7, 18:17). Here, it appears to be synonymous with the far more common ἔθνος (used some 162 times in the NT). Both terms refer to Gentiles (that is, pagans or unbelievers). Since the issue here is the support for the itinerant missionaries, and there is no indication that the writer would want to forbid receiving support from the Gentile converts to Christianity (cf. Paul's reception of support from Gentile converts in 1 Cor. 9:14, Phil. 4:10–18), ἐθνικῶν must refer to Gentile and Jewish unbelievers, (i.e., pagans). So God's servants accept no support from non-Christians (NET; Brown, *Johannine Epistles*, 713; Lieu, *2 and 3 John*, 108).

need of nails, students in need of a power cord, people in need of straw. Today, support for such individuals should exceed merely the provision of food and shelter. Culturally, God's servants are in need of monetary support not only to provide food and shelter for them and their families, but also transportation, various forms of insurance (even the dreaded health insurance), and other culture necessities. Yet, many today are inadequately supported to do their job.

Let me ask the following of us as a church: Who are we? Are we a Demetrius? Are we a Diotrephes? Are we a Gaius? How would we cast ourselves as a community? Are we the good? Are we the bad? Or are we the faithful? Would you consider us to be a community who is *faithful* in lavishly supporting God's vocationally called servants? Or would you confess we struggle with or perhaps even begrudge supporting God's servants? Do we border on depriving God's servants and their families the means to live comfortably? Are we a church that withholds prayer, love, and praise from people who actually give money to support people? Or are we a church more prone to praise people who wish to contribute to the construction of lavish buildings, ornately furnished rooms, or memorial gardens? Do we sing, "this world is not my home, I'm just a-passing through, my treasures are laid up somewhere beyond the blue . . ." and yet make it a point to leave a memorial treasure or two behind with our names engraved on them while people who serve God and whose efforts are eternal bound are left floundering financially in this present world.

Do you find it easier to give to projects rather than to people? Are we a church that believes it is God's responsibility to keep his servants humble and our responsibility to keep them poor? Let me read 3 John 8, what God has spoken through John:

> [8]Therefore we ought (*we all ought as a church*) to support such people (*God's vocationally called servants*), so that we might become co-workers with *them* in the truth (*namely Jesus*).

It seems we as a community ought to make it a priority to provide, without hesitation and yet with intention, not only the everyday necessities of our preachers, teachers, and missionaries, but to go beyond those twenty-first-century necessities. Our intention should be so that we might become co-workers with them in the truth, co-workers with Jesus.

How might 3 John alter our community's perspective in the way we currently provide for God's vocationally-called preachers, teachers, and missionaries? How do we measure up? *Do our attitudes about giving generously to God's servants distinguish us as the bad or the faithful.* Can we do better?

Chapter in Review

In this chapter, "Communicating the General Letters" we learned how to move from one outline to another as presented on several occasions throughout these past three chapters, and that all communication begins at the clause level and progresses in the following manner.

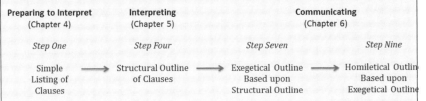

Preparing to Interpret (Chapter 4)	Interpreting (Chapter 5)	Communicating (Chapter 6)	
Step One	*Step Four*	*Step Seven*	*Step Nine*
Simple Listing of Clauses	→ Structural Outline of Clauses	→ Exegetical Outline Based upon Structural Outline	→ Homiletical Outline Based upon Exegetical Outline

We emphasized how interpreting the General Letters clause-by-clause helps to ensure, prevent, and perhaps even protect us from wandering from what the text actually says. Thus, we are more prone to honor the authors (divine and human) when we work to communicate the text first exegetically, wrestle with communicating the central idea of a text, and then communicate the text homiletically in order to affect our twenty-first-century audiences. The question is simply: How great is your commitment to be one of God's vocationally called servants with highly developed skills in interpretation and communication so that you too might become a person worthy of lavish support from God's people?

7

FROM EXEGESIS TO EXPOSITION
OF THE GENERAL LETTERS

The Chapter at a Glance

Jude vv.5–7
    Greek Text
    Text-Critical Issue
    Structural Outline with Simple Translation
    Exegetical Outline
    Exposition

Hebrews 10:19–25
    Contextual Orientation
    Greek Text
    Structural Outline
    Exegetical Outline
    Exposition

AS WE BEGIN THIS CHAPTER "From Exegesis to Exposition of the General Letters," it is helpful to bear in mind that we are pulling together the previous six chapters with special attention given to the nine steps of interpretation discussed in chapters four through six. Nevertheless, there will be opportunities to telescope some steps to save space. For instance, step one that involves the listing of clauses where verbs and verbals are underlined and a simple translation appears under each clause will be combined with step four where both will be represented under *Structural Outline* and the other aspects of exegesis learned throughout the other steps are telescoped throughout the *Exposition*.

Preparing to Interpret (Chapter 4)	Interpreting (Chapter 5)	Communicating (Chapter 6)	
Step One	*Step Four*	*Step Seven*	*Step Nine*
Simple Listing of Clauses	Structural Outline of Clauses	Exegetical Outline Based on Structural Outline	Homiletical Outline Based on Exegetical Outline

Thus this chapter provides an exposition of two passages: Jude vv.5–7 and Hebrews 10:19–25. Since each passage chosen occurs within the middle of its respective letter, each discussion begins with a contextual orientation. The Greek text is presented followed by a textual issue, a structural outline, and an exegetical outline based upon the structural outline. The exposition serves to communicate the exegesis. Although space does not allow for a homiletical outline, a comparison of this chapter's exposition with the homily in step nine will make for an easy transition to create your own sermon.

JUDE VV.5–7

After his customary, and yet affirming epistolary salutation and greeting (vv.1–2), Jude discloses his purpose for writing his letter. He admonishes Judean followers of Jesus to stand firm in their faith rather than succumb to and join with godless people (e.g., Jewish rebels or Zealots; vv.3–4) who conspire to revolt against Rome.[1] Then, in a vituperative manner, Jude leaves no stone unturned in his scathing descriptions of these godless people (vv.5–16).[2]

Jude 5–16 divides naturally into four sections: verses 5–7, verses 8–10, verses 11–13, and verses 14–16. The focus here is Jude vv.5–7. Jude begins with a mitigated expectation[3] to remember (v.5a–b) three notorious rebellions of the past: rebellion of the Israelites against God's

---

1   The assumption is that Jude wrote his letter sometime between 62–66 CE, just prior to the Jewish revolt against the Roman Empire (66–73 BCE) led by Zealots. See chapter two, "Background for the General Letters." See also Herbert W. Bateman IV, *Jude,* Evangelical Exegetical Commentary, edited by Hall Harris (Bellingham, WA: Logos, 2013).

2   For discussions about the vituperative letter writing see chapter one, "Genre of the General Letters."

3   A mitigated exhortation softens expectation in order to make it more palatable to the listener or reader. A similar exhortation occurred in 3 John v.6. See chapter six "Communicating the General Letters," page 217 n. 12.

leading in the wilderness (v.5c–d), rebellion of angelic beings against God's heavenly placement (v.6), and rebellion of Gentiles against God's marital norms (v.7). All share the same outcome, divine judgment. Thus, Jude vv.5–7 is a call to remember that divine judgment exists for any who rebel.

Greek Text

⁵ Ὑπομνῆσαι δὲ ὑμᾶς βούλομαι, εἰδότας ἅπαξ πάντα, ὅτι [ὁ] κύριος* λαὸν ἐκ γῆς Αἰγύπτου σώσας τὸ δεύτερον τοὺς μὴ πιστεύσαντας ἀπώλεσεν, ⁶ ἀγγέλους τε τοὺς μὴ τηρήσαντας τὴν ἑαυτῶν ἀρχὴν ἀλλὰ ἀπολιπόντας τὸ ἴδιον οἰκητήριον εἰς κρίσιν μεγάλης ἡμέρας δεσμοῖς ἀϊδίοις ὑπὸ ζόφον τετήρηκεν· ⁷ ὡς Σόδομα καὶ Γόμορρα καὶ αἱ περὶ αὐτὰς πόλεις, τὸν ὅμοιον τρόπον τούτοις ἐκπορνεύσασαι καὶ ἀπελθοῦσαι ὀπίσω σαρκὸς ἑτέρας, πρόκεινται δεῖγμα πυρὸς αἰωνίου δίκην ὑπέχουσαι.

Text–Critical Issue

Verse 5 Variant★: Does the text read "the **Lord**" ([ὁ] κύριος) or does it read "**Jesus**" (Ἰησοῦς)? The presence of Lord or Jesus is a theological issue. On the one hand, the external evidence supporting Ἰησοῦς is impressive (A B 33 81 322 323 65 1241 1739 1881 2298 2344) and is favored by some contemporary Greek texts and English translations.[4] On the other hand, internal evidence causes many to reject the external evidence. (1) The mention of "Jesus" without the title "Christ" is unparalleled in Jude. (2) The mention of Jesus as the one who delivers the exodus generation is unparalleled in the New Testament (yet, cf. 1 Cor. 10:4). (3) The second example of divine judgment on angelic beings kept for judgment appears to be executed by God in that just as believers are kept for Jesus by God (v.1b), fallen angels are kept for judgment (v.6a). Furthermore, the [ὁ] κύριος reading has external support (ℵ ψ C* 630 1505). Of particular significance is the split reading within the Alexandrian family (ℵ C* vs. B A) "Admittedly," says Metzger, "Ἰησοῦς is the best attested reading among Greek and versional witnesses," but argues in favor of the internal evidence. Thus in keeping with contemporary Greek texts and English translations "the Lord" ([ὁ] κύριος) is preferred, though "Lord" might be interpreted to be Jesus.[5]

---

4   Robinson and Peirpont in *The New Testament in the Original Greek: Byzantine Textform 2005*, SBL's *The Greek New Testament* and subsequently several English translation (ESV, NET, NLT^SE) also support the "Jesus" rendering. For a defense for "Jesus" as the original reading see Jarl Fossum, "Kyrios Jesus as the Angel of the Lord in Jude 5," *NTS* 33 (1987): 226–43; Carroll D. Osborne, "The Text of Jude 5," *Biblica* 62 (1981): 107–15.

5   NA²⁷,²⁸, UBS⁴, Hodges and Farstad in *The Greek New Testament According to the Majority Text*, and subsequently several English translation (KJV, ASV, NRSV, NIV, CEB, WEB) favor the

Structural Outline with Simple Translation

⁵ᵃ **Ὑπομνῆσαι** δὲ ὑμᾶς **βούλομαι**,⁶
⁵ᵃ Now I want (wish) to remind you
                          |
                    ⁵ᵇ **εἰδότας**⁷ ἅπαξ πάντα,⁸
                    ⁵ᵇ although you know all *these things*

⁵ᶜ **ὅτι** [ὁ] κύριος . . . τὸ δεύτερον τοὺς μὴ πιστεύσαντας **ἀπώλεσεν**⁹
⁵ᶜ that the Lord . . . destroyed those who did not believe the second time.
                  |
            ⁵ᵈ λαὸν ἐκ γῆς Αἰγύπτου σώσας
            ⁵ᵈ who saved [once] the people out of the land of Egypt
    |
⁶ᵃ [**ὅτι**] ἀγγέλους τε . . . εἰς κρίσιν μεγάλης ἡμέρας δεσμοῖς ἀϊδίοις ὑπὸ ζόφον
τετήρηκεν·¹⁰

___

    [ὁ] κύριος reading. For a defense of "Lord" see Metzger, *A Textual Commentary on the Greek New Testament*, 657. Landon, *A Text-Critical Study of the Epistle of Jude*, 75–76.

6   Structurally, verse 5 has four clauses. The first independent clause is governed by the verb "I wish" (βούλομαι). βούλομαι is a first singular present middle indicative from βούλομαι that means, "I will" or "I want." The second, ὑπομνῆσαι is an aorist active infinitive from ὑπομιμνήσκω that means, "I remind." Semantically, the indicative is a potential indicative or a mitigated assertion, the infinitive is a complementary infinitive that completes the verbal idea of what Jude desires from his recipients.

7   The governing verb of this dependent clause is "*although you* know" (εἰδότας). εἰδότας is a perfect active participle masculine plural accusative from οιδα, which means, "I know." Semantically, it is a perfect with a present force. Syntactically, it functions as an adverbial participle modifying "I want to remind" (ὑπομνῆσαι . . . βούλομαι) that, as an adverbial participle has a concessive semantical force "although you know."

8   Interpreting any demonstrative pronoun is often problematic in the NT. Syntactically, the ὅτι clause is an adjectival clause modifying "all *things*" (πάντα). Semantically, ὅτι is epexegetical in that ὅτι completes the idea of "all things" (πάντα). Thus, here in Jude "that" (ὅτι) provides a threefold content of what is common knowledge to Judean Jews: the exodus event (v.5b), the fallen angels (v. 6), and Sodom and Gomorrah (v.7).

9   The governing verb of this dependent clause is "destroyed" (ἀπώλεσεν) and frames Jude's discussion about the divine judgment executed on God's chosen people for their disbelief. It is a third singular aorist active indicative from ἀπόλλυμι that means, "I destroy, or "I lose." Syntactically, "he [God] destroyed" (ἀπώλεσεν) governs the dependent clause. Semantically, nearly all translations render the aorist as a constative aorist, which describes the event as a whole with no interest in the internal workings of the action. It stresses the fact that the event occurred, namely people died.

10   Structurally, verse 6 has three clauses. One [ὅτι] dependent clause (v.6a) governed by the verb "he has kept" (τετήρηκεν) and two adjectival dependent clauses (v.6b & c) in that they modify "angels" (ἀγγέλους). "He has kept" (τετήρηκεν) is third singular perfect active indicative from τηρέω, which means, "I keep" or "I guard." Syntactically, "he has kept" (τετήρηκεν) functions as the verb of this dependent clause with an assumed subject, "he." Semantically, it is rendered as an extensive perfect that emphasizes the completed action with continuing results, which means God locked them up in the past and they remain locked up.

^{6a} and *that* angels . . . he has kept in eternal chains in realms of darkness for the great Day of Judgment.

|

^{6b} τοὺς μὴ τηρήσαντας τὴν ἑαυτῶν ἀρχὴν
^{6b} those who did not keep their own domain

|

^{6c} ἀλλὰ ἀπολιπόντας τὸ ἴδιον οἰκητήριον
^{6c} but *who* abandoned their own place of residence

|

^{7a} [**ὅτι**] ὡς Σόδομα καὶ Γόμορρα καὶ αἱ περὶ αὐτὰς πόλεις, . . . **πρόκεινται**¹¹ δεῖγμα
^{7a} *that* similarly Sodom and Gomorrah and the cities around them . . . are *now* set as an example

^{7b} τὸν ὅμοιον τρόπον τούτοις ἐκπορνεύσασαι
^{7b} who practiced immorality in the same way as these (Sodom & Gomorrah)

|

^{7c} καὶ ἀπελθοῦσαι ὀπίσω σαρκὸς ἑτέρας,
^{7c} and who went after different flesh

^{7d} πυρὸς αἰωνίου δίκην **ὑπέχουσαι.**
^{7d} by suffering a punishment of eternal fire.

Exegetical Outline

Subject: The call to remember ancient Jewish testimonies . . .

Complement: . . . serves to remind Judean believers that divine consequences exist for anyone who rebel against God.

I. **A Call to Remember:** (ὑπομνῆσαι . . . βούλομαι) Jude expects Judeans to keep in mind their ancient Jewish testimonies (v.5a).

II. **Rebellion Ends in Divine Judgment:** Jude recalls various forms of judgment that occurred to those who resisted God's leading, left their prescribed residence, and ignored his marital expectations (vv. 5b–7).

---

11 Structurally, verse 7 has four clauses. One [ὅτι] dependent clause (v.7a) governed by the verb "exhibited" (πρόκεινται) and three dependent clauses. Two clauses (v.7b & c) are adjectival in that they modify "cities" (πόλεις). The third (v.7d) is a dependent adverbial clause that modifies the verb "exhibited" (πρόκεινται) in the first dependent clause (v.7a) Thus, the dependent clause with the verb "exhibited" (πρόκεινται) frames Jude's discussion about God's judgment executed on Gentiles for their societal perversions.

A. Divine Judgment of **Rebellion against God's Leading:**
(ἀπώλεσεν) God's judgment of the Israelites who rebelled
against God at Kadesh Barnea was physical death (v.5b).

B. Divine Judgment of **Rebellion against God's Prescribed
Residence:** (τετήρηκεν) God's judgment of the angels who
rebelled and left heaven was incarceration until a future day of
judgment (v.6).

C. Divine Judgment of **Rebellion against God's Marital
Norms:** (πρόκεινται) God's judgment of Gentiles who rejected
God's marital norms was death and eternal humiliation (v.7).

Exposition: A Call to Remember (Jude vv.5–7)

A Call to Remember. Jude begins with an expressed desire (βούλομαι) to remember (ὑπομνῆσαι) or to keep something in mind (v.5a). The
call to remember, however, is not an unusual expectation for a Judean.
Remembering the past was to govern the life of every Jew. For instance,
the Jewish people were to remember the Exodus: "Remember that you
were slaves in Egypt and the LORD your God redeemed you" (Deut.
15:15). The way Jewish people remember their deliverance from Egypt
is by celebrating the Passover, the Feast of Unleavened Bread, and the
Feast of Tabernacles.[12] In the minds of some, failure to remember God's
exploits on Israel's behalf was a form of godlessness (Jos *Ant.* 2.9.3 §
214). So Jude's request is not unusual.

As a result, many historical events were common knowledge. Jude
realizes his readers "know all these *things*" (εἰδότας πάντα) he is about
to write. The phrase, "all these *things*" (πάντα) points forward to God's
execution of judgment on those who rebelled, namely, the exodus
generation (v.5c), fallen angels (v.6), and Sodom and Gomorrah (v.7).
Thus, Jude opens with an expressed desire to remember a few well-
known past events that did not end well.

Rebellion Ends in Divine Judgment. Having expressed his expectation to remember, Jude features three rebellions that ended in
judgment: the exodus generation (v.5c), angels (v.6), and Sodom and
Gomorrah (v.7). Each appeared frequently in canonical and noncanonical Jewish literature. Jude, however, presents his own version of

---

12 There were three major festivals. The first was the Passover and Feast of Unleavened Bread.
The second was the Feast of Weeks (Pentecost), which occurred on the sixth of Sivan in
order to dedicate to God the firstfruits of the wheat harvest the fiftieth day after Passover (Ex.
23:16; 34:22; Lev. 23:16; Num. 28:26; Deut. 16:9–10; Acts 1:11; 2:7). Finally, there was the
Feast of Tabernacles, which foreshadowed peace and prosperity (Zech. 14:16). See Gleason
L. Archer Jr., *A Survey of Old Testament Introduction* (Chicago: Moody, 1974), 242.

these events in a manner that extends beyond the traditional record in Hebrew Scriptures.[13] His choices, therefore, were not arbitrary but calculated in order to tackle the godless rebels circulating among Judean churches.

Jude first recalls the *divine judgment of the exodus rebellion against God's leading*. It is a story about deliverance from Egypt and great hopes that only ends with God's judgment of Israel at Kadesh-Barnea (v.5c–d). Their disbelief started with a few, spread to others, and ended in punishment for many. Attention is first given to God's deliverance of Israel from Egypt (v.5d)[14] and then to the rebellion and divine judgment (v.5c).

<u>Israelite Deliverance.</u> Jude recalls that the Lord "saved the people out of the land of Egypt." Historically, God's deliverance of Israel began with Moses. Moses was God's man who led the Israelites successfully out of Egypt (Ex. 7:1–12:42; cf. Ps. 135:8), avoided recapture (Ex. 13:17–15:21; cf. Pss. 66:5; 78:13), provided for the needs of people (Ex. 15:22–17:7; cf. Ps 78:14–16), and mediated a covenant with God (Ex. 19:1–20:21; 24:1–8). Yet Jude draws attention to God's "deliverance" (σώσας)[15] that occurred "once" (ἅπαξ). The term "once" (ἅπαξ) specifies God's deliverance from Egypt to be unique, decisive, and never to be repeated.[16] This momentous deliverance occurred at Passover (Ex. 12:1–42) and again at the sea (Ex. 14:1–15:21; cf. 4Q122.1–5; Jos *Ant.* 3.12.6 § 297), but rebellion followed.

---

13   Although his presentation differs in emphasis, Jude echoes presentations evident in other Judean texts: *Sirach* 16:5–8, 3 Maccabees 2:4–7, and Damascus document 2:17–3:12. Similarly, the author of Hebrews chapter 11 echoes catalogs of Jewish ancestors found in other second temple sources like 1 Maccabees 2:51–64 and *Sirach* 44–50.

14   The prepositional phrase "out of Egypt" (ἐκ γῆς Αἰγύπτου) occurs throughout Scripture recalling Israel's deliverance from Egypt (Judg. 2:12, 6:8, 19:30; Dan. 9:15; Acts 7:40; Heb. 8:9).

15   The aorist active nominative participle σώσας could be rendered two other ways: (1) as a dependent adverbial clause to the main verb "he destroyed" (ἀπώλεσεν) and thereby translated "although God saved (σώσας) the people out of the land of Egypt once"; and (2) as an independent verb and thereby translated "the Lord delivered (σώσας) his people out of Egypt" (NIV; Life Application Bible; Davids, 46; Harrington, 194; Schreiner, 441). The rendering in this commentary is that of a dependent adjectival clause modifying "the Lord" ([ὁ] κύριος) and thereby translated "who once saved (σώσας) a people out of the Land of Egypt" (NAB; cf. NASB).

16   "Once" (ἅπαξ) may convey a numeral concept of being stoned once (2 Cor. 11:25) or of high priests entering the Holy of Holies once a year (Heb. 9:7). It may convey the idea of "once again" as in a series of giving gifts (Phil. 4:16), visiting a community of believers (1 Thess. 2:18), or recurring earthquakes (Heb. 12:26–27). It also conveys a unique and unrepeatable event in Jesus' life (Heb. 9:26, 27, 28; 10:2; 1 Peter 3:18). In Jude, "once" (ἅπαξ) is used to convey a unique and unrepeatable event. In Jude 1:3, the emphasis is on God's final revelation, which appears to be similar to Hebrews 1:1–2. In Jude v.5, the emphasis is on God's deliverance from Egypt that was unique, decisive, and never to be repeated.

Israelite Rebellion. Jude then moves to remembering their rebellion, namely, that the Lord "destroyed those who did not believe a *second time*." Unfortunately, there is no shortage of rebellion in the wilderness. In the book of Numbers, Miriam and Aaron rebelled against Moses and his choice of an Ethiopian wife (12:1–1); Korah, along with Dathan and Abiram rebelled against Moses' leadership (16:1–35); and people rebelled against Moses by way of their perpetual complaints about their circumstances (11:1–15). All were divinely judged. The first judgment was by way of leprosy (12:10, 13–16), and the latter two by death (16:20–35; 11:3, 31–34). Consequently, there is no shortage of *segmented* rebellion.

Yet there are two extensive rebellions worthy of consideration. Exodus records the first at the Red Sea when Pharaoh was in rapid pursuit of his recently released Jewish slaves (14:5–7). All the people cried out, "Is it because there are no graves in Egypt that you have taken us away to die in the desert? What in the world have you done to us by bringing us out of Egypt? Isn't this what we told you in Egypt, 'Leave us alone so that we can serve the Egyptians, because it is better for us to serve the Egyptians than to die in the desert!'" (14:11–12; NET). God obviously overlooked the revolt for he parted the sea, the Jewish people crossed the sea on dry ground (14:22), the sea destroyed Egypt's army (14:23–28), and the Israelites were "delivered" from the Egyptians (14:29–31; cf. Jos *Ant.* 3.12.6 § 297). The second massive rebellion, however, was not without its consequences and appears to be the one to which Jude alludes.

As God's people were camped at Kadesh-Barnea with Canaan before them, namely, the land God had promised them to inhabit (Deut. 12:9–10; Josh. 21:44), Israel again rebelled against God's leading. According to Numbers, twelve men, one man per tribe, spied out the land for forty days (13:1–25). When they returned to report their findings, only two expressed confidence in subduing Canaan (13:26–30). The others expressed great reservations, which resulted in the Jewish people to fear, to mummer against Moses, Aaron, and God, and to make plans to elect new leaders and return to Egypt (13:31–14:4). All the people cried out, "If only we had died in the land of Egypt, or if only we had perished in this wilderness! Why has the LORD brought us into this land only to fall by the sword, that our wives and our children should become plunder? Would it not be better for us to return to Egypt? So they said to one another, 'Let's appoint a leader and return to Egypt" (14:2b–4; NET). So their mutiny was rooted in their disbelief in both God and his appointed leader, Moses.

Despite the plea of Moses, Aaron, Joshua, and Caleb not to rebel against God, the people ignored their appeals and wanted to stone them (14:5–10a). They wanted to murder God's anointed one,

Moses. Israel rebelled against God's desire to lead them into the land of promise. Ten disbelieving spies led an entire community to doubt God's ability to deliver (cf. Jos *Ant.* 3.14.1–15.1 §§ 300–14).[17] So God pronounced punishment on people twenty years of age and older: they were to wander in the wilderness for forty years (the number of days they spent spying out the land) until they died in the desert south of Canaan (14:10b–35). Thus, Jude's first historical memory recalls the ancient testimony about the Exodus community, a community that was persuaded by a few to disbelieve in God's leading. As a result, God punished them.

Divine Punishment of Israel. Jude reminds his readers that "he (God) destroyed" them. The verb "destroyed" (ἀπώλεσεν) could speak of eternal destruction (Matt. 10:28).[18] But it speaks most commonly of physical death, particularly when used to describe Exodus accounts. For instance, the Egyptian armies' pursuit of the Jewish people leaving Egypt came to an abrupt end: "what he [God] did to the Egyptian army, to their horses and chariots, how he made the water of the Red Sea flow over them as they pursued you, so that the LORD has destroyed (ἀπώλεσεν) them to this day" (e.g., LXX, Deut. 11:4 [NRSV; cf. 4Q 122.1–5). Noncanonical retellings of the Exodus event also consider "destroy" to mean physical death. For instance, in speaking of God's judgment of Korah Josephus avers, "Moses, after these men were destroyed (ἀπολωλότας), was desirous that the memory of this judgment might be delivered down to posterity, and that future ages might be acquainted with it" (e.g., *Ant.* 4.3.4 § 57; of Dathan, *Ant.* 4.3.3 § 52; cf. Philo *Moses* 2.281).[19] So when Jude says, "God destroyed" (ἀπώλεσσεν) the Israelites for disbelief, he means God pronounced a penalty of physical death.

In summary, Jude's first historical memory highlights God's judgment of Israel, namely, the exodus generation who disbelieved that

---

17   Hebrews 3:7–4:14 also refers to this event. Yet unlike Hebrews 3:7–4:14 where the followers of Jesus are warned **not** *to become like those followers of God at Kadesh-barnea,* Jude warns his readers that there are people who were like those ten spies at Kadesh-barnea in their congregation.

18   Annihilation or utter destruction appears more commonly with the noun form, which seems to speak of an eternal state of torment for ungodly people (2 Peter 3:7) and the beast and people whose names are not written in the book of Life (Rev. 17:8, 11). It also speaks of people who attempt to thwart God's program (Judas, John 17:12; Antichrist, 1 Thess. 2:3) and distort God's message (2 Peter 2:3, 3:16). It is used of those who oppose the church at Philippi (Phil. 1:28 and 3:19). BDAG 127, ἀπώλεια; *TDNT* (1983), ἀπώλεια. Jude, however, does not use the noun but rather the verb, which tends to be more in keeping with physical death.

19   The verb form (ἀπόλλυμι) speaks often of being killed in battle (Jos *Ant.* 6.14.5.354; 10.1.3§14; 10.7.4§119; 11.8.3 § 316; 15.5.3 § 145; *War* 2.3.3.50; 2.22.1 § 650; 7.3.1.38). Yet it is also used of killing Jesus (Matt. 2:13; 12:14; 27:20; Mark 3:6; 11:18; Luke 19:47), and of being worked to death (*PTebt* II 278.25), of divine judgment (Jos *Ant.* 4.6.12 § 155). See also BDAG 127 ἀπόλλυμι; *TDNT* (1983), ἀπόλλυμι.

God would lead them victoriously from Kadesh-Barnea into the land of promise. Thus, disbelief and their rebellion ended in physical death.

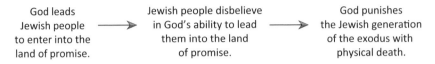

Second, Jude recalls the *divine judgment of the angelic rebellion against God's prescribed residence* (v.6). Unlike the first event about Israel's rebellion against God's leading, the second recalls angels who left their heavenly residence. It is a sobering story about angels who spread their wings to experience new but God forbidden territories only to be locked up pending a future judgment day. Attention is first given to the celestial rebellion itself (v.6b, c) and then to God's execution of judgment (v.6a).

Celestial Rebellion. Naturally, the statements, "those who did not keep their own domain but *who* abandoned their own place of residence" modify "angels" (ἀγγέλους) mentioned in the previous clause. These phrases are essential to understanding the celestial rebellion. First, who are these angels? The angels (ἀγγέλους) appear to be those alluded to in Genesis 6:1–4. Genesis recalls a period of time when men and women were reproducing according to God's expressed expectations (Gen. 6:1; cf. 1:28). During this time, a group referred to as the "sons of God" decided that they too wanted to join in the reproduction process, but there were divine repercussions (Gen. 6:1–4).[20] Although some debate surrounds the identity of the "sons of God," Jewish tradition identifies them as angels. Job speaks of "sons of god" as angelic beings (1:6; 2:1; 38:7). More pointedly, however, Jewish retellings of Genesis 6 identify "sons of God" as angels.[21] Three sources *Jubilees*, 1Q Genesis Apocryphon, and *1 Enoch* make it clear that Jude's learned and restated version of the Genesis account is that the "sons of God" of Genesis 6 are celestial beings, "children of heaven."

Second, what does Jude emphasize concerning the angelic rebellion? Jewish sources draw attention to angels who desired women, left

---

20   Although assumed here that the "sons of God" in Genesis 6:1–4 are angelic beings, some believe they are human beings. See Lyle Eslinger, "A Contextual Identification of the *bene ha'elohim and benoth ha'adam* in Genesis 6:1–4," *JSOT* 13 (1979): 65–73. Nevertheless during Jude's timeframe, the general consensus was that "sons of God" were angelic beings. See Erik W. Larson, "The LXX and Enoch: Influence and Interpretation in Early Jewish Literature" and James C. VanderKam, "Response: Jubilees and Enoch," both may be found in *Enoch and Qumran Origins: New Light on a Forgotten Connection*, edited by Gabriele Boccaccini (Grand Rapids: Eerdmans, 2005), 84–89; 162–70. Thus, the point is simply this: First-century Judeans understood "sons of god" to be "angels of god."

21   In keeping with the Hebrew texts, "sons of God" (בהאלהים) is rendered "angels of God" (ἄγγελοι θεοῦ) in the Old Greek LXX (3ʳᵈ BCE) and Josephus (*Ant.* 1.3.1. §§ 72–73).

heaven, took women for wives, and procreated with women (*1 Enoch* 6:1–6; 7:1–6). So Jude's readers were aware of the various forms of rebellion, the subsequent manner by which these angels led people astray, and their punishment. Yet what aspect of this multifaceted rebellion does Jude underscore? Jude's stress is found in a twofold statement that resembles a synonymous form of parallelism.[22]

> 6b τοὺς μὴ τηρήσαντας τὴν ἑαυτῶν ἀρχὴν
> 6b those who did not keep their own domain

> 6c ἀλλὰ ἀπολιπόντας τὸ ἴδιον οἰκητήριον
> 6c but *who* abandoned their own place of residence

On the one hand, the similar wording of "those who did not keep" (τηρήσαντας)[23] and "those who abandoned" (ἀπολιπόντας)[24] underscores the act of leaving somewhere. In fact, the latter clause echoes *1 Enoch* where the author includes in his retelling of the event: "who left (ἀπολιπόντες) the highest heaven" (12:4; cf. 15:3). On the other hand, the latter half of both clauses, namely, "their own domain" (τὴν ἑαυτῶν ἀρχήν) and "their own residence" (τὸ ἴδιον οἰκητήριον), draws our attention from whence they left. "The language," as Schreiner rightly observes, "is rather vague."[25] Consequently, there are several different ways to render "domain" (ἀρχήν) and "residence" (οἰκητήριον).

First, the noun "domain" (ἀρχήν) could mean they were authority figures, or cosmic rulers. For instance, one Qumran text avers, "peace and blessing for the lot of God, to exalt the authority of Michael among the gods and the dominion of Israel among all flesh" (1QM 17:7–8).[26]

---

22   Bauckham also views these two clauses to be in synonymous parallelism. (see Bauckham, *Jude, 2 Peter*, 11, 52). As we shall see, Jude recounts this second type of rebellion to be a refusal to accept God's desired place in the heavens.

23   "Those who did not keep" (τηρήσαντας) is an aorist active participle masculine plural accusative from τηρέω that means, "I keep" or "I guard." Syntactically, the participle is functioning adjectivally modifying "angels" (ἀγγέλους). Semantically, it is a constative aorist that merely identifies the angelic event of leaving as a whole with no particular emphasis on its beginning, end, or continuation.

24   "Those who abandoned" (ἀπολιπόντας) is an aorist active participle masculine plural accusative from ἀπολείπω that means, "I leave." Syntactically, the participle is functioning adjectivally modifying "angels" (ἀγγέλους). Semantically, it is a constative aorist that merely identifies the angelic event of leaving as a whole with no particular emphasis on its beginning, end, or continuation.

25   Thomas R. Schreiner, *1, 2 Peter, Jude*, NAC (Nashville: B&H, 2003), 448.

26   See *1 Enoch* 82:10–20; 1QM 10:12. Several commentators appear to support the idea that the angels did not keep their position of heavenly powers they at one time exercised over the world: Bauckham, *Jude, 2 Peter*, 52; Davids, *The Letters of 2 Peter, Jude*, 50; Norman Hillyer, *1 and 2 Peter, Jude*, NIBC (Peabody, MA: Hendrickson, 1992), 242; J.N.D. Kelly, *A Commentary on the Epistles of Peter and Jude*, Thornapple Commentaries (Grand Rapids: Baker, 1981), 257.

Naturally, Michael is the archangel who will appear later in Jude v.9. The point to be made here is simply that an angel is given authority or "position of authority" (CEB). Thus, the term *might* mean angels did not keep their office or position of rulership. Yet Jude's parallelism seems to suggest that these celestial beings did not stay within their sphere of official activity, they did not maintain their rightful place of influence, or quite simply they did not remain in their proper domain. In essence, they left heaven (cf. *1 Enoch* 12:4).[27] Likewise, the noun "residence" (οἰκητήριον) or "home" is translated numerous ways.[28] Yet no matter how it is translated angels refused to stay put. Jude recalls one aspect of the ancient testimony about these rebellious angels, namely, that they rejected God's prescribed heavenly residence. So, God punished them.

<u>Divine Punishment of Angels.</u> The angelic rebellion ended in judgment. Jude avers, that God "has kept angels in eternal chains in darkness for the judgment of the great day." Four questions need to be addressed here. First, who issued the judgment? Although "angels" (ἀγγέλους)[29] is placed first in this dependent clause, they are not the subject but rather the objects being kept (τετήρηκεν). The assumed subject is included in the verb "*he* has kept" (τετήρηκεν). Who, however, is "he"? Some translations say "Jesus" (ESV, NET) is the subject, while others say "God" (NET-SE), and still others say "Lord" (KJV, ASV, NAB, NRSV, NASB, NIV, WEB). Yet the verb "keep" (τηρέω) is an important term in Jude. Whereas the *angels did not keep* their place (v. 6b,c), so *God now keeps them* in their place (v.6a). Similarly, whereas *God keeps followers* for Jesus (v.1), *believers are to keep* themselves for God (v.21).

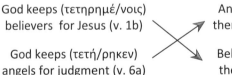

God keeps (τετηρημέ/νοις)
believers for Jesus (v. 1b)

Angels did not keep (τηρή/σαντας)
themselves in God's domain (v. 6b,c)

God keeps (τετή/ρηκεν)
angels for judgment (v. 6a)

Believers are to keep (τηρή/σατε)
themselves in God's love (v. 21a)

---

27   BDAG (138d 7 ἀρχή) lists both possibilities. Several commentators appear to support the idea that Jude is merely saying they left heaven: Gene L. Green, *Jude and 2 Peter*, BECNT (Grand Rapids: Baker, 2008), 68; Schreiner, *1, 2 Peter, Jude*, 448; NET. The synonymous parallelism would seem to best support this option: they are merely two clauses that say the same thing just with different terms.

28   For instance, "their own habitation" (KJV), "their proper dwelling" (NRSV, ESV; cf. ASV), "their own dwelling place" (WEB), "their own place of residence" or "home" (NET; cf. NIV, CEB), and "the place where they belonged" (NLT^SE).

29   The noun "angels" (ἀγγέλους) is an masculine plural accusative and thereby functions grammatically as the direct object to the verb "he has kept" (τετήρηκεν), which is third singular perfect active indicative τηρέω. Semantically, "he has kept" is an extensive perfect emphasizing the completed action of a past action of the current imprisonment of the angels waiting divine judgment.

Accordingly, the person of the Godhead who keeps "the called for Jesus" (v.1b) is the very one who has kept and continues to keep (τε-τήρηκεν) these seditious beings. It is God the Father who guards the rebellious angels.

Second, what is the judgment? Jude contends that God has kept these defiant angels "in eternal chains" (δεσμοῖς ἀϊδίοις). It is not unusual to read about people bound in chains and imprisoned either as a criminal or a prisoner of war.[30] In Jude, however, angels are shackled in "eternal chains" (δεσμοῖς ἀϊδίοις). Whereas Jude's version about angelic rebels includes being bound in chains, no such punishment of the "sons of god" is mentioned in Genesis 6. Bauckham muses this concept is "very prominent in the tradition of the fall of the Watchers."[31] So like a criminal or a prisoner of war, angelic rebels are chained, cast into a dark prison, and incapable of moving about freely. Is this binding, however, literal, and what does "eternal" (ἀϊδίοις) mean when they appear to be released "for judgment of the great day" (εἰς κρίσιν μεγάλης ἡμέρας)? Perhaps "we are not intended to imagine," as Hillyer concludes, "a literal dungeon in which fallen angels are fettered. Rather, Jude is vividly depicting the misery of their conditions."[32] Whether understood literally or figuratively, Jude's point is that God has kept and continues to keep angelic rebels in some sort of confined custody.

Third, where does the judgment occur? Although the confinement is "in darkness" (ὑπὸ ζόφον), once again no such description occurs in Genesis 6. Nevertheless, the concept is common in the Enoch tradi-

---

30   In the LXX many references use the noun "bind" (δεσμός; MT Hebrew (רסא) for literal imprisonment (of Israelites in Egypt, Lev. 26:13; of Manasseh in Assyria, 2 Chron. 33:11; Prayer of Manasseh 10; of Zedekiah in Babylon, 1 *Esdras* 1:40; of Jewish people in Egypt, 3 Macc. 3:25). Yet there are references to figurative bindings (of sin, Isa. 52:2; Jer. 2:20; of women, Eccl. 7:26). In the New Testament, the idea of being bound for literal imprisonment describes the situations of both Peter and Paul (Acts 12:7; 16:22–27) as well as in Josephus (of Josephus in Egypt, *Ant.* 10.7.5 § 122; of Jeremiah in Jerusalem, *Ant.* 10.7.5 § 122; of Aristobulus in Rome, *Ant.* 14.7.4 § 123; of Herod Agrippa in Rome, *War* 1.9.6 § 181; etc.). At Masada they would rather commit suicide than to be placed in chains and taken to Rome (Jos *War* 7.9.1 §§ 389–406). In fact, Josephus recalls how the rebel leader John of Gischala, one of several who lead a Jewish insurrection against Rome *circa* 67–68 CE, was captured and then describes his imprisonment to be the equivalent to "eternal chains" (δεσμοῖς αἰωνίοις; *War* 6.9.4 § 434).

31   For instance, "And to Michael God said, 'Make known to Semyaz and the others who are with him, who fornicated with the women, that they will die together with them in all their defilement . . . bind them for seventy generations underneath the rocks of the ground until the day of their judgment and of their consummation, until the eternal judgment is concluded'" (*1 Enoch* 10:12; cf. 4Q202 f1iv:5–10). *1 Enoch* 10:12 was translated by E. Isaac in *The Old Testament Pseudepigrapha*, Volume One, edited by James H. Charlesworth (Garden City: Doubleday, 1985), 17. See Bauckham, *Jude, 2 Peter*, 53.

32   Hillyer, *1 and 2 Peter, Jude*, 242. See also Schreiner (*1, 2, Peter, Jude*, 448) who agrees with Hillyer.

tion.[33] So where is this "darkness" (KJV, ASV, NASB, NIV)?[34] On the one hand, Jude's description "in darkness" may refer to a second heaven.[35] On the other hand, the location of "the realms of darkness" (ζόφος) may be beneath the earth. Perhaps, "in darkness" (ὑπὸ ζόφον) refers to the "underworld" (CEB) or "nether world" (RSV: "nether darkness").[36] For instance, in Homer's *Iliad* the god Hades rules the world below, "the *darkness* (ζόφον) of the realms under the earth" (15:191).[37] Perhaps, the underworld is an abyss alluded to when Enoch describes, "I then saw one . . . seizing that first star binding his hands and feet, and throwing him into an abyss—this abyss was narrow and deep, empty and dark" (88:1; cf. 54:3–5).[38] Perhaps, it is merely some sort of pit or cistern,[39] or a sort of grave.[40] Regardless of whether "in

---

33   For instance in *2 Enoch* we read, "And those men picked me up and brought me up to the second heaven. And they showed me, and I saw a darkness greater than earthly darkness. And there I perceived prisoners under guard, hanging up, waiting for her measureless judgment. And those angels have the appearance of darkness itself, more than earthly darkness" (71–2; cp 18:1–5). Translation of *2 Enoch* 7:1–2 is by F. I. Anderson, "2 (Slavonic Apocalypse of) Enoch" in *The Old Testament Pseudepigrapha*, Volume One, edited by James H. Charlesworth (Garden City: Doubleday, 1985), 112.

34   Other possible English renders are "deepest darkness" (NRSV), "gloomy darkness" (ESV; cf. NAB), "utter darkness" (NET), or "prisons of darkness" (NET-SE).

35   Bauckham, *Jude, 2 Peter*; Davids, *The Letters of 2 Peter and Jude*, 51; Kelly, *A Commentary in the Epistles of Peter and Jude*, 257.

36   G. Green supports the netherworld perspective with selected statements in Greek classical literature from Aeschylus who wrote, "As for me, I depart for the darkness beneath the earth" (*Persians*, 839) and Euripides who wrote, "Forever in the nether gloom" (*Hippolytus*, 1416). See G. Green, *Jude & 2 Peter*, 70. People who favor a Greek underworld view are Donald Senior and Daniel Harrington, *1 Peter, Jude and 2 Peter*, SP, vol. 17. (Collegeville, MN: The Litrugical Press, 2003), 196 and perhaps Bauckham, *Jude, 2 Peter*, 52–53.

37   In Homer's Iliad the heaven and earth are divided into three parts. Neptune dwells in the sea, Hades took the darkness of the realms under the earth, and Zeus took to the air, sky, and clouds (15.184–199). The Greek for 15.191 reads: Ἀιδιης δ ἔλαχε ζόφον ἠερόεντα. See Walter Leaf, editor, *The Iliad*, vol II (London: Macmillan, 1902), 117. Translation from *The Iliad of Homer The Odyssey* in Great Books of the Western World (Chicago, IL: Encyclopaedia Britannica, 1952). Liddell and Scott (1983 reprint), ζόφος. BDAG 429b 2, ζόφος.

38   For instance, after an archangel bound Azaz'el/Semyaz in *1 Enoch* 10, "he made a hole in the desert which was in Duda'el and cast him there; he threw on top of him rugged and sharp rocks. And he covered his face in order that he may not see light" (10:4–5), and again it is said he is placed "underneath the rocks of the ground" (10:11–12; cf. 14:5). *1 Enoch* 88:1 is translated by E. Isaac in *The Old Testament Pseudepigrapha*, 64.

39   For instance, in *1 Enoch*, the "darkness" in which Semyaz alias Azaz'el is buried (10:4–5; 11–12) may be nothing more than a cistern similar to the one Jeremiah was placed (Jer. 38:6–13; Jos *Ant.* 10.7.5 § 122), or in Isaiah where heavenly forces and earthly kings are imprisoned in a pit (e.g., "cistern," see NET note) until a period of judgment (Isa. 24:21–22).

40   *1 Enoch* 10:11–12 is translated by E. Isaac in *The Old Testament Pseudepigrapha*, 18. Moo even goes so far as to conclude, "Jude probably has this passage in mind as he writes Jude 6." Douglas Moo, *2 Peter and Jude*, NIV Application Commentary (Grand Rapids: Zondervan, 1996), 241.

darkness" (ὑπὸ ζόφον) means some deep underworld, an abyss, a cistern, or some grave the point is clear: seditious angels lost their freedom, were placed in darkness, and are no longer able to perceive and take part in any of the happenings in heaven or on earth.

Finally, when will the judgment end? The current confinement will end on a specified day of judgment. Once again, Jude's reference of angelic punishment "for judgment of the great day" (εἰς κρίσιν μεγάλης ἡμέρας) is not in Genesis 6:1–4. Perhaps, this embellishment is derived from Joel's "the day of the LORD comes—that great and terrible day" (Joel 2:31; 3:4 NET), or another Hebrew prophet because this concept resonates among many prophets (Isa. 13:6, 9; Joel 2:11; Amos 5:18, 20; Zeph. 14; Mal. 4:5).[41] Although possible, Jude's portrayal seems similar to *1 Enoch*. The "judgment of the great day" (εἰς κρίσιν μεγάλης ἡμέρας) is God's righteous judgment, namely, fallen angels lead into "the bottom of the fire—and in torment—the prison (where) they will be locked up forever" (10:13–14).[42] Regardless, celestial beings remain incarcerated until God's appointed judgment day.

In summary, Jude's second historical memory highlights God's judgment of angels, who rejected their heavenly residence. "For this sin," concludes Richard, "they are banished from heaven and condemned to imprisonment in darkness within the earth with chains (*1 Enoch* 10:4–6; 14:5; 54:3–5) until the ominous 'great day of judgment' (*1 Enoch* 10:12; 22:11)."[43]

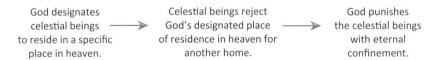

God designates celestial beings to reside in a specific place in heaven. → Celestial beings reject God's designated place of residence in heaven for another home. → God punishes the celestial beings with eternal confinement.

Jude's third and final memory recalls the *divine judgment of Gentiles who reject God's marital norms* (v.7). As it was with the exodus community and

---

41 Davids (*The Letters of 2 Peter and Jude*, 51) draws attention the similar terminology between Jude and the OT prophets, but "The Day of the Lord" in Hebrew Scriptures speaks more of a longer duration of judgment and ought not to be confused with Jude's reference to God's judgment of the great day for it is more in keeping with God's final great white throne judgment of Revelation 20:11–15.

42 *1 Enoch* 10:13–14 is translated by E. Isaac in *The Old Testament Pseudepigrapha*, 18. See also *1 Enoch* 10:12–13; 16:3; 21:10; *2 Enoch* 18:6. Of particular significance is the location of the sinful before judgment day, the judgment day itself, and the events after judgment day: "sinners are set apart when they die and are buried in the earth and judgment has not been executed upon them in their lifetime . . . until the great day of Judgment—and to the accursed (there will be) plague and pain forever, and the retribution of their spirits. They will bind them there forever . . ." (*1 Enoch* 22:10–11; cf. Luke 16).

43 Earl J. Richard, *Reading 1 Peter, Jude, and 2 Peter: A Literary and Theological Commentary* (Macon, GA: Smyth & Helwys Publishing, 2000), 256.

the angels, the Gentile rebellion began with a few, spread to others, and ended in punishment for many. Attention is first given to the Gentile rebellion (v.7b, c) and then to God's execution of judgment (v.7a, d).

Gentile Rebellion. Jude describes the rebellion with two statements: "those who practiced immorality in the same way as these" and "those who went after different flesh." Both refer back to the "cities" (πόλεις).[44] Yet only two cities are named, Sodom and Gomorrah. Although Hebrew Scriptures and extrabiblical literature refer frequently to Sodom and Gomorrah, they often limit discussions to their location within Canaanite territory (Gen. 10:19) and to the wealth of the surrounding land (Gen. 13:10; cf. Philo *Abr.* 227). Yet today the meaning of their names and their exact location remain a mystery.[45]

Also debated is the sin for which these cities are judged.[46] While it is clear they were judged for sexual perversions (Jub. 16:5–6; 20:5–6; *TNap* 3:4; perhaps T. Levi 14:6), Josephus describes them as people who "grew proud, on account of their riches and great wealth: they became unjust towards men, and impious towards God, insomuch that they did not call to mind the advantages they received from him: they hated strangers, and abused themselves with Sodomitical practices" (*Ant.* 1.11.1 § 194; cf. Gen. 19:2–11).[47] Yet what sin or rebellion does Jude emphasize? Although it would seem the synonymous parallelism (see note #22) identifies the nature of the Gentile rebellion, both phrases baffle twenty-first-century interpreters.

> [7b] τὸν ὅμοιον τρόπον τούτοις ἐκπορνεύσασαι
>
> [7b] who practiced immorality in the same way as these (Sodom & Gomorrah)

---

44   The term "cities" (πόλεις) is a metonymy, or more specifically, a metonymy of subject where "cities" is stated for an attribute or adjunct of it, namely "cities" equal "people." Similar occurrences exist in 1 John where "world" equals "people" ("world" equals "people"; cf. 2:2, 3:1, 4:1, 5:19) and in 1 John 3:12 "if our *heart* condemns us" ("heart" = conscience). Bullinger's *Figures of Speech*, 587–89.

45   Compare Anson F. Rainey and R Steven Notley, *The Sacred Bridge: Carta's Atlas of the Biblical World* (Jerusalem: Carta, 2006), 15, 113–14 and Steve Collins, "Rethinking the Location of Zoar: An Exercise in Biblical Geography, *Biblical Research Bulletin: The Academic Journal of Trinity Southwest University* 6.3 (2006): 1–7.

46   Some Jewish literature limits their sin to depraved sexual activities (Gen. 19:1–13, 23–25; cf. Jub. 16:5–6; 20:5–6). Josephus even muses "they resolved themselves to enjoy these beautiful boys by force and violence" (*Ant.* 1.11.3–4 § 200–04; cp Philo, *Abel* 122; *Dreams* 1:85). And yet their sins are also expanded to include pride (Ezek. 16:49a), arrogance (*Sir.* 16:8; 3 Macc. 2:5), disregard for the poor (Ezek. 16:49b), hatred of foreigners (Jos *Ant.* 1.11.1 § 194), and moral debauchery in general (Ezek. 16:46–48; 3 Macc. 2:5).

47   Certainly sins of hospitality (Gen. 19:2–3, 8; Wisd. Sol. 19:14–15), resentment toward Lot's ethnicity (Gen. 19:9; Jos *Ant.* 1 § 194), and satisfying their homosexual urges (Gen. 19:4–5; Jos *Ant.* 1.11.3–4 §§ 200–04) are evident in Genesis.

^{7c} καὶ ἀπελθοῦσαι ὀπίσω σαρκὸς ἑτέρας,
^{7c} and who went after different flesh

First, what does the term "immorality" (ἐκπορνεύω) mean? As presented in chapter four, "who practiced immorality" (ἐκπορνεύσασαι)[48] involves an array of unacceptable forms of extramarital sex. Thus, the best rendering is "immoral *sexual relations*" (CEB; cf. ESV, NIV, NET, WEB). Another challenge in defining the Gentile rebellion is the phrase "in the same way as these" (τὸν ὅμοιον τρόπον τούτοις). To what does the word "these" (τούτοις) refer? Many consider the word "these" (τούτοις) to refer back to the "angels" (ἀγγέλους) in verse 6 (cf. NET).[49] Some suggest that an interpretive paraphrase might be "the cities practiced immoral *sexual relations* like the angels." Yet Jude's depiction of the angels in verse 6 does not highlight sexual perversions but rather underscores a *refusal* to remain in heaven. Thus, the grammatical connection to the angles is somewhat elusive. So if not the angels, what then is the referent of "these" (τούτοις)? "These" (τούτοις) more pointedly refers to the cities of Sodom and Gomorrah (Σόδομα καὶ Γόμορρα).[50] An interpretive paraphrase would be "the cities practiced immoral *sexual relations* like Sodom and Gomorrah." Jude's point then is "neighboring towns" (NLT^{SE}) practiced similar immoral behavior as those of Sodom and Gomorrah. The negative behavior of two cities influenced other neighboring cities. Finally, what does "different flesh" (σαρκὸς ἑτέρας) mean? As presented in chapter four, "who went" (ἀπελθοῦσαι)[51] joined

---

48   The term "who practiced immorality" (ἐκπορνεύσασαι) is an aorist active participle feminine plural nominative from ἐκπορνεύω that means, "I live immorally." Syntactically, the participle functions adjectivally and modifies the feminine plural nominative "cities" (πόλεις). Semantically, it is a constative aorist that identifies immorality as a whole with no particular emphasis on its beginning, end, or continuation.

49   The demonstrative pronoun "these" (τούτοις) could be declined as a masculine plural dative from οὗτος, which means "this" or "this one." The closest word that "these" (τούτοις) modify in this sentence is "angels" (ἀγγέλους). The noun "angels" (ἀγγέλους) is a masculine plural accusative that functions grammatically as the direct object to the verb "he has kept" (τετήρηκεν) in verse 6.

50   The demonstrative pronoun "these" (τούτοις) could be declined as a neuter plural dative from οὗτος. The closest antecedent is "Sodom" (Σόδομα), which is also neuter or both "Sodom and Gomorrah" (Σόδομα καὶ Γόμορρα). It is not unusual for neuters to have antecedents of mixed gender or sometimes even purely masculine gender (cf. Rom. 2:14; 1 Cor. 6:10–11). Furthermore, some translations (cf. KJV, ESV,) consider "these" (τούτοις) to refer back to "Sodom and Gomorrah" (Σόδομα καὶ Γόμορρα).

51   The term that is translated "who went after" (ἀπελθοῦσαι) is an aorist active participle feminine plural nominative from ἀπέρχομαι that means, "I go after" or I depart." Syntactically, the participle is functioning adjectivally modifying feminine plural nominative "cities" (πόλεις). Semantically, it is a constative aorist that merely identifies the act of attaining something, in this case man after men, as a whole with no particular emphasis on its beginning, end, or continuation.

with the phrase "after different flesh" (ὀπίσω σαρκὸς ἑτέρας) simply means that Gentile residents of these cities, rather than sleeping with their wives (spouses), flesh of their flesh (cf. Gen. 2:23; cf. Eph. 5:28–31), went after "different flesh" (woman or man) and thereby practiced forms of sexual whoredom that spans sexual activities like marriage to foreign women, premarital sex, adultery, prostitution, orgies, cultic prostitution, and homosexuality. This rendering upholds the integrity of the parallelism between the two clauses. Thus, Jude draws attention to an unhealthy orientation to "free sex." Consequently, the only connection with the angels is that like the angles who **rejected** God's heavenly residence, these Gentiles **rejected** God's marital expectations (cf. Rom. 2:14). Jude recalls the rebellion of the Gentiles to underscore a lifestyle that veers away from God's path of living rightly within a marriage relationship. So God punished them.

Divine Punishment. The judgment against the Gentiles is vague. Jude says "*that* similarly Sodom and Gomorrah and the cities around them . . . , are *now* set as an example by suffering a punishment of eternal fire." First, what exactly is God's punishment? Jude says, "they *now* set as an example" (πρόκεινται δεῖγμα).[52] Although the phrase seldom denotes being placed on display as an example, Josephus describes Jehoiachin as a public example for John of Gischala (a leading rebel in the Jewish revolt) concerning how to behave when he was faced with the threat of Jerusalem's destruction by Rome.[53] Most translations emphasize Sodom and Gomorrah serving as a negative example.[54] Consequently, these Gentile cities were placed on public display to encourage Judeans to honor God's marital norms.

---

52   "They *now* set" (πρόκεινται) is third plural present middle indicative from πρόκειμαι, which means, "I set before" or "I lie before." Syntactically, "they *now* set" (πρόκεινται) functions as the main verb of this dependent clause with an assumed subject, "they." Semantically, it is rendered as a progressive present: "they are *now* set"; however, customary present is also possible: "they are *continually* set."

53   Jehoiachin was king when Nebuchadnezzar invaded Judea in December 598 BCE, laid siege on Jerusalem, and captured it in March 597 BCE. Josephus avers, "But still, John, it is never dishonorable to repent, and amend what has been done amiss, even at the last. You have a "good example set" before you in Jehoiachin, the king of the Jews. He, when of old his conduct had brought the Babylonian's arm upon him, of his own free will left the city before it was taken, and with his family endured voluntary captivity" (*War* 6.2.1§103–04; cf. Philo *Moses* 1:48).

54   The rendering "they serve as a warning" (NLT^SE; cf. CEB) concurs with Jewish literature. Sodom and Gomorrah symbolized the sort of judgment to expect for any sinful city (Jer. 49:18; 50:40): Jew (Amos 4:11; T. Levi 14:6) or Gentile (Zeph. 2:9). The sins of the prophets such as adultery, living lies, and encouragement of evildoers prior to the destruction of the first temple are, in God's eyes, typical of the people of Sodom and Gomorrah (Jer. 23:14). Others declared that "Just as the Sodomites were destroyed from the earth, so all who serve idols will be destroyed" (4Q221 f2i:3; cf. 4Q223 224 f2ii:53). Later, Jesus equates Galilean rejection of him and his ministry in the cities of Capernaum as sin whose judgment will be more terrible than that of Sodom and Gomorrah (Matt. 10:15; 11:23–24; cf. Luke 10:12; 17:29; Rom. 9:29).

Second, how did God punish these cities? Jude says, "by suffering" (ὑπέχουσαι)[55] a "*divine* punishment" (δίκην). A similar combination of "suffer" (ὑπέχω) and "punishment" (δίκην) occurs in Josephus.
Although he employs the term to speak of suffering under the judicial
decisions of a king (*Ant.* 6.3.5 § 42; cf. 13.8.1 § 232), he also uses it
to describe God's people suffering divine judgment of the flood (*Ant.*
1.3.8 § 99) and a plague for rebellion (*Ant.* 4.4.1 § 61; cf. 17.5.6 § 129).
Jude also regards the punishment suffered at Sodom, Gomorrah, and
the other urban centers as *divine* punishment.[56] According to Genesis,
they were destroyed with fire. Jude, however, transforms the literal
term "fire" into a figure of speech when he writes "eternal fire" (πυρὸς αἰωνίου). Yet "eternal fire" has a twofold nuance. On the one
hand, the geographical area where the urban infernos occurred remained desolate. So "eternal fire" could be conceived as a warning.
The fiery destruction of Sodom and Gomorrah was so dreadful it was
an eternal warning for all subsequent generations to beware lest it happen to them: "You consumed with 'fire and sulfur' (πυρὶ καὶ θείῳ) the
people of Sodom who acted arrogantly, who were notorious for their
vices; and you made them an example (παράδειγμα) to those who
should come afterward" (3 Macc. 2:5; cf. Philo *Moses* 2.56; Jos *War* 4.
§ 483).[57] On the other hand, "eternal fire" could be a periphrasis for
hell. So, "eternal fire" is used rather than "hell."[58] The eternal form of

55   "By suffering" (ὑπέχουσαι) is a present active participle feminine plural nominative from
      ὑπέχω, which means, "I suffer." Syntactically, "by suffering" (ὑπέχουσαι) functions as
      an adverbial participle that modifies the verb "they now set" (πρόκεινται) of the previous
      dependent clause. Semantically, the participle "suffering" (ὑπέχουσαι) is a participle of means
      explaining how these Gentile centers are displayed as an example to modify sexual conduct.

56   The noun "punishment" (δίκην) is frequently used to describe judgment: against Egypt (Wisd.
      Sol. 18:11); against anyone who ignores God and practices sexual immorality, idolatry (Wisd.
      Sol. 14:22–31; cf. 1:8); against the Jewish nation for Jason's changing the nation's way of life
      (4 Macc. 4:21); against a tyrant for an unjustified murder and other heinous crimes (4 Macc.
      11:2; 18:22; cf. 12:12 where divine judgment involves "intense and eternal fire and tortures" (4
      Macc. 18:22). There appears, however, an instance where the term conveys the idea of a request
      of substitution whereby divine judgment of the Jewish nation be passed on to Eleazer (4 Macc.
      6:28), and that people are excused from divine judgment when fearing a king (4 Macc. 8:22).

57   The figure of example is when, according to Bullinger, "we conclude a sentence by
      employing an example as a precedent to be followed or avoided." For example, Luke writes
      "On that day, anyone who is on the roof, with his goods in the house, must not come down
      to take them away, and likewise the person in the field must not turn back. Remember Lot's
      wife" (17:31–32). "Remember Lot's wife" (i.e., do not look back) is the example. Here in
      Jude it is the fiery destruction of Gentile urban dwellers. See Bullinger's *Figures of Speech Used
      in the Bible*, 467.

58   This figure of speech is called a periphrasis or circumlocution. "The figure is so called,"
      avers Bullinger, "because more words that are necessary are used to describe anything." For
      instance, "in the city of David" is a periphrasis for Bethlehem (Luke 2:11), or "this fruit of
      the vine" is a periphrasis for wine (Matt. 26:29). Here in Jude "eternal fire" is a periphrasis
      for hell. See Bullinger's *Figures of Speech Used in the Bible*, 419–22.

punishment occurs elsewhere for tyrants: "justice has laid up for you intense and eternal fire and tortures, and *these throughout all time will never let you go*" (4 Macc. 12:12; cf. 1QS 2.8; Matt. 18:8; Rev. 20:11–15). "Jude means," according to Bauckham, "the still burning site of the cities is a warning picture of the eternal fires of hell."[59] As a consequence, Jewish literature describes the affect of God's punishment on the land as a "smoking wasteland, plants bearing fruit that does not ripen and a pillar of salt standing as a monument to an unbelieving soul" (Wisd. Sol. 10:6–8; cf. Deut 29:22–23; 32:32; Philo *Moses* 2.56). Schreiner avers, "This fire functions as an example because it is a type or anticipation of what is to come for all those who reject God. The destruction of Sodom and Gomorrah is not merely a historical curiosity; it functions typologically as a prophecy of what is in store for the rebellious."[60] Perhaps "eternal fire" serves as both a temporal warning for the present in order to avoid the eschatological perils of eternal flames associated with hell. As it happened to the Gentiles, so it may happen to any Judean who rejects God's marital standards.

In summary, Jude's final historical memory highlights God's judgment of Gentiles. Jude draws specific attention to the marital misconduct in urban centers, which involved many types of extramarital sex. Their rejection of God's marital expectations was an act of rebellion that ended in entire cities being destroyed by fire and thereby set as an example.

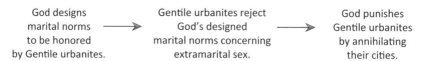

In conclusion, the central theological theme of Jude vv.5–7 is simply that God judges rebellion impartially and in various ways. Jude demonstrates God's impartiality in the divine judgment of Jew, angels, and Gentile alike. He identifies three different types of rebellion: disbelief in God's leading, rejecting God's prescribed residence (= placement within the Roman Empire), and rejecting God's mari-

---

59   Bauckham, *Jude, 2 Peter, 55*; cf. Harrington who sees "eternal fire" a periphrasis for hellfire" (*Jude and 2 Peter*, 197). What appears to drive this periphrasis sense is the presupposition that Jude speaks to the sexual misconduct of angels, who in turn will suffer the eternal fires of hell where angelic beings are eventually cast for their sexual misconduct (*1 Enoch* 10:13–14; 20:1–7; cf. Rev 20:10). See Davids, *The Letter of 2 Peter and Jude*, 53–54; Hillyer, *1 and 2 Peter, Jude*, 244–46; Steven J. Kraftchick, *Jude, 2 Peter*, ANTC (Nashville: Abingdon, 2002), 39–40; Moo, *2 Peter and Jude*, 241–42.

60   Schreiner (*1, 2 Peter, Jude*, 453) says, "the brimstone, salt, and wasted nature of the land function as a warning for Israel and the church elsewhere in the Scriptures (Deut. 29:23; Jer. 49:17–18; cf. Isa. 34:9–10; Ezek. 38:22; Rev. 14:10–11; 19:3; 20:10)." See also E. K. Lee, "Words Denoting 'Pattern' in the New Testament," *NTS* 8 (1961–62): 167.

tal standards. Jude then exemplifies types of punishment: physical death, imprisonment, and total destruction of cities.

Groups	Types of Rebellion	Types of Punishment
Jewish People	Disbelief in God's Leading	Physical Death and No Entrance into the Land of Promise
Angelic Beings	Rejection of God's Designated Placement or Station	Imprisonment and No Longer Able to Interact in Heaven or on Earth
Gentile People	Rejection of God's Design of Societal Sexual Behavior	Total Destruction of Urban Cities and Their Inhabitants

As indicated earlier, Jude's literary grouping of the disbelieving Exodus generation, the seditious celestial beings, and the Gentile cities of Sodom and Gomorrah is not unique to Jude. This theme of rebellion followed by judgment occurs in numerous Jewish writings.[61] What is unique to Jude is his intention? Jude desires that Judeans remember that whether a person is an Israelite, angel, or Gentile urbanite, God punishes rebellion impartially and in various ways. His point to the Judeans to whom he writes is simply: Do not join in the Zealot insurrection against Rome.

HEBREWS 10:19–25

Contextual Orientation

Hebrews 10:19–25 stands in literary parallel with Hebrews 4:14–16.[62] Whereas Hebrews 4:14–16 is positioned to introduce a major

---

61   For instance, *the Damascus Document* (CD) appeals to the three historical tragedies in "the Admonition," where the text speaks of God's future punishment of wicked backsliders. They are used to warn readers to stay firm in the Jewish tradition and not to stray from it. In 3 Maccabees, these historical disasters about God's judgment are placed in the midst of an intercessory prayer for divine intervention against Gentiles who profane the temple. In Jude, they are used to remember that God judges the rebellious, impartially, and decisively. Thus Richard rightly concludes, "Examination of these shows no signs of literary borrowing by Jude" though there is in fact cultural, conceptual, and literary parallels.

62   This inclusio, a figure of speech that brackets a passage of text with the same set of words at the beginning and end, occurs throughout Hebrews, was first introduced in chapter five,

unit of thought or central theological theme that explains both *the appointment and the offering of Jesus as royal priest* (5:1–7:28), Hebrews 10:19–25 is situated to close the unit with a repeated exhortation to "draw near" (10:22; cf. 4:16) and to "hold fast" (10:23; cf. 4:14). The author opens verse 19 by addressing his readers directly as "brothers *and sisters*" (ἀδελφοί; cf. 3:1, 12) with whom he too shares in benefits of the offerings of Jesus whom God has appointed as royal priest. Consequently, the inferential structural marker, "therefore" (οὖν), signals the author's conclusion to the entire section and thereby makes, eventually, three motivational and emotive appeals: *let us* draw near to God (v.22), *let us* hold fast to the confession of faith (v.23), and *let us* encourage one another (vv.24–25) based solely upon Jesus who has put into effect a new way to enter God's presence (vv.19–20) and his presiding /ruling influence as royal-priest (v.21). Thus, the author has reasoned expectations for the community to worship God together, persevere together, and consider others together.

Greek Text[63]

> [19] Ἔχοντες οὖν, ἀδελφοί, παρρησίαν εἰς τὴν εἴσοδον τῶν ἁγίων ἐν τῷ αἵματι Ἰησοῦ, [20] ἣν ἐνεκαίνισεν ἡμῖν ὁδὸν πρόσφατον καὶ ζῶσαν διὰ τοῦ καταπετάσματος, τοῦτ᾽ ἔστιν τῆς σαρκὸς αὐτοῦ, [21] καὶ ἱερέα μέγαν ἐπὶ τὸν οἶκον τοῦ θεοῦ, [22] προσερχώμεθα μετὰ ἀληθινῆς καρδίας ἐν πληροφορίᾳ πίστεως, ῥεραντισμένοι τὰς καρδίας ἀπὸ συνειδήσεως πονηρᾶς καὶ λελουσμένοι τὸ σῶμα ὕδατι καθαρῷ· [23] κατέχωμεν τὴν ὁμολογίαν τῆς ἐλπίδος ἀκλινῆ, πιστὸς γὰρ ὁ ἐπαγγειλάμενος· [24] καὶ κατανοῶμεν ἀλλήλους εἰς παροξυσμὸν ἀγάπης καὶ καλῶν ἔργων, [25] μὴ ἐγκαταλείποντες τὴν ἐπισυναγωγὴν ἑαυτῶν, καθὼς ἔθος τισίν, ἀλλὰ παρακαλοῦντες, καὶ τοσούτῳ μᾶλλον ὅσῳ βλέπετε ἐγγίζουσαν τὴν ἡμέραν.

Structural Outline

> [19] **Ἔχοντες** οὖν, ἀδελφοί, παρρησίαν εἰς τὴν εἴσοδον τῶν ἁγίων ἐν τῷ αἵματι Ἰησοῦ,[64]
> Therefore brothers and sisters, *because* we have confidence to enter God's presence by the blood of Jesus

---

"Interpreting the General Letters," 188.

63 There are no textual variants of consequence in Hebrews 10:19–25. For a listing of text-critical issues see Bateman, "Major Textual Issues in Hebrews" in *Charts on the Book of Hebrews*, 176–84.

64 Structurally, verse 19 is a dependent clause governed by the verbal ἔχοντες, a present active nominative masculine plural participle from ἔχω meaning "I have." Syntactically, it functions as an adverbial participle modifying the three subsequent hortatory subjunctives "let us come together" (προσερχώμεθα), "let us hold on" (κατέχωμεν), and "let us consider" (κατανοῶμεν). Semantically, it functions as a causal adverbial participle and thereby providing the motivational reasoning for the subsequent hortatory subjunctives.

²⁰ (ἣν ἐνεκαίνισεν ἡμῖν) ὁδὸν πρόσφατον καὶ **ζῶσαν** διὰ τοῦ καταπετάσματος,⁶⁵

by a fresh and **_living_** way (that he <u>opened</u> for us) through the curtain

τοῦτ᾽ ἔστιν τῆς σαρκὸς
αὐτοῦ,

<u>that is</u>, through his flesh

²¹ καὶ (**ἔχοντες**) ἱερέα μέγαν ἐπὶ τὸν οἶκον τοῦ θεοῦ,⁶⁶
²¹ and (_because_ we have) a great priest over the house of God,

²²ᵃ **προσερχώμεθα** μετὰ ἀληθινῆς καρδίας ἐν πληροφορίᾳ πίστεως,⁶⁷
²²ᵃ let us come together to worship with a true heart with full assurance of faith,

|

²²ᵇ **ῥεραντισμένοι** τὰς καρδίας ἀπὸ συνειδήσεως πονηρᾶς⁶⁸
²²ᵇ _because_ our hearts have been sprinkled _clean_ from an evil conscience,

|

²²ᶜ καὶ **λελουσμένοι** τὸ σῶμα ὕδατι καθαρῷ·⁶⁹
²²ᶜ and _because_ our bodies have been washed in pure water;

²³ᵃ **κατέχωμεν** τὴν ὁμολογίαν τῆς ἐλπίδος ἀκλινῆ,⁷⁰
²³ᵃ let us hold fast to the confession of our hope without wavering,

|

---

65 There are obviously three verbs underlined. The first is part of the relative clause and in parenthesis, the second is the participle, and the third is part of a demonstrative pronoun clause also in parenthesis. The verb of consequence to be noted is ζῶσαν. It is a present active accusative feminine singular participle ζαω meaning "I live." Syntactically, it is functioning as an adverb modifying "because we have" (ἔχοντες).

66 The verbal governing the clause is an elliptical ἔχοντες. See note 64 above.

67 The verb governing this independent clause is προσερχώμεθα. It is a first-person plural present middle (deponent) subjunctive from προσέρχομαι meaning "I washed." Syntactically, it functions as the main verb of the clause. Semantically, it is functioning as a hortatory subjunctive "let us come together" (προσερχώμεθα).

68 The verbal governing this dependent clause is ῥεραντισμένοι. It is a perfect passive nominative masculine plural participle from ραντιζω meaning "I washed." Syntactically, it functions as an adverbial participle modifying the hortatory subjunctives "let us come together" (προσερχώμεθα). Semantically, it is functioning as a causal adverbial participle and thereby providing a reason for believers to come together to worship God.

69 The verbal governing this dependent clause is λελουσμένοι. It is a perfect passive nominative masculine plural participle from ραντι meaning "I wash." Syntactically, it functions as an adverbial participle modifying the hortatory subjunctives "let us come together" (προσερχώμεθα). Semantically, it is functioning as a causal adverbial participle and thereby providing a reason for believers to come together to worship God.

70 The verb governing this independent clause is κατέχωμεν. It is a first-person plural present active subjunctive from κατέχω meaning "I hold." Syntactically, it functions as the main verb of the clause. Semantically, it functions as a hortatory subjunctive "let us come hold on" (κατέχωμεν).

23b πιστὸς **γὰρ** ὁ ἐπαγγειλάμενος (**ἐστίν**)·[71]
23b for the one who has promised is faithful;

24 καὶ **κατανοῶμεν** ἀλλήλους εἰς παροξυσμὸν ἀγάπης καὶ καλῶν ἔργων,[72]
24 and <u>let us consider</u> one another for provocation to love and to do good deeds,

|

25a μὴ **ἐγκαταλείποντες** τὴν ἐπισυναγωγὴν ἑαυτῶν,[73]
25a not *by* abandoning our meeting together *as community*,

|

25b **καθὼς** (**ἐστίν**) ἔθος τισίν,[74]
25b as (*is*) the habit of some *people*,

|

25c **ἀλλὰ παρακαλοῦντες**,[75]
25c but *by* encouraging *one another*,

|

25d **καὶ** τοσούτῳ μᾶλλον ὅσῳ **βλέπετε ἐγγίζουσαν** τὴν ἡμέραν.
25d and even more so *because* you see the day.

Exegetical Outline

Subject   Based upon the free and safe access to God through Jesus who presides as royal priest . . .

Complement   . . . followers of Jesus are expected to worship, persevere, and consider seriously others as community.

---

71   The structural marker is an explanatory "for" (γάρ) with an elliptical equative verb, "is" (ἐστίν).

72   The verb governing this independent clause is κατανοῶμεν. It is a first-person plural present active subjunctive from κατανοέω meaning "I hold." Syntactically, it functions as the main verb of the clause. Semantically, it functions as a hortatory subjunctive "let us consider" (κατανοῶμεν).

73   The verbal governing this clause is ἐγκαταλείποντες. It is a present active nominative masculine plural participle ἐγκαταλείπω meaning "I forsake" or "I desert." Syntactically, it functions as an adverb modifying "let us consider" (κατανοῶμεν). Semantically, it functions as an adverbial participle of means.

74   The structural marker is a comparative "as" (καθώς) with an elliptical equative verb, "is" (ἐστίν).

75   The verbal governing this clause is παρακαλοῦντες. It is a present active nominative masculine plural participle παρακαλεω meaning "I urge" or "I encourage." Syntactically, it functions as an adverb modifying "let us consider" (κατανοῶμεν). Semantically, it functions as an adverbial participle of means.

I.   **Jesus' Work and Appointment:** Jesus has put into effect a free and safe access to God as royal priest ruling over God's kingdom (10:19–21).

    A. **Free Access via Jesus:** A free and safe access into God's presence exists through the sacrificial death of Jesus (vv. 19–20).

        1. Free Access to God (ἔχοντες): Followers of Jesus have free and safe access before God's presence (v. 19a, 20a).

        2. The Means of Free Access (ζῶσαν): The means by which followers have a free and safe access into God's presence is through Jesus' sacrificial death (v. 19b, 20b).

    B. **Royal Priest** (ἔχοντες): Jesus as great royal priest presides *over* God's kingdom (v. 21).

II. **Three Expectations:** The community is expected to worship God, persevere in their confession of faith, and consider each other to love (10:22–25).

    A. **Worship:** The community is expected to seize the opportunity to corporately worship God with stability of faith because of their spiritual purification (10:22).

        1. Expectation (προσερχώμεθα): Seize the opportunity to worship God (v. 22a).

        2. Reason (ῥεραντισμένοι/ λελουσμένοι): The reason to seize the opportunity to worship God is because of spiritual purification (v. 22bc).

    B. **Persevere:** The community is expected to persevere in their confession of Jesus because God keeps his promises (10:23).

        1. Expectation (κατέχωμεν): Persevere in the confession of Jesus (v. 23a).

        2. Reason (γὰρ): The reason to persevere is because God is faithful to his promise (v. 23b).

    C. **Consider Others:** The community is expected to consider seriously rousing people to love and do good deeds by building community confidence because of the Son's judgment is coming near (10:24–25).

1. Expectation (κατανοῶμεν): The community is expected
   to consider seriously rousing people to love and do good
   deeds (v. 24).

2. How (ἐγκαταλείποντες): The expectation to consider seriously rousing people to love and do good deeds is not by
   neglecting to meet to together (v. 25a).

3. How (παρακαλοῦντες): The expectation to consider seriously rousing people to love and do good deeds is by building community confidence (v. 25b).

4. Reason (ἐγγίζουσαν): The expectation to consider seriously rousing people to love and do good deeds is because of
   the Son's judgment is coming near (v. 25c).

Exposition: Reasoned Expectations for Community Worship and Support

Jesus' Work and Appointment (vv.19–20). The author of Hebrews
crafts this concluding collection of verses by opening with two causal
summary statements: (1) "*because* we have (ἔχοντες) confidence to enter
God's presence by the blood of Jesus" and (2) "*because* we have (elliptical
ἔχοντες) a great priest over the house of God." The first sums up Jesus'
superior offering (vv.19–20) described in Hebrews 8:1–10:18, while
the second succinctly restates Jesus' appointment as royal priest (v.21)
taught in Hebrews 5:1–7:28.

First, *Jesus provides free and safe access to God* (vv.19a, 20a). The author avers, that followers of Jesus have "confidence (παρρησίαν) to enter
God's presence" (v.19a). The term "confidence" (παρρησίαν) has already occurred twice before in Hebrews (3:6; 4:16) and yet interpreted
differently. On the one hand, the noun "confidence" in 3:6 conveys
the idea of *conviction*, a *resolve*, or a *determination* that "takes possession
of" or "holds firmly to" one's status as members of God's house ("we
are of his house"). It involves being courageous, steady, or true to
one's convictions. The house (i.e., kingdom) is ruled over by the divine royal Son (3:6a; cf. 1:1–14) whose function is that of royal priest
(3:1; 5:4–5; 10:21; cf. 1 Macc. 13:42; T. Levi 8:14, 18:2–14). Thus,
"hold firmly to our confidence" might be rendered "hold firmly to
our *resolve* about the Christ,"[76] or perhaps paraphrased as a prohibition

---

76   Gareth L. Cockerill, *Hebrews: A Bible Commentary in the Wesleyan Tradition* (Indianapolis, IN:
     Wesleyan Publishing House, 1999), 92.

"Do not give up your *citizen's rights*."[77] On the other hand, two possible interpretations exist for "confidence" in 4:16, which has its parallel in 10:19. Some translations suggest that the noun "confidence" (παρρησίαν) conveys the idea of speaking boldly and quite openly with God (KJV, ASV, NRSV, WEB, NLT[SE]). This emphasis appears in Proverbs where the author depicts Wisdom as speaking "openly" (LXX, παρρεσία) in the public square (1:20). Similarly, the same emphasis existed in the Greco-Roman world. The full citizen alone has the right to say anything "openly" in the midst of a gathering of people. It is also used to express emotions or sufferings "openly" in public (3 Macc. 4:1). Yet "confidence" (παρρησίαν) might better be understood as approaching God's throne in "safety" or "security." In the LXX, "safety" exists for the poor (Ps. 11:5 [12:5]) and for the repentant (Job 22:26; 1 John 3:21) before God. When discussing human relations, "confidence" (παρρησίαν) expresses "security," which is evident in the mutual confidence between two brothers (*P. Mich.* 502.9, 12) and between a husband and a wife (Jos *Ant.* 2.4.4 § 52). This latter understanding appears to be the case for both Hebrews 4:15 and 10:19. In 4:15, Jesus as royal priest can "sympathize" (συμπαθέω)[78] with our "weaknesses" or human frailties (ἀσθένεια)[79] and thereby provides a sense of "safety" or "security" to approach God's throne. Certainly Jesus' "intercession" for believers provides "safety" in approaching God.

This latter perspective would seem to be supported from Hebrews 7:25 where the author describes Jesus as "living to *intercede* on behalf

---

77 Paul Ellingworth, *The Epistle to the Hebrews: A Commentary on the Greek Text*, NIGTC (Grand Rapids: Eerdmans, 1993), 211.

78 The term "sympathize" (συμπαθέω) occurs in the New Testament only in Hebrews (1:15, 10:34). Extra–biblical usage reveals a sense of tenderness as exercised between family members: mothers with children (4 Macc. 14:13–14, 15:4; Jos *War* 6.3.4 § 211) and brothers with brothers (4 Macc. 13:23). This deep affection of family relationships intensifies during or because of trouble or suffering: mothers with children (4 Macc. 15:7, 11–15) and sons with mothers (Jos *Ant.* 13.8.1 § 233). Here in Hebrews, the term "sympathize" emphasizes Jesus' deep affection associated with attitudes of a high priest or his attitude toward his fellow human family members (2:14–18). Due to his own human experience, the divine royal Son "understands" (NLT) or "sympathizes" intensely with being human, particularly as it pertains to human weaknesses.

79 The term "weakness" (ἀσθένεια) often signals physical illness (Matt. 8:17; Luke 5:15, 8:2, 13:11, 12; John 5:5, 11:4; Acts 28:9; Heb. 11:34; cf. 2 Macc. 9:21–22; Philo *Virt.* 25). In Hebrews 4:15, it accents human frailty of an earthly-bodily existence (cf. Philo *Mos.* 1:184, 1 Cor. 15:42–45; *EDNT* 1:170–71), particularly human limitations, human temptation, human suffering, and human death (Heb. 2:17–16, 5:7–8; cf. 12:2b–3a). Although ἀσθένεια may convey a person's moral weakness or sin (5:2, 7:28), experiencing human limitations and temptation are differentiated from those who succumb to them in Hebrews. It was said of the expected Messiah that, "He will not be weak (ἀσθένεια), nor waver in his trust of God" (Pss. Sol. 17:42). Jesus, the royal high priest, is able to empathize with the believer's intellectual and moral stress to obey God (4:14), yet he himself was obedient to God and without sin (Heb. 7:26–27; cf. 2 Cor. 5:21; Phil. 2:5–8).

of" (ζῶν εἰς τὸ ἐντυγχάνειν ὑπέρ) those who come to God through him (δι' αὐτοῦ τῷ θεῷ). The verb ἐντυγχάω "belongs primarily to the conceptual world of the ruler's court" (*EDNT* 2:461). On the one hand, ἐντυγχάω could mean to make an *accusation against* someone in the form of an "appeal." The Maccabees appealed to Rome against King Demetrius (1 Macc. 8:32), Jews appealed to King Antiochus against Menelaus' murder of Onias (2 Macc. 4:36), malcontents appealed to King Alexander against Jonathan Maccabee (1 Macc. 10:61–64, 11:25; cf. Acts 25:24), and Elijah pleads with God against Israel (Rom. 11:2). On the other hand, ἐντυγχάω could mean "intercede." "Moses . . . interceded with God to save [the nation of Israel] from their desperate afflictions . . ." (Philo *Mos.* 1.173; cf. *POxy* 31:2597.6–10). Yet, whenever ἐντυγχάω is used with "for" or "on behalf of" (ὑπέρ), it carries significant theological import. In Romans 8:34, before a heavenly court, Jesus the royal priest "*intercedes* on behalf of us" therefore no one can bring a charge against the saint. In Hebrews 7:25, before God's heavenly court (cf. Heb. 1:3, 8–9, 13; 8:1), Jesus, the royal priest "intercedes" continually (present tense; cf. 2:17–18; 4:14–16) for believers. Thus, followers of Jesus have a free and safe access to enter "into the holy of holies" (εἰς τὴν εἴσοδον τῶν ἁγίων), which in turn parallels the phrase "through the curtain" (διὰ τοῦ καταπετάσματος) in verse 20a.

Typically, the "curtain" or "veil" (καταπετάσμα) in the LXX is the second inner curtain of the tabernacle.[80] In Hebrews, however, the "curtain" appears three times and each time differently (6:19; 9:3; 10:20). In 6:19, the author says, "a *hope* which reaches inside behind the curtain" (NET). Here the concept of *hope* is personified as having entered behind the veil of the innermost part of God's *heavenly sanctuary* where Jesus himself has also entered (cf. Heb. 6:20; 9:12, 24).[81] In 9:3, the author avers, "and after the second curtain there was a tent called the holy of holies" (NET). The veil is the literal one that separates the innermost part of the Holy of Holies from the Holy Place within the *earthly sanctu*-

---

80 See Exodus 26:31–33; 37:3–5[36:35–37], 40:3, 21–27 (cf. 2 Par. [2 Chron.] 3:14; cf. Philo *Mos.* 2:95; Jos *War* 5.5.4 § 212). For a more detailed overview of the tabernacle in extrabiblical material and Hebrews see Herbert W. Bateman, "The Tabernacle in Exodus," "The Tabernacle's Sanctuary in the Old Testament," and "The Old Testament Tabernacle's Sanctuary Compared with Hebrews" in *Charts on the Book of Hebrews*, 75–78.

81 The tabernacle, Solomon's temple, and Herod's temple of Jesus' day were at one time the focus of worship in Jewish history. All were believed to be the abode of God's presence (tabernacle: Ex. 40:34–38, Lev. 16:2, 12–13, 15; Solomon's temple: 2 Chron. 7:1–3; Ezek. 10:3–4, 18–19; Jos *Ant.* 8.4.2 § 106; second temple: cf. 2 Macc. 1:18–2:18). In Jesus' day, the temple was considered functionally identical with a heavenly sanctuary (Jub. 31:14; 4Q400 – 407; 11Q17; Heb. 8:4–5; cf. 1 Enoch 14:10–14, 14:14–22). In addition, temple priests regarded themselves in God's service like the angels (Jub. 31:14–15; 4Q400–407, 11Q17; Mal. 2:7, Eccl. 5:6 [see NET n 9], 4Q511 frag. 35:1–5; perhaps, Jos *Ant.* 9.10.4 § 226–27, Philo *SpecLeg* 1.113b–116). (See *EDSS* 2:921–27; Eskola, 65–83).

ary. Here in 10:20, the author once again appeals to the curtain, this time figuratively: "through the curtain, that is, through his flesh" (NET). The author defines the curtain to be "the flesh of the Jesus," which is also a figure of speech.[82] Perhaps a symbolic equivalence exists with the curtain of the temple that was violently torn at the time of Jesus' death on the cross (Mark 15:38) and thereby symbolically serves to eliminate a parallel hindrance to the true heavenly tabernacle. Regardless, to get to God during the previous era meant to go through the literal curtain that separated the Holy Place from the Holy of Holies. In Hebrews 10:20, to get to God means to go through Jesus, which is clearly evident in the next two paralleled statements (letters B and B[1]).

A		ἔχοντες παρρησίαν εἰς τὴν εἴσοδον τῶν ἁγίων we have free and safe access into God's presence (v. 19a)
	B	ἐν τῷ αἵματι Ἰησοῦ by the blood of Jesus (v. 19b)
	B[1]	ὁδὸν πρόσφατον καὶ ζῶσαν by a fresh and living way (v. 20a)
A[1]		διὰ τοῦ καταπετάσματος through the curtain (that is, his flesh) (v. 20b)

The means by which this free and safe access has occurred is "by the blood of Jesus" (ἐν τῷ αἵματι Ἰησοῦ), which is paralleled with "by a fresh and living way" (ὁδὸν πρόσφατον καὶ ζῶσαν). The "blood of Jesus" (τῷ αἵματι Ἰησοῦ) and "new way" (ὁδὸν πρόσφατον) echoes the author's previous and lengthy discussion about Jesus and his ushering in the "new covenant" (διαθήκης καινῆς; 9:1–28). Thus, the author's first compelling basis is simply that all believers have a free and safe access into God's presence by way of the sacrificial death of Jesus whereby he inaugurated a new covenantal relationship with God (vv.19–20).

The second reason to worship God is equally compelling: *Jesus as great royal priest presides* over *God's kingdom* (v.21). The author describes Jesus as "a great priest over the house of God" (v.21a). Naturally, the statement succinctly recalls Jesus' status as royal priest according to the order of Melchizedek (5:5–7).[83] Earlier in chapter seven, the au-

---

82 This figure of speech involves changing the literal rendering into something else. In the case of "flesh" it tends to be considered a synecdoche whereby an exchange of one idea takes the place of another. More specifically, the part (e.g., "flesh") is put for the whole (e.g., the body or person of Jesus). The author of Hebrews has already used this figure for Jesus in 2:14.

83 New Testament recollections of Melchizedek occur only in Hebrews (5:6, 10; 6:20; 7:1, 10, 11, 15, 17). The infrequent yet distinct reference to Melchizedek in the OT (Gen. 14, Ps

thor expanded the significance of his application by drawing attention to Melchizedek's *kingship* and *priesthood* with particular stress on his priestly functions (he blessed Abraham, and he received a tithe from Abraham, vv.4, 6–7, 9–10). Commenting briefly on Melchizedek as king, the author interprets his name, "king of righteousness" (mel-ech = Hebrew word for "king"; *zedek* = Hebrew word for "righteousness") and describes the sort of king he was, a king of peace. Clearly, he did not descend from Levi (v.6a), and in fact Scripture's silence about Melchizedek's descendants depicts him as someone who was beyond history (v.3). These carefully chosen facts about Melchizedek and their typological application to Jesus serve to reinforce Jesus as an eternal royal priest (5:6; 6:20; 7:17; cf. divine royal priest concept in 1:2–3, 5–13).[84] Furthermore, Jesus is a "great priest *over* God's house," which evokes the comparison between Moses who served *in* God's house and Jesus who currently rules *over* God's house (i.e., kingdom; 3:1–6). Thus, Jesus presently presides *over* God's inaugurated kingdom.[85] Based upon these two previously established and extremely compelling facts about Jesus' superior offering (vv.19–20; cf. 8:1–10:18) and his appointment as royal priest (v.21; cf. 5:1–7:28), the author ushers three significant expectations for worship.

    Three Expectations (vv. 22–25). The threefold expectation progresses from God, to self, and ends with others: worship God (v.22), persevere in your confession about Jesus (v. 23), and consider others (vv.24–25). First, *followers of Jesus are expected to come together to worship God*, "let us draw near *to God* with a sincere heart with full assurance of faith" (v.22a). The English translation "let us draw near" (προσερ-χώμεθα) might also be rendered "let us approach," or more flexibly "let us go right into" (NLT^SE) God's presence. Regardless, it echoes Hebrews 4:16, yet with a nuanced difference. Whereas 4:16 emphasizes approaching God in prayer for mercy and help in times of trouble, 10:22 stresses a broader perspective that naturally includes prayer, but also corporate (the hortatory subjunctive "*let us*") and individual worship (through the individual cleansing, v.22bc). The manner in which believers approach God is "with a true heart in full assurance of faith." Some translations render "true heart" (ἀληθινῆς καρδίας) as

---

110), coupled with the unparalleled descriptions of Melchizedek and his royal-priesthood in Hebrews, makes him profoundly important. For unlike the Aaronite and Zadokite priesthoods (5:1–3; cf. 7:11–14, 23, 28a) Jesus' priesthood of the Melchizedekian order is superior (5:5–10; cf. 7:15–17, 20–22, 24–27, 28b).

84 See previous discussion on pages 189–91 as well as Herbert W. Bateman IV, "Psalm 45:6–7 and Its Christological Contributions to Hebrews," *TJ* 22NS (2001): 3–21.

85 For a theological canonical picture about Jesus as the one through whom God has inaugurated his kingdom and how the letter of Hebrews contributes to it, see Chapter three, "The Theology of the General Letters," 103–20.

"sincere heart" (NASB[95], NIV, NET, NLT[SE]), but the points remain the same. It connotes an honest and devoted attitude toward God, namely a full assurance of trust in God (cf. 6:11).

The reason for worshiping God with all honesty is because God has spiritually purified those who follow Jesus (v.22bc). The parallel construction concerning "hearts being sprinkled *clean*" (ῥεραντισμένοι τὰς καρδίας) and "bodies being washed" (λελουσμένοι τὸ σῶμα) brings to mind several differing Old and New Testament images.

> [22b] **ῥεραντισμένοι** τὰς καρδίας ἀπὸ συνειδήσεως πονηρᾶς
> [22b] *because our* hearts have been sprinkled *clean* from an evil conscience,

> [22c] καὶ **λελουσμένοι** τὸ σῶμα ὕδατι καθαρῷ
> [22c] and *because our bodies* have been washed in pure water

Although some may associate the language of verse 22b with the consecration of priests (Ex. 29:14; Lev. 8:6), others connect the imagery with Moses sprinkling the people with blood at the inauguration of the first covenant at Sinai (Ex. 24:3–8). Thus in contrast to the Exodus event at Sinai, followers of Jesus are sprinkled with the blood of the royal priest and thereby partners in the new covenant (Heb. 9:19).[86] Similarly, some may associate "our bodies having been washed in pure water" in verse 22c with the symbol of water baptism.[87] Yet others see the connection with the discussion of the new covenant in Ezekiel 36:25–26.[88]

> I will sprinkle you with pure water and you will be clean from all your impurities. I will purify you from all your idols. I will give you a new heart, and I will put a new spirit within you. I will remove the heart of stone from your body and give you a heart of flesh. (NET)

---

86   Peter T. O'Brien, *The Letter to the Hebrews*, PNTC (Grand Rapids: Eerdmans, 2010), 368. For my discussion of the verb "inaugurate" (ἐγκαίνιζω) see chapter 3 "The Theology of the General Letters," 106, n. 35 and 99, n. 19.

87   E.g., Harold W. Attridge, *The Epistle to the Hebrews: A Commentary on the Epistle to the Hebrews*, Hermeneia (Philadelphia: Fortress Press, 1989), 289; F. F. Bruce, *The Epistle to the Hebrews*, NICNT (Grand Rapids: Eerdmans, 1990), 255; William L Lane, *Hebrews 9–13*, WBC (Dallas, TX: Word, 1991), 287; Ellingworth, *The Epistle to the Hebrews*, 523–24; Alan C. Mitchell, Hebrews, SP (Collegeville, MN: Liturgical Press, 1989), 211–12, 214; Craig R. Koester, *Hebrews: A New Translation with Introduction and Commentary*, AB (Garden City, NY: Doubleday, 2001), 445, 449.

88   E.g., John Calvin, *The Epistle of Paul the Apostle to the Hebrews and the First and Second Epistles of St. Peter*, translated by William B. Johnston, ed. by David W. Torrance and Thomas F. Torrance (Grand Rapids: Eerdmans, 1963), 142; O'Brien, *The Letter to the Hebrews*, 368; David L. Allen, *Hebrews*, NAC (Nashville, TN: Broadman & Holman, 2010), 515–16.

The inner cleansing of a believer has occurred via the Spirit of God (Heb. 9:13–14; cf. 8:10; 10:16). Thus again, a contrast exists with the old covenant whereby it has been superseded via the inauguration of the new covenant. Consequently, the author of Hebrews emphasizes the internal cleansing and the indwelling spirit of God that has occurred through the divine work of God. Therefore, followers of Jesus ought not to hesitate in coming together before God to worship but rather should embrace it because the spiritual purification through Jesus is the basis for entering safely into God's presence.

Second, *followers of Jesus are expected to persevere in their believing faith about Jesus*, "let us hold fast to the confession of our hope without wavering (v.23a). The English translation "let us hold fast (κατέχωμεν: KJV, NASB, RSV, NRSV, NET, ESV), might also be rendered "let us hold firmly" (NIV), or "let us hold unwaveringly" (κατέχωμεν along with ἀκλινῆ: NET). This expectation echoes previous appearances of the verb "hold fast" (κατέχω).

> But Christ is faithful as a son over God's house. We are of his house (i.e., kingdom), if in fact (ἐάν) *we hold firmly* (κατάσχωμεν) to our confidence and the hope we take pride in (3:6, NET).

> For we have become partners with Christ, if in fact (ἐάνπερ) we *hold* our initial confidence *firm* (κατάσχωμεν) until the end (3:14, NET).

> And *let us hold* (κατέχωμεν) unwaveringly to the hope that we confess, for the one who made the promise is trustworthy (10:23, NET).

The act to "hold firmly" (κατεχω) then conveys an expectation to "be strong" or "stand firm" for what you believe, unite in *adhering strongly to* their confession about Jesus, God's royal priest,[89] which in turn defines "hope" as something objective: hope was previously personified in 6:19 as entering in behind the curtain. Thus, our hope rests in Jesus who presides as royal priest.

The reason (γὰρ) for a strong adherence to Jesus who currently functions as royal priest is found in God himself: "for the one who has promised is faithful" (v.23b). Stated simply, God, the one who makes promises, keeps them. References to "promise," which are "a declaration to do something [along] with an obligation to carry

---

89   In Hebrews 2:1, the community is exhorted to "pay close attention" to those teachings (see 2:1). The Son's appointment to exercise rule over God's house in 3:6 reinforces the teachings about the divine Davidite presented in chapter one (particularly 1:2, 8–9). The author further develops and exhorts the community to embrace the Son's role as royal priest (3:1). Thus as members of Christ's house (perhaps kingdom 1:8–9), the community is expected to *retain* or *keep in their memory* what they had been taught about the Son.

out what is stated," appear regularly in Hebrews.[90] Without exception, the author of Hebrews draws particular attention upon God as the one who makes promises and upon the believing community as recipients or heirs of those promises through Jesus (cf. 1:14; 6:12, 17; 9:15). Two types of promises appear to exist in Hebrews: (1) fulfilled (realized)[91] and (2) unfulfilled (unrealized).[92] Here in 10:23, the emphasis is on God as a keeper of a promise that has as a basis the inaugurated promises as well as the anticipation of a complete consummation yet to come through Jesus.

Finally, *followers of Jesus are expected to consider others*, "let us consider how to encourage one another to love and good deeds" (v.23a). The expectation "let us consider" (κατανοῶμεν) conveys a process that is more than a mere glance in a mirror whereby reflection is quickly forgotten upon leaving the mirror (James 1:23–24), but rather one that takes seriously the situation before him as Abraham did when he considered the deadness of his body and yet acted (Rom. 4:19). The object of consideration is other people (ἀλλήλους). This consideration for other people is followed by an emotive expression: "for provocation" (εἰς παροξυσμὸν). Generally, it conveys the idea of intense anger (Deut. 29:27 LXX) or a strong disagreement between two people (as in the case of Paul and Barnabas, Acts 15:39). Thus, the expectation is to look deeply and thoughtfully into ways to stimulate (or provide opportunities for) fellow followers of Jesus to love others and to do good deeds.

Fulfilling the author's expectation is twofold. On the one hand, people who do not worship together as community makes the author's expectation difficult to fulfill. All followers of Jesus are to be

---

90 BDAG 355d & 356b. Two forms of the word promise appear in Hebrews: ἐπαγγελία: 6:12, 15, 17; 7:6; 8:6; 9:15; 10:36; 11:9 [twice], 13, 17, 33, 39; and ἐπαγγέλλομαι: 6:13, 10:23, 11:11, 12:26). See also "Era of Fulfillment in the General Letters," pages 103–18.

91 The Jewish cultural-theological underpinnings of the author are clearly evident in Hebrews 6:12–20: (1) God makes promises to people and (2) Abraham received one of those promises from God (Mic. 7:20, Bar. 2:34, Odes Sol. 9:73; cf. Pss. Sol. 9:9–11). The paraphrase of Genesis 22:17 in verse 14 restates *one* aspect of God's promise to Abraham, namely that Abraham would be the father of a great nation (cf. Gen. 12:2–3; 15:5; 17:5). The emphasis, however, is not on how Abraham himself inherited the promise, because that issue is unclear in the text. What is clear is the emphasis on his perseverance. *All who faithfully persevere in Jesus*—the one through whom God's promises to Abraham are fulfilled (6:20)—*are the realized heirs of Abraham* (cf. Rom. 4:13–22; Gal. 3:29).

92 Hebrews 4:8; 9:15; 11:9, 13; 12:26 are examples of unrealized or promises yet to come. For instance in 9:15, the author speaks broadly of "the promise" (τὴν ἐπαγγελίαν) in connection with an "eternal inheritance" (τῆς αἰωνίου κληρονομίας). People who have been invited (οἱ κεκλημένοι τῆς αἰωνίου κληρονομίας), namely, those who are partners of the heavenly calling (3:1), will not only enter the heavenly place-of-rest where Sabbath celebration occurs (4:8), but much more. Later, when the author resumes the theme of a promised inheritance, he mentions entrance into the eternal city (11:9–10, 13–16; 12:22–24).

valued, loved, and encouraged within community. The way every follower of Jesus can be considered is "by *not* abandoning our meeting together as community" (v.25a). Difficulty arises when people are no-shows. And yet, no-shows tend to be a no-show for a reason: persecution (10:32–34), apathy (3:7–15; 4:1; 5:11–14), and apostasy (6:4–8). Some people then are in the habit of not showing up and thereby could be heading in a direction that may end in an uncomfortable and restless situation (cf. 4:1–13; 10:26–31).[93] Thus, the first way to fulfill the author's final expectation is simply: Do not stop worshiping with other people. On the other hand, and in contrast (ἀλλὰ) with the previous way, the way to consider seriously rousing people to love and good deeds is by mutual encouragement: "encourage *one another*" (παρακαλοῦντες; v. 25b). This concept is woven throughout the letter via both the noun (παράκλησις; 6:18; 12:5; 13:22) and the verb (παρακαλέω; 3:13; 10:25; 13:19, 22). The term sometimes appears in a context that warrants the idea of "strong *encouragement*" (6:18; 13:19), other times mutual exhortation (3:13), still other times elements of both exhortation and encouragement (12:5), which appears to be the case here and has been exemplified throughout the letter (13:22).[94] The reason for considering seriously rousing people to love and good deeds is because "the day is drawing near" (v.25c). The reference is a common one for the coming judgment of God.

In conclusion, based upon the fact that Jesus has put into effect a free and safe access to God as royal priest ruling over God's kingdom (10:19–21), three expectations exist for the community: worship God together, persevere together, and consider others together.

---

93 For various perspectives concerning the warning passages in Hebrews, see Herbert W. Bateman IV, editor, *Four Views on the Warning Passages in Hebrews* (Grand Rapids: Kregel, 2007).

94 Hebrews 12:5 has the element of exhortation and encouragement in the OT citation from Proverbs 3:11–12 (cited only here in the NT) are reasons for this split rendering. The identification of the community as "My son" is assuring (cf. 2:10), but the more salient admonition is that as "son" they are not to treat lightly the Lord's educative discipline (*paideia*, cf. Deut. 8:5), which the author defines as suffering ("endure your suffering as discipline," 12:7). Extra–biblical material favors the latter rendering and also reveals a similar paternal discipline of the father / God to educate a son / beloved one (of God: Philo *Congr.* 177; Sir. 22:27–23:6; Judith 8:27; cf. Ps. 94[93]:10; of Wisdom: Sir. 4:11, 17–19). Finally, the vividly forceful application that follows Proverbs 3:11–12 is a reminder that sonship and suffering are linked together (12:7–13; cf. Jesus in 5:8–9). Thus this *exhortation* from Proverbs 3:11–12, addressed to this Christian community of believers (vv.1–6), as well as the subsequent application (vv.7–13), serves to remind them that sonship entails educative discipline/suffering, which evidences that they belong to the Lord.

Chapter in Review

We began by stating the goal of this chapter to be pulling together the previous six chapters of this book with special attention give to chapters four through six. It provided an exposition of two passages: Jude vv.5–7 and Hebrews 10:19–25.

- First, we examined Jude vv.5–7, which was a call to remember that divine judgment exists for any who rebel.

- Second, we examined Hebrews 10:19–25, which served as a summary statement for Hebrews 4:14–10:25 through the author issued three expectations for the community to worship God together, persevere together, and consider others together that is based upon Jesus' salvific work and appointment as royal priest.

8

SELECTED SOURCES

As we begin this chapter on "Selected Sources," it is helpful to bear in mind that we merely wish to create a composite list of sources for future study of the General Letters. Please take into consideration that the sources reflect evidence *about* the text. So whenever you appeal to any one of these sources for help make it a point to recognize the author's reasoning. Furthermore, isolate the support cited from the text that validates his or her reasoning. Validation comes from the text and is <u>not</u> based upon an author's name.[1] Finally, check all supporting evidence, especially passage citations. A common error is that some people may leave out key texts that oppose a view of the problem.

SOURCES FOR COMPREHENDING FIRST-CENTURY LETTER-WRITING

Grassmick, John D. "Epistolary Genre: Reading Ancient Letters," in *Interpreting the New Testament Text: Introduction to the Art and Science of Exegesis*, 221–39. Wheaton, IL: Crossway, 2006.

Klauck, Hans-Josef. *Ancient Letters and the New Testament: A Guide to Content and Exegesis*. Waco, TX: Baylor University Press, 2006.

---

1   Carson refers to such simplistic appeals to authority as a logical fallacy. See D. A. Carson, *Exegetical Fallacies*, second edition (Grand Rapids: Baker, 1996), 122–23.

Malherbe, Abraham J. *Ancient Epistolary Theorists.* SBL Sources for Biblical Study 19. Atlanta: Scholars Press, 1988.

Oxyrhynchus Papyri, http://163.1.169.40/cgi–bin/library?site=loca lhost&a=p&p=about&c=POxy&ct=0&l=en&w=utf-8 (accessed February 2, 2011).

Poster, Carol and Linda C. Mitchell, editors. *Letter-Writing Manuals and Instruction from Antiquity to the Present.* Columbia, SC: University of South Carolina Press, 2007.

Stowers, Stanley K. *Letter Writing in Greco-Roman Antiquity.* Literature of Early Christianity, edited by Wayne A. Meeks. Philadelphia, PA: Westminster, 1986.

White, John L. *Light from Ancient Letters. Foundations and Facets: New Testament.* Philadelphia, PA: Fortress, 1986.

Wilder, Terry L. *Pseudonymity, The New Testament, and Deception: An Inquiry into Intention and Reception.* Lanham, MD: University Press of America, 2004.

SOURCES FOR GROUNDING THE TEXT HISTORICALLY

Barclay, John M. G. *Jews in the Mediterranean Diaspora from Alexander to Trajan.* Edinburgh, England: T & T Clark, 1996.

Bateman IV, Herbert W., Darrell L. Bock, Gordon H. Johnston. *Jesus the Messiah: Tracing the Promises, Expectations, and Coming of Israel's King.* Grand Rapids: Kregel, 2012.

deSilva, David A. *Introducing the Apocrypha: Message, Context and Significance.* Grand Rapids: Baker Academic, 2002.

Charlesworth, James H. ed. *The Old Testament Pseudepigrapha,* 2 volumes. New York: Doubleday, 1985.

Collins, John J. and Gregory E. Sterling, editors. *Hellenism in the Land of Israel.* Christianity and Judaism in Antiquity Series, vol. 13. Notre Dame: University Press, 2001.

Fantin, Joseph D. "Background Studies: Grounding the Text in Reality," in *Interpreting the New Testament Text: Introduction to the*

Art and Science of Exegesis, edited by Darrell L. Bock and Buist M. Fanning, 167–96. Wheaton, IL: Crossway, 2006.

Ferguson, Everett. *Backgrounds of Early Christianity*. 3rd edition. Grand Rapids: Eerdmans, 2003.

Gagarin, Michael, editor. *The Oxford Encyclopedia of Ancient Greece and Rome*, 7 volumes. Oxford, New York: Oxford University Press, 2010.

Grabbe, Lester L. *First Century Judaism: Jewish Religion and History in the Second Temple Period*. Edinburgh, England: T&T Clark, 1996.

_____. *The Maccabean Revolt: Anatomy of a Biblical Revolution*. Wilmington, DE: 1988.

Hess, Richard S. and M. Daniel Carroll R. eds. *Israel's Messiah in the Bible and the Dead Sea Scrolls*. Grand Rapids: Baker, 2003.

Hengel, Martin. *The Zealots: Investigations into the Jewish Freedom Movement in the Period from Herod I until 70 A.D.* Translated by David Smith. Edinburgh: T&T Clark, 1989.

Mason, Steve. *Josephus and the New Testament*. Peabody, MA: Hendrickson, 2nd edition, 2003.

Metzger, Bruce M. and Roland E. Murphy, ed. The *New Oxford Annotated Apocrypha*, New Revised Standard Version. New York: Cambridge University Press, 1991.

Richardson, Peter. *Herod: King of the Jews and Friend of the Romans*. South Carolina: University Press, 1996.

Schiff, Stacy. *Cleopatra: A Life*. New York: Little Brown and Company, 2010.

Seager, Robin. *Pompey the Great*. 2nd edition. Oxford: Blackwell Publishing, 2002.

Saldarini, Anthony J. *Pharisees, Scribes and Sadducees in Palestinian Society*. Grand Rapids: Eerdmans, 1988; reprint; 2001.

Suetonius, Gaius. *The Twelve Caesars*. Translated by Robert Graves. New York: Penguin Classics, 1957; revised edition, 2007.

VanderKam, James C. *The Dead Sea Scrolls Today*. Grand Rapids: Eerdmans, 1994.

_____. *From Joshua to Caiaphas: High Priests after the Exile*. Minneapolis, MN: Fortress, 2005.

Wise, Michael; Abegg, Martin; Cook, Edward. *The Dead Sea Scrolls: A New Translation*. San Francisco: Harper, 1996.

SOURCES FOR BUILDING A BIBLICAL THEOLOGY

Bateman IV, Herbert W. gen ed. *Three Central Issues in Contemporary Dispensationalism: A Comparison of Traditional and Progressive Views*. Grand Rapids: Kregel, 1999.

Blaising, C. A., and Bock, D. L. ed. *Dispensationalism, Israel, and the Church*. Grand Rapids: Zondervan, 1992.

Caird, G. B. *New Testament Theology*. Editor L. D. Hurst. Oxford, Great Britain: Clarendon, 1994.

Fanning, Buist L. "Theological Analysis: Building Biblical Theology," in *Interpreting the New Testament Text: Introduction to the Art and Science of Exegesis*, edited by Darrell L. Bock and Buist M. Fanning, 277–91. Wheaton, IL: Crossway, 2006.

_____. "A Theology of Hebrews," in *A Biblical Theology of the New Testament*, edited by Roy B. Zuck and Darrell L. Bock, 369–415. Chicago: Moody, 1994.

_____. "A Theology of James," in *A Biblical Theology of the New Testament*, edited by Roy B. Zuck and Darrell L. Bock, 417–35. Chicago: Moody, 1994.

_____. "A Theology of Peter and Jude," in *A Biblical Theology of the New Testament*, edited by Roy B. Zuck and Darrell L. Bock, 437–71. Chicago: Moody, 1994.

Harris, W. Hall. "A Theology of John's Writings," in *A Biblical Theology of the New Testament*, edited by Roy B. Zuck and Darrell L. Bock, 167–42. Chicago: Moody, 1994.

Jobes, Karen H. *Letters to the Church: A Survey of Hebrews and the General Epistles*. Grand Rapids: Zondervan, 2011.

Ladd, George Eldon. *A Theology of the New Testament*. Rev. ed. Edited by Donald A. Hagner. Grand Rapids: Eerdmans, 1993.

Marshall, I. Howard. *New Testament Theology: Many Witnesses, One Gospel*. Downers Grove, IL: InterVarsity Press, 2004.

Osborne, Grant R. *The Hermeneutical Spiral: A Comprehensive Introduction to Biblical Interpretation*. Downers Grove, IL: InterVarsity Press, 1991.

SOURCES FOR INTERPRETING TEXTUAL PROBLEMS

Aland, Kurt and Barbara Aland. *The Text of the New Testament*, translated by Erroll F. Rhodes. Grand Rapids: Eerdmans, 1987.

Bateman IV, Herbert W. "Manuscript Evidence for Hebrews," in *Charts on the Book of Hebrews*. Kregel Charts of the Bible and Theology. Grand Rapids: Kregel, 2012.

_____. "Consistently Cited Witnesses for Hebrews," in *Charts on the Book of Hebrews*. Kregel Charts of the Bible and Theology. Grand Rapids: Kregel, 2012.

_____. "Classification & Dates of Manuscript Evidence for Hebrews," in *Charts on the Book of Hebrews*. Kregel Charts of the Bible and Theology. Grand Rapids: Kregel, 2012.

_____. "Major Textual Issues Hebrews," in *Charts on the Book of Hebrews*. Kregel Charts of the Bible and Theology. Grand Rapids: Kregel, 2012.

_____. "Manuscript Text-Types and Witnesses of the Johannine Epistles," in *A Workbook for Intermediate Greek: Grammar, Exegesis, and Commentary on 1–3 John*, 602–05. Grand Rapids: Kregel, 2008.

Elliott, J. K. "In Defense of Thoroughgoing Eclecticism in New Testament Textual Criticism." *Restoration Quarterly* 21:2 (1978): 95–115.

Ehrman, Bruce. "New Testament Textual Criticism: Quest for Methodology" (M.Div. Thesis, Princeton Theological Seminary, 1981).

Epp, Eldon Jay. *Studies in the Theory of New Testament Textual Criticism.* Grand Rapids: Eerdmans, 1993.

Greenlee, J. Harold. *Introduction to New Testament Textual Criticism.* Grand Rapids: Eerdmans, 1989.

Hodges, Zane C. "Modern Textual Criticism and the Majority Text: A Response." *Journal of the Evangelical Theological Society* 21 (1978): 143–55.

Kilpatrick, G. D. "Atticism and the Text of the Greek New Testament," in *Neutestamentliche Aufsätze: Festschrift fur Prof. Josef Schmid zum 70. Geburstag.* Edited by J. Blinzler, O. Kuss and F. Mussner. Regensburg, 1963.

Metzger, Bruce M. *The Text of the New Testament: Its Transmission, Corruption, and Restoration.* Third Enlarged Edition. New York: Oxford University Press, 1992.

_____. *A Textual Commentary on the Greek New Testament,* 2nd edition. New York: United Bible Society, 1994.

Metzger, Bruce M. and Bart D. Ehrman. *The Text of the New Testament: Its Transmission, Corruption, and Restoration.* Fourth Edition. New York: Oxford University Press, 2005.

Nestle-Aland, *Novum Testamenum Graece,* 27th and 28th editions. New York: United Bible Society, 1993, 2012.

_____. *The Greek New Testament,* 4th revised edition. Edited by Kurt Aland, Matthew Black, et al. Peabody, MA: Hendrickson, 2001.

Pickering, W. N. "The Majority Text and the Original Text: a Response to Gordon D. Fee," in *The Majority Text: Essays and Reviews in the Continuing Debate,* 25–41. Edited by Theodore P. Letis. Fort Wayne, IN: The Institute for Reformation Biblical Studies, 1987.

Wallace, Daniel B. "Laying a Foundation: New Testament Textual Criticism," 33–56. In *Interpreting the New Testament Text: Introduction to the Art and Science of Exegesis*, edited by Darrell L. Bock and Buist M. Fanning. Wheaton, IL: Crossway, 2006.

_____. "The Majority Text and the Original Text: Are They Identical?" *Bibliotheca Sacra* 148 (1991): 151–69.

Wasserman, Tommy. *The Epistle of Jude: Its Text and Transmission*. Coniectanea Biblica New Testeament Series 43. Stockholm, Sweden: Almqvist & Wiksell International, 2006.

SOURCES FOR INTERPRETING STRUCTURE, STYLE, SYNTAX, AND SEMANTICS

Adam, A. K. M. *James: A Handbook on the Greek Text*. Waco, TX: Baylor University Press, 2013.

Bateman, Herbert W. "3 John: Tracing the Flow of Thought," in *Interpreting the New Testament Text: Introduction to the Art and Science of Exegesis*, 449–61. Wheaton, IL: Crossway, 2006.

_____. *A Workbook for Intermediate Greek: Grammar, Exegesis, and Commentary on 1–3 John*. Grand Rapids: Kregel, 2008.

Black, David Alan. *It's Still Greek to Me: An Easy-to-Understand Guide to Intermediate Greek*. Grand Rapids: Baker, 1998.

Blass, F., and Debrunner, A. *A Greek Grammar of the New Testament and Other Early Christian Literature*. Translation and revision of the 9th–10th German edition, by Robert W. Funk. Chicago: University of Chicago Press, 1961.

Brooks, James A. and Carlton L. Winbery. *Syntax of New Testament Greek*. Lanham, MD: University Press of America, 1979.

Burton, Ernest De Witt. *Syntax of the Moods and Tenses in New Testament Greek*, 2nd Edition. Chicago: University of Chicago Press, 1893.

Cully, Martin M. *I, II, III John: A Handbook on the Greek Text*. Waco, TX: Baylor University Press, 2004.

Dana, H. E. and Julius R. Mantey. *A Manual Grammar of the Greek New Testament*. Ontario: The Macmillan Company, 1955.

Davids, Peter H. *II Peter and Jude: A Handbook on the Greek Text*. Waco, TX: Baylor University Press, 2011.

Dubis, Mark. *I Peter: A Handbook on the Greek Text*. Waco, TX: Baylor University Press, 2010.

Greenlee, J. Harold. *A Concise Exegetical Grammar of New Testament Greek*. Grand Rapids: Eerdmans 1986.

Guthrie, George H. and J. Scott Duvall, *Biblical Greek Exegesis: A Guided Approach to Learning Intermediate and Advanced Greek*. Grand Rapids: Zondervan, 1988.

Hanna, Robert. *A Grammatical Aid to the Greek New Testament*. Grand Rapids: Baker Book House, 1983.

Moule, C. F. D. *An Idiom Book of New Testament Greek*. Second edition. Cambridge University Press, 1959.

Moulton, James Hope. *A Grammar of New Testament Greek. Vol. 3: Syntax*, by Nigel Turner. Edinburgh, England: T & T Clark, 1963.

Osborne, Grant R. *The Hermeneutical Spiral: A Comprehensive Introduction to Biblical Interpretation*. Downers Grove, IL: InterVarsity Press, 1991.

Porter, Stanley E. *Idioms of the Greek New Testament*. Sheffield: JSOT Press, 1992.

Robertson, A. T. *A Grammar of New Testament Greek in Light of Historical Research*. Fourth edition, Nashville, TN: Broadman Press, 1923.

Smith, Jay E. "Sentence Diagramming, Clausal Layouts, and Exegetical Outlining," in *Interpreting the New Testament Text: Introduction to the Art and Science of Exegesis*, edited by Darrell L. Bock and Buist M. Fanning, 73–134. Wheaton, IL: Crossway, 2006.

Turner, Niger. *A Grammar of New Testament Greek*, Volume 4, *Style*. Edinburgh, England: T & T Clark, 1976, 1980.

Wallace, Daniel B. *Greek Grammar Beyond the Basics: An Exegetical Syntax of the New Testament*. Grand Rapids: Zondervan Publishing House, 1996.

_____. *The Basics of New Testament Greek Syntax: An Intermediate Greek Grammar*. Grand Rapids: Zondervan Publishing House, 2000.

Young, Richard A. *Intermediate New Testament Greek: A Linguistic and Exegetical Approach*. Nashville, TN: Broadman & Holman, 1994.

Zerwick, Maximilian. *Biblical Greek: Illustrated by Examples*. Translated and adapted by Joseph Smith. Rome: Scripta Pontificii Instituti Biblici, 1963.

SOURCES FOR INTERPRETING GREEK WORDS

Balz, Horst and Gerhard Schneider. *Exegetical Dictionary of the New Testament*. 3 Volumes. Grand Rapids: Eerdmans, 1990–93.

Bateman, Herbert W. "Figure of Speech in Johannine Literature," in *A Workbook for Intermediate Greek: Grammar, Exegesis, and Commentary on 1–3 John*, 606–12. Grand Rapids: Kregel, 2008.

_____. "Literary Devices of Additions Used in Hebrews," in *Charts on the Book of Hebrews*. Kregel Charts of the Bible and Theology. Grand Rapids: Kregel, 2011.

_____. "Literary Devices of Change Used in Hebrews," in *Charts on the Book of Hebrews*. Kregel Charts of the Bible and Theology. Grand Rapids: Kregel, 2011.

_____. "Literary Devices of Omission Used in Hebrews," in *Charts on the Book of Hebrews*. Kregel Charts of the Bible and Theology. Grand Rapids: Kregel, 2011.

Bock, Darrell L. "Lexical Analysis: Studies in Words," in *Interpreting the New Testament Text: Introduction to the Art and Science of Exegesis*, edited by Darrell L. Bock and Buist M. Fanning, 135–53. Wheaton, IL: Crossway, 2006.

Bullinger, E. W. *Figures of Speech Used in the Bible: Explained and Illustrated*. Grand Rapids: Baker, 1968; tenth edition, 1984.

Brown, Colin. *New International Dictionary of the New Testament Text*. Two volumes. Grand Rapids: Zondervan, 1977.

Kittel, Gerhard, Editor. *Theological Dictionary of the New Testament*. Ten Volumes. Translated and edited by Geoffrey W. Bromiley. Grand Rapids: Wm. B. Eerdmans Publishing Company, repr. 1983.

Liddell, Henry George and Robert Scott. *A Greek-English Lexicon*. Oxford: Claredon, 1968. (all Ancient Greek, from 900 BCE to 600 CE)

Moule, C. F. D. *An Idiom Book of New Testament Greek*. 2nd edition. Cambridge University Press, 1959.

Moulton, James H. and George Milligan. *The Vocabulary of the Greek New Testament*. Grand Rapids: Eerdmans, 1980.

Porter, Stanley E. *Idioms of the Greek New Testament*. Sheffield, England: JSOT Press, 1992.

Spicq, Ceslas. *Theological Lexicon of the New Testament*. Three Volumes. Translated and edited by James D. Ernest. Peabody, MA: Hendrickson, 1994.

SOURCES FOR IMPROVING COMMUNICATION

Adam, Peter. *Speaking God's Words: A Practical Theology of Expository Preaching*. Downers Grove, IL: InterVarsity, 1996.

Arthurs, Jeffrey D. *Preaching with Variety*. Grand Rapids: Kregel, 2007.

Doriani, Daniel M. *Putting the Truth to Work: The Theory and Practice of Biblical Application*. Phillipsburg, NJ: P&R Publishing, 2001.

Matthews, Alice. *Preaching That Speaks to Women*. Grand Rapids: Baker, 2003.

Ralston, Timothy J. "Scripture in Worship: An Indispensable Symbol of Covenant," in *Authentic Worship: Hearing Scripture's Voice, Applying Its Truth*, edited by Herbert W. Bateman IV, 195–222. Grand Rapids: Kregel, 2002.

_____. "Showing the Relevance: Application, Ethics, and Preaching," in *Interpreting the New Testament Text: Introduction to the*

Art and Science of Exegesis, edited by Darrell L. Bock and Buist M. Fanning, 293–310. Wheaton, IL: Crossway, 2006.

Ramesh, Richard. *Preparing Expository Sermons: A Seven-Step Method for Biblical Preaching*. Rev. ed. Grand Rapids: Baker, 2001.

Robinson, Haddon W. *Biblical Preaching: The Development and Delivery of Expository Messages*. Second edition. Grand Rapids: Baker, 2001.

Robinson, Haddon W. and Torrey Robinson. *It's All In How You Tell It: Preaching First-Person Expository Messages*. Grand Rapids: Baker, 2003.

Sunukjian, Donald R. *Invitation to Biblical Preaching: Proclaiming Truth with Clarity and Relevance*. Grand Rapids: Kregel, 2007.

Warren, Timothy. "Paradigm for Preachers," *Bibliotheca Sacra* 148 (October–December 1991): 463–90.

GUIDE FOR CHOOSING COMMENTARIES

As you know, there is a host of commentaries available today. In truth, the proliferation of commentaries is more staggering than the number of English translations on the market. Nevertheless, there are notable differences between the commentaries available today. In fact, we might group commentaries into four types: devotional, popular, expositional, and exegetical. First, there are *the devotional commentaries*, which tend to be more directed to application. Ironside's, Warren Wiersbe's, and John McAuthur's commentaries tend to be *transcribed sermons or devotional commentaries*. Second there are *the popular commentaries*, which tend to be based on an English text and tend not to solve exegetical issues. For example, some popular commentaries are based on the RV or RSV: New Century Bible Commentary. Other commentaries are based on the NIV: The College Press NIV Commentary, the New International Biblical Commentary, and The NIV Application Commentary. At least one, Cornerstone Biblical Commentary, interacts with the NLT. They all tend to be written for a popular audience. These two types of commentaries have *limited* value for doing exegetical work. Yet that is not the case for the next two types of commentaries.

The third type of commentary is the *expositional commentary*. These commentaries are generally semi-technical in that they tend to major on the major problems of the text and thereby limit explanations to the contemporary author's view. The *Expositor's Bible Commentary*, the IVP New Testament Commentary, and the Tyndale New Testament Commentaries are expositional commentaries. Expositional commentaries help pinpoint major issues in any given passage. If the author of an expositional commentary pauses to ponder a problem in the text, it is important, ought to be read carefully, and perhaps should even be evaluated by way of a more critical commentary. The fourth type of commentary is *the critical commentary*, which provides technical discussions on any given passage. The following chart is a list of some of the more significant commentary series. Provided is a descriptive purpose for each series and a list identifying the named commentators who contributed to the respective series concerning the General Letters.

A Guide to New Testament Commentary Series		
Commentary Series	**Stated Purpose or Description of the Series**	**General Letters**
Abingdon New Testament Commentaries	This series provides readers with a compact critical examination of the writings of the New Testament. The target audience is upper-level college or university students as well as pastors and other church leaders. Contributors come from a wide range of ecclesiastical affiliations and confessional stances. It is not a verse-by-verse commentary but is arranged by literary unit and is thereby *expositional*.	Hebrews: Pfitzner (1997) James: Sleeper (1998) 1 Peter: Boring (1999) Johannine Letters: Rensberger (1997) 2 Peter, Jude: Kraftchick (2002)
Anchor Bible	The AB is a technical/*critical* commentary series whose quality varies depending on the book. The commentary is arranged as a verse-by-verse commentary with interpretive translations, critical notes, and expositional sections. The series is moderate-liberal.	Hebrews: Koester (2001) James: Johnson (2005) 1 Peter: Elliott (2000) Johannine Letters: Brown (1982) 2 Peter, and Jude: Neyrey (1993)

A Guide to New Testament Commentary Series		
Commentary Series	**Stated Purpose or Description of the Series**	**General Letters**

Baker Exegetical Commentary on the New Testament	The BECNT is intended to address the needs of the pastor and others involved in preaching and teaching the New Testament. The series is evangelical and contributors come from a variety of theological traditions that share a belief in the trustworthiness and unity of Scripture. It is a *critical* commentary series of great value.	Hebrews: Forthcoming
		James: McCartney (2009)
		1 Peter: Jobes (2005)
		Johannine Letters:
		  Yarbrough (2008)
		2 Peter, Jude:
		  Green (2008)

Evangelical Exegetical Commentary	The EEC is a *critical* commentary on the entire Bible for Evangelicals in digital form available wherever Logos Bible Software's platform is available. While upholding the Bible as God's inspired Word, it engages in rigorous critical scholarship, reveals the biblical theology for each book, and provides a poignant application suitable for pastors and scholars.	Hebrews:
		  Fanning (forthcoming)
		James:
		  Varner
		1 Peter:
		  Glenny (forthcoming)
		Johannine Letters
		  Derickson
		Jude & 2 Peter:
		  Bateman

Hermeneia	The Hermeneia series represents a moderate-liberal perspective. They are technical, historical, and very *critical*. They are well footnoted with a bibliography. These volumes are strong in matters of historical background and texts from the ancient world that are relevant to the passage, but weak (at times) in *detailed* exegesis. Its quality is highly regarded by critics in that virtually every volume is regarded as a standard commentary. Many of these volumes are translated from standard German commentaries.	Hebrews:
		  Attridge (1989)
		James:
		  Dibelius/Greeven (1976)
		1 Peter:
		  Achtemeier (1996)
		Johannine Letters:
		  Strecker (1995)
		2 Peter, Jude:
		  Not Available

A Guide to New Testament Commentary Series		
Commentary Series	**Stated Purpose or Description of the Series**	**General Letters**
International Critical Commentary	The ICC is a technical series whose contributors range from conservative to liberal. Most volumes are good, but some older volumes are not as helpful (cf. old Matthew, Mark, John, Revelation). A new edition of the series is currently being produced. It is truly a *critical* commentary.	Hebrews: Moffat (1924) James: Ropes (1916) Petrine Letters/Jude: Bigg (1909) Johannine Leters: Brooke (1912)
The Interpretation Series	The Interpretation Series integrates the results of historical and theological analysis of the biblical text. The contributors offer moderate-to-liberal theological analysis in an expository format, while still being applicable to the church. A brief bibliography is located at the end of each commentary, All expository essays focus on the RS/RSV. The target audience is pastors and teachers in a local church context and by nature a *popular* series.	Hebrews: Long (1997) Johannine Letters: Smith (1992) 1, 2 Peter, James, Jude: Perkins (1995)
The IVP New Testament Commentary	The IVP New Testament Commentary is a biblical *expositional* commentary that is extremely user-friendly for pastors. Contributors represent a range of theological traditions but are united by a common commitment to the authority of Scripture for Christian faith and practice.	Hebrews: Stedman (1992) James: Stulac (1993) 1 Peter: Marshall (1991) Johannine Letters: Thomson (1992) 2 Peter, Jude: Harvey/Tower (2009)

A Guide to New Testament Commentary Series		
Commentary Series	Stated Purpose or Description of the Series	General Letters
The New American Commentary	The NAC series updates An American Commentary. It examines the text *critically* and emphasizes the theological unity of each book and the contribution each book makes to Scripture as a whole. While concentrating on theological exegesis, the series also seeks to provide a practical, applicable exposition suited for the twenty-first-century church. There is a clear commitment to the inerrancy of Scripture and to the classic Christian tradition.	Hebrews: Allen (2010) James: Richardson (1997) 1, 2 Peter, Jude: Schreiner (2003) Johannine Letters: Akin (2001)
New International Biblical Commentary	The NIBCNT series strives to make each commentary accessible to the Christian community at large and is thereby written with the broader concerns of the universal church in mind. The series purposely uses the NIV as the basis for its series because of its popularity with lay Bible students and pastors. Thus, it is a self-proclaimed *popular* commentary.	Hebrews: Hagner (1990) James: Davids (1989) 1, 2 Peter, Jude: Hillyer (1991) Johannine Letters: Johnson (1993)
New International Commentary of the New Testament	The NICNT is a conservative series whose volumes vary greatly in quality and approach: some technical and critical, others more homiletical. Weaker volumes have been redone. Thus the series is a mix, though it tends to be more *expositional*.	Hebrews: Cockerill (2012) James: McKnight (2011) 1 Peter: Davids (1990) Johannine Letters: Marshall (1978)
New International Greek Testament Commentary	The NIGTC is a *critical* commentary series based on the Greek text written by conservative, international scholars. The volumes thus far are all excellent. It represents a British conservative point of view and also will point the reader not only to the Greek text and critical discussion of it, but also to key periodical literature.	Hebrews: Ellingworth (1993) James: Davids (1982) 1 Peter: Forthcoming Johannine Letters: Forthcoming 2 Peter, Jude: Forthcoming

A Guide to New Testament Commentary Series		
Commentary Series	**Stated Purpose or Description of the Series**	**General Letters**
The NIV Application Commentary	The NIV Application Commentary is committed to bringing an ancient message into our contemporary context. The focus is on application, and yet it helps the reader think through the process of moving from an original meaning of a passage to its contemporary significance. Contrary to their claim, they appear to be a *popular* commentary in that they are based upon the NIV text.	Hebrews: Guthrie (1998) James: Nystrom (1997) 1 Peter: McKnight (1996) Johannine Letters: Burge (1996) 2 Peter, Jude: Moo (1996)
Pillar New Testament Commentary	The PNT seek to make clear the text of Scripture that blends exegesis and exposition with biblical theology and contemporary relevance of the Bible. The series represents a verse-by-verse presentation of the text in a non-technical manner, though the presentations are not sermonic. The target audience is the pastor, teacher, and students. All commentaries on the General Letters are readable and are a cross between an *expositional* and a *critical* commentary.	Hebrews: O'Brien (2010) James: Moo (2000) 1 Peter: Forthcoming Johannine Letters: Kruse (2000) 2 Peter, Jude: Davids (2006)
Reading the New Testament	The RNT is a relatively new literary and theological commentary series that expresses some non-evangelical views. Nevertheless, the series presents cutting-edge research in a popular format for upper-level undergraduates, seminarians, seminary educated pastors, and educated laypersons. Although the commentaries are not verse-by-verse, they interact with current grammatical, structural, semantical, literary, and theological issues well.	Hebrews: Isaacs (2002) James: Isaacs (2002) 1, 2 Peter, Jude: Richard (2000) Johannine Letters: Forthcoming

A Guide to New Testament Commentary Series		
Commentary Series	**Stated Purpose or Description of the Series**	**General Letters**
Sacra Pagina	Written by an international team of biblical scholars the Sacra Pagina ("Sacred Page") series is intended for biblical professionals, graduate students, theologians, clergy, and religious educators. It provides sound critical analysis and is written in an *exposition* format in that the series is not an overly critical or technical. Yet the work evaluates key issues of the text, is reader-friendly, and offers helpful insights into the text.	Hebrews: Mitchell (2007) James: Hartin (2003) 1, 2 Peter, Jude: Senior / Harrington (2003) Johannine Letters: Painter (2002)
Two Horizons New Testament Commentary	The Two Horizons series offers both theological exegesis and theological reflection. Theological exegesis includes attention to syntactical, historical, social–scientific, political, and canonical issues. Theological reflection investigates what each NT book contributes to biblical theology. Its target audience is students, pastors, and Christian leaders who seek to engage in theological interpretation and thus this commentary series is *expositional*.	Hebrews: Forthcoming James: Forthcoming 1 Peter: J. Green (2007) Johannine Letters: Forthcoming 2 Peter/Jude: Reese (2007)
Tyndale New Testament Commentaries	The TNTC were produced by the British Tyndale Society and are representative of British Conservatives, though newer volumes include American participants. The volumes are more *expositional* than technical.	Hebrews: Guthrie (2009) James: Moo (2009) 1 Peter: Grudem (2009) Johannine Letters: Stott (1988) 2 Peter/Jude: M. Green (1987)

A Guide to New Testament Commentary Series		
Commentary Series	**Stated Purpose or Description of the Series**	**General Letters**
Word Biblical Commentary (WBC)	The WBC series is a technical, conservative, and critical commentary that represents a wing of American conservatism. They interact with *critical* studies at a scholarly level, and most volumes are good. They all contain full bibliographies that point to helpful monographs and articles.	Hebrews: Lane (1991) James: Martin (1988) 1 Peter: Michaels (1988) Johannine Letters: Smalley (1984) 2 Peter/Jude: Bauckham (1983)

At times, many of these commentaries are a mix between critical and expositional commentaries. Yet like all the books listed in this chapter, all commentaries need to be used critically and with a theological sensitivity to their differing perspectives. The following bibliography for commentaries not only lists those mentioned above, but includes many other works. It is not exhaustive, merely a selective listing.

Hebrews

Allen, David. *Hebrews*. The New American Commentary. Nashville, TN: Broadman & Holman, 2010.

Anderson, David R. *The King-Priest of Psalm 110 in Hebrews*. Studies in Biblical Literature 21. New York: Peter Lang, 2001.

Attridge, Harold W. *The Epistle to the Hebrews: A Commentary on the Epistle to the Hebrews*. Hermeneia. Philadelphia: Fortress Press, 1989.

Bateman IV, Herbert W. *Early Jewish Hermeneutics and Hebrews 1:5–13*. New York: Peter Lang, 1997.

_____, editor. *The Warning Passages in Hebrews: Four Perspectives*. Grand Rapids: Kregel, 2007.

Bruce, F. F. *The Epistle to the Hebrews*. Rev. ed. New International Commentary on the New Testament. Grand Rapids: Eerdmans, 1990.

Buck, Daniel E. "The Rhetorical Arrangement and Function of OT Citations in the Book of Hebrews: Uncovering Their Role in the Paraenetic Discourse of Access." Ph.D. dissertation, Dallas Theological Seminary, 2001.

Cockerill, Gareth L. *The Epistle to the Hebrews*. The New International Commentary on the New Testament. Grand Rapids: Eerdmans, 2012.

_____, *Hebrews: A Bible Commentary in the Wesleyan Tradition*. Indianapolis, IN: Wesleyan Publishing House, 1999.

D'Angelo, Mary Rose. *Moses the Letter to the Hebrews*. SBL Dissertation Series 42. Missoula, MO: Scholars Press, 1979.

deSilva, David A. *Perseverance in Gratitude: A Socio-Rhetorical Commentary on the Epistle "to the Hebrews."* Grand Rapids: Eerdmans, 2000.

Ellingworth, Paul. *The Epistle to the Hebrews: A Commentary on the Greek Text*. New International Greek Testament Commentary. Grand Rapids: Eerdmans, 1993.

Gheorghita, Radu. *The Role of the Septuagint in Hebrews: An Investigation of its Influence with Special Consideration to the Use of Hab 2:3-4 in Heb 10:37-38*. Wissenschaftliche Untersuchungen zum Neuen Testament 2. Reihe. Tübingen: Mohr Siebeck, 2003.

Gordon, Robert P. *Hebrews. Readings: A New Biblical Commentary*. Sheffield Academic Press, 2000.

Guthrie, Donald. *Hebrews*. Tyndale New Testament Commentaries. Grand Rapids: Eerdmans, 1983, reprint 2007.

Guthrie, George. *Hebrews*. The NIV Application Commentary. Grand Rapids: Zondervan, 1998.

Hagner, Donald A. *Hebrews*. New International Biblical Commentary. Peabody, MA: Hendrickson, 1983, 1990.

Hughes, Philip Edgcumbe. *A Commentary on the Epistle to the Hebrews*. Grand Rapids: Eerdmans, 1977, 1983.

Isaacs, Marie E. *Reading Hebrews and James: A Literary and Theological Commentary*. Macon, GA: Smyth & Helwys Publishing, 2002.

Johnson, Luke Timothy. *Hebrews: A Commentary*. The New Testament Library. Louisville: Westminster John Knox Press, 2006.

Käsemann, Ernst. *The Wandering People of God: An Investigation of the Letter to the Hebrews*. Translation by Roy A. Harrisville and Irving L. Sandberg. Minneapolis: Augsburg, 1984.

Koester, Craig R. *Hebrews: A New Translation with Introduction and Commentary*. The Anchor Bible. Garden City, NY: Doubleday, 2001.

Kurianal, James. *Jesus Our High Priest: Ps 110, 4 as the Substructure of Heb 5, 1–7, 28*. European University Studies. New York: Peter Lang, 2000.

Lanansma, Jon. *I Will Give You Rest: The Rest Motif in the New Testament with Special Reference to Mt 11 and Heb 3–4*. 98 Wissenschaftliche Untersuchungen zum Neuen Testament 2. Reihe. Tübingen: Mohr Siebeck, 1997.

Lane, William L. *Hebrews*. 2 vols. Word Biblical Commentary, vol. 47A-B. Dallas, TX: Word, 1991.

Long, Thomas G. *Hebrews*. Interpretation: A Bible Commentary for Teaching and Preaching. Louisville, KY: John Knox, 1997.

Mitchell, Alan C. *Hebrews*. Sacra Pagina, vol. 13. Collegeville, MN: The Litrugical Press, 2007.

Montefiore, Hugh. *A Commentary on the Epistle to the Hebrews*. Harper's New Testament Commentary. San Francisco: Harper & Row, 1964; 1987.

O'Brien, Peter T. *Letter to the Hebrews*. Pillar New Testament Commentary. Grand Rapids: Eerdmans, 2010.

Pfitzner, Victor C. *Hebrews*. Abingdon New Testament Commentaries. Nashville: Abingdon, 1997.

Rhee, Victor (Sung Yul). "The Concept of Faith in the Overall Context of the Book of Hebrews." Ph.D. dissertation, Dallas Theological Seminary, 1996.

Stedman, Ray C. *Hebrews*. IVP New Testament Commentary Series. Downers Grove, IL: InterVarsity, 1992.

Westcott, Brooke Foss. *The Epistle to the Hebrews*. London, England: MacMillan, 1909.

James

Adamson, James. *The Epistle of James*. The New International Commentary on the New Testament. Grand Rapids: Eerdmans, 1976.

Baker, William. *Personal Speech-Ethics in the Epistle of James*. Wissenschaftliche Untersuchungen zum Neuen Testament. Tübingen, Germany: Mohr Siebeck, 1995.

_____. *Sticks and Stones: The Discipleship of Our Speech*. Downers Grove, IL: InterVarsity, 1996.

Blomberg, Craig L, and Mariam J. Kamell. *James*. Zondervan Exegetical Commentary on the New Testament. Grand Rapids: Zondervan, 2008.

Davids, Peter H. *James*. New International Biblical Commentary, vol. 15. Peabody, MA: Hendrickson, 1989.

Dibelius, Martin and Heinrich Greeven. *James*. Hermeneia. Translated by Michael A. Williams. Philadelphia, PA: Fortress Press, 1976.

Hartin, Patrick and Daniel Harrington. *James*. Sacra Pagina, vol. 14. Collegeville, MN: The Litrugical Press, 2003.

Isaacs, Marie E. *Reading Hebrews and James: A Literary and Theological Commentary*. Macon, GA: Smyth & Helwys Publishing, 2002.

Johnson, Luke Timothy. *The Letter of James: A New Translation with Introduction and Commentary*. Anchor Bible, vol. 37A. New York: Doubleday, 1995.

Laws, Sophie. *A Commentary of the Epistle of James*. Harper's New Testament Commentaries. New York: Harper & Row, 1980.

Martin, Ralph P. *James*. Word Biblical Commentary, vol. 48. Dallas, TX: Word, 1988.

McCartney, Dan G. *James*. Exegetical Commentary on the New Testament. Grand Rapids: Baker, 2009.

McKnight, Scot. *The Letter of James*. The New International Commentary on the New Testament. Grand Rapids: Eerdmans, 2011.

Moo, Douglas J. *The Letter of James*. Pillar New Testament Commentary. Grand Rapids: Eerdmans, 2000.

_____. *James*. Tyndale New Testament Commentaries. Grand Rapids: Eerdmans, 2007.

Nystrom, David P. *James*. The NIV Application Commentary. Grand Rapids: Zondervan, 1997.

Painter, John and David A. deSilva. *James and Jude*. Paideia Commentary on the New Testament. Grand Rapids: Baker, 2012.

Richardson, Kurt A. *James*. The New American Commentary, vol. 36. Nashville, TN: Broadman & Holman, 1997.

Sleeper, C. Freeman. *James*. Abingdon New Testament Commentaries. Nashville, TN: Abingdon, 1998.

Tasker, R. V. G. *James*. Tyndale New Testament Commentaries. Grand Rapids: Eerdmans, 1983.

Taylor, Mark. *A Text-Linguistic Investigation into the Discourse Structure of James*. New York: T&T Clark, 2006.

Varner, William. *James*. The Evangelical Exegetical Commentary, edited by Hall Harris. Bellingham, WA: Logos, 2012.

Webb, Robert L. and John Kloppenburg. *Reading James with New Eyes: Methodological Reassessments of the Letter of James*. London, England: T & T Clark, 2007.

1 Peter

Achtemeier, Paul J. *1 Peter*. Hermenia. Minneapolis, MN: Fortress Press, 1996.

Boring, M. Eugene. *1 Peter*. Abingdon New Testament Commentaries. Nashville, TN: Abingdon, 1999.

Davids, Peter H. *The First Epistle of Peter*. New International Commentary on the New Testament. Grand Rapids: Eerdmans, 1990.

Elliott, John H. *1 Peter: A New Translation with Introduction and Commentary*. The Anchor Bible. Garden City, NY: Doubleday, 2000.

Goppelt, Leonhard. *A Commentary on 1 Peter*. Edited by Ferdinand Hahn. Translated and augmented by John E. Alsup. Grand Rapids: Eerdmans, 1993.

Green, Gene L. *Jude and 2 Peter*. Baker Exegetical Commentary on the New Testament. Grand Rapids: Baker Academic, 2008.

Green, Joel B. *1 Peter*. The Two Horizons New Testament Commentary. Grand Rapids: Eerdmans, 2007.

Grudem, Wayne. *1 Peter*. Tyndale New Testament Commentaries. Grand Rapids: Eerdmans, 2007.

Harvey, Robert and Philip H. Tower. *2 Peter and Jude*. The IVP New Testament Commentary Series. Downers Grove, IL: InterVarsity, 2009.

Hillyer, Norman. *1 and 2 Peter, Jude*. New International Biblical Commentary. Peabody, MA: Hendrickson, 1992.

Jobes, Karen H. *1 Peter*. Exegetical Commentary on the New Testament. Grand Rapids: Baker, 2005.

Marshall, I. Howard. *1 Peter*. IVP New Testament Commentary Series. Downers Grove, IL: InterVarsity, 1991.

McKnight, Scott. *1 Peter*. The NIV Application Commentary. Grand Rapids: Zondervan, 1996.

Michaels, J. Ramsey. *1 Peter*. Word Biblical Commentary, vol. 49. Waco, TX: Word, 1988.

Scaggs, R. *The Pentecostal Commentary on 1 Peter, 2 Peter, Jude*. New York: T&T Clark, 2004.

Schreiner, Thomas R. *1, 2 Peter, Jude*. New American Commentary, vol. 37. Nashville, TN: Broadman & Holman, 2003.

Selwyn, Edward. *The First Epistle of St. Peter*. Thornapple Commentaries. Grand Rapids: Baker, 1947, 1981, 1983.

Senior, Donald and Daniel Harrington. *1 Peter, Jude and 2 Peter*. Sacra Pagina, vol. 17. Collegeville, MN: The Liturgical Press, 2003.

Stibbs, A. M. and A. F. Walls. *1 Peter*. Tyndale New Testament Commentaries. Grand Rapids: Eerdmans, 1959, reprint 1983.

Richard, Earl J. *Reading 1 Peter, Jude, and 2 Peter: A Literary and Theological Commentary*. Macon, GA: Smyth & Helwys Publishing, 2000.

Johannine Epistles

Akin, Daniel. *1, 2, 3, John*. The New American Commentary, vol. 38. Nashville, TN: Broadman & Holman, 2001.

Bateman, Herbert W. *A Workbook for Intermediate Greek: Grammar, Exegesis, and Commentary on 1–3 John*. Grand Rapids: Kregel, 2008.

Baugh, S. M. *A First John Reader: Intermediate Greek Reading Notes and Grammar*. Phillipsburg: NJ: P&R Publishing, 1999.

Brown, Raymond E. *The Epistles of John*. The Anchor Bible. Garden City, NY: Doubleday, 1982.

Bruce, F. F. *The Epistles of John*. New International Commentary of the New Testament. Grand Rapids: Eerdmans, 1970.

Burge, Gary M. *Letters of John*. The NIV Application Commentary. Grand Rapids: Zondervan, 1996.

Bultmann, Rudolf. *The Johannine Epistles*. Philadelphia, PA: Fortress, 1973.

Culpepper, R. Alan. *The Gospel and Letters of John*. Nashville, TN: Abingdon, 1998.

Derickson, Gary. *1, 2, 3 John*. The Evangelical Exegetical Commentary, edited by Hall Harris. Bellingham, WA: Logos, 2012.

Hass, C. and M. deJonge, J. L. Swellengrebal. *A Translator's Handbook on the Letters of John*. Volume 13. London: United Bible Societies, 1972.

Houlden, J. L. *A Commentary on the Johannine Epistles*. rev. 2nd ed. Black's New Testament Commentaries. New York: Harper & Row, 1973, London: A & C Black, 1974.

Johnson, Thomas F. *1, 2 and 3 John*. New International Biblical Commentary. Peabody, MA: Hendrickson, 1993.

Jones, Peter Rhea. *1, 2, & 3 John*. Smyth & Helwys Bible Commentary. Macon, GA: Smyth & Helwys Publishing, 2009.

Kruse, Colin G. *The Letters of John*. The Pillar New Testament Commentary. Grand Rapids: Eerdmans, 2000.

Lieu, Judith M. *The Second and Third Epistles of John*. Edinburgh, England: T&T Clark, 1986.

_____. *I, II, & III John: A Commentary*. The New Testament Library. Louisville, KY: John Knox Press, 2008.

Marshall, I. Howard. *The Epistles of John*. New International Commentary on the New Testament. Grand Rapids: Eerdmans, 1978.

Painter, John. *1, 2, and 3, John*. Sacra Pagina, vol. 18. Collegeville, MN: The Litrugical Press, 2002.

Rensberger, David. *1 John, 2 John, 3 John*. Abingdon New Testament Commentaries. Nashville, TN: Abington, 1997.

Smalley, Stephen S. *1, 2, 3, John*. Word Biblical Commentary, Volume 51. Waco, TX: Word Books, 1984.

Smith, Dale Moody. *First, Second, and Third John*. Interpretation: A Bible Commentary for Teaching and Preaching. Louisville, KY: John Knox, 1992.

Stott, John R. W. *The Letters of John*. The Tyndale New Testament Commentaries. Grand Rapids: Eerdmans, 1964, 1988, reprint 2007.

Strecker, Georg. *The Johannine Letters*. Hermeneia. Translated by Linda M. Maloney. Edited by Harold Attridge. Minneapolis: Fortress Press, 1995.

Westcott, Brooke Foss. *The Epistles of St. John*. Grand Rapids: Eerdmans, 1966 (reprint from 1892 third edition).

Yarbrough, Robert W. *1–3 John*. Exegetical Commentary on the New Testament. Grand Rapids: Baker, 2008.

2 Peter and Jude

Bateman IV, Herbert W. *Jude*. The Evangelical Exegetical Commentary, edited by Hall Harris. Bellingham, WA: Logos, 2013.

Bauckham, Richard J. *2 Peter, Jude*. Word Biblical Commentary Series, vol. 50. Waco, TX: Word, 1983.

Davids, Peter. *The Letter of 2 Peter and Jude*. Pillar New Testament Commentary. Grand Rapids: Eerdmans, 2006.

Donelson, Lewis R. *I & II Peter and Jude: A Commentary*. The New Testament Library. Louisville, KY: John Knox Press, 2010.

Grant, Michael. *Saint Peter: A Biography*. New York: Scribner, 1994.

Green, Gene L. *Jude and 2 Peter*. Baker Exegetical Commentary on the New Testament. Grand Rapids: Baker Academic, 2008.

Green, Michael. *2 Peter and Jude*. Tyndale New Testament Commentaries. Grand Rapids: Eerdmans, 1968, 1987, reprint 2007.

Hillyer, Norman. *1 and 2 Peter, Jude*. New International Biblical Commentary. Peabody, MA: Hendrickson, 1992.

Kelly, J.N.D. *A Commentary on the Epistles of Peter and Jude.* Thornapple Commentaries. Grand Rapids: Baker, 1981.

Kraftchick, Steven J. *Jude, 2 Peter*. Abingdon New Testament Commentaries. Nashville, TN: Abingdon, 2002.

Moo, Douglas. *2 Peter and Jude*. The NIV Application Commentary. Grand Rapids: Zondervan, 1996.

Neyrey, Jerome. *2 Peter, and Jude: A New Translation with Introduction and Commentary*. The Anchor Bible Commentary. New Haven: Yale, 1993.

Painter, John and David A. deSilva. *James and Jude*. Paideia Commentary on the New Testament. Grand Rapids: Baker, 2012.

Pheme, Perkins. *First and Second Peter, James, and Jude.* Interpretation: A Bible Commentary for Teaching and Preaching. Louisville, KY: John Knox, 1995.

Reese, Ruth-Ann. *2 Peter and Jude* in The Two Horizons New Testament Commentary. Grand Rapids: Eerdmans, 2007.

Richard, Earl J. *Reading 1 Peter, Jude, and 2 Peter: A Literary and Theological Commentary*. Macon, GA: Smyth & Helwys Publishing, 2000.

Scaggs, R. *The Pentecostal Commentary on 1 Peter, 2 Peter, Jude.* New York: T&T Clark, 2004.

Schreiner, Thomas. *1, 2 Peter, Jude*. New American Commentary Series, vol. 37. Nashville, TN: Broadman & Holman, 2003.

Senior, Donald and Daniel Harrington. *1 Peter, Jude and 2 Peter*. Sacra Pagina, vol. 17. Collegeville, MN: The Liturgical Press, 2003.

GLOSSARY

amillennialism. The teaching that the return of Christ is followed immediately by the eternal state without a milliennial kingdom on earth.

anarthrous. A noun or adjective without an article.

Apocrypha. A closed and focused collection of ancient various literary books written in Semitic languages except for the Wisdom of Solomon.

apocalypticism. A genre in which the author reports dreams or visions, given through an angelic mediator, which reveal heavenly mysteries that explain earthly realities (e.g., portions of Daniel, 1 Enoch, 4 Ezra, Revelation).

apodosis. The second clause in a conditional construction.

application. The process of exploring how to engage and move a twenty-first century audience to embrace scripture's meaning as it was initially heard by it original audience so that it will affect and perhaps change current attitudes and behavior.

articular. A noun or adjective that has an article.

biblical covenant. An arrangement in which God enters into an agreement with people that ultimately reveals his eschatological program (e.g., the Abrahamic, Davidic, and New covenants).

clause. A group of words that contains a subject and a predicate.

Covenant Theology. The theological system that understands salvation history as governed by a covenant of works and a covenant of grace.

chiasmus. A form of symmetric literary structure in which the second half of a literary unit mirrors the first half (e.g., A B C // C' B' A').

contextualization. Speaking or acting in a way that reflects the historical, literary, and cultural context of the addressee and facilitates understanding and relationship.

dependent clause. A clause that cannot stand alone and has a subordinate relationship to another clause.

dispensation. A term that applies generally to direction, administration, or provision.

ellipsis. The omission of any element of language that renders a sentence technically "ungrammatical" yet still understandable in its context.

eschatology. Events pertaining to the future, particularly those that culminate an era of history.

exegesis. The process of interpreting the text.

external textual evidence. The textual witnesses that support various textual readings.

genre. A group of texts with common literary characteristics (e.g., opening salutation, body, closing salutation = a letter).

grammatical function. The way in which a word or dependent clause functions in a sentence (e.g., subject, verb, or direct object).

hendiadys. Two formally coordinate terms that express a single concept in which one of the components defines the other.

hypocatastasus. A declaration that implies a comparison.

inclusio. A compositional technique in which certain words or phrases appear at both the beginning and end of a literary unit to mark it out as a distinct structural unit.

independent clause. A clause that has a subject and verb, can stand alone, and is not subordinate to another clause.

metaphor. A declaration that one thing is or represents another.

metonymy. The exchange of one idea for another idea logically associated with it (e.g., cause for effect).

millennium. The period of time when Christ rules on earth as God's royal priest as described in Revelation 20:2–7.

mood. The author's portrayal of certainty of the verbal action from actuality (indicative mood) to potentiality (optative mood).

Muratorian Canon (*ca.* 160–180). An anonymous eighth-century Latin document that represents the first known authorized collection of the NT by the Christian Church and may present a consensus viewpoint on the NT canon in the Western Church near the end of the second century.

parallelism. A relationship of correspondence that exists between one logical-syntactical unit in the verse with another, completing, contrasting, continuing or describing another clause within a verse.

premillennialism. The teaching that Christ will return before his millennial rule on earth.

progressive dispensationalism. A hermeneutical framework used to guide biblical interpretation chronologically according to successive dispensations in distinguishable and yet complementary progressive stages.

protasis. The first clause in a conditional construction.

Pseudepigrapha. A modern collection of ancient writings that are helpful reading for an understanding of early Judaism (250 BCE to 200 CE) and early Christianity.

Qumran scrolls. A collection of over 800 scroll fragments found in eleven caves near Qumran dating from the mid-third-century BCE to 135 CE that are part of a larger collection of scrolls found near the Dead Sea.

semantic function. The way in which a word functions in its immediate context.

Septuagint. The Greek translation of the Old Testament (abbreviated LXX), which tradition reports was completed in seventy-two days by seventy-two elders in Egypt.

synecdoche. The exchange of one idea for another idea internally associated with it (e.g., part for whole).

syntactic function. The way in which a dependent clause functions within a sentence (e.g., substantivally, adjectivally, adverbially).

tense. The author's presentation of verbal action with reference to its aspect (continuous, undefined, perfect) and sometimes its time.

textual criticism. The study of existing manuscripts for the purpose of determining the exact wording of the original New Testament text.

validation. The process of identifying, evaluating, deciding, and supporting a decision between two or more interpretations of any given passage of Scripture.

voice. The way in which the subject is related to the action expressed by the verb (e.g., active voice performs the action, middle voice reveals the subject's participation in the action, passive voice identifies the subject reception of the action).